I0609053

Robert Slater

Telegraphic Code

To ensure Secrecy in the transmission of Telegrams

Robert Slater

Telegraphic Code
To ensure Secrecy in the transmission of Telegrams

ISBN/EAN: 9783337188627

Printed in Europe, USA, Canada, Australia, Japan

Cover: Foto ©ninafisch / pixelio.de

More available books at **www.hansebooks.com**

TELEGRAPHIC
CODE,

TO ENSURE

SECRESY

IN THE

𝕮ransmission of 𝕮elegrams.

BY

ROBERT SLATER,

SECRETARY OF THE

Société du Cable Transatlantique Français, Limited.

(French Atlantic Telegraphic Company).

THIRD EDITION.

LONDON:

PRINTED AND PUBLISHED BY

W R. GRAY,

6, LOMBARD COURT, E.C.

1888.

INTRODUCTION.

On the 1st February, 1870, the telegraph system throughout the United Kingdom passes into the hands of the Government, who will work the lines by Post Office officials. In other words, those who have hitherto so judiciously and satisfactorily managed the delivery of our sealed letters will in future be entrusted also with the transmission and delivery of our open letters in the shape of telegraphic communications, which will thus be exposed not only to the gaze of public officials, but from the necessity of the case must be read by them. Now in large or small communities (particularly perhaps in the latter) there are always to be found prying spirits, curious as to the affairs of their neighbours, which they think they can manage so much better than the parties chiefly interested, and proverbially inclined to gossip.

With every disposition on the part of the Post Office authorities to work the telegraphs in such a manner as shall command the confidence of the public, and justify them in entrusting their dispatches to them,—and this disposition certainly exists in no ordinary degree,—the community will frequently have occasion to employ

the telegraph in the transmission of messages
which they will be most anxious to forward in
such terms as shall be unintelligible to the
operators through whose hands they pass.
Already in the transmission of commercial in-
telligence it has been found absolutely necessary
to conceal the news communicated from all but
the receivers of the messages, and particularly is
this the case in the instance of submarine cables,
whilst an additional reason for the employment
of apparently unintelligible messages is found in
the charges of submarine cables, which has ren--
dered those using them alive to the fact that;
by a well-selected code, one word or figure may
be made to represent much more than it ex-
presses.

The compiler of the present vocabulary would
draw attention to the fact that by his system
messages can be communicated in a form unintelligible to the operator, and can be sent either
in the form of unconnected words or of series of
figures, whilst either the words or the figures can
be used in conjunction with a prearranged code.
The simplicity of the mode of using the vocabulary is a great advantage which cannot fail to be
evident to those employing it, whilst the nume-
rous combinations of which the vocabulary is
capable gives those using it the means of select-
ing upwards of a million different keys, thus
effectually concealing their messages from all
but those with whom a key has been pre-arranged.
In the following pages the mode of using the

work is illustrated, and, for a reason which will be more evident on reading page xiv., one sentence has been adopted throughout, showing how an alteration of the system of the key will vary the message.

The vocabulary embraces from A to Z 24000 words, in addition to which 1000 more words have been added, expressing Christian names, some surnames in common use, the names of heathen deities, heroes, &c., and some geographical names, all of which are so arranged that they may be used advantageously in code messages. They thus afford in themselves some clue to any error which may possibly creep into messages during transit, for even telegraph operators, skilful as they are, are fallible; besides which earth currents at times act in such a subtle manner during the transmission of a message that the signals may be mis-read, and a different value be ascribed to them by the reader-off from that which was actually given in as it were to the wire by the sender.

The following examples commence with a simple form of cipher, viz., by the addition and then by the subtraction of a pre-arranged number, afterwards by the transposition of the numbers, then in a more complex form by the combination of these two methods, and finally by a variation in the series of figures, whereby it will be seen that one and the same word in a sentence does not by any means involve the necessity for employing the same cipher, thus almost entirely preventing the possibility of a message being deciphered by those skilful investigators who by long practice have acquired wondrous facility in reading off messages which the senders had hoped were concealed from all the world but those they were intended for.

The sentence selected for illustration in the following pages is—

"The Queen is the supreme power in the Realm."

EXAMPLE I.

The Queen is the supreme power in the Realm.

Add any number below 25000 (say, for instance,) 5555 to the numbers opposite to those words it is desired to transmit. Where the result exceeds 25000, deduct that number, or, in other words, commence the alphabet again.

Word to be transmitted.	No. in Vocabulary.	Plus 5555.	Representing in Vocabulary.
The	22313	27868	Bounteous
Queen	18095	23650	wedge
is	12370	17925	purifying
the	22313	27868	bounteous
supreme	21953	27508	biography
power	17056	22611	transparent
in	11426	16981	posed
the	22313	27868	bounteous
Realm	18419	23974	yoke

The message being transmitted :—

Bounteous wedge purifying bounteous biography transparent posed bounteous yoke,

the receiver reverses the operation, adding 25000 to the number where it is below that to be deducted.

Word received.	No. in Vocabulary.	Minus 5555.	Representing in Vocabulary.
Bounteous	02868	22313	The
wedge	23650	18095	Queen
purifying	17925	12370	is
bounteous	02868	22313	the
biography	02508	21953	supreme
transparent	22611	17056	power
posed	16981	11426	in
bounteous	02868	22313	the
yoke	23974	18419	Realm

EXAMPLE II.

The Queen is the supreme power in the Realm.

Subtract any number below 25000 (say, for instance,) 5555 from the numbers opposite to those words it is desired to transmit. Where this number exceeds the numbers in question, add 25000.

Word to be transmitted.	No. in Vocabulary.	Minus 5555.	Representing in Vocabulary.
The	22313	16758	Plenty
Queen	18095	12540	judging
is	12370	06815	diatribe
the	22313	16758	plenty
supreme	21953	16398	perspective
power	17056	11501	inciter
in	11426	05871	crispate
the	22313	16758	plenty
Realm	18419	12864	lagoon

The message being transmitted :—

Plenty judging diatribe plenty perspective inciter crispate plenty lagoon,

the receiver reverses the operation.

Word received.	No. in Vocabulary.	Add 5555.	Representing in Vocabulary.
Plenty	16758	22313	The
Judging	12540	18095	Queen
diatribe	06815	12370	is
plenty	16758	22313	the
perspective	16398	21953	supreme
inciter	11501	17056	power
crispate	05871	11426	in
plenty	16758	22313	the
lagoon	12864	18419	Realm

EXAMPLE III.

The Queen is the supreme power in the Realm.

The three last figures representing the word transmitted are transposed. Thus, in place of sending 12345, the number transmitted is 12453.

Word to be transmitted.	No. in Vocabulary.	Transposed.	Representing in Vocabulary.
The	22313	22133	Talking
Queen	18095	18950	remonstrated
is	12370	12703	kinks
the	22313	22133	talking
supreme	21953	21539	starch
power	17056	17560	promised
in	11426	11264	imparted
the	22313	22133	talking
Realm	18419	18194	quote

The message being transmitted :—

Talking remonstrated kinks talking starch promised imparted talking quote,

the receiver reverses the operation.

Word received.	No. in Vocabulary.	Transposed.	Representing in Vocabulary.
Talking	22133	22313	The
remonstrated	18950	18095	Queen
kinks	12703	12370	is
talking	22133	22313	the
starch	21539	21953	supreme
promised	17560	17056	power
imparted	11264	11426	in
talking	22133	22313	the
quote	18194	18419	Realm

EXAMPLE IV.

The Queen is the supreme power in the Realm.

Add as before 5555, and transpose the three right hand figures, as in Example III.

Word to be transmitted.	No. in Vocabulary.	Add 5555.	Transposed.	Representing in Vocabulary.
The	22313	27868	27688	Blundered
Queen	18095	23650	23506	waft
is	12370	17925	17259	presage
the	22313	27868	27688	blundered
supreme	21953	27508	27085	basalt
power	17056	22611	22116	tadpole
in	11426	16981	16819	pneumonia
the	22313	27868	27688	blundered
Realm	18419	23974	23749	why

The message being transmitted reads :—

Blundered waft presage blundered basalt tadpole pneumonia blundered why,

the receiver reverses the operation.

Word received.	No. in Vocabulary.	Transposed.	Deduct 5555.	Representing in Vocabulary.
Blundered	02688	02868	22313	The
waft	23506	23650	18095	Queen
presage	17259	17925	12370	is
blundered	02688	02868	22313	the
basalt	02085	02508	21953	supreme
tadpole	22116	22611	17056	power
pneumonia	16819	16981	11426	in
blundered	02688	02868	22313	the
why	23749	23974	18419	Realm

EXAMPLE V.

The Queen is the supreme power in the Realm.

Subtract as before 5555, and transpose the three right hand figures, as in Example III.

Word to be transmitted.	No. in Vocabulary.	Minus 5555.	Transposed.	Representing in Vocabulary.
The	22313	16758	16587	Pillaging
Queen	18095	12540	12405	jackass
is	12370	06815	06158	darn
the	22313	16758	16587	pillaging
supreme	21953	16398	16983	posing
power	17056	11501	11015	hulk
in	11426	05871	05718	cousin
the	22313	16758	16587	pillaging
Realm	18419	12864	12648	ketch

The message being transmitted :—

Pillaging jackass darn pillaging posing hulk cousin pillaging ketch,

the receiver reverses the operation.

Word received.	No. in Vocabulary.	Transposed.	Add 5555.	Representing in Vocabulary.
Pillaging	16587	16758	22313	The
jackass	12405	12540	18095	Queen
darn	06158	06815	12370	is
pillaging	16587	16758	22313	the
posing	16983	16398	21953	supreme
hulk	11015	11501	17056	power
cousin	05718	05871	11426	in
pillaging	16587	16758	22313	the
ketch	12648	12864	18419	Realm

EXAMPLE VI.

The Queen is the supreme power in the Realm.

The series of five figures representing the message are transmitted in series of four figures.

Word to be transmitted.	No. in Vocabulary.	Altered Series.	Representing in Vocabulary.
The	22313	2231	Begged
Queen	18095	3180	bulging
		9512	freak
is	12370	3702	catamaran
the	22313	2313	beneath
		2195	bedstead
supreme	21953	3170	build
power	17056	5611	corrupting
in	11426	4262	claimed
		2313	beneath
the	22313	1841	autumn
realm	18419	9000	few

The message being transmitted :—

Begged bulging freak catamaran beneath bedstead build corrupting claimed beneath autumn few,

the receiver reverses the operation.

Word received.	No. in Vocabulary.	Altered Series.	Representing in Vocabulary.
Begged	2231	22313	The
bulging	3180	18095	Queen
freak	9512	12370	is
catamaran	3702		
beneath	2313	22313	the
bedstead	2195		
build	3170	21953	supreme
corrupting	5611	17056	power
claimed	4262	11426	in
beneath	2313		
autumn	1841	22313	the
few	9000	18419	Realm

EXAMPLE VII.
The Queen is the supreme power in the Realm.

The series of five figures are converted into series of four figures, as in Example VI., the three right hand figures being transposed, as in Example III.

Word to be transmitted.	No. in Vocabulary.	Altered Series.	Transposed.	Representing in Vocabulary.
The	22313	2231	2312	Bends
Queen	18095	3180	3801	celestially
is	12370	9512	9125	fivefold
the	22313	3702	3027	brigade
supreme	21953	2313	2133	bays
power	17056	2195	2951	Brazilian
in	11426	3170	3701	catalogue
the	22313	5611	5116	conjecturing
Realm	18419	4262	4622	come
		2313	2133	bays
		1841	1418	Areopagus
		9000	9000	few

The message being transmitted :—

Bends celestially fivefold brigade bays Brazilian catalogue conjecturing come bays Areopagus few,

the receiver reverses the operation.

Word received.	No. in Vocabulary.	Transposed.	Altered Series.	Representing in Vocabulary.
Bends	2312	2231	22313	The
celestially	3801	3180	18095	Queen
fivefold	9125	9512	12370	is
brigade	3027	3702		
bays	2133	2313	22313	the
Brazilian	2951	2195	21953	supreme
catalogue	3701	3170		
conjecturing	5116	5611	17056	power
come	4622	4262	11426	in
bays	2133	2313	22313	the
Areopagus	1418	1841		
few	9000	9000	18419	Realm

EXAMPLE VIII.
The Queen is the supreme power in the Realm.

The series of five being converted into series of four figures, and transposed, as in Example VII., add 1 to the first result, 2 to the second, 3 to the third, and so on, according to the number of words transmitted.

Word to be transmitted.	No. in Vocabulary.	Altered Series.	Transposed.	With Addition.	Representing in Vocabulary
The	22313	2231	2312	2313	Beneath
Queen	18095	3180	3801	3803	celibate
is	12370	9512	9125	9128	fixed ness
		3702	3027	3031	brigandine
the	22313	2313	2133	2138	beaconage
supreme	21953	2195	2951	2957	breadth
		3170	3701	3708	catch
power	17056	5611	5116	5124	conjugation
in	11426	4262	4622	4631	comfort
		2313	2133	2143	beaker
the	22313	1841	1418	1429	argument
Realm	18419	9000	9000	9012	fiddler

The message being transmitted :—
Beneath celibate fixedness brigandine beaconage breadth catch conjugation comfort beaker argument fiddler,
the receiver reverses the operation.

Word received.	No. in Vocabulary.	After Deduction.	Transposed.	Altered Series.	Representing in Vocabulary
Beneath	2313	2312	2231	22313	The
celibate	3803	3801	3180	18095	Queen
fixedness	9128	9125	9512	12370	is
brigandine	3031	3027	3702	22313	the
beaconage	2138	2133	2313	21953	supreme
breadth	2957	2951	2195	17056	power
catch	3708	3701	3170	11426	in
conjugation	5124	5116	5611	22313	the
comfort	4631	4622	4262	18419	Realm
beaker	2143	2133	2313		
argument	1429	1418	1841		
fiddler	9012	9000	9000		

EXAMPLE IX.

The practical effect of the last Illustration in concealing the meaning of a message from all who have not the Key, is shown in the present Example by transposing the Message itself, so that it shall read "In the Realm, the Queen is the supreme power."

Word to be transmitted.	No. in Vocabulary.	Altered Series.	Transposed.	With additions.	Representing in Vocabulary.
In	11426	1142	1421	1422	Argentine
the	22313	6223	6232	6234	decay
Realm	18419	1318	1183	1186	antispasmodic
the	22313	4192	4921	4925	conclude
Queen	18095	2313	2133	2138	beaconage
is	12370	1809	1098	1104	anomalous
the	22313	5123	5231	5238	constitutional
supreme	21953	7022	7220	7228	dissenter
power.	17056	3132	3321	3330	caffre
		1953	1539	1549	ascribable
		1705	1057	1068	anneal
		6000	6000	6012	cupping

This Message which (with the exception of a single word) differs entirely from that given under the previous Illustration being transmitted :—

Argentine decay antispasmodic conclude beaconage anomalous constitutional dissenter caffre ascribable anneal cupping—

the receiver reverses the operation.

Word received.	No. in Vocabulary.	After deduction.	Transposed.	Altered Series.	Representing in Vocabulary.
Argentine	1422	1421	1142	11426	In
decay	6234	6232	6223	22313	the
antispasmodic	1186	1183	1318	18419	Realm
conclude	4925	4921	4192	22313	the
beaconage	2138	2133	2313	18095	Queen
anomalous	1104	1098	1809	12370	is
constitutional	5238	5231	5123	22313	the
dissenter	7228	7220	7022	21953	supreme
Caffre	3330	3321	3132	17056	power.
ascribable	1549	1539	1953		
anneal	1068	1057	1705		
cupping	6012	6000	6000		

Further examples are unnecessary, as the reader will readily see from the preceding, that a very large number of keys, amounting to some millions in number, may be employed, besides which others can be arranged by using the numbers at the head of the pages, folios, or sheets of four pages, taking advantage or not of the words in each column, which are arranged in fifties. The ingenuity of those making use of the book may be exercised in devising these. For further information, however, the number of words under each letter is here subjoined:—

A	1900
B	1400
C	2800
D	1500
E	1100
F	1000
G	700
H	700
I	1300
J	200
K	200
L	900
M	1200
N	400
O	500
P	2200
Q	200
R	1600
S	2300
T	700
U	400
V	300
W	450
X, Y, and Z ...	50
	24000

NUMBERED VOCABULARY

FOR

TELEGRAPHIC USE.

I	A	(I)	ABR

A	00001	Abides	00051
Aback	00002	Abiding	00052
Abacus	00003	Ability	00053
Abaft	00004	Abject	00054
Abalienate	00005	Abjection	00055
Abandon	00006	Abjectly	00056
Abandoned	00007	Abjectness	00057
Abandonee	00008	Abjudicate	00058
Abandoner	00009	Abjuration	00059
Abandonment ...	00010	Abjure	00060
Abase	00011	Abjurer	00061
Abasement	00012	Ablation...	00062
Abash	00013	Ablative...	00063
Abate	00014	Ablaze	00064
Abated	00015	Able	00065
Abates	00016	Abluent	00066
Abattoir	00017	Ablution...	00067
Abbacy	00018	Ably	00068
Abbé	00019	Abnegate	00069
Abbess	00020	Abnegation	00070
Abbey	00021	Abnormal	00071
Abbot	00022	Aboard	00072
Abbreviate	00023	Abode	00073
Abbreviated	00024	Abodement	00074
Abbreviation	00025	Abolish	00075
Abbreviature	00026	Abolished	00076
Abdicate...	00027	Abolisher	00077
Abdicated	00028	Abolishes	00078
Abdicates	00029	Abolishing	00079
Abdicating	00030	Abolition	00080
Abdication	00031	Abolitionist	00081
Abdomen	00032	Abominable	00082
Abdominal	00033	Abominably	00083
Abduce	00034	Abominate	00084
Abduct	00035	Abominated	00085
Abduction	00036	Abominates	00086
Aberrance	00037	Abomination	00087
Aberrant...	00038	Aboriginal	00088
Abet	00039	Aborigines	00089
Abetment	00040	Abortion...	00090
Abeyance	00041	Abortive...	00091
Abgregate	00042	Abound	00092
Abhor	00043	Abounding	00093
Abhorred	00044	About	00094
Abhorrence	00045	Above	00095
Abhorrently	00046	Abrade	00096
Abhorrer	00047	Abrahamic	00097
Abhorring	00048	Abrasion...	00098
Abhors	00049	Abreast	00099
Abide	00050	Abrenunciation ...	00100

ABR	(1)	ACC	2

Abridge ...	...	...	00101	Abstracter	00151
Abridged	...	...	00102	Abstraction	00152
Abridger...	...	...	00103	Abstractive	00153
Abridgement ...	...	...	00104	Abstractly	00154
Abroad ...	...	...	00105	Abstruse	00155
Abrogate	...	...	00106	Abstrusely	00156
Abrogated	...	...	00107	Absurd	00157
Abrupt ...	...	...	00108	Absurdity	00158
Abruptly	...	...	00109	Absurdly	00159
Abscess ...	...	...	00110	Abundance	00160
Abscond...	...	...	00111	Abundant	00161
Absconded	...	...	00112	Abundantly	00162
Absconding	...	...	00113	Abuse	00163
Absconds	...	...	00114	Abused	00164
Absence ...	...	...	00115	Abuser	00165
Absent ...	...	...	00116	Abuses	00166
Absentee	...	...	00117	Abusive	00167
Absenter...	...	...	00118	Abusing	00168
Absist ...	...	...	00119	Abut	00169
Absisted ...	...	...	00120	Abutment	00170
Absolute...	...	...	00121	Abuts	00171
Absolutely	...	...	00122	Abutting...	00172
Absolution	...	...	00123	Abyss	00173
Absolutism	...	...	00124	Acacia	00174
Absolutory	...	...	00125	Academic	00175
Absolve ...	...	...	00126	Academical	00176
Absolved	...	...	00127	Academician	00177
Absolver...	...	...	00128	Academist	00178
Absolving	...	...	00129	Academy	00179
Absonant	...	...	00130	Acataleptic	00180
Absorb ...	...	...	00131	Accede	00181
Absorbable	...	...	00132	Acceded	00182
Absorbed	...	...	00133	Accedes	00183
Absorbent	...	...	00134	Acceding	00184
Absorbing	...	...	00135	Accelerate	00185
Absorbs ...	...	...	00136	Accelerated	00186
Absorption	...	...	00137	Accelerates	00187
Abstain ...	...	...	00138	Accelerating	00188
Abstained	...	...	00139	Acceleration	00189
Abstaining	...	...	00140	Accelerative	00190
Abstains ...	...	...	00141	Accent	00191
Abstemious	...	...	00142	Accentual	00192
Abstention	...	...	00143	Accentuate	00193
Absterge...	...	...	00144	Accentuation	00194
Abstergent	...	...	00145	Accept	00195
Abstinence	...	...	00146	Acceptable	00196
Abstorted	...	...	00147	Acceptance	00197
Abstract ...	...	...	00148	Accepted	00198
Abstracted	...	...	00149	Accepter...	00199
Abstractedly ...	...	00150	Accepting	00200

3	ACC	(2)	ACH

Accepts	00201	Accountant	00251
Access	00202	Accounted	00252
Accessibility	00203	Accounting	00253
Accessible	00204	Accounts	00254
Accession	00205	Accoutre...	00255
Accessorial	00206	Accoutred	00256
Accessorily	00207	Accoutrements ...	00257
Accessory	00208	Accredit	00258
Accident...	00209	Accredited	00259
Accidental	00210	Accrescent	00260
Accipient	00211	Accretion	00261
Acclaim	00212	Accretive	00262
Acclamation	00213	Accrue	00263
Acclamatory	00214	Accrued	00264
Acclimatize	00215	Accruement	00265
Acclivity...	00216	Accruing...	00266
Accolade...	00217	Accubation	00267
Accommodable ...	00218	Accumulate	00268
Accommodableness .	00219	Accumulated	00269
Accommodate ...	00220	Accumulates	00270
Accommodated ...	00221	Accumulative ...	00271
Accommodately ...	00222	Accumulator	00272
Accommodates ...	00223	Accuracy	00273
Accommodating ...	00224	Accurate...	00274
Accommodation ...	00225	Accurately	00275
Accommodator ...	00226	Accurse	00276
Accompanied	00227	Accursed...	00277
Accompanier	00228	Accusable	00278
Accompaniment ...	00229	Accusant...	00279
Accompany	00230	Accusation	00280
Accomplice	00231	Accusative	00281
Accomplish	00232	Accusatory	00282
Accomplished ...	00233	Accuse	00283
Accomplishment ...	00234	Accuser	00284
Accord	00235	Accused	00285
Accordance	00236	Accusing	00286
Accordant	00237	Accustom	00287
Accorded	00238	Accustomed	00288
Accorder...	00239	Ace	00289
According	00240	Acerbity	00290
Accordingly	00241	Acetic	00291
Accordion	00242	Acetous	00292
Accords	00243	Ache	00293
Accouchement ...	00244	Achievable	00294
Accoucheur	00245	Achievance	00295
Accoucheuse	00246	Achieve	00296
Account	00247	Achieved...	00297
Accountability ...	00248	Achievement	00298
Accountable	00249	Achiever	00299
Accountably	00250	Achieving	00300

ACH	(2)	ADD	4
Aching	00301	Acrimonious	00351
Achromatic	00302	Acrimony	00352
Acicular	00303	Across	00353
Acid	00304	Acrostic	00354
Acidiferous	00305	Act	00355
Acidification	00306	Actiniform	00356
Acidify	00307	Action	00357
Acidimeter	00308	Actionable	00358
Acidity	00309	Activate	00359
Acidulate	00310	Active	00360
Acidulous	00311	Activity	00361
Aciform	00312	Actless	00362
Acknowledge	00313	Actor	00363
Acknowledged ...	00314	Actress	00364
Acknowledger ...	00315	Actual	00365
Acknowleges	00316	Actualize	00366
Acknowledging ...	00317	Actually	00367
Acknowledgment ...	00318	Actuary	00368
Acme	00319	Actuate	00369
Acolyte	00320	Actuated	00370
Aconite	00321	Acumen	00371
Acorn	00322	Acute	00372
Acoustic	00323	Acuteness	00373
Acoustics	00324	Adage	00374
Acquaint	00325	Adagio	00375
Acquaintable	00326	Adamant	00376
Acquaintance	00327	Adamantean	00377
Acquainted	00328	Adamantine	00378
Acquainting	00329	Adapt	00379
Acquaints	00330	Adaptable	00380
Acquiesce	00331	Adapted	00381
Acquiesced	00332	Adapter	00382
Acquiescent	00333	Adapting	00383
Acquiesces	00334	Adapts	00384
Acquiescing	00335	Add	00385
Acquirability	00336	Addable	00386
Acquirable	00337	Added	00387
Acquire	00338	Addenda	00388
Acquired	00339	Adder	00389
Acquirement	00340	Addict	00390
Acquirer	00341	Addicted	00391
Acquisition	00342	Adding	00392
Acquisitive	00343	Addition	00393
Acquisitiveness ...	00344	Additional	00394
Acquit	00345	Additionally	00395
Acquittal	00346	Addle	00396
Acquittance	00347	Addled	00397
Acquitted	00348	Address	00398
Acre	00349	Addressed	00399
Acrid	00350	Addresser	00400

Addressing	...	00401	Admeasurement	...	00451
Adds	...	00402	Admensuration	...	00452
Adduce	...	00403	Administer	...	00453
Adducer	...	00404	Administered	...	00454
Adducible	...	00405	Administerial	...	00455
Ademption	...	00406	Administering	...	00456
Adept	...	00407	Administrable	...	00457
Adequacy	...	00408	Administration	...	00458
Adequate	...	00409	Administrator	...	00459
Adequately	...	00410	Administratrix	...	00460
Adhere	...	00411	Admirable	...	00461
Adhered	...	00412	Admirably	...	00462
Adherence	...	00413	Admiral	...	00463
Adherent	...	00414	Admiralty	...	00464
Adheres	...	00415	Admiration	...	00465
Adhering	...	00416	Admire	...	00466
Adhesion	...	00417	Admired	...	00467
Adhesive	...	00418	Admirer	...	00468
Adieu	...	00419	Admires	...	00469
Adipose	...	00420	Admiring	...	00470
Adit	...	00421	Admiringly	...	00471
Adjacency	...	00422	Admissible	...	00472
Adjacent	...	00423	Admissibly	...	00473
Adjacently	...	00424	Admission	...	00474
Adjective	...	00425	Admit	...	00475
Adjoin	...	00426	Admits	...	00476
Adjoined	...	00427	Admittance	...	00477
Adjoining	...	00428	Admitted	...	00478
Adjoins	...	00429	Admitting	...	00479
Adjourn	...	00430	Admix	...	00480
Adjourned	...	00431	Admonish	...	00481
Adjourning	...	00432	Admonisher	...	00482
Adjournment	...	00433	Admonished	...	00483
Adjudge	...	00434	Admonishing	...	00484
Adjudicate	...	00435	Admonition	...	00485
Adjunct	...	00436	Admonitory	...	00486
Adjunction	...	00437	Ado	...	00487
Adjunctive	...	00438	Adolescence	...	00488
Adjunctly	...	00439	Adolescent	...	00489
Adjuration	...	00440	Adopt	...	00490
Adjure	...	00441	Adopted	...	00491
Adjurer	...	00442	Adoption	...	00492
Adjust	...	00443	Adoptive	...	00493
Adjusted	...	00444	Adorable	...	00494
Adjuster	...	00445	Adorably	...	00495
Adjustive	...	00446	Adoration	...	00496
Adjustment	...	00447	Adore	...	00497
Adjutant	...	00448	Adorer	...	00498
Adjutantcy	...	00449	Adorn	...	00499
Admeasure	...	00450	Adorner	...	00500

ADR	(3)	AFF	6

Adrift	00501	Advocates	00551
Adroit	00502	Advocating	00552
Adroitly	00503	Advolation	00553
Adulation	00504	Advowee	00554
Adulator...	00505	Advowson	00555
Adult	00506	Adze	00556
Adulterate	00507	Ægis	00557
Adulterated	00508	Æneid	00558
Adulteration	00509	Aerate	00559
Adulterer	00510	Aerated	00560
Adulteress	00511	Aerial	00561
Adulterous	00512	Aeriform...	00562
Adultery...	00513	Aerify	00563
Advance	00514	Aerolite	00564
Advanced	00515	Aerology...	00565
Advancement... ...	00516	Aeronaut...	00566
Advancing	00517	Aeronautics	00567
Advantage	00518	Aerostatic	00568
Advantageous ...	00519	Aerostatics	00569
Advent	00520	Aesthetic	00570
Adventitious	00521	Aesthetics	00571
Adventive	00522	Afar...	00572
Adventual	00523	Afeard	00573
Adventure	00524	Affability	00574
Adventurer	00525	Affable	00575
Adventurous	00526	Affair	00576
Adventurously ...	00527	Affect	00577
Adverb	00528	Affectation	00578
Adversary	00529	Affected	00579
Adverse	00530	Affectedly	00580
Adversely	00531	Affecting...	00581
Adversity	00532	Affection...	00582
Advert	00533	Affectionate	00583
Advertence	00534	Affectionately... ...	00584
Advertent	00535	Affectioned	00585
Advertise	00536	Affiance	00586
Advertised	00537	Affianced	00587
Advertisement ...	00538	Affiancer...	00588
Advertiser	00539	Affidavit	00589
Advice	00540	Affiliate	00590
Advisable	00541	Affiliated...	00591
Advise	00542	Affiliation	00592
Advised	00543	Affinity	00593
Advisedly ...	00544	Affirm	00594
Adviser	00545	Affirmant	00595
Advises	00546	Affirmation	00596
Advising...	00547	Affirmative	00597
Advocacy	00548	Affirmed...	00598
Advocate	00549	Affirmer	00599
Advocated	00550	Affirms	00600

Affix	00601	Agenda 00651
Affixed	00602	Agent 00652
Affixture...	00603	Agglomerate 00653
Afflict	00604	Agglutinate 00654
Afflicted	00605	Agglutinative... ... 00655
Afflicter	00606	Aggrandize 00656
Afflicting	00607	Aggrandizement ... 00657
Affliction	00608	Aggrandizer 00658
Afflictive...	00609	Aggravate 00659
Affluence	00610	Aggravated 00660
Affluent	00611	Aggravates 00661
Afflux	00612	Aggravating 00662
Afford	00613	Aggravation 00663
Afforded	00614	Aggregate 00664
Affording	00615	Aggregately 00665
Affords	00616	Aggregative 00666
Affranchise	00617	Aggregator 00667
Affranchisement ...	00618	Aggress 00668
Affray	00619	Aggressive 00669
Affronted	00620	Aggressor 00670
Afront	00621	Aggrievance 00671
Affronter...	00622	Aggrieve... 00672
Affronting	00623	Aghast 00673
Affrontive	00624	Agile 00674
Afloat	00625	Agility 00675
Atoot	00626	Agitate 00676
Afore	00627	Agitated 00677
Aforegoing	00628	Agitates 00678
Aforehand	00629	Agitating 00679
Aforementioned ...	00630	Agitator 00680
Aforenamed	00631	Aglutition 00681
Aforesaid	00632	Agnate 00682
Aforethought... ...	00633	Ago... 00683
Aforetime	00634	Agonize 00684
Afraid	00635	Agony 00685
Afresh	00636	Agrarian... 00686
African	00637	Agrarianism 00687
Aft	00638	Agree 00688
After	00639	Agreeable 00689
Afternoon	00640	Agreeability 00690
Afterwards	00641	Agreeably 00691
Aga...	00642	Agreed 00692
Again	00643	Agreeing... 00693
Against	00644	Agreement 00694
Agape	00645	Agrees 00695
Agate	00646	Agricultural 00696
Agaze	00647	Agriculture 00697
Age...	00648	Agriculturist 00698
Aged	00649	Aground... 00699
Agency	00650	Ague 00700

AGU				(4)	ALL			8
Aguish	...	...	...	00701	Alibi	00751
Ah ...	...	...	...	00702	Alien	00752
Aha...	...	...	...	00703	Alienable	00753
Aid ...	...	...	...	00704	Alienage...	00754
Aided	...	...	...	00705	Alienate	00755
Aide-de-camp		...	...	00706	Alienated	00756
Aiding	...	...	...	00707	Alienation	00757
Aidless	...	...	...	00708	Alight	00758
Aids	...	...	...	00709	Alike	00759
Ail ...	...	...	...	00710	Aliment	00760
Ailing	...	...	...	00711	Alimentary	00761
Ailment ...	...	...	00712	Alimentation	00762
Aim...	...	...	...	00713	Alimony	00763
Aimed	...	...	...	00714	Aliquant	00764
Aiming	...	...	...	00715	Aliquot	00765
Aimless ...	...	...	00716	Aliture	00766
Air ...	...	...	...	00717	Alive	00767
Aired	...	...	...	00718	Alkalescency	00768
Airily	...	...	...	00719	Alkali	00769
Airing	...	...	...	00720	Alkalify	00770
Airy	...	...	...	00721	Alkaligenous	00771
Aisle	...	...	...	00722	Alkaline	00772
Ajar	...	...	...	00723	Alkaloid	00773
Akin	...	...	...	00724	Alkoran	00774
Alabaster	...	...	00725	All	00775
Alacrity ...	...	...	00726	Allah	00776
Alarm	...	...	...	00727	Allay	00777
Alarmed...	...	...	00728	Allayed	00778
Alarming	...	...	00729	Allays	00779
Alarmist	...	...	00730	Allegation	00780
Alarms ...	...	...	00731	Allege	00781
Alas	...	...	...	00732	Allegiance	00782
Alb ...	...	...	...	00733	Alleging	00783
Albatross	...	...	00734	Allegorical	00784
Albeit	...	...	...	00735	Allegorist	00785
Albescent	...	...	00736	Allegorize	00786
Albion	...	...	...	00737	Allegory...	00787
Album	...	...	...	00738	Allegro	00788
Albumen	...	...	00739	Allelujah	00789
Alchemical	...	...	00740	Alleviate...	00790
Alchemy...	...	...	00741	Alleviated	00791
Alcohol ...	...	...	00742	Alleviation	00792
Alcoholization		...	00743	Alleviative	00793
Alcove	..	...	...	00744	Alley	00794
Alderman	...	...	00745	Alliance	00795
Ale ...	...	...	...	00746	Allies	00796
Alert	...	...	...	00747	Alligator...	00797
Algebra ...	...	...	00748	Alliteration	00798
Alguazil ...	...	...	00749	Alliterative	00799
Alias	...	...	...	00750	Allocate	00800

Allocated	... ...	00801
Allocation	... ...	00802
Allocution	... ...	00803
Allopathic	... ...	00804
Allopathist	... ...	00805
Allopathy	... ...	00806
Allot	... ...	00807
Allotment	... ...	00808
Allotted ...	... ...	00809
Allow	... ...	00810
Allowable	... ...	00811
Allowance	... ...	00812
Allowed ...	... ...	00813
Allowing	... ...	00814
Allows	... ...	00815
Alloy	... ...	00816
Allude	... ...	00817
Alluded ...	... ...	00818
Alludes ...	... ...	00819
Alluding...	... ...	00820
Alluminate	... ...	00821
Allure	... ...	00822
Allurement	... ...	00823
Allurer ...	... ...	00824
Alluring ...	... ...	00825
Allusion ...	... ...	00826
Alluvial ...	... ...	00827
Alluvium	... ...	00828
Ally	... ...	00829
Almanac	... ...	00830
Almightily	... ...	00831
Almightiness ...	...	00832
Almighty	... ...	00833
Almond ...	... ...	00834
Almoner...	... ...	00835
Almonry	... ...	00836
Almost ...	... ...	00837
Alms	... ...	00838
Alnage ...	... ...	00839
Aloe	... ...	00840
Aloft	... ...	00841
Alone	... ...	00842
Along	... ...	00843
Aloof	... ...	00844
Aloud	... ...	00845
Alp ...	... ...	00846
Alpaca	... ...	00847
Alpha	... ...	00848
Alphabet	... ...	00849
Alphabetical ...	...	00850

Alpine	... ...	00851
Already ...	... ...	00852
Also	... ...	00853
Altar	... ...	00854
Alter	... ...	00855
Alterable	... ...	00856
Alterableness...	...	00857
Alteration	... ...	00858
Alterative	... ...	00859
Altercate	... ...	00860
Altercation	... ...	00861
Altered ...	... ...	00862
Alterer ...	... ...	00863
Altering ...	... ...	00864
Alternate	... ...	00865
Alternately	... ...	00866
Alternation	... ...	00867
Alternative	... ...	00868
Alters	... ...	00869
Although	... ...	00870
Altitude ...	... ...	00871
Alto	... ...	00872
Altogether	... ...	00873
Alum	... ...	00874
Alumina...	... ...	00875
Aluminite	... ...	00876
Aluminous	... ...	00877
Aluminium	... ...	00878
Alumnus	... ...	00879
Always ...	... ...	00880
Am ...	... ...	00881
Amain	... ...	00882
Amalgamate ...	...	00883
Amalgamation	...	00884
Amanuensis ...	...	00885
Amaranth	... ...	00886
Amass	... ...	00887
Amassment	... ...	00888
Amateur...	... ...	00889
Amatory	... ...	00890
Amaze	... ...	00891
Amazed ...	... ...	00892
Amazedness ...	...	00893
Amazement	... ...	00894
Amazing	... ...	00895
Amazon ...	... ...	00896
Ambassador ...	...	00897
Ambassadress	...	00898
Amber ...	... ...	00899
Ambergris	... ...	00900

AMB	(5)	ANA	10
Ambidexter	00901	Among	00951
Ambidextrous ...	00902	Amorous...	00952
Ambient...	00903	Amorphous	00953
Ambiguity	00904	Amount	00954
Ambiguous	00905	Amounted	00955
Ambit	00906	Amounting	00956
Ambition	00907	Amounts...	00957
Ambitionless	00908	Amour	00958
Ambitious	00909	Amphibiology ...	00959
Ambitiously	00910	Amphibious	00960
Amble	00911	Amphibological ...	00961
Ambrosia	00912	Amphitheatre... ...	00962
Ambrosial	00913	Ample	00963
Ambulance	00914	Ampliate...	00964
Ambulate	00915	Amplification	00965
Ambulator	00916	Amplified	00966
Ambulatory	00917	Amplifier	00967
Ambush	00918	Amplify	00968
Ameer	00919	Amplitude	00969
Ameliorate	00920	Amply	00970
Amelioration	00921	Amputate	00971
Amen	00922	Amputated	00972
Amenable	00923	Amputation	00973
Amend	00924	Amulet	00974
Amendatory	00925	Amuse	00975
Amende	00926	Amused	00976
Amended	00927	Amusement	00977
Amending	00928	Amuser	00978
Amendment	00929	Amusing...	00979
Amends	00930	An	00980
Amenity	00931	Anabaptist	00981
Amerce	00932	Anachronism	00982
Amercement	00933	Anacreontic	00983
American	00934	Anagram	00984
Americanize	00935	Analectic	00985
Amethyst	00936	Analogical	00986
Amiability	00937	Analogism	00987
Amiable	00938	Analogist	00988
Amiably	00939	Analogous	00989
Amicable	00940	Analogue	00990
Amicably	00941	Analogy	00991
Amical	00942	Analysis	00992
Amid	00943	Analyst	00993
Amidships	00944	Analytical	00994
Amiss	00945	Analytics...	00995
Amity	00946	Analyze	00996
Ammonia	00947	Anarch	00997
Ammoniac	00948	Anarchical	00998
Ammunition	00949	Anarchism	00999
Amnesty...	00950	Anarchist	01000

Anarchy	01001	Animalcule	01051
Anathema	01002	Animalism	01052
Anathematism ...	01003	Animalize	01053
Anathematization ...	01004	Animate	01054
Anathematize... ...	01005	Animated	01055
Anatomical	01006	Animation	01056
Anatomist	01007	Animator	01057
Anatomize	01008	Animosity	01058
Anatomy	01009	Animus	01059
Ancestor...	01010	Anise	01060
Ancestral	01011	Anisette	01061
Ancestress	01012	Anker	01062
Ancestry...	01013	Ankle	01063
Anchor	01014	Anklet	01064
Anchorage	01015	Annal	01065
Anchored	01016	Annalist	01066
Anchoret	01017	Annals	01067
Anchovy...	01018	Anneal	01068
Ancient	01019	Annectant	01069
Anciently	01020	Annex	01070
Ancillary	01021	Annexation	01071
And...	01022	Annexed...	01072
Anecdotal	01023	Annihilate	01073
Anecdote	01024	Annihilated	01074
Anele	01025	Annihilation	01075
Anelectric	01026	Anniversary	01076
Anemometer	01027	Annotate	01077
Anent	01028	Annotation	01078
Aneurism	01029	Annotator	01079
Anew	01030	Announce	01080
Angel	01031	Announced	01081
Angelic	01032	Announcement ...	01082
Anger	01033	Announces	01083
Angina	01034	Announcing	01084
Angle	01035	Annoy	01085
Angler	01036	Annoyance	01086
Anglican...	01037	Annoyed...	01087
Anglice	01038	Annoying	01088
Anglicism	01039	Annoys	01089
Anglicize	01040	Annual	01090
Angling	01041	Annually	01091
Angrily	01042	Annuitant	01092
Angry	01043	Annuity	01093
Anguineal	01044	Annul	01094
Anguish	01045	Annular	01095
Angular	01046	Annulled	01096
Anile	01047	Annulment	01097
Animadversion ...	01048	Annunciate	01098
Animadvert	01049	Annunciation ...	01099
Animal	01050	Anodyne...	01100

Anoint	01101	Anticipated 01151
Anointed	01102	Anticipates 01152
Anointing	01103	Anticipating 01153
Anomalous	01104	Anticipation 01154
Anomaly	01105	Anticipator 01155
Anon	01106	Anticonstitutional ... 01156
Anonymous	01107	Anticontagious ... 01157
Another	01108	Antidotal 01158
Answer	01109	Antidote... 01159
Answerable	01110	Antiloquy 01160
Answered	01111	Antimonial 01161
Answerer	01112	Antimony 01162
Answering	01113	Antipapal 01163
Answerless	01114	Antipathetic 01164
Answers	01115	Antipathy 01165
Ant	01116	Antipatriotic 01166
Antagonism	01117	Antiphlogistic ... 01167
Antagonist	01118	Antiphon 01168
Antagonistic	01119	Antiphony 01169
Antagonize	01120	Antiphrasis 01170
Antarctic	01121	Antiphysical 01171
Ante	01122	Antipodal 01172
Antecede	01123	Antipodes 01173
Antecedence	01124	Antiquarian 01174
Antecedent	01125	Antiquarianism ... 01175
Antecedently	01126	Antiquary 01176
Anteceding	01127	Antiquate 01177
Antecessor	01128	Antiquated 01178
Antechamber	01129	Antique 01179
Antedate...	01130	Antiquities 01180
Antedated	01131	Antiquity 01181
Antediluvian	01132	Antiscriptural... ... 01182
Antelope...	01133	Antiseptic 01183
Antemeridian... ...	01134	Antislavery 01184
Antennæ...	01135	Antisocial 01185
Antenuptial	01136	Antispasmodic ... 01186
Antepast...	01137	Antithesis 01187
Anterior	01138	Antitype... 01188
Anteroom	01139	Antler 01189
Anthem	01140	Anus 01190
Anthology	01141	Anvil 01191
Anthomania	01142	Anxietude 01192
Anthropography ...	01143	Anxiety 01193
Anthropology... ...	01144	Anxious 01194
Anthropophagi ...	01145	Any... 01195
Anthropophagy ...	01146	Anywise 01196
Antibilious	01147	Apace 01197
Antic	01148	Apart 01198
Antichrist	01149	Apartment 01199
Anticipate	01150	Apathetic 01200

13	APA	(7)	APP

Apathist	01201	Appeared 01251
Apathy	01202	Appearing 01252
Ape...	01203	Appears 01253
Aperient...	01204	Appeasable 01254
Aperitive	01205	Appease 01255
Aperture...	01206	Appeasive 01256
Apex	01207	Appellant 01257
Aphlogistic	01208	Appellation 01258
Aphorism	01209	Appellatory 01259
Aphorist...	01210	Appellee... 01260
Apiary	01211	Appellor... 01261
Apiece	01212	Append 01262
Apish	01213	Appendage 01263
Apocalypse	01214	Appendancy 01264
Apocrypha	01215	Appended 01265
Apocryphal	01216	Appendix 01266
Apogee	01217	Appertain 01267
Apologetic	01218	Appertained 01268
Apologist	01219	Appertaining 01269
Apologize	01220	Appetite... 01270
Apologizing	01221	Applaud... 01271
Apologue	01222	Applauded 01272
Apology	01223	Applauder 01273
Apoplectic	01224	Applause 01274
Apoplexy	01225	Apple 01275
Apostasy	01226	Appliance 01276
Apostate...	01227	Applicable 01277
Apostle	01228	Applicant 01278
Apostolic	01229	Application 01279
Apostrophe	01230	Applicatory 01280
Apothecary	01231	Applied 01281
Apothegm	01232	Applies 01282
Apothegmatize ...	01233	Apply 01283
Apotheosis	01234	Applying 01284
Apotheosize	01235	Appoint 01285
Appal	01236	Appointed 01286
Appalled	01237	Appointing 01287
Appalling	01238	Appointment 01288
Apparatus	01239	Appoints 01289
Apparel	01240	Apportion 01290
Apparent	01241	Apposite... 01291
Apparently	01242	Appraisal 01292
Apparition	01243	Appraise... 01293
Appeal	01244	Appraisement ... 01294
Appealed	01245	Appraiser 01295
Appealer	01246	Appreciable 01296
Appealing	01247	Appreciate 01297
Appeals	01248	Appreciated 01298
Appear	01249	Appreciation 01299
Appearance	01250	Apprehend 01300

APP	(7)	ARC	14

Apprehended...	...	01301	Arable	01351
Apprehending	...	01302	Arbalist	01352
Apprehensible	...	01303	Arbiter	01353
Apprehension...	...	01304	Arbitrament	01354
Apprehensive...	...	01305	Arbitrarily	01355
Apprentice ...	...	01306	Arbitrary	01356
Apprenticeship	...	01307	Arbitrate	01357
Apprise	...	01308	Arbitration	01358
Apprised ...	...	01309	Arbitrator	01359
Approach ...	...	01310	Arbitrement	01360
Approached ...	...	01311	Arboreous	01361
Approacher ...	...	01312	Arborescence... ...	01362
Approaching ...	...	01313	Arboretum	01363
Approbate ...	...	01314	Arboriculture ...	01364
Approbation ...	...	01315	Arbour	01365
Appropinquate	...	01316	Arc	01366
Appropriable...	...	01317	Arcade	01367
Appropriate ...	...	01318	Arcanum...	01368
Appropriated...	...	01319	Arch	01369
Appropriation	...	01320	Archæologic	01370
Appropriator ...	...	01321	Archæologist	01371
Approvable ...	...	01322	Archæology	01372
Approval ...	...	01323	Archaic	01373
Approve	...	01324	Archaism	01374
Approved ...	...	01325	Archangel	01375
Approvement...	...	01326	Archbishop	01376
Approves ...	...	01327	Archbishopric ...	01377
Approving ...	...	01328	Archdeacon	01378
Approximate ...	...	01329	Archdeaconry ...	01379
Approximation	...	01330	Archdiocese	01380
Appulse	...	01331	Archduchy	01381
Appulsive ...	...	01332	Archduke	01382
Appurtenance	...	01333	Archenemy	01383
Apricot	...	01334	Archer	01384
April	...	01335	Archery	01385
Apron	...	01336	Archetype	01386
Apropos	...	01337	Archfiend	01387
Apt	...	01338	Archheresy	01388
Apter	...	01339	Archidiaconal ...	01389
Aptitude... ...	...	01340	Archiepiscopal ...	01390
Aptly	...	01341	Archimandrite ...	01391
Aptness	...	01342	Arching	01392
Aquarium ...	...	01343	Archipelago	01393
Aquatic	...	01344	Architect	01394
Aqueduct ...	...	01345	Architective ...	01395
Aqueous ...	...	01346	Architectural	01396
Aquiline	...	01347	Architecture	01397
Aquose	...	01348	Archives	01398
Arab	...	01349	Archlike	01399
Arabesque ...	...	01350	Archly	01400

15	ARC	(8)	ARR

Archness...	...	...	01401	Armature	... ...	01451
Archstone	...	...	01402	Armed ...	... ...	01452
Archway...	...	...	01403	Arming ...	... ...	01453
Archwise	...	...	01404	Armful ...	... ...	01454
Arctic ...	...	...	01405	Armhole	... ...	01455
Arcubalist	...	...	01406	Armistice	... ...	01456
Ardency...	...	...	01407	Armless ...	... ...	01457
Ardent ...	...	...	01408	Armlet ...	... ...	01458
Ardour ...	...	...	01409	Armorial	... ...	01459
Arduous ...	...	...	01410	Armorist...	... ...	01460
Are	...	...	01411	Armour ...	... ...	01461
Area ...	...	...	01412	Arms ...	... ...	01462
Areal ...	...	...	01413	Army ...	... ...	01463
Arefaction	...	...	01414	Aroma ...	... ...	01464
Arefy ...	...	...	01415	Aromatic	... ...	01465
Arena ...	...	...	01416	Arose ...	... ...	01466
Arenose ...	...	...	01417	Around ...	... ...	01467
Areopagus	...	...	01418	Arouse ...	... ...	01468
Argent ...	...	...	01419	Arquebusade	...	01469
Argentation	...	...	01420	Arquebuse	... ...	01470
Argentiferous...	...	...	01421	Arrack ...	... ...	01471
Argentine	...	...	01422	Arraign ...	... ...	01472
Argil ...	...	...	01423	Arraigned	... ...	01473
Argosy ...	...	...	01424	Arraignment ...	...	01474
Argue ...	...	...	01425	Arrange ...	... ...	01475
Argued ...	...	...	01426	Arranged	... ...	01476
Arguer ...	...	...	01427	Arrangement ...	...	01477
Arguing ...	...	...	01428	Arranger...	... ...	01478
Argument	...	...	01429	Arranges...	... ...	01479
Argumentable	...	...	01430	Arranging	... ...	01480
Argumentative	...	...	01431	Arrant ...	... ...	01481
Aria ...	...	...	01432	Arras ...	... ...	01482
Arianism...	...	...	01433	Array ...	... ...	01483
Arid ...	...	...	01434	Arrear ...	... ...	01484
Aridity ...	...	...	01435	Arrest ...	... ...	01485
Arietta ...	...	...	01436	Arrestation	... ...	01486
Aright ...	...	...	01437	Arrested ...	... ...	01487
Arise ...	...	...	01438	Arrester ...	... ...	01488
Arisen ...	...	...	01439	Arrival ...	... ...	01489
Arises ...	...	...	01440	Arrive ...	... ...	01490
Aristocracy	...	...	01441	Arrived ...	... ...	01491
Aristocrat	...	...	01442	Arrives ...	... ...	01492
Aristocratic	...	...	01443	Arriving ...	... ...	01493
Aristotelian	...	...	01444	Arrogance	... ...	01494
Arithmetic	...	...	01445	Arrogant	... ...	01495
Arithmetician	...	...	01446	Arrogantly	... ...	01496
Ark	...	...	01447	Arrogate...	... ...	01497
Arm ..	...	...	01448	Arrosion ...	... ...	01498
Armada ...	...	...	01449	Arrow ...	... ...	01499
Armament	...	...	01450	Arrowy ...	... ...	01500

Arsenal	01501	Ascribed	01551
Arsenic	01502	Ascribing	01552
Arsenical	01503	Ascription	01553
Arsenicate	01504	Ash	01554
Arson	01505	Ashamed	01555
Art	01506	Ashes	01556
Artery	01507	Ashore	01557
Artful	01508	Ashy	01558
Artfully	01509	Asiatic	01559
Artichoke	01510	Aside	01560
Article	01511	Asinine	01561
Articularly	01512	Ask	01562
Articulate	01513	Askance	01563
Articulately	01514	Asked	01564
Articulation	01515	Askew	01565
Artifice	01516	Asking	01566
Artificer	01517	Asks	01567
Artificial	01518	Aslant	01568
Artificially	01519	Asleep	01569
Artillery	01520	Aslope	01570
Artilleryman	01521	Asp	01571
Artisan	01522	Asparagus	01572
Artist	01523	Aspect	01573
Artistic	01524	Aspen	01574
Artistically	01525	Asperate	01575
Artless	01526	Asperity	01576
Artlessly	01527	Asperse	01577
As	01528	Asperser	01578
Asafetida	01529	Aspersion	01579
Asbestine	01530	Asphalte	01580
Asbestos	01531	Asphyxia	01581
Ascend	01532	Aspirant	01582
Ascendant	01533	Aspirate	01583
Ascended	01534	Aspirated	01584
Ascendency	01535	Aspiration	01585
Ascending	01536	Aspire	01586
Ascends	01537	Aspired	01587
Ascension	01538	Aspirer	01588
Ascensive	01539	Aspiring	01589
Ascent	01540	Asquint	01590
Ascertain	01541	Ass	01591
Ascertainable	01542	Assail	01592
Ascertained	01543	Assailant	01593
Ascertaining	01544	Assailed	01594
Ascertainment	01545	Assailing	01595
Ascertains	01546	Assails	01596
Ascetic	01547	Assassin	01597
Asceticism	01548	Assassinate	01598
Ascribable	01549	Assassinated	01599
Ascribe	01550	Assassination	01600

17	ASS			(9)		AT	
Assault	...	...	01601	Associable	...	...	01651
Assaulted	...	...	01602	Associate	...	...	01652
Assay	...	...	01603	Associated	...	...	01653
Assayer	...	...	01604	Association	...	...	01654
Assemblage	...	...	01605	Assonance	...	...	01655
Assemblance	...	...	01606	Assort	...	...	01656
Assemble	...	...	01607	Assorted	...	...	01657
Assembled	...	...	01608	Assortment	...	...	01658
Assembling	...	...	01609	Assuage	...	...	01659
Assembly	...	...	01610	Assuagement	...	...	01660
Assent	...	...	01611	Assuasive	...	...	01661
Assented	...	...	01612	Assuetude	...	...	01662
Assenter	...	...	01613	Assume	...	...	01663
Assenting	...	...	01614	Assumed	...	...	01664
Assents	...	...	01615	Assumes	...	...	01665
Assert	...	...	01616	Assuming	...	...	01666
Asserted	...	...	01617	Assumption	...	...	01667
Asserting	...	...	01618	Assurance	...	...	01668
Assertion	...	...	01619	Assure	...	...	01669
Assertively	...	...	01620	Assured	...	...	01670
Assertor	...	...	01621	Assuredly	...	...	01671
Asserts	...	...	01622	Assuring	...	...	01672
Assess	...	...	01623	Asterisk	...	...	01673
Assessable	...	...	01624	Astern	...	...	01674
Assessed	...	...	01625	Asteroidal	...	...	01675
Assessment	...	...	01626	Asthma	...	...	01676
Assessor	...	...	01627	Astonish	...	...	01677
Assets	...	...	01628	Astonished	...	...	01678
Asseverate	...	...	01629	Astonishes	...	...	01679
Asseverated	...	...	01630	Astonishing	...	...	01680
Asseveration	...	...	01631	Astonishment	...	01681
Assiduity	...	...	01632	Astound	...	...	01682
Assiduous	...	...	01633	Astounded	...	...	01683
Assiege	...	...	01634	Astounding	...	...	01684
Assign	...	...	01635	Astral	...	...	01685
Assignable	...	...	01636	Astray	...	...	01686
Assignation	...	...	01637	Astride	...	...	01687
Assigned	...	...	01638	Astringe	...	...	01688
Assignee	...	...	01639	Astringent	...	...	01689
Assignment	...	...	01640	Astrologer	...	...	01690
Assimilate	...	..	01641	Astrologically	...	01691
Assimilated	...	...	01642	Astrology	...	...	01692
Assimilation	...	...	01643	Astronomer	...	...	01693
Assist	...	...	01644	Astronomical	...	...	01694
Assistance	...	...	01645	Astronomy	...	...	01695
Assistant	...	...	01646	Astute	...	...	01696
Assisted	...	...	01647	Astuteness	...	...	01697
Assisting	...	...	01648	Asunder	...	...	01698
Assists	...	...	01649	Asylum	...	...	01699
Assize	...	...	01650	At	...	...	01700

Ataghan...	01701	Attended 01751
Ate	01702	Attending 01752
Athanasian	01703	Attention 01753
Atheism	01704	Attentive 01754
Atheist	01705	Attently 01755
Athirst	01706	Attenuate 01756
Athlete	01707	Attenuated 01757
Athletic	01708	Attenuation 01758
Athwart	01709	Attest 01759
Atlas	01710	Attestation 01760
Atmosphere	01711	Attested 01761
Atmospherical ...	01712	Attesting 01762
Atom	01713	Attestor 01763
Atomism	01714	Attests 01764
Atomist	01715	Attic 01765
Atomize	01716	Attire 01766
Atomy	01717	Attired 01767
Atone	01718	Attirer 01768
Atonement	01719	Attitude 01769
Atones	01720	Attitudinal 01770
Atoning	01721	Attorney... 01771
Atrabilarian	01722	Attract 01772
Atrabiliary	01723	Attracted 01773
Atrocious	01724	Attracting 01774
Atrocity	01725	Attractingly 01775
Atrophy	01726	Attraction 01776
Attach	01727	Attractive 01777
Attaché	01728	Attractor 01778
Attached	01729	Attracts 01779
Attaches...	01730	Attribute 01780
Attaching	01731	Attributed 01781
Attachment	01732	Attributes 01782
Attack	01733	Attributive 01783
Attacked	01734	Attrition... 01784
Attacking	01735	Attune 01785
Attain	01736	Auburn 01786
Attainder	01737	Auction 01787
Attained	01738	Auctioneer 01788
Attaining	01739	Audacious 01789
Attainment	01740	Audacity... 01790
Attaint	01741	Audible 01791
Attainted	01742	Audibly 01792
Attemper	01743	Audience 01793
Attempt	01744	Audit 01794
Attempted	01745	Auditor 01795
Attempting	01746	Auditory... 01796
Attempts	01747	Auger 01797
Attend	01748	Aught 01798
Attendance	01749	Augmentation ... 01799
Attendant	01750	Augmented 01800

Augmenter	...	...	01801
Augmenting	...	...	01802
Augur	...	...	01803
Augury	...	...	01804
August	...	...	01805
Augustness	...	...	01806
Aulic	..	...	01807
Aunt	...	...	01808
Auricle	...	...	01809
Auricular	...	...	01810
Auriferous	...	...	01811
Auriform	...	...	01812
Aurist	...	...	01813
Auscultation	...	...	01814
Auspicate	...	...	01815
Auspices...	...	...	01816
Auspicious	...	...	01817
Austere	...	...	01818
Austerity...	...	...	01819
Australasian	...	...	01820
Australian	...	...	01821
Austrian	...	...	01822
Authentic	...	...	01823
Authenticate	...	...	01824
Authenticated	...	...	01825
Authentication	...	...	01826
Authenticity	...	...	01827
Author	...	...	01828
Authoress	...	...	01829
Authoritative	...	...	01830
Authority	...	...	01831
Authorize	...	...	01832
Authorized	...	...	01833
Autobiographical	...	...	01834
Autobiography	...	...	01835
Autocracy	...	...	01836
Autocrat...	...	...	01837
Autograph	...	...	01838
Autographic	...	...	01839
Automaton	...	...	01840
Autumn	...	...	01841
Auxiliary	...	...	01842
Auxiliaries	...	...	01843
Avail	...	...	01844
Available	...	...	01845
Availed	...	...	01846
Availing...	...	...	01847
Avalanche	...	...	01848
Avarice	...	...	01849
Avaricious	...	...	01850
Ave...	...	...	01851
Avenge	...	...	01852
Avenged...	...	...	01853
Avenger	...	...	01854
Avenging	...	...	01855
Avenue	...	...	01856
Aver	...	...	01857
Average	...	...	01858
Averment	...	...	01859
Averse	...	...	01860
Aversion	...	...	01861
Avert	...	...	01862
Averted	...	...	01863
Aviary	...	..	01864
Avidity	...	...	01865
Avocation	...	...	01866
Avoid	...	...	01867
Avoidance	...	...	01868
Avoided	...	...	01869
Avoiding	...	...	01870
Avoids	...	...	01871
Avow	..	...	01872
Avowal	...	...	01873
Avowedly	...	...	01874
Await	...	...	01875
Awaiting...	...	...	01876
Awaited	...	...	01877
Awake	...	...	01878
Awakes	...	...	01879
Award	...	...	01880
Awarded...	...	...	01881
Aware...	...	...	01882
Away	...	...	01883
Awe	...	...	01884
Awful	...	...	01885
Awfully	...	...	01886
Awhile	...	...	01887
Awkward	...	...	01888
Awkwardly	...	...	01889
Awl...	...	...	01890
Awless	...	...	01891
Awning	...	...	01892
Awoke	...	...	01893
Awry	...	...	01894
Axe...	...	...	01895
Axiom	...	...	01896
Axis	...	...	01897
Axle	...	...	01898
Aye...	...	...	01899
Azure	...	...	01900

B	(10)	BAN	20

B	01901	Bailed	01951
Babble	01902	Bailee	01952
Babbler	01903	Bailie	01953
Babe	01904	Bailiff	01954
Baboon	01905	Bailiwick	01955
Baby	01906	Bailment...	01956
Babyhood	01907	Bairn	01957
Babyish	01908	Bait...	01958
Baccalaureate... ...	01909	Baited	01959
Bacchanalia	01910	Baize	01960
Bacchanalian	01911	Bake	01961
Bacchant	01912	Baked	01962
Bacchic	01913	Baker	01963
Bachelor...	01914	Balance	01964
Bachelorship	01915	Balanced...	01965
Back	01916	Balances...	01966
Backbite...	01917	Balancing	01967
Backbiter	01918	Balcony	01968
Backbiting	01919	Bald	01969
Backbone	01920	Balderdash	01970
Backed	01921	Baldrick...	01971
Backer	01922	Bale...	01972
Backgammon... ...	01923	Baleful	01973
Backslide	01924	Balister	01974
Backslider	01925	Balk	01975
Backstairs	01926	Balked	01976
Backward	01927	Ball...	01977
Backwards	01928	Ballad	01978
Backwardly	01929	Ballast	01979
Backwoodsman ...	01930	Ballastage	01980
Bacon	01931	Ballasted	01981
Baconian	01932	Ballet	01982
Bad	01933	Balloon	01983
Bade	01934	Balloonist	01984
Badge	01935	Ballot	01985
Badger	01936	Balloting...	01986
Badgered	01937	Ballotted...	01987
Badinage	01938	Balm	01988
Badly	01939	Balmy	01989
Baffle	01940	Balsam	01990
Baffled	01941	Baluster	01991
Bag...	01942	Balustrade	01992
Bagatelle	01943	Bamboo	01993
Baggage	01944	Bamboozle	01994
Bagged	01945	Bamboozled	01995
Bagnio	01946	Ban...	01996
Bagpipe	01947	Banco	01997
Bail...	01948	Band	01998
Bailable	01949	Bandage...	01999
Bailbond...	01950	Bandana...	02000

Bandbox...	...	...	02001	Bargain ...	...	...	02051
Banded	...	...	02002	Bargained	...	...	02052
Bandit	...	...	02003	Barge	...	...	02053
Banditti ...	...	...	02004	Barger	...	...	02054
Bandrol	...	...	02005	Bark	...	...	02055
Bandy	...	...	02006	Barker	...	...	02056
Bane	...	...	02007	Barking ...	...	...	02057
Baneful	...	...	02008	Barley	...	...	02058
Bang	...	...	02009	Barm	...	...	02059
Banish	...	...	02010	Barmaid ...	...	...	02060
Banished...	...	...	02011	Barn	...	...	02061
Banisher ...	...	...	02012	Barnacle...	...	...	02062
Banishment	...	...	02013	Barometer	...	...	02063
Bank	...	...	02014	Baron	...	...	02064
Bankable	...	...	02015	Baronage	...	...	02065
Banker	...	...	02016	Baroness	...	...	02066
Banking ...	...	...	02017	Baronet ...	...	...	02067
Bankrupt	...	...	02018	Baronetage	...	...	02068
Bankruptcy	...	...	02019	Baronetcy	...	...	02069
Banner	...	...	02020	Baronial ...	...	...	02070
Banneret...	...	...	02021	Barony	...	...	02071
Banns	...	...	02022	Barouche	...	...	02072
Banquet ...	...	...	02023	Barrack ...	...	...	02073
Bantam	...	...	02024	Barratry ...	...	...	02074
Banter	...	...	02025	Barrel	...	...	02075
Banterer ...	...	...	02026	Barren	...	...	02076
Bantling ...	...	...	02027	Barrenness	...	...	02077
Banyan	...	...	02028	Barricade	...	...	02078
Baptism ...	...	...	02029	Barrier	...	...	02079
Baptist	...	...	02030	Barrister...	...	...	02080
Baptistery	...	...	02031	Barrow	...	...	02081
Baptize	...	...	02032	Barter	...	...	02082
Baptized ...	...	...	02033	Bartered ...	...	...	02083
Bar ...	...	...	02034	Barytone...	...	...	02084
Barb	...	...	02035	Basalt	...	...	02085
Barbacan	...	...	02036	Basinet	...	...	02086
Barbarian	...	...	02037	Base	...	...	02087
Barbaric ...	...	...	02038	Based	...	...	02088
Barbarism	...	...	02039	Basely	...	...	02089
Barbarity	...	...	02040	Basement	...	...	02090
Barbarous	...	...	02041	Baseness	...	...	02091
Barbed	...	...	02042	Bashaw	...	...	02092
Barber	...	...	02043	Bashful	...	...	02093
Bard	...	...	02044	Basilisk ...	...	...	02094
Bare	...	...	02045	Basin	...	...	02095
Barebone	...	...	02046	Basined	...	...	02096
Bared	...	...	02047	Basis	...	...	02097
Barefaced	...	...	02048	Bask	...	...	02098
Barely	...	...	02049	Basket	...	...	02099
Bareness...	...	...	02050	Bass...	...	...	02100

Bassinet	...	...	02101	Bearer	...	...	02151
Bassoon	...	...	02102	Bearing	...	...	02152
Bastard	...	...	02103	Bearish	...	...	02153
Bastardize	...	...	02104	Beast	...	...	02154
Baste	...	...	02105	Beastliness	...	...	02155
Bastinado	...	...	02106	Beastly	...	...	02156
Bastion	...	...	02107	Beat	...	...	02157
Bat ...	...	...	02108	Beats	...	...	02158
Batable	...	...	02109	Beaten	...	...	02159
Batch	...	...	02110	Beater	...	...	02160
Bath	...	...	02111	Beatific	...	...	02161
Bathe	...	...	02112	Beatify	...	...	02162
Bather	...	...	02113	Beating	...	...	02163
Bathos	...	...	02114	Beatitude	...	...	02164
Batiste	...	...	02115	Beau	...	...	02165
Battalion	...	...	02116	Beauteous	...	...	02166
Batten	...	...	02117	Beautiful	...	...	02167
Batter	...	...	02118	Beautifully	...	...	02168
Battered	...	...	02119	Beautify	...	...	02169
Battery	...	...	02120	Beauty	...	...	02170
Battle	...	...	02121	Beaver	...	...	02171
Battledore	...	...	02122	Becalm	...	...	02172
Battlement	...	...	02123	Becalmed	...	...	02173
Battling	...	...	02124	Becalming	...	...	02174
Battue	...	...	02125	Became	...	...	02175
Bavarian	...	...	02126	Because	...	...	02176
Bawble	...	...	02127	Bechance	...	...	02177
Bawl	...	...	02128	Beck	...	...	02178
Bawled	...	...	02129	Beckon	...	...	02179
Bawler	...	...	02130	Beckoned	...	...	02180
Bay ...	...	...	02131	Becloud	...	...	02181
Bayonet	...	...	02132	Become	...	...	02182
Bays	...	...	02133	Becomes	...	...	02183
Bazaar	...	...	02134	Becoming	...	...	02184
Be ...	...	...	02135	Bed ...	...	...	02185
Beach	...	...	02136	Bedding	...	...	02186
Beacon	...	...	02137	Bedeck	...	...	02187
Beaconage	...	...	02138	Bedew	...	...	02188
Bead	...	...	02139	Bedim	...	...	02189
Beadle	...	...	02140	Bedizen	...	...	02190
Beagle	...	...	02141	Bedlam	...	...	02191
Beak	...	...	02142	Bedlamite	...	...	02192
Beaker	...	...	02143	Bedouin	...	...	02193
Beam	...	...	02144	Bedridden	...	...	02194
Beaming	...	...	02145	Bedstead	...	...	02195
Bean	...	...	02146	Bedtick	...	...	02196
Bear	...	...	02147	Bedtime	...	...	02197
Bearable	...	...	02148	Bedwarf	...	...	02198
Beard	...	...	02149	Bee	...	...	02199
Beardless	...	...	02150	Beef	...	...	02200

Beef-eater	...	...	02201	Behaving	 02251
Beef-steak	...	...	02202	Behead ...	 02252
Beelzebub	...	...	02203	Beheaded	 02253
Been	...	...	02204	Beheld ...	 02254
Beer	...	...	02205	Behemoth	 02255
Beeswax	...	...	02206	Behest ...	 02256
Beetle	...	...	02207	Behind ...	 02257
Beetling	...	...	02208	Behindhand	 02258
Beeves	...	...	02209	Behold ...	 02259
Befall	...	...	02210	Beholding	 02260
Befallen	...	...	02211	Beholden	 02261
Befit	...	...	02212	Beholder	 02262
Befitting	...	...	02213	Behoof ...	 02263
Befogged	...	...	02214	Behoove ...	 02264
Befool	...	...	02215	Behooves	 02265
Before	...	...	02216	Being	 02266
Beforehand	...	...	02217	Belabour ...	 02267
Beforetime	...	...	02218	Belated ...	 02268
Befoul	...	...	02219	Belay	 02269
Befriend	...	...	02220	Belch	 02270
Befriended	...	...	02221	Belching ...	 02271
Befringe	...	...	02222	Beldam ...	 02272
Beg ...	...	...	02223	Beleaguer	 02273
Began	...	...	02224	Belectured	 02274
Beget	...	...	02225	Belfry	 02275
Begets	...	...	02226	Belgian	 02276
Begetting	...	...	02227	Belial	 02277
Beggar	...	...	02228	Belie	 02278
Beggarly	...	...	02229	Belied	 02279
Beggary	...	...	02230	Belief	 02280
Begged	...	...	02231	Believe	 02281
Begging	...	...	02232	Believer ...	 02282
Begin	...	...	02233	Believed ...	 02283
Begins	...	...	02234	Believes ...	 02284
Beginner	...	...	02235	Believing	 02285
Beginning	...	...	02236	Bell	 02286
Begone	...	...	02237	Belladonna	 02287
Begotten	...	...	02238	Belle	 02288
Begrime	...	...	02239	Bellicose	 02289
Begrudge	...	...	02240	Bellied ...	 02290
Begs	...	...	02241	Belligerent	 02291
Beguile	...	...	02242	Bellow ...	 02292
Beguilement	...	...	02243	Bellows ...	 02293
Begum	...	...	02244	Belly	 02294
Begun	...	...	02245	Belock ...	 02295
Behalf	...	...	02246	Belong ...	 02296
Behave	...	...	02247	Belonged	 02297
Behaved	...	...	02248	Belonging	 02298
Behaves	...	...	02249	Belongs ...	 02299
Behaviour	...	...	02250	Below	 02300

BEL	(12)	BET	24

Belt...	02301	Bereft	02351
Belted	02302	Bergamot	02352
Bemask	02303	Bernouse...	02353
Bemoan	02304	Berry	02354
Bemoaned	02305	Berth	02355
Bemoaning	02306	Bescrawl...	02356
Bemuddle	02307	Bescreen	02357
Bench	02308	Beseech	02358
Bencher	02309	Beseecher	02359
Bend	02310	Beseeching	02360
Bending	02311	Beseem	02361
Bends	02312	Beset	02362
Beneath	02313	Besetting	02363
Benedict...	02314	Beshrew	02364
Benedictine	02315	Beshrouded	02365
Benediction	02316	Beside	02366
Benedictory	02317	Besides	02367
Benefaction	02318	Besiege	02368
Benefactor	02319	Besieged	02369
Benefactress	02320	Besieger	02370
Benefice	02321	Besieging	02371
Beneficed	02322	Besmear	02372
Beneficence	02323	Besmeared	02373
Beneficent	02324	Besmoke...	02374
Beneficial	02325	Besom	02375
Beneficiary	02326	Besot	02376
Benefit	02327	Besought	02377
Benevolence	02328	Besottedly	02378
Benevolent	02329	Bespangle	02379
Benevolently	02330	Bespatter	02380
Bengalee...	02331	Bespeak	02381
Benight	02332	Best...	02382
Benighted	02333	Bestial	02383
Benign	02334	Bestialize	02384
Benignant	02335	Bestially	02385
Benignity	02336	Bestir	02386
Benignly...	02337	Bestow	02387
Bent	02338	Bestowal...	02388
Benumb	02339	Bestowed	02389
Benumbed	02340	Bestower...	02390
Beplaster	02341	Bestowing	02391
Bepowder	02342	Bestride	02392
Bepraise	02343	Bestud	02393
Bequeath	02344	Bet	02394
Bequeathed	02345	Betake	02395
Bequeather	02346	Betaken	02396
Bequest	02347	Betel	02397
Bere	02348	Bethink	02398
Bereave	02349	Betide	02399
Bereavement	02350	Betimes	02400

Betoken	02401	Biceps	02451
Betook	02402	Bicker	02452
Betrap	02403	Bickerer	02453
Betray	02404	Bickering	02454
Betrayal	02405	Bid	02455
Betrayer	02406	Bids...	02456
Betroth	02407	Bidden	02457
Betrothed	02408	Bidder	02458
Betrothment ...	02409	Bidding	02459
Betted	02410	Bide	02460
Better	02411	Biennial	02461
Bettered	02412	Biennially	02462
Bettering	02413	Bier...	02463
Betting	02414	Biffin	02464
Between	02415	Bifold	02465
Betwixt	02416	Biform	02466
Bevel	02417	Bifurcate... ...	02467
Bevelling	02418	Bifurcation ...	02468
Beverage... ...	02419	Big	02469
Bevy	02420	Bigamist	02470
Bewail	02421	Bigamy	02471
Bewailed... ...	02422	Bight	02472
Bewailing	02423	Bigness	02473
Beware	02424	Bigot	02474
Bewilder... ...	02425	Bigotedly	02475
Bewildered ...	02426	Bigotry	02476
Bewilderment ...	02427	Bilateral	02477
Bewitch	02428	Bilberry	02478
Bewitched	02429	Bilbo	02479
Bewitchery	02430	Bile	02480
Bewitching	02431	Bilge	02481
Bey...	02432	Biliary	02482
Beylick	02433	Bilingual... ...	02483
Beyond	02434	Bilious	02484
Bezonian... ...	02435	Bilk...	02485
Bias...	02436	Bill	02486
Biassed	02437	Billet	02487
Bib	02438	Billiards	02488
Bibber	02439	Billing	02489
Bible	02440	Billingsgate ...	02490
Biblical	02441	Billion	02491
Biblicist	02442	Billow	02492
Bibliographer...	02443	Billowy	02493
Bibliography ...	02444	Bimanous ...	02494
Bibliomania ...	02445	Bin	02495
Bibliomaniac ...	02446	Binary	02496
Bibulous... ...	02447	Binate	02497
Bicapitated ...	02448	Bind	02498
Bicarbonate ...	02449	Binder	02499
Bicephalous ...	02450	Binding	02500

| BIN | (13) | BLA | 26 |

Binds	02501	Blackamoor	02551
Binnacle...	02502	Blackball	02552
Binocular	02503	Blackballed	02553
Biodynamics	02504	Blackberry	02554
Biographer	02505	Blackbird	02555
Biographical	02506	Blacken	02556
Biographically ...	02507	Blackened	02557
Biography	02508	Blackfriar	02558
Biology	02509	Blackguard	02559
Biped	02510	Blacking...	02560
Bipedal	02511	Blackleg...	02561
Bipolar	02512	Blackness	02562
Birch	02513	Blacksmith	02563
Bird...	02514	Blackthorn	02564
Birman	02515	Bladder	02565
Birth	02516	Blade	02566
Birthday...	02517	Blain	02567
Birthplace	02518	Blamable	02568
Birthright	02519	Blamably	02569
Bis	02520	Blame	02570
Biscuit	02521	Blamed	02571
Bisect	02522	Blames	02572
Bisected	02523	Blamefully	02573
Bisection...	02524	Blameless	02574
Bishop	02525	Blamer	02575
Bishopric	02526	Blaming	02576
Bismuth	02527	Blanch	02577
Bison	02528	Blancher	02578
Bissextile	02529	Blanching	02579
Bit	02530	Bland	02580
Bitch	02531	Blandiloquence ...	02581
Bite...	02532	Blandish...	02582
Bites	02533	Blandisher	02583
Bitten	02534	Blandishment... ...	02584
Biter	02535	Blandness	02585
Biting	02536	Blank	02586
Bitter	02537	Blanket	02587
Bitterly	02538	Blanketing	02588
Bittern	02539	Blankly	02589
Bitterness	02540	Blarney	02590
Bitters	02541	Blaspheme	02591
Bitumen	02542	Blasphemer	02592
Bituminate	02543	Blasphemous	02593
Bituminize	02544	Blasphemy	02594
Bituminous	02545	Blast	02595
Bivalve	02546	Blasted	02596
Bivouac	02547	Blatant	02597
Bizarre	02548	Blaze	02598
Blab	02549	Blazing	02599
Black	02550	Blazon	02600

| 27 | BLA | (14) | BLU | ` |

Blazoner ...	...	...	02601
Bleach ...	...	...	02602
Bleached...	...	...	02603
Bleachery	...	...	02604
Bleaching	...	...	02605
Bleak ...	...	...	02606
Blear ...	...	...	02607
Bled ...	...	...	02608
Bleat ...	...	...	02609
Bleed ...	...	...	02610
Bleeds ...	...	...	02611
Bleeding...	...	...	02612
Blemish ...	...	...	02613
Blemished	...	...	02614
Blench ...	...	...	02615
Blenching	...	...	02616
Blend ...	...	...	02617
Blended ...	...	...	02618
Blending...	...	...	02619
Blends ...	...	...	02620
Bless ...	...	...	02621
Blessed ...	...	...	02622
Blessedness	...	...	02623
Blessing ...	...	...	02624
Blest ...	...	...	02625
Blew ...	...	...	02626
Blight ...	...	...	02627
Blighted ...	...	...	02628
Blind ...	...	...	02629
Blinded ...	...	...	02630
Blinding ...	...	...	02631
Blindfold	...	...	02632
Blindly ...	...	...	02633
Blindness	...	...	02634
Blink ...	...	...	02635
Blinkers ...	...	...	02636
Bliss ...	...	...	02637
Blissful ...	...	...	02638
Blister ...	...	...	02639
Blistered...	...	...	02640
Blithe ...	...	...	02641
Blithely ...	...	...	02642
Blithesome	...	...	02643
Bloat ...	...	...	02644
Bloated ...	...	...	02645
Bloater ...	...	...	02646
Block ...	...	...	02647
Blocked ...	...	...	02648
Blocking...	...	...	02649
Blockade	...	...	02650

Blockhead	...	...	02651
Blonde ...	...	...	02652
Blood ...	...	...	02653
Bloodily ...	...	...	02654
Bloodless	...	...	02655
Bloodletting	...	...	02656
Bloodshed	...	...	02657
Bloodshot	...	...	02658
Bloodstone	...	...	02659
Bloodsucker	...	...	02660
Bloodthirsty	...	...	02661
Bloody ...	...	...	02662
Bloom ...	...	...	02663
Blooming	...	...	02664
Blossom ...	...	...	02665
Blot... ...	...	...	02666
Blotch ...	...	...	02667
Blotchy ...	...	...	02668
Blotted ...	...	...	02669
Blotting ...	...	...	02670
Blouse ...	...	...	02671
Blow ...	...	...	02672
Blower ...	...	...	02673
Blowing ...	...	...	02674
Blown ...	...	...	02675
Blow-pipe	...	...	02676
Blows ...	...	...	02677
Blowy ...	...	...	02678
Blowzy ...	...	...	02679
Blubber ...	...	...	02680
Bludgeon	...	...	02681
Blue ...	...	...	02682
Bluff ...	...	...	02683
Bluffness...	...	...	02684
Bluish ...	...	...	02685
Blunder ...	...	...	02686
Blunderbuss	...	...	02687
Blundered	...	...	02688
Blunderer	...	...	02689
Blundering	...	...	02690
Blunt ...	...	...	02691
Blunted ...	...	...	02692
Bluntness	...	...	02693
Blur... ...	...	...	02694
Blurt ...	...	...	02695
Blush ...	...	...	02696
Blushed ...	...	...	02697
Blushes ...	...	...	02698
Blushing...	...	...	02699
Bluster ..	...	...	02700

BLU			(14)	BOO			28
Blusterer...	...	...	02701	Boldness...	...	...	02751
Blustering	...	...	02702	Bolero	...	...	02752
Boa ...	...	...	02703	Bolivian ...	...	...	02753
Boar	...	...	02704	Boll...	...	...	02754
Board	...	...	02705	Bolled	...	...	02755
Boarded ...	...	...	02706	Bolster	...	...	02756
Boarder	...	...	02707	Bolstered	...	...	02757
Boarish ...	...	...	02708	Bolt...	...	...	02758
Boast	...	...	02709	Bolted	...	...	02759
Boasted ...	...	...	02710	Bolter	...	...	02760
Boaster ...	...	...	02711	Bolting	...	...	02761
Boastful ...	...	...	02712	Bolts	...	...	02762
Boasting ...	...	...	02713	Bolus	...	...	02763
Boastingly	...	...	02714	Bomb	...	...	02764
Boasts	...	...	02715	Bombardier	...	...	02765
Boat	...	...	02716	Bombardment		...	02766
Boating ...	...	...	02717	Bombasin	...	...	02767
Boatman...	...	...	02718	Bombast	...	...	02768
Boatswain	...	...	02719	Bombastic	...	...	02769
Bob ...	...	...	02720	Bonapartist	...	...	02770
Bobbin ...	...	...	02721	Bond	...	...	02771
Bobbinet...	...	...	02722	Bondage...	...	...	02772
Bobstays...	...	...	02723	Bonded ...	...	...	02773
Bobtail ...	...	...	02724	Bonding ...	...	...	02774
Bode	...	...	02725	Bondmaid	...	...	02775
Boded	...	...	02726	Bondman	...	...	02776
Bodice	...	...	02727	Bondsman	...	...	02777
Bodiless ...	...	...	02728	Bone	...	...	02778
Bodily	...	...	02729	Boned	...	...	02779
Boding	...	...	02730	Boneless ...	...	...	02780
Bodkin ...	...	...	02731	Bonfire	...	...	02781
Bodleian...	...	...	02732	Bonnet	...	...	02782
Body	...	...	02733	Bonnily ...	...	...	02783
Bog...	...	...	02734	Bonny	...	...	02784
Boggle	...	...	02735	Bonus	...	...	02785
Boggler	...	...	02736	Bony	...	...	02786
Boggy	...	...	02737	Booby	...	...	02787
Bogle	...	...	02738	Book	...	...	02788
Bohea	...	...	02739	Bookbinder	...	...	02789
Bohemian	...	...	02740	Bookbinding ...	...	...	02790
Boil	...	...	02741	Booked ...	...	...	02791
Boiled	...	...	02742	Booking ...	...	...	02792
Boiler	...	...	02743	Bookish ...	...	...	02793
Boiling	...	...	02744	Bookseller	...	...	02794
Boils	...	...	02745	Bookstall	...	...	02795
Boisterous	...	...	02746	Bookworm	...	...	02796
Boisterously	...	...	02747	Boom	...	...	02797
Bold	...	...	02748	Boomerang	...	...	02798
Bolden	...	...	02749	Booming...	...	...	02799
Boldly	...	...	02750	Boon	..	...	02800

Boor	02801	Bottled 02851
Boorish	02802	Bottling 02852
Boose	02803	Bottom 02853
Boot	02804	Bottomless 02854
Booted	02805	Boudoir 02855
Booth	02806	Bough 02856
Bootless	02807	Bought 02857
Boots	02808	Boulevard 02858
Booty	02809	Bounce 02859
Boracite	02810	Bouncer 02860
Borax	02811	Bouncing 02861
Border	02812	Bound 02862
Bordered	02813	Boundary 02863
Borderer	02814	Bounden 02864
Bordering	02815	Bounding 02865
Bore	02816	Boundless 02866
Boreas	02817	Boundlessly 02867
Borecole	02818	Bounteous 02868
Bored	02819	Bounteousness ... 02869
Borer	02820	Bountiful 02870
Born	02821	Bounty 02871
Borne	02822	Bouquet 02872
Borough	02823	Bourn 02873
Borrow	02824	Bout 02874
Borrowed	02825	Bow 02875
Borrower	02826	Bowed 02876
Borrowing	02827	Bowel 02877
Borrows	02828	Bowels 02878
Bosh	02829	Bower 02879
Bosket	02830	Bowl 02880
Bosky	02831	Bowler 02881
Bosom	02832	Bowling 02882
Boss	02833	Bowman 02883
Bossed	02834	Bowse 02884
Botanical	02835	Bowsprit 02885
Botanically	02836	Box 02886
Botanist	02837	Boxer 02887
Botanize	02838	Boxing 02888
Botany	02839	Boy 02889
Botch	02840	Boyhood 02890
Botched	02841	Boyish 02891
Botcher	02842	Boyishly 02892
Botchery	02843	Brace 02893
Both	02844	Braced 02894
Bother	02845	Bracelet 02895
Botheration	02846	Brachial 02896
Bothered	02847	Bracing 02897
Bothering	02848	Bracket 02898
Bothers	02849	Brackish 02899
Bottle	02850	Brad 02900

Brag	...	...	...	02901	Brazilian	...	...	02951
Braggadocio	...	...	02902	Brazing	...	...	...	02952
Braggart	...	...	...	02903	Breach	...	...	...	02953
Bragger	...	...	...	02904	Breached	...	...	02954
Bragging	...	...	02905	Bread	...	...	...	02955
Brahma	...	...	02906	Breadstuff	...	...	02956
Brahmin	...	...	02907	Breadth	...	...	...	02957
Brahminical	...	...	02908	Break	...	...	...	02958
Brahminism	...	...	02909	Breakage	...	...	02959
Braid	...	...	...	02910	Breaker	...	...	...	02960
Brain	...	...	...	02911	Breakfast	...	...	02961
Brainless	...	...	02912	Breaking	...	...	02962
Brake	...	...	...	02913	Breakneck	...	...	02963
Braky	...	...	...	02914	Breaks	...	...	...	02964
Bramble	...	...	02915	Breakwater	...	...	02965
Bran	...	...	...	02916	Breast	...	...	...	02966
Branch	...	...	02917	Breasted	...	...	02967
Branched	...	...	02918	Breastwork	...	...	02968
Branching	...	...	02919	Breath	...	...	...	02969
Branchless	...	...	02920	Breathe	...	...	02970
Branchlet	...	...	02921	Breather	...	...	02971
Brand	...	...	...	02922	Breathing	...	...	02972
Branded	...	...	02923	Breathless	...	...	02973
Brandied	...	...	02924	Bred	...	...	...	02974
Brandish	...	...	02925	Breech	...	...	...	02975
Brandished	...	...	02926	Breeches	...	...	02976
Brandisher	...	...	02927	Breed	...	...	...	02977
Brandishing	...	...	02928	Breeder	...	...	02978
Brandy	...	...	...	02929	Breeding	...	...	02979
Brasier	...	...	...	02930	Breeds	...	...	...	02980
Brass	...	...	...	02931	Breeze	...	...	...	02981
Brat	...	...	...	02932	Breezy	...	...	...	02982
Braunite	...	...	02933	Brethren	...	...	02983
Bravado	...	...	02934	Brettices	...	...	02984
Brave	...	...	...	02935	Breve	...	...	...	02985
Braved	...	...	...	02936	Brevet	...	...	...	02986
Bravely	...	...	02937	Brevetcy	...	...	02987
Bravery	...	...	02938	Breviary	...	...	02988
Braving	...	...	02939	Brevity	...	...	...	02989
Bravo	...	...	...	02940	Brew	...	...	...	02990
Bravura	...	...	02941	Brewage	...	...	02991
Brawl	...	...	...	02942	Brewed	...	...	02992
Brawler	...	...	02943	Brewer	...	...	...	02993
Brawling	...	...	02944	Brewery	...	...	02994
Brawn	...	...	...	02945	Brewing	...	...	02995
Brawny	...	...	02946	Briarean	...	...	02996
Bray	...	...	...	02947	Bribe	...	...	...	02997
Braying	...	...	02948	Bribed	...	...	...	02998
Brazen	...	...	...	02949	Briber	...	...	...	02999
Brazenness	...	...	02950	Bribery	...	...	...	03000

Bribing	03001	Brink	03051
Brick	03002	Briny	03052
Bricked	03003	Brisk	03053
Brickbat	03004	Brisket	03054
Brickbuilt	03005	Briskly	03055
Bricklayer	03006	Briskness	03056
Bricklaying	03007	Bristle	03057
Brickmaker	03008	Bristling	03058
Bridal	03009	Bristly	03059
Bride	03010	Britannic	03060
Bridecake	03011	British	03061
Bridechamber ...	03012	Briton	03062
Bridegroom	03013	Brittle	03063
Bridesmaid	03014	Britzka	03064
Bridesman	03015	Broach	03065
Bridge	03016	Broached	03066
Bridged	03017	Broacher	03067
Bridgeless	03018	Broaching	03068
Bridle	03019	Broad	03069
Brief	03020	Broadcast	03070
Briefless	03021	Broadcloth	03071
Briefly	03022	Broadly	03072
Briefness	03023	Broadness	03073
Brier	03024	Broadside	03074
Briery	03025	Broadsword	03075
Brig	03026	Broadwise	03076
Brigade	03027	Brocade	03077
Brigadier	03028	Brocaded	03078
Brigand	03029	Brocage	03079
Brigandage	03030	Broccoli	03080
Brigandine	03031	Brochure	03081
Brigantine	03032	Brogue	03082
Bright	03033	Broil	03083
Brighten	03034	Broiling	03084
Brightly	03035	Broke	03085
Brightness	03036	Broken	03086
Brilliancy	03037	Broker	03087
Brilliant	03038	Brokerage	03088
Brilliantly	03039	Bromine	03089
Brim	03040	Bronchia	03090
Brimful	03041	Bronchial	03091
Brimless	03042	Bronchitis	03092
Brimmer	03043	Bronze	03093
Brimstone	03044	Bronzed	03094
Brindled	03045	Bronzing	03095
Brine	03046	Brooch	03096
Bring	03047	Brood	03097
Bringing	03048	Brooding	03098
Brings	03049	Brook	03099
Brinish	03050	Broom	03100

Broth 03101	Bucolical 03151
Brother 03102	Bud... 03152
Brotherhood 03103	Budded 05153
Brotherly 03104	Buddha 03154
Brought 03105	Budding 03155
Brow 03106	Budge 03156
Browbeat 03107	Budget 03157
Browless... 03108	Buff 03158
Brown 03109	Buffalo 03159
Brownish 03110	Buffer 03160
Brownist... 03111	Buffet 03161
Browse 03112	Buffeting... 03162
Browsing 03113	Buffoon 03163
Bruin 03114	Buffoonery 03164
Bruise 03115	Bug 03165
Bruised 03116	Bugbear 03166
Bruiser 03117	Buggy 03167
Brumal 03118	Bugle 03168
Brunette... 03119	Buhl 03169
Brunt 03120	Build 03170
Brush 03121	Builder 03171
Brusher 03122	Building 03172
Brushing 03123	Built 03173
Brushwood 03124	Bulb 03174
Brushy 03125	Bulbaceous 03175
Brusque 03126	Bulbiferous 03176
Brutal 03127	Bulbous 03177
Brutalism 03128	Bulge 03178
Brutality 03129	Bulged 03179
Brutalize 03130	Bulging 03180
Brutally 03131	Bulk 03181
Brute 03132	Bulkhead 03182
Brutify 03133	Bulkiness 03183
Brutish 03134	Bulky 03184
Bryony 03135	Bull 03185
Bubble 03136	Bullet 03186
Bubbler 03137	Bulletin 03187
Bubbling ... ., 03138	Bullied 03188
Buccaneer ... ~. 03139	Bullion 03189
Bucentaur 03140	Bullock 03190
Bucephalus 03141	Bully 03191
Buck 03142	Bulrush 03192
Bucket 03143	Bulwark 03193
Buckle 03144	Bumbailiff 03194
Buckler 03145	Bumboat... 03195
Buckram 03146	Bump 03196
Buckskin 03147	Bumper 03197
Buckthorn 03148	Bumpkin... 03198
Buckwheat 03149	Bun 03199
Bucolic 03150	Bunch 03200

Bundle	03201	Burying 03251
Bundled	03202	Bush 03252
Bung	03203	Bushel 03253
Bunged	03204	Bushman... 03254
Bungalow	03205	Bushy 03255
Bunghole	03206	Busied 03256
Bungle	03207	Busily 03257
Bungled	03208	Business 03258
Bungler	03209	Buskin 03259
Bungling...	03210	Bust... 03260
Bunion	03211	Bustard 03261
Bunting	03212	Bustle 03262
Buoy	03213	Bustler 03263
Buoyancy	03214	Bustling 03264
Buoyant	03215	Busy 03265
Buoyed	03216	Busybody 03266
Bur	03217	But 03267
Burden	03218	Butcher 03268
Burdensome	03219	Butcherly 03269
Bureau	03220	Butchery... 03270
Bureaucracy	03221	Butler 03271
Burgess	03222	Butlery 03272
Burgh	03223	Butt 03273
Burgher	03224	Butter 03274
Burglar	03225	Buttercup 03275
Burglary	03226	Butterfly 03276
Burial	03227	Buttermilk 03277
Buried	03228	Buttery 03278
Burin	03229	Buttock 03279
Burke	03230	Button 03280
Burlesque	03231	Buttoned... 03281
Burlesquer	03232	Buttress 03282
Burletta	03233	Butts 03283
Burly	03234	Buxom 03284
Burn	03235	Buxomly 03285
Burned	03236	Buy 03286
Burner	03237	Buyer 03287
Burning	03238	Buying 03288
Burnish	03239	Buys 03289
Burnished	03240	Buzz 03290
Burnisher	03241	Buzzard 03291
Burns	03242	Buzzer 03292
Burnt	03243	Buzzing 03293
Burrow	03244	By 03294
Bursar	03245	Bye 03295
Bursary	03246	Bygone 03296
Burst	03247	By-stander 03297
Bursting	03248	By-way 03298
Bursts	03249	By-word 03299
Bury	03250	Byzantine 03300

C	03301	Calculable 03351
Cab...	03302	Calculate 03352
Cabal	03303	Calculated 03353
Cabalistical	03304	Calculating 03354
Caballer	03305	Calculation 03355
Cabbage...	03306	Calculator 03356
Cabin	03307	Calculus 03357
Cabinet	03308	Caldron 03358
Cable	03309	Caleche 03359
Cabman	03310	Caledonian 03360
Caboose	03311	Calefacient 03361
Cabriolet	03312	Calefactor 03362
Cacao	03313	Calendar 03363
Cachinnation... ...	03314	Calender... 03364
Cackle	03315	Calendrer 03365
Cacoethes	03316	Calends 03366
Cactus	03317	Calescence 03367
Cad...	03318	Calf... 03368
Cadaverous	03319	Calibre 03369
Caddy	03320	Calico 03370
Cadence	03321	Calid 03371
Cadenza	03322	Calidity 03372
Cadet	03323	Californian 03373
Cadger	03324	Caliph 03374
Cadi	03325	Calisthenics 03375
Cadmium	03326	Call... 03376
Caduceus	03327	Called 03377
Cæsura	03328	Calligraphist 03378
Café	03329	Calligraphy 03379
Caffre	03330	Calling 03380
Caftan	03331	Callosity... 03381
Cage	03332	Callous 03382
Caique	03333	Callousness 03383
Cairn	03334	Callow 03384
Caisson	03335	Calls 03385
Caitiff	03336	Calm 03386
Cajole	03337	Calmed 03387
Cajoled	03338	Calmly 03388
Cajoler	03339	Calmness 03389
Cajolery	03340	Calomel 03390
Cake	03341	Caloric 03391
Caked	03342	Calorific 03392
Calabash...	03343	Calorimeter 03393
Calamitous	03344	Calorimotor 03394
Calamity...	03345	Calotype... 03395
Calcareous	03346	Calumet 03396
Calcinable	03347	Calumniate 03397
Calcination	03348	Calumniated 03398
Calcine	03349	Calumniates 03399
Calcium	03350	Calumniating... ... 03400

Calumniation	03401	Cane 03451
Calumniator	03402	Canescent 03452
Calumnious	03403	Canicular 03453
Calumny...	03404	Canine 03454
Calvary	03405	Caning 03455
Calve	03406	Canister 03456
Calvinist	03407	Canker 03457
Calyx	03408	Cankered 03458
Cambist	03409	Cankeredly 03459
Camboose	03410	Cannabis 03460
Cambrian	03411	Cannel 03461
Cambric	03412	Cannibal... 03462
Came	03413	Cannibalism 03463
Camel	03414	Cannon 03464
Camelia	03415	Cannonade 03465
Camelopard	03416	Cannonaded 03466
Cameo	03417	Cannonading 03467
Camera	03418	Cannular 03468
Cameronians	03419	Canny 03469
Camisade	03420	Canoe 03470
Camlet	03421	Canon 03471
Camp	03422	Canonical 03472
Campaign	03423	Canonicals 03473
Campaigner	03424	Canonization 03474
Camped	03425	Canonize... 03475
Campestral	03426	Canonized 03476
Camphene	03427	Canonry 03477
Camphor	03428	Canopied 03478
Camphorated... ...	03429	Canopy 03479
Can	03430	Cant 03480
Canadian	03431	Cantab 03481
Canal	03432	Cantata 03482
Canary	03433	Canteen 03483
Cancel	03434	Canter 03484
Cancelled	03435	Cantering 03485
Cancelling	03436	Cantharides 03486
Cancels	03437	Canticle 03487
Cancer	03438	Canting 03488
Cancerous	03439	Canto 03489
Candelabrum... ...	03440	Canton 03490
Candent	03441	Cantonment 03491
Candid	03442	Canvas 03492
Candidate	03443	Canvassed 03493
Candidly...	03444	Canvasser 03494
Candied	03445	Canvassing 03495
Candify	03446	Canzonet.. 03496
Candle	03447	Caoutchouc 03497
Candlemas	03448	Cap 03498
Candour	03449	Capability 03499
Candy	03450	Capable 03500

CAP	(18)	CAR	36

Capacious	03501	Capuchin	03551
Capaciously	03502	Car	03552
Capacitate	03503	Carabine...	03553
Capacitated	03504	Carabineer	03554
Capacity	03505	Caracole	03555
Caparison	03506	Carat	03556
Cape	03507	Caravan	03557
Capelan	03508	Caravansary	03558
Caper	03509	Caraway	03559
Capias	03510	Carbon	03560
Capillary...	03511	Carbonaceous... ...	03561
Capital	03512	Carbonate	03562
Capitalist	03513	Carbonic...	03563
Capitalized	03514	Carboniferous... ...	03564
Capitally...	03515	Carbonize	03565
Capitation	03516	Carbonized	03566
Capitular	03517	Carbuncle	03567
Capitularly	03518	Carcass	03568
Capitulate	03519	Card	03569
Capitulated	03520	Cardamom	03570
Capitulation	03521	Cardboard	03571
Capitulator	03522	Carded	03572
Capon	03523	Carder	03573
Capped	03524	Cardiac	03574
Caprice	03525	Cardinal	03575
Capricious	03526	Carding	03576
Capriciously ...	02527	Carditis	03577
Capriciousness ...	03528	Care	03578
Capsicum	03529	Cared	03579
Capsize	03530	Careen	03580
Capsized...	03531	Careened	03581
Capsizing	03532	Career	03582
Capstan	03533	Careful	03583
Capsular...	03534	Carefulness	03584
Capsule	03535	Careless	03585
Captain	03536	Carelessness	03586
Captaincy	03537	Cares	03587
Caption	03538	Caress	03588
Captious	03539	Caressed...	03589
Captiously	03540	Caressing	03590
Captiousness	03541	Caressingly	03591
Captivate	03542	Cargo	03592
Captivated	03543	Caricature	03593
Captivating	03544	Caricatured	03594
Captivation	03545	Caricaturist	03595
Captive	03546	Caring	03596
Captivity	03547	Cariosity...	03597
Captor	03548	Carious	03598
Capture	03549	Carline	03599
Captured	03550	Carman	03600

37	CAR	(19)	CAT

Carmelite	...	...	03601	Carving	03651
Carmine ...	...	...	03602	Caryatides	03652
Carnage ...	...	...	03603	Cascade	03653
Carnal	...	...	03604	Case	03654
Carnality	...	...	03605	Casement	03655
Carnalize	...	...	03606	Cash	03656
Carnation	...	...	03607	Cashed	03657
Carnival ...	...	...	03608	Cashier	03658
Carnivora	...	...	03609	Cashiered	03659
Carol	...	...	03610	Cashmere	03660
Carotid ...	...	...	03611	Casing	03661
Carousal ...	...	...	03612	Casino	03662
Carouse ...	...	...	03613	Cask	03663
Carouser ...	...	...	03614	Casket	03664
Carousing	...	...	03615	Casque	03665
Carp	...	...	03616	Cassation	03666
Carpenter	...	...	03617	Cassia	03667
Carpentering	...	...	03618	Cassimere	03668
Carpentry	...	...	03619	Cassinette	03669
Carper	...	...	03620	Cassock	03670
Carpet	...	...	03621	Cassowary	03671
Carpeting	...	...	03622	Cast	03672
Carping ..	...	...	03623	Castanets	03673
Carpingly	...	...	03624	Castaway	03674
Carriage ...	...	...	03625	Caste	03675
Carried ...	...	...	03626	Castellan	03676
Carrier	...	...	03627	Castellated	03677
Carries ...	...	...	03628	Caster	03678
Carrion ...	...	...	03629	Casters	03679
Carrot	...	...	03630	Castigate	03680
Carroty ...	...	...	03631	Castigation	03681
Carry	...	...	03632	Castigator	03682
Carrying ...	...	...	03633	Castilian	03683
Cart	...	...	03634	Casting	03684
Cartage ...	...	...	03635	Castle	03685
Carte	...	...	03636	Castled	03686
Carted	...	...	03637	Castor	03687
Cartel	...	...	03638	Castrate	03688
Carter	...	...	03639	Castration	03689
Carthusian	...	...	03640	Casts	03690
Cartilage ...	...	...	03641	Casual	03691
Carting ...	...	...	03642	Casually	03692
Cartographer ...	...	...	03643	Casualty	03693
Cartography ...	...	...	03644	Casuist	03694
Cartoon ...	...	...	03645	Casuistry	03695
Cartouch ...	...	...	03646	Cat	03696
Cartridge	...	...	03647	Cataclysm	03697
Carve	...	...	03648	Catacomb	03698
Carved ...	...	...	03649	Catadioptric	03699
Carver ...	...	...	03650	Catalepsis	03700

Catalogue	03701	
Catamaran	03702	
Catapult	03703	
Cataract	03704	
Catarrh	03705	
Catastrophe	03706	
Catcall	03707	
Catch	03708	
Catches	03709	
Catching...	03710	
Catchpenny	03711	
Catchword	03712	
Catechetical	03713	
Catechise	03714	
Catechised	03715	
Catechism	03716	
Catechumen	03717	
Categorical	03718	
Categorize	03719	
Category...	03720	
Catenary...	03721	
Catenation	03722	
Cater	03723	
Caterer	03724	
Caterpillar	03725	
Caterwaul	03726	
Catgut	03727	
Cathedra...	03728	
Cathedral	03729	
Catheter	03730	
Catholic	03731	
Catholicism	03732	
Catholicity	03733	
Catoptrics	03734	
Cattle	03735	
Caucasian	03736	
Caudal	03737	
Caudle	03738	
Caught	03739	
Caul	03740	
Cauliflower	03741	
Caulk	03742	
Caulked	03743	
Caulker	03744	
Caulking...	03745	
Causal	03746	
Causality	03747	
Causation	03748	
Cause	03749	
Caused	03750	
Causeless	03751	
Causes	03752	
Causeway	03753	
Causing	03754	
Caustic	03755	
Cauter	03756	
Cauterization	03757	
Cauterize	03758	
Cauterized	03759	
Cautery	03760	
Caution	03761	
Cautioned	03762	
Cautious	03763	
Cavalcade	03764	
Cavalier	03765	
Cavalry	03766	
Cavatina...	03767	
Cave	03768	
Caveat	03769	
Caveator...	03770	
Cavern	03771	
Cavernous	03772	
Caviare	03773	
Cavil	03774	
Cavilled	03775	
Caviller	03776	
Cavilling...	03777	
Cavity	03778	
Caw...	03779	
Cawing	03780	
Cease	03781	
Ceased	03782	
Ceaseless...	03783	
Ceases	03784	
Ceasing	03785	
Cedar	03786	
Cede	03787	
Ceded	03788	
Ceding	03789	
Ceil...	03790	
Ceiling	03791	
Celebrant	03792	
Celebrate	03793	
Celebrated	03794	
Celebrating	03795	
Celebration	03796	
Celebrity...	03797	
Celerity	03798	
Celery	03799	
Celestial	03800	

39	CEL			(20)		CHA		
Celestially	...	...	03801	Cerebral ...	...	...	03851
Celibacy ...	...	...	03802	Cerebrum	...	...	03852
Celibate ...	...	...	03803	Cerement	...	...	03853
Cell ...	...	...	03804	Ceremonial	...	...	03854
Cellar	...	...	03805	Ceremonious ...	...	...	03855
Cellarage	...	...	03806	Ceremony	...	...	03856
Cellaret ...	...	...	03807	Certain ...	...	...	03857
Cellular ...	...	...	03808	Certainly	...	...	03858
Cellule	...	...	03809	Certificate	...	...	03859
Celtic	...	...	03810	Certificated	...	...	03860
Cement ...	...	...	03811	Certified ...	...	...	03861
Cementation ...	...	...	03812	Certifies ...	...	...	03862
Cemented	...	...	03813	Certify ...	...	...	03863
Cemetery	...	...	03814	Certiorari	...	...	03864
Cenobite...	...	...	03815	Certitude	...	...	03865
Cenotaph	...	...	03816	Cerulean ...	...	...	03866
Cense	...	...	03817	Ceruse ...	...	...	03867
Censer	...	...	03818	Cervical ...	...	..	03868
Censor	...	...	03819	Cessation	...	...	03869
Censorial...	...	...	03820	Cession ...	...	...	03870
Censorious	...	..	03821	Cesspool...	...	...	03871
Censorship	...	...	03822	Cesura	...	...	03872
Censurable	...	...	03823	Chablis ...	...	...	03873
Censure ...	...	...	03824	Chafe	...	...	03874
Censured	...	...	03825	Chafer	...	...	03875
Census	...	...	03826	Chaff	...	...	03876
Cent	...	...	03827	Chaffinch	...	...	03877
Centage ...	...	...	03828	Chaffing ...	...	...	03878
Centaur ...	...	...	03829	Chafing ...	...	...	03879
Centenarian	...	...	03830	Chagrin ...	...	...	03880
Centenary	...	...	03831	Chain	...	...	03881
Centennial	...	...	03832	Chained ...	...	...	03882
Centesimal	...	...	03833	Chair	...	...	03883
Centigrade	...	...	03834	Chaired ...	...	...	03884
Centipede	...	...	03835	Chairman	...	...	03885
Central ...	...	...	03836	Chaise ...	...	...	03886
Centrality	...	...	03837	Chalcedony	...	...	03887
Centralize	...	...	03838	Chaldron	...	...	03888
Centralized	...	...	03839	Chalice ...	...	...	03889
Centre	...	...	03840	Chalk	...	...	03890
Centred ...	...	...	03841	Challenge	...	...	03891
Centrifugal	...	...	03842	Challenged	...	...	03892
Centripetal	...	...	03843	Challenges	...	...	03893
Centuple...	...	...	03844	Challenging	...	...	03894
Century ...	...	...	03845	Challis ...	...	...	03895
Cephalitis	...	...	03846	Chalybeate	...	...	03896
Cerated ...	...	...	03847	Chamber...	...	...	03897
Cerberus...	...	...	03848	Chamberlain ...	...	...	03898
Cere	...	...	03849	Chameleon	...	...	03899
Cereal	...	...	03850	Chamois...	...	...	03900

CHA	(20)	CHA	40
Chamomile	03901	Chargeable	03951
Champ	03902	Charged	03952
Champagne	03903	Charger	03953
Champaign	03904	Charges	03954
Champion	03905	Charging	03955
Championship ...	03906	Charily	03956
Chance	03907	Chariness	03957
Chanced	03908	Charing	03958
Chancel	03909	Chariot	03959
Chancellor	03910	Charioteer	03960
Chancellorship ...	03911	Charitable	03961
Chancery	03912	Charitably	03962
Chandelier	03913	Charity	03963
Chandler	03914	Charivari	03964
Chandlery	03915	Charlatan	03965
Change	03916	Charlatanism	03966
Changed	03917	Charm	03967
Changes	03918	Charmed	03968
Changeable	03919	Charmer	03969
Changeless	03920	Charming	03970
Changeling	03921	Charmless	03971
Changing	03922	Charnel	03972
Channel	03923	Charred	03973
Chant	03924	Chart	03974
Chanted	03925	Charta	03975
Chanter	03926	Charter	03976
Chanticleer	03927	Chartered	03977
Chantry	03928	Chartering	03978
Chaos	03929	Chartism	03979
Chaotic	03930	Chartist	03980
Chap	03931	Chartreux	03981
Chapel	03932	Chary	03982
Chapelry	03933	Chase	03983
Chaperon	03934	Chased	03984
Chapiter	03935	Chaser	03985
Chaplain	03936	Chasing	03986
Chaplaincy	03937	Chasm	03987
Chaplet	03938	Chasseur	03988
Chapman	03939	Chaste	03989
Chapped	03940	Chastely	03990
Chapter	03941	Chasten	03991
Char	03942	Chastened	03992
Character	03943	Chasteness	03993
Characteristic ...	03944	Chastening	03994
Characteristically ...	03945	Chastise	03995
Characterize	03946	Chastised	03996
Characterized	03947	Chastisement	03997
Charade	03948	Chastiser	03998
Charcoal	03949	Chastising	03999
Charge	03950	Chastity	04000

41	CHA	(21)	CHI	
Chasuble	... ...	04001	Chevalier	04051
Chat	... ...	04002	Chew	04052
Chateau ...	... ...	04003	Chewed	04053
Chattel ...	... ...	04004	Chewing...	04054
Chatter ...	... ...	04005	Chibook	04055
Chatterer	... ...	04006	Chicane	04056
Chattering	... ...	04007	Chicanery	04057
Chatty ...	... ...	04008	Chicken	04058
Cheap ...	... ...	04009	Chicory	04059
Cheapen...	... ...	04010	Chidden	04060
Cheapened	... ...	04011	Chide	04061
Cheapener	... ...	04012	Chider	04062
Cheaply...	... ...	04013	Chiding	04063
Cheapness	... ...	04014	Chidingly	04064
Cheat ...	... ...	04015	Chief	04065
Cheated ...	... ...	04016	Chiefly	04066
Cheating...	... ...	04017	Chieftain	04067
Cheats ...	... ...	04018	Chiffonier	04068
Check ...	... ...	04019	Chilblain	04069
Checked...	... ...	04020	Child	04070
Checker ...	... ...	04021	Childbearing	04071
Checkless	... ...	04022	Childbirth	04072
Checkmate	... ...	04023	Childhood	04073
Chedder ...	... ...	04024	Childish	04074
Cheek ...	... ...	04025	Childless... ...	04075
Cheer ...	... ...	04026	Childlike	04076
Cheerful ...	... ...	04027	Children	04077
Cheerfully	... ...	04028	Chilian	04078
Cheerily ...	... ...	04029	Chill	04079
Cheering...	... ...	04030	Chilled	04080
Cheeringly	... ...	04031	Chilliness	04081
Cheerless	... ...	04032	Chillingly	04082
Cheery ...	... ...	04033	Chilly	04083
Cheese ...	... ...	04034	Chiltern	04084
Cheese-monger	...	04035	Chime	04085
Chemical	... ...	04036	Chimer	04086
Chemise ...	... ...	04037	Chimera... ...	04087
Chemist ...	... ...	04038	Chimerical	04088
Chemistry	... ...	04039	Chimney... ...	04089
Cheque ...	... ...	04040	Chin	04090
Cherish ...	... ...	04041	China	04091
Cherished	... ...	04042	Chinchilla	04092
Cherisher	... ...	04043	Chine	04093
Cheroot ...	... ...	04044	Chinese	04094
Cherry ...	... ...	04045	Chink	04095
Cherub ...	... ...	04046	Chintz	04096
Cherubim	... ...	04047	Chip	04097
Chess ...	... ...	04048	Chipped	04098
Chest ...	... ...	04049	Chipping	04099
Chestnut...	... ...	04050	Chirographer	04100

CHI	(21)	CIN	42

Chirography	... ...	04101	Christianlike	04151
Chiropodist	... ...	04102	Christmas	04152
Chirp	...	04103	Chroma	04153
Chirrup ...	... ...	04104	Chromatic	04154
Chisel ...	... ...	04105	Chronic	04155
Chiselled	... ...	04106	Chronicle	04156
Chisleu ...	... ...	04107	Chronicler	04157
Chit ...	... ...	04108	Chronological ...	04158
Chivalrous	... ...	04109	Chronology	04159
Chivalry...	... ...	04110	Chronometer	04160
Chloride...	... ...	04111	Chrysalis	04161
Chloroform	... ...	04112	Chrysolite	04162
Chocolate	... ...	04113	Chrysoprase	04163
Choice ...	... ...	04114	Chub	04164
Choicely...	... ...	04115	Chubby	04165
Choir ...	... ...	04116	Chuck	04166
Choke ...	... ...	04117	Chucked...	04167
Choked ...	... ...	04118	Chuckle	04168
Choking...	... ...	04119	Chum	04169
Choky ...	... ...	04120	Chump	04170
Choler ...	... ...	04121	Church	04171
Cholera ...	... ...	04122	Churchdom	04172
Choleraic	... ...	04123	Churching	04173
Choleric ...	... ...	04124	Churchman	04174
Cholerine	... ...	04125	Churchwarden ...	04175
Choose ...	... ...	04126	Churchyard	04176
Chooser ...	... ...	04127	Churl	04177
Chooses ...	... ...	04128	Churlish	04178
Choosing	... ...	04129	Churn	04179
Chop ...	... ...	04130	Chyle	04180
Chopper...	... ...	04131	Chyme	04181
Chops ...	... ...	04132	Cicatrice...	04182
Choral ...	... ...	04133	Cicatrize	04183
Chord ...	... ...	04134	Cicatrized	04184
Chorister	... ...	04135	Cicerone...	04185
Chorus ...	... ...	04136	Cid	04186
Chose ...	... ...	04137	Cider	04187
Chosen ...	... ...	04138	Cigar	04188
Chough ...	... ...	04139	Ciliary	04189
Chouse ...	... ...	04140	Cimmerian	04190
Chrism ...	... ...	04141	Cinchona	04191
Chrismal...	... ...	04142	Cincture	04192
Christ ...	... ...	04143	Cinder	04193
Christen ...	... ...	04144	Cindery	04194
Christened	... ...	04145	Cindrous...	04195
Christendom	.. ...	04146	Cinefaction	04196
Christening	... ...	04147	Cinereous	04197
Christian	... ...	04148	Cingalese	04198
Christianity	... ...	04149	Cinnabar...	04199
Christianize	... ...	04150	Cinnamon	04200

43	CIN	(22)	CLA	
Cinque	04201	Civic	04251
Cipher	04202	Civil	04252
Circassian	04203	Civilian	04253
Circle	04204	Civility	04254
Circlet	04205	Civilization	04255
Circling	04206	Civilize	04256
Circuit	04207	Civilized	04257
Circuitous	04208	Clack	04258
Circular	04209	Clad	04259
Circulate...	04210	Claim	04260
Circulated	04211	Claimant	04261
Circulation	04212	Claimed	04262
Circumambient ...	04213	Claiming	04263
Circumambulate ...	04214	Claims	04264
Circumcise	04215	Clam	04265
Circumcised ...	04216	Clamber...	04266
Circumcision ...	04217	Clammy	04267
Circumference ...	04218	Clamorous	04268
Circumflex	04219	Clamour...	04269
Circumjacent	04220	Clamp	04270
Circumlocution ...	04221	Clamped...	04271
Circumnavigate ...	04222	Clan	04272
Circumnavigator ...	04223	Clandestine	04273
Circumscribe	04224	Clandestinely... ...	04274
Circumscribed ...	04225	Clang	04275
Circumspect	04226	Clangour	04276
Circumspection ...	04227	Clank	04277
Circumstance... ...	04228	Clannish...	04278
Circumstantial ...	04229	Clanship...	04279
Circumstantially ...	04230	Clap	04280
Circumstantiate ...	04231	Clapped	04281
Circumvent	04232	Clapper	04282
Circumvented ...	04233	Clapping	04283
Circumvention ...	04234	Claret	04284
Circus	04235	Clarification	04285
Cisalpine...	04236	Clarified...	04286
Cistercian	04237	Clarifier	04287
Cistern	04238	Clarify	04288
Cit	04239	Clarionet	04289
Citable	04240	Clash	04290
Citadel	04241	Clashed	04291
Citation	04242	Clashing...	04292
Cite...	04243	Clasp	04293
Cited	04244	Clasped	04294
Citizen	04245	Class	04295
Citizenship	04246	Classed	04296
Citrate	04247	Classic	04297
Citron	04248	Classics	04298
City...	04249	Classically	04299
Civet	04250	Classification... ...	04300

Classified	... ...	04301
Classify	... ...	04302
Clatter	... ...	04303
Clatterer	... ...	04304
Clattering	... ...	04305
Clause	... ...	04306
Clavicle	... ...	04307
Claw	... ...	04308
Clawed	... ...	04309
Clay	... ...	04310
Clayey	... ...	04311
Claymore	... ...	04312
Clean	... ...	04313
Cleaned	... ...	04314
Cleaner	... ...	04315
Cleanliness	... ...	04316
Cleanness	... ...	04317
Cleanse	... ...	04318
Cleansing	... ...	04319
Clear	... ...	04320
Clearance	... ...	04321
Cleared	... ...	04322
Clearing	... ...	04323
Clearly	... ...	04324
Clearness	... ...	04325
Cleavable	... ...	04326
Cleavage	... ...	04327
Cleave	... ...	04328
Cleaver	... ...	04329
Cleaving	... ...	04330
Cleft	... ...	04331
Clemency	... ...	04332
Clement	... ...	04333
Clemently	... ...	04334
Clergy	... ...	04335
Clergyman	... ...	04336
Clerical	... ...	04337
Clerk	... ...	04338
Clerkly	... ...	04339
Clever	... ...	04340
Cleverly	... ...	04341
Cleverness	... ...	04342
Clew	... ...	04343
Click	... ...	04344
Client	... ...	04345
Cliff	... ...	04346
Climacteric	... ...	04347
Climate	... ...	04348
Climatic	... ...	04349
Climatize	... ...	04350

Climax	... ...	04351
Climb	... ...	04352
Climbed	... ...	04353
Climber	... ...	04354
Climbing	... ...	04355
Clime	... ...	04356
Clinch	... ...	04357
Clinched	... ...	04358
Clincher	... ...	04359
Cling	... ...	04360
Clinging	... ...	04361
Clinical	... ...	04362
Clink	... ...	04363
Clip..	... ...	04364
Clipped	... .	04365
Clipper	... ...	04366
Clipping	... ...	04367
Clique	... ...	04368
Cloak	... ...	04369
Cloaked	... ...	04370
Clock	... ...	04371
Clod	... ...	04372
Clodhopper	... ...	04373
Clog	... ...	04374
Clogged	... ...	04375
Cloggy	... ...	04376
Cloister	... ...	04377
Cloistered	... ...	04378
Close	... ...	04379
Closed	... ...	04380
Closely	... ...	04381
Closeness	... ...	04382
Closet	... ...	04383
Closing	... ...	04384
Clot	... ...	04385
Cloth	... ...	04386
Clothe	... ...	04387
Clothes	... ...	04388
Clothier	... ...	04389
Clothing	... ...	04390
Clotted	... ...	04391
Cloud	... ...	04392
Clouded	... ...	04393
Cloudily	... ...	04394
Cloudless	... ...	04395
Cloudy	... ...	04396
Clout	... ...	04397
Clove	... ...	04398
Cloven	... ...	04399
Clover	... ...	04400

45 CLO	(23)	COG	
Clown	04401	Cobalt	04451
Clownish	04402	Cobble	04452
Cloy	04403	Cobbled	04453
Club	04404	Cobbler	04454
Clubbed	04405	Coble	04455
Clubbist	04406	Cobweb	04456
Cluck	04407	Cobwebbed	04457
Clucking...	04408	Cochineal	04458
Clump	04409	Cock	04459
Clumsily...	04410	Cockade	04460
Clumsiness	04411	Cockatoo	04461
Clumsy	04412	Cockatrice	04462
Clung	04413	Cocked	04463
Cluster	04414	Cockle	04464
Clustered	04415	Cockled	04465
Clutch	04416	Cockney...	04466
Clyster	04417	Cockneyism	04467
Co	04418	Cockpit	04468
Coach	04419	Cockroach	04469
Coachman	04420	Cockswain	04470
Coactive...	04421	Cocoa	04471
Coadjutor	04422	Cocoon	04472
Coadjutorship ...	04423	Cod	04473
Coagent	04424	Code	04474
Coagulability... ...	04425	Codex	04475
Coagulant	04426	Codicil	04476
Coagulate	04427	Codification	04477
Coagulated	04428	Codified	04478
Coagulation	04429	Codify	04479
Coal	04430	Coefficient	04480
Coalesce...	04431	Coemption	04481
Coalescence	04432	Coequal	04482
Coalescent	04433	Coerce	04483
Coalition	04434	Coerced	04484
Coaly	04435	Coercible	04485
Coamings	04436	Coercion...	04486
Coannex...	04437	Coercive...	04487
Coarse	04438	Coeternal	04488
Coarsely...	04439	Coeternity	04489
Coarseness	04440	Coeval	04490
Coast	04441	Coexist	04491
Coaster	04442	Coexistent	04492
Coasting...	04443	Coextensive	04493
Coat	04444	Coffee	04494
Coated	04445	Coffer	04495
Coating	04446	Coffin	04496
Coax	04447	Cog	04497
Coaxer	04448	Cogency	04498
Coaxing	04449	Cogent	04499
Cob	04450	Cogently...	04500

| COG | (23) | COL. | 46 |

Cogitate	04501	Collation	04551
Cogitation	04502	Collator	04552
Cogitative	04503	Colleague	04553
Cognac	04504	Collect	04554
Cognate	04505	Collecting	04555
Cognizance	04506	Collects	04556
Cognizant	04507	Collected	04557
Cognomen	04508	Collection	04558
Cognovit...	04509	Collective	04559
Cohabit	04510	Collectively	04560
Cohabitation	04511	Collector	04561
Coheir	04512	College	04562
Coheiress	04513	Collegian	04563
Cohere	04514	Collegiate	04564
Coherence	04515	Collide	04565
Coherent	04516	Collided...	04566
Coherently	04517	Collier	04567
Cohesion	04518	Colliery	04568
Cohesive...	04519	Collimator	04569
Cohesively	04520	Collision...	04570
Cohibition	04521	Collitigant	04571
Coil...	04522	Collocate	04572
Coiled	04523	Collocated	04573
Coin	04524	Colloquial	04574
Coinage	04525	Colloquialism ...	04575
Coined	04526	Colloquy	04576
Coincide...	04527	Collude	04577
Coincided	04528	Colluder...	04578
Coincidence	04529	Collusion	04579
Coincident	04530	Collusive	04580
Coincider	04531	Colon	04581
Coinciding	04532	Colonel	04582
Coiner	04533	Colonial	04583
Coining	04534	Colonist	04584
Coinheritance ...	04535	Colonisation	04585
Coir...	04536	Colonise...	04586
Coition	04537	Colonising	04587
Coke	04538	Colonnade	04588
Cold	04539	Colony	04589
Coldly	04540	Colossal	04590
Coldness...	04541	Collosseum	04591
Colic	04542	Colossus...	04592
Collapse	04543	Colour	04593
Collapsed	04544	Colourable	04594
Collar	04545	Coloured	04595
Collared	04546	Colourless	04596
Collate	04547	Colours	04597
Collated	04548	Colt	04598
Collateral	04549	Columbine	04599
Collaterally	04550	Column	04600

Columnar	... ...	04601
Colza	... ...	04602
Coma	... ...	04603
Comate	... ...	04604
Comatose	... ...	04605
Comb	... ...	04606
Combed	... ...	04607
Combat	... ...	04608
Combatant	... ...	04609
Combative	... ...	04610
Combativeness	...	04611
Combinable	... ...	04612
Combination	... ...	04613
Combine	... ...	04614
Combined	... ...	04615
Combiner	... ...	04616
Combing	... ...	04617
Combining	... ...	04618
Combustibility	...	04619
Combustible	... ...	04620
Combustion	... ...	04621
Come	... ...	04622
Comedian	... ...	04623
Comedy	... ...	04624
Comely	... ...	04625
Comer	... ...	04626
Comes	... ...	04627
Comet	... ...	04628
Cometary	... ...	04629
Comfit	... ...	04630
Comfort	... ...	04631
Comfortable	... ...	04632
Comforted	... ...	04633
Comforter	... ...	04634
Comfortless	... ...	04635
Comic	... ...	04636
Comical	... ...	04637
Comically	... ...	04638
Coming	... ...	04639
Comma	... ...	04640
Command	... ...	04641
Commandant	... ...	04642
Commandatory	...	04643
Commanded	... ...	04644
Commander	... ...	04645
Commandership	...	04646
Commanding	... ...	04647
Commandment	...	04648
Commemorable	...	04649
Commemorate	...	04650

Commemorated	...	04651
Commemoration	...	04652
Commemorative	...	04653
Commence	... ...	04654
Commenced	... ...	04655
Commencement	...	04656
Commences	... ...	04657
Commencing	... ...	04658
Commend	... ...	04659
Commendable	...	04660
Commendation	...	04661
Commendatory	...	04662
Commended	... ...	04663
Commensurate	...	04664
Commensurately	...	04665
Comment	... ...	04666
Commented	... ...	04667
Commentary	... ...	04668
Commentative	...	04669
Commentator	... ...	04670
Commenter	... ...	04671
Commerce	... ...	04672
Commercial	... ...	04673
Commercially	... ...	04674
Commination	... ...	04675
Comminatory	... ...	04676
Commingle	... ...	04677
Commiserate	... ...	04678
Commiserated	...	04679
Commiseration	...	04680
Commiserator	...	04681
Commissariat	... ...	04682
Commissary	... ...	04683
Commission	... ...	04684
Commissioned	...	04685
Commissioner	...	04686
Commit	... ...	04687
Committal	... ...	04688
Committed	... ...	04689
Committee	... ...	04690
Commix	... ...	04691
Commixture	... ...	04692
Commodious	... ...	04693
Commodiously	...	04694
Commodity	... ...	04695
Commodore	... ...	04696
Common	... ...	04697
Commonalty	... ...	04698
Commoner	... ...	04699
Commonly	... ...	04700

COM	(24)	COM	48

Commonplace	...	04701	Compeer...	04751
Commons	04702		Compel	04752
Commonwealth	...	04703	Compelled	04753
Commotion	04704		Compeller	04754
Commune	04705		Compelling	04755
Communed	04706		Compels	04756
Communicability ...	04707		Compendium	04757
Communicable ...	04708		Compendious... ...	04758
Communicably ...	04709		Compensate	04759
Communicant ...	04710		Compensated... ...	04760
Communicate... ...	04711		Compensates	04761
Communicated ...	04712		Compensation ...	04762
Communication ...	04713		Compensatory ...	04763
Communicative ...	04714		Compete...	04764
Communicativeness	04715		Competed	04765
Communicator ...	04716		Competes	04766
Communing	04717		Competence	04767
Communion	04718		Competency	04768
Communism	04719		Competent	04769
Community	04720		Competently	04770
Commutability ...	04721		Competing	04771
Commutable	04722		Competition	04772
Commute	04723		Competitive	04773
Compact...	04724		Competitor	04774
Compactly	04725		Compilation	04775
Compactness	04726		Compile	04776
Companion	04727		Compiled	04777
Companionable ...	04728		Compiler	04778
Companionless ...	04729		Complacency	04779
Companionship ...	04730		Complacent	04780
Company	04731		Complacently... ...	04781
Comparable	04732		Complain	04782
Comparably	04733		Complainant	04783
Comparative	04734		Complained	04784
Comparatively ...	04735		Complaining	04785
Compare	04736		Complains	04786
Compared	04737		Complaint	04787
Comparer	04738		Complaisance... ...	04788
Compares	04739		Complaisant	04789
Comparing	04740		Complement	04790
Comparison	04741		Complemental ...	04791
Compartment... ...	04742		Complete	04792
Compass...	04743		Completed	04793
Compasses	04744		Completely	04794
Compassion	04745		Completeness... ...	04795
Compassionate ...	04746		Completes	04796
Compassionately ...	04747		Completing	04797
Compatibility... ...	04748		Completion	04798
Compatible	04749		Complex...	04799
Compatriot	04750		Complexion	04800

49	COM	(25)	CON	
Complexity	... ...	04801	Compromises	04851
Complexly	... ...	04802	Compromising ...	04852
Compliable	... ...	04803	Comptroller	04853
Compliance	... ...	04804	Compulsatory ...	04854
Compliant	... ...	04805	Compulsion	04855
Complicate	... ...	04806	Compulsive	04856
Complicated	... ...	04807	Compulsively... ...	04857
Complication		04808	Compulsorily	04858
Complicity	... ...	04809	Compulsory	04859
Complied	... ...	04810	Compunction	04860
Complies	... ...	04811	Compunctious ...	04861
Compliment		04812	Computable	04862
Complimental	...	04813	Computate	04863
Complimentary	...	04814	Computation	04864
Complimented	...	04815	Compute...	04865
Complimenter	...	04816	Computer	04866
Compline	...	04817	Comrade...	04867
Complot...	... ..	04818	Comradeship	04868
Comply ...	... ...	04819	Con...	04869
Complying	... ...	04820	Concatenate	04870
Component	... ...	04821	Concatenation ...	04871
Comport...	... ...	04822	Concave	04872
Comported	... ...	04823	Concavity	04873
Compose...	... ...	04824	Conceal	04874
Composed	... ...	04825	Concealer	04875
Composer	... ...	04826	Concealing	04876
Composing	... ...	04827	Concealment	04877
Composite	... ...	04828	Concede	04878
Composition		04829	Conceded	04879
Compositor	... ,...	04830	Concedes	04880
Composure	... ...	04831	Conceding	04881
Compound	... ...	04832	Conceit	04882
Compounded		04833	Conceited	04883
Compounder		04834	Conceivable	04884
Compounding	...	04835	Conceive...	04885
Compounds		04836	Conceived	04886
Comprehend		04837	Conceiving	04887
Comprehended	...	04838	Concentrate	04888
Comprehending	...	04839	Concentrated	04889
Comprehends... ...		04840	Concentration ...	04890
Comprehensible ...		04841	Concentrative... ...	04891
Comprehensibly ...		04842	Concentre	04892
Comprehension ...		04843	Concentric	04893
Comprehensive ...		04844	Conception	04894
Compress		04845	Concern	04895
Compressed		04846	Concerned	04896
Compression		04847	Concernedly	04897
Comprise		04848	Concerning	04898
Comprising		04849	Concernment	04899
Compromise		04850	Concerns...	04900

CON	(25)	CON	50
Concert	04901	Concupiscence ...	04951
Concerted	04902	Concupiscent	04952
Concertina	04903	Concur	04953
Concession	04904	Concurrence	04954
Concessionaire ...	04905	Concurrent	04955
Concessionary ...	04906	Concurrently	04956
Concessive	04907	Concurring	04957
Concessively ...	04908	Concussion	04958
Concessory	04909	Condemn	04959
Conch	04910	Condemnable... ...	04960
Conchological ...	04911	Condemnation ...	04961
Conchologist	04912	Condemnatory ...	04962
Conchology	04913	Condemned	04963
Conciliate	04914	Condemning	04964
Conciliating	04915	Condensability ...	04965
Conciliative ...	04916	Condensable	04966
Conciliation	04917	Condensate	04967
Conciliator	04918	Condensated	04968
Conciliatory	04919	Condensating	04969
Concise	04920	Condensation	04970
Concisely	04921	Condensative	04971
Conciseness	04922	Condense	04972
Conclamation... ...	04923	Condenser	04973
Conclave	04924	Condensity	04974
Conclude	04925	Condescend	04975
Concluded	04926	Condescending ...	04976
Concluder	04927	Condescension ...	04977
Concludes	04928	Condign	04978
Concluding	04929	Condignly	04979
Concludingly	04930	Condiment	04980
Conclusible	04931	Condition	04981
Conclusion	04932	Conditional	04082
Conclusive	04933	Conditionally	04983
Conclusory	04934	Condolatory	04984
Concoct	04935	Condole	04985
Concocted	04936	Condolence	04986
Concocting	04937	Condoling	04987
Concoction	04938	Condone...	04988
Concomitant	04939	Conduce	04989
Concord	04940	Conduces	04990
Concordance	04941	Conducive	04991
Concordant	04942	Conduct	04992
Concordat	04943	Conducted	04993
Concourse	04944	Conductible	04994
Concrescence	04945	Conductive	04995
Concrete...	04946	Conductor	04996
Concretely	04947	Conduit	04997
Concretion	04948	Cone	04998
Concubinage	04949	Confab	04999
Concubine	04950	Confabulate	05000

51	CON	(26)	CON

Confect	05001	Confluent	05051
Confection	05002	Conform...	05052
Confectioner	05003	Conformable	05053
Confederacy	05004	Conformation ...	05054
Confederate	05005	Conformed	05055
Confederated	05006	Conforming	05056
Confederation... ...	05007	Conformist	05057
Confer	05008	Conformity	05058
Conference	05009	Confound	05059
Conferring	05010	Confounded	05060
Confess	05011	Confounding	05061
Confessed	05012	Confraternity... ...	05062
Confessedly	05013	Confront...	05063
Confessing	05014	Confrontation ...	05064
Confession	05015	Confronting	05065
Confessional	05016	Confuse	05066
Confessor	05017	Confused	05067
Confidant	05018	Confusedly	05068
Confide	05019	Confusing	05069
Confidence	05020	Confusion	05070
Confident	05021	Confutable	05071
Confidential	05022	Confutation	05072
Confidentially	05023	Confutative	05073
Confidently	05024	Confute	05074
Confider	05025	Confuting	05075
Confiding	05026	Congé	05076
Configurate	05027	Congeal	05077
Configuration... ...	05028	Congealing	05078
Confine	05029	Congealment	05079
Confined...	05030	Congelation	05080
Confineless	05031	Congener	05081
Confinement	05032	Congeneracy	05082
Confines	05033	Congeneric	05083
Confirm	05034	Congenial	05084
Confirmation	05035	Congeniality	05085
Confirmative	05036	Congenialize	05086
Confirmed	05037	Congenital	05087
Confirming	05038	Congeries	05088
Confirms...	05039	Congestion	05089
Confiscable	05040	Conglomerate ...	05090
Confiscate	05041	Conglomeration ...	05091
Confiscation	05042	Congo	05092
Confiscated	05043	Congratulate	05093
Confiscating	05044	Congratulation ...	05094
Confiscator	05045	Congratulatory ...	05095
Conflagration... ...	05046	Congregate	05096
Conflict	05047	Congregating... ...	05097
Conflicting	05048	Congregation... ...	05098
Conflictive	05049	Congregational ...	05099
Confluence	05050	Congregationalist ...	05100

CON	(26)	CON	52

Congress...	05101	Conquering	05151
Congressional ...	05102	Conqueringly	05152
Congressive	05103	Conqueror	05153
Congreve	05104	Conquest...	05154
Congruence	05105	Consanguineous ...	05155
Congruent	05106	Consanguinity ...	05156
Congruity	05107	Conscience ...	05157
Congruous	05108	Conscienceless ...	05158
Conical	05109	Conscientious... ...	05159
Conically	05110	Conscionable	05160
Conics	05111	Conscious	05161
Conifer	05112	Conscript	05162
Coniform	05113	Conscription	05163
Conjecturally... ...	05114	Consecrate	05164
Conjecture	05115	Consecrated	05165
Conjecturing ...	05116	Consecration	05166
Conjoin	05117	Consecratory	05167
Conjoined	05118	Consecutive	05168
Conjoining	05119	Consent	05169
Conjoint	05120	Consentaneous ...	05170
Conjointly	05121	Consentient	05171
Conjugal...	05122	Consenting	05172
Conjugate	05123	Consentingly ...	05173
Conjugation	05124	Consequence	05174
Conjunct...	05125	Consequent	05175
Conjunction	05126	Consequential ...	05176
Conjunctive	05127	Consequently... ...	05177
Conjunctly	05128	Conservable	05178
Conjuncture	05129	Conservation	05179
Conjuration	05130	Conservatism... ...	05180
Conjure	05131	Conservative	05181
Conjurer...	05132	Conservatoire... ...	05182
Connate	05133	Conservator	05183
Connect	05134	Conservatory	05184
Connected	05135	Conserve...	05185
Connectedly	05136	Consider...	05186
Connecting	05137	Considerable	05187
Connection	05138	Considerate	05188
Connectively	05139	Considerately... ...	05189
Connivance	05140	Consideration... ...	05190
Connive	05141	Considering	05191
Conniver...	05142	Consign	05192
Conniving	05143	Consigned	05193
Connoisseur	05144	Consignee	05194
Connotate	05145	Consigning	05195
Connotation	05146	Consignment	05196
Connote	05147	Consignor	05197
Connubial	05148	Consist	05198
Conquer	05149	Consistency	05199
Conquered	05150	Consistent	05200

Consisting	05201	
Consistorial	05202	
Consistory	05203	
Consolable	05204	
Consolation	05205	
Consolatory	05206	
Console	05207	
Consoler	05208	
Consolidate	05209	
Consolidated	05210	
Consolidation... ...	05211	
Consoling	05212	
Consols	05213	
Consonance	05214	
Consonant	05215	
Consort	05216	
Conspicuity	05217	
Conspicuous	05218	
Conspicuously ...	05219	
Conspiracy	05220	
Conspiration	05221	
Conspirator	05222	
Conspire...	05223	
Conspiring	05224	
Constable	05225	
Constabulary	05226	
Constancy	05227	
Constant	05228	
Constantly	05229	
Constellation	05230	
Consternation ...	05231	
Constipated	05232	
Constituency	05233	
Constituent	05234	
Constitute	05235	
Constituting	05236	
Constitution	05237	
Constitutional ...	05238	
Constitutionalist ...	05239	
Constitutive	05240	
Constrain	05241	
Constrainedly ...	05242	
Constraining	05243	
Constraint	05244	
Constrict...	05245	
Constricted	05246	
Constriction	05247	
Constrictive	05248	
Constrictor	05249	
Construct	05250	
Constructed	05251
Constructer	05252
Constructing	05253
Construction	05254
Constructive	05255
Constructure	05256
Construe...	05257
Construing	05258
Consubsist	05259
Consubstantialist ...	05260
Consubstantiality ...	05261
Consubstantiate ...	05262
Consubstantiated ...	05263
Consubstantiation ...	05264
Consuetude	05265
Consul	05266
Consulage	05267
Consular...	05268
Consulate	05269
Consult	05270
Consultation	05271
Consulted	05272
Consulting	05273
Consumable	05274
Consume	05275
Consumed	05276
Consumer	05277
Consuming	05278
Consummate	05279
Consummation ...	05280
Consumption	05281
Consumptive	05282
Contact	05283
Contagion	05284
Contagious	05285
Contain	05286
Contained	05287
Containing	05288
Contaminate	05289
Contaminated ...	05290
Contamination ...	05291
Contankerous... ...	05292
Contemn...	05293
Contemner	05294
Contemning	05295
Contemplate	05296
Contemplated ...	05297
Contemplating ...	05298
Contemplation ...	05299
Contemplative ...	05300

CON	(27)	CON	54

Contemplator... ...	05301	Contract...	05351
Contemporaneous ...	05302	Contracted	05352
Contemporary ...	05303	Contractile	05353
Contempt	05304	Contracting	05354
Contemptible... ...	05305	Contraction	05355
Contemptibly... ...	05306	Contractor	05356
Contemptuous ...	05307	Contradict	05357
Contend	05308	Contradicted	05358
Contender	05309	Contradicting ...	05359
Contending	05310	Contradiction ...	05360
Content	05311	Contradictorily ...	05361
Contented	05312	Contradictory ...	05362
Contenting	05313	Contradistinction ...	05363
Contention	05314	Contradistinguish ...	05364
Contentious	05315	Contradistinguished	05365
Contentless	05316	Contralto	05366
Contentment	05317	Contraries	05367
Contents...	05318	Contrariety	05368
Conterminable ...	05319	Contrarily	05369
Conterminous ...	05320	Contrariwise	05370
Contest	05321	Contrary...	05371
Contesting	05322	Contrast	05372
Contestable	05323	Contrasted ... · ...	05373
Contested	05324	Contrasting	05374
Context	05325	Contravene	05375
Contiguity	05326	Contravening... ...	05376
Contiguous	05327	Contravention ...	05377
Continence	05328	Contretemps	05378
Continent	05329	Contributable ...	05379
Continental	05330	Contribute	05380
Contingency	05331	Contributed	05381
Contingent	05332	Contributing	05382
Continuable	05333	Contribution	05383
Continual	05334	Contributive	05384
Continually	05335	Contributor	05385
Continuance	05336	Contrite	05386
Continuation	05337	Contrition	05387
Continue	05338	Contrivance	05388
Continued	05339	Contrive...	05389
Continuer	05340	Contrived	05390
Continuing	05341	Contriving	05391
Continuity	05342	Contriver	05392
Continuous	05343	Control	05393
Contort	05344	Controllable	05394
Contorted	05345	Controller	05395
Contortion	05346	Controllership ...	05396
Contour	05347	Controlling	05397
Contra	05348	Controversial... ...	05398
Contraband	05349	Controversialist ...	05399
Contrabandist ...	05350	Controversially ...	05400

Controversion	...	05401
Controversy ...	...	05402
Controvert ...	...	05403
Controverted ...	...	05404
Controverter ...	...	05405
Controvertible	...	05406
Controverting	...	05407
Contumacious	...	05408
Contumacy ...	...	05409
Contumelious...	...	05410
Contumely ...	...	05411
Contuse	...	05412
Contused ...	...	05413
Contusion ...	...	05414
Conundrum ...	...	05415
Convalescence	...	05416
Convalescent ...	...	05417
Convenable ...	...	05418
Convene	...	05419
Convened ...	...	05420
Convener ...	...	05421
Convenience ...	...	05422
Convenient ...	...	05423
Convening ...	...	05424
Convent	...	05425
Conventicle ...	...	05426
Convention ...	...	05427
Conventional ...	...	05428
Conventionally	...	05429
Conventual ...	...	05430
Converge... ...	...	05431
Convergence ...	...	05432
Converging ...	...	05433
Conversable ...	...	05434
Cohversably ...	...	05435
Conversant ...	...	05436
Conversation ...	...	05437
Conversational	...	05438
Conversazione	...	05439
Converse ...	...	05440
Conversely ...	...	05441
Conversion ...	...	05442
Conversive ...	...	05443
Convert	...	05444
Converted ...	...	05445
Converter ...	...	05446
Converting ...	...	05447
Convertibility...	...	05448
Convex	...	05449
Convexly ...	...	05450

Convey	...	05451
Conveyance ...	...	05452
Conveyancer ...	...	05453
Conveyancing	...	05454
Conveyed ...	...	05455
Conveying ...	...	05456
Convict	...	05457
Convicted ...	...	05458
Convicting ...	...	05459
Conviction ...	...	05460
Convince... ...	...	05461
Convinced ...	...	05462
Convincing ...	...	05463
Convivial ...	...	05464
Convivialist ...	...	05465
Convocate ...	...	05466
Convocation ...	...	05467
Convocational	...	05468
Convoke... ...	...	05469
Convoked ..	...	05470
Convoking ...	...	05471
Convolute ...	...	05472
Convoy	...	05473
Convulse... ...	...	05474
Convulsed ...	...	05475
Convulsion ...	...	05476
Convulsive ...	...	05477
Coo	...	05478
Cooing	...	05479
Cook	...	05480
Cooked	...	05481
Cooking	...	05482
Cookery	...	05483
Cool	...	05484
Cooled	...	05485
Cooling	...	05486
Cooler	..	05487
Coolish	...	05488
Coolness... ...	...	05489
Coop	...	05490
Cooped	...	05491
Cooper	...	05492
Co-operate ...	...	05493
Co-operating ...	...	05494
Co-operation ...	...	05495
Coopering ...	...	05496
Co-ordinate ...	...	05497
Co-ordinately...	...	05498
Copaiba	...	05499
Cope	...	05500

COP	(28)	COR	56

Copeck	05501	Cornea	05551
Copernican	05502	Cornelian	05552
Copestone	05503	Corneous	05553
Copied	05504	Corner	05554
Copier	05505	Cornet	05555
Coping	05506	Cornetcy...	05556
Copious	05507	Cornice	05557
Copiously	05508	Cornish	05558
Copiousness	05509	Cornucopia	05559
Copper	05510	Cornute	05560
Copperas	05511	Corolla	05561
Coppered	05512	Corollary	05562
Coppice	05513	Corona	05563
Coptic	05514	Coronal	05564
Copula	05515	Coronation	05565
Copulate...	05516	Coroner	05566
Copulative	05517	Coronet	05567
Copy	05518	Corporal...	05568
Copyhold	05519	Corporally	05569
Copyholder	05520	Corporate	05570
Copyist	05521	Corporation	05571
Copyright	05522	Corporeal	05572
Coquet	05523	Corporealist	05573
Coquetry	05524	Corps	05574
Coquette	05525	Corpse	05575
Coquettish	05526	Corpulence	05576
Coral	05527	Corpulent	05577
Coralline	05528	Corpus	05578
Cord	05529	Correct	05579
Cordage	05530	Corrected	05580
Cordate	05531	Correcting	05581
Corded	05532	Correction	05582
Cordial	05533	Corrective	05583
Cordiality	05534	Correctly	05584
Cordially	05535	Corregidor	05585
Cordovan	05536	Correlate	05586
Corduroy	05537	Correlation	05587
Cordwain	05538	Correlative	05588
Cordwainer	05539	Correlatively	05589
Core	05540	Correspond	05590
Coregent	05541	Correspondence ...	05591
Corelation	05542	Correspondent ...	05592
Corinthian	05543	Corresponding ...	05593
Cork	05544	Corridor...	05594
Corked	05545	Corrigible	05595
Corking	05546	Corroborant	05596
Corkscrew	05547	Corroborate	05597
Corky	05548	Corroborated... ...	05598
Cormorant	05549	Corroborating ...	05599
Corn	05550	Corrode	05600

57	COR	(29)		COU	
Corroded	 05601		Cough ...	... ...	05651
Corroding	 05602		Coughed...	... ...	05652
Corrosive	 05603		Could ...	... ...	05653
Corrugate	 05604		Coulter ...	... ...	05654
Corrugated	 05605		Council ...	... ...	05655
Corrugator	 05606		Councillor	... ...	05656
Corrupt ...	 05607		Counsel ...	... ...	05657
Corrupted	 05608		Counselled	... ...	05658
Corrupter	 05609		Counsellor	... ...	05659
Corruptible	 05610		Count ...	... ...	05660
Corrupting	 05611		Counted ...	... ...	05661
Corruption	 05612		Countenance ...	...	05662
Corruptly	 05613		Countenanced	...	05663
Corsair ...	 05614		Counter ...	... ...	05664
Corselet ...	 05615		Counteract	... ...	05665
Corset	 05616		Counteracting	...	05666
Cortege ...	 05617		Counteraction	...	05667
Cortes ...	 05618		Counteractive	...	05668
Coruscant	 05619		Counterbalance	...	05669
Coruscate	 05620		Counterfeit ...	...	05670
Coruscation ...	... 05621		Counterfeited...	...	05671
Corvette ...	 05622		Counterfeiting	...	05672
Corypheus	 05623		Counterfeitly ...	...	05673
Co-sentient	 05624		Countermand...	...	05674
Cosmetic	 05625		Countermanded	...	05675
Cosmic ...	 05626		Countermanding	...	05676
Cosmically	 05627		Countermarch	...	05677
Cosmogony ...	... 05628		Countermine ...	...	05678
Cosmography	... 05629		Counterpane ...	...	05679
Cosmopolitan...	... 05630		Counterpart ...	...	05680
Cosmorama ...	... 05631		Counterplead...	...	05681
Cossack ...	 05632		Counterplot ...	...	05682
Cost	 05633		Counterpoint ...	...	05683
Costermonger	... 05634		Counterpoise ...	...	05684
Costing ...	 05635		Countersign ...	...	05685
Costive ...	 05636		Countersigned	...	05686
Costs ...	 05637		Countervail ...	...	05687
Costliness	 05638		Countess...	... ...	05688
Costly ...	 05639		Counting	... ...	05689
Costume...	 05640		Countless	... ...	05690
Cot ...	 05641		Countrified	... ...	05691
Coterie ...	 05642		Country ...	... ...	05692
Cotillon ...	 05643		Countryman	... ...	05693
Cottage ...	 05644		County ...	... ...	05694
Cottager...	 05645		Couple ...	... ...	05695
Cotter ...	 05646		Coupled ...	... ...	05696
Cotton ...	 05647		Couplet ...	... ...	05697
Couch ...	 05648		Coupling	... ...	05698
Couchant	 05649		Coupon ...	... ...	05699
Coughing	 05650		Courage ...	... ...	05700

COU	(29)	CRA	58

Courageous	05701	Cozened	05751
Courageously... ...	05702	Cozener	05752
Courant	05703	Cozy	05753
Courier	05704	Crab	05754
Course	05705	Crabbed	05755
Courser	05706	Crack	05756
Court	05707	Cracked	05757
Courteous	05708	Cracker	05758
Courtesan	05709	Cracking...	05759
Courtesy...	05710	Crackle	05760
Courtier	05711	Crackling	05761
Courting...	05712	Cracknel...	05762
Courtlike	05713	Cradle	05763
Courtliness	05714	Cradled	05764
Courtly	05715	Craft	05765
Courtship	05716	Craftily	05766
Courtyard	05717	Craftsman	05767
Cousin	05718	Crafty	05768
Cousinly	05719	Crag	05769
Cove	05720	Cragged	05770
Covenant	05721	Cram	05771
Covenanter	05722	Crammed	05772
Cover	05723	Cramming	05773
Covered	05724	Cramp	05774
Covering...	05725	Cramped...	05775
Coverlet	05726	Cranberry	05776
Covert	05727	Crane	05777
Covertly	05728	Craniological	05778
Coverture	05729	Craniologist	05779
Covet	05730	Craniology	05780
Coveting...	05731	Cranium	05781
Covetous	05732	Crank	05782
Covetousness	05733	Crankness	05783
Covey	05734	Cranny	05784
Cow...	05735	Crape	05785
Coward	05736	Craped	05786
Cowardice	05737	Crash	05787
Cowed	05738	Crass	05788
Cower	05739	Crassitude	05789
Cowl	05740	Crater	05790
Cowled	05741	Crateriform	05791
Cowry	05742	Cravat	05792
Cowslip	05743	Crave	05793
Coxcomb	05744	Craven	05794
Coxcombry	05745	Craving	05795
Coy	05746	Crawl	05796
Coyish	05747	Crawling...	05797
Coyness	05748	Crayon	05798
Coz	05749	Crazed	05799
Cozen	05750	Crazy	05800

Creak 05801	Cricket 05851
Creaking... 05802	Cricketer 05852
Cream 05803	Crier 05853
Creamy 05804	Cries 05854
Crease 05805	Crime 05855
Creased 05806	Criminal... 05856
Create 05807	Criminating 05857
Created 05808	Criminality 05858
Creating... 05809	Criminate 05859
Creation... 05810	Crimination 05860
Creative 05811	Crimp 05861
Creator 05812	Crimping 05862
Creature... 05813	Crimson 05863
Credence 05814	Cringe 05864
Credential 05815	Cringing... 05865
Credibility 05816	Crinkle 05866
Credible... 05817	Crinoline 05867
Credibly... 05818	Cripple 05868
Credit 05819	Crisis 05869
Credited... 05820	Crisp 05870
Creditable 05821	Crispate 05871
Creditably 05822	Crisped 05872
Creditor 05823	Crisply 05873
Credulity 05824	Criterion... 05874
Credulous 05825	Critic 05875
Creed 05826	Critical 05876
Creek 05827	Critically 05877
Creep 05828	Criticise 05878
Creeper 05829	Criticiser 05879
Creeping 05830	Criticising 05880
Creeps 05831	Criticism... 05881
Cremation 05832	Critique 05882
Creole 05833	Croak 05883
Creosote... 05834	Croaker 05884
Crepitation 05835	Croaking 05885
Crept 05836	Croaks 05886
Crescent... 05837	Crochet 05887
Cress 05838	Crock 05888
Cresset 05839	Crockery 05889
Crest 05840	Crocodile 05890
Crestless... 05841	Crocus 05891
Cretaceous 05842	Croft 05892
Cretin 05843	Cromlech 05893
Crevasse... 05844	Crone 05894
Crevice 05845	Crony 05895
Crew 05846	Crook 05896
Crib 05847	Crooked... 05897
Cribbage 05848	Crop 05898
Crick 05849	Cropper 05899
Cricked 05850	Croquet 05900

CRO			(30)	CUM			60
Crore	...	...	05901	Crustily	...	...	05951
Crosier	...	...	05902	Crusty	...	...	05952
Cross	...	...	05903	Crutch	...	...	05953
Crossed	...	...	05904	Cry	...	...	05954
Crosses	...	...	05905	Crying	...	...	05955
Crossing	...	...	05906	Crypt	...	...	05956
Crossness	...	...	05907	Cryptogamic	...	...	05957
Crotchet	...	...	05908	Crystal	...	...	05958
Crotchety	...	...	05909	Crystalline	...	...	05959
Crouch	...	...	05910	Crystallize	...	...	05960
Croup	...	...	05911	Crystallized	...	...	05961
Croupier	...	...	05912	Cub	...	...	05962
Crow	...	...	05913	Cuban	...	...	05963
Crowd	...	...	05914	Cubature	...	...	05964
Crowded	...	...	05915	Cube	...	...	05965
Crowding	...	...	05916	Cubical	...	...	05966
Crowing	...	...	05917	Cubicular	...	...	05967
Crown	...	...	05918	Cubit	...	...	05968
Crowning	...	...	05919	Cuckold	...	...	05969
Crucial	...	...	05920	Cuckoo	...	...	05970
Crucible	...	...	05921	Cucumber	...	...	05971
Crucified	...	...	05922	Cud	...	...	05972
Crucifix	...	...	05923	Cuddle	...	...	05973
Crucifixion	...	...	05924	Cudgel	...	...	05974
Cruciform	...	...	05925	Cue	...	...	05975
Crucify	...	...	05926	Cuff	...	...	05976
Crude	...	...	05927	Cuirass	...	...	05977
Crudely	...	...	05928	Cuirassier	...	...	05978
Cruel	...	...	05929	Cuisine	...	...	05979
Cruelty	...	...	05930	Culinary	...	...	05980
Cruet	...	...	05931	Cull	...	...	05981
Cruise	...	...	05932	Cullender	...	...	05982
Cruiser	...	...	05933	Culling	...	...	05983
Cruising	...	...	05934	Culminate	...	...	05984
Crumb	...	...	05935	Culminating	...	...	05985
Crumble	...	...	05936	Culmination	...	...	05986
Crumpet	...	...	05937	Culpability	...	...	05987
Crumple	...	...	05938	Culpable	...	...	05988
Crumpled	...	...	05939	Culpably	...	...	05989
Crumpling	...	...	05940	Culprit	...	...	05990
Crunch	...	...	05941	Cultivate	...	...	05991
Crupper	...	...	05942	Cultivated	...	...	05992
Crusade	...	...	05943	Cultivating	...	...	05993
Cruse	...	...	05944	Cultivation	...	...	05994
Crush	...	...	05945	Cultivator	...	...	05995
Crushed	...	...	05946	Culture	...	...	05996
Crusher	...	...	05947	Culvert	...	...	05997
Crushing	...	...	05948	Cumber	...	...	05998
Crust	...	...	05949	Cumbersome	...	...	05999
Crustacea	...	...	05950	Cumbrance	...	...	06000

DI	CUM	(31)	CZA	

Cumbrous	... ...	06001	Curtailing	... ...	06051
Cumulate	... ...	06002	Curtain ...	... ...	06052
Cumulation	... ...	06003	Curtained	... ...	06053
Cumulative	... ...	06004	Curtly ...	... ...	06054
Cuneiform	... ...	06005	Curtness ...	... ...	06055
Cunning...	... ...	06006	Curtsy ...	... ...	06056
Cunningly	... ...	06007	Curvature	... ...	06057
Cup... ...	... ...	06008	Curve ...	... ...	06058
Cupidity ...	... ...	06009	Curved ...	... ...	06059
Cupola ...	... ...	06010	Curvet ...	... ...	06060
Cupped ...	... ...	06011	Curvilinear	... ...	06061
Cupping ...	... ...	06012	Curving ...	... ...	06062
Cupreous	... ...	06013	Cushion ...	... ...	06063
Cur	... ...	06014	Cushioned	... ...	06064
Curable ...	... ...	06015	Cusp ...	... ...	06065
Curaçoa ...	... ...	06016	Custard ...	... ...	06066
Curacy ...	... ...	06017	Custodian	... ...	06067
Curate ...	... ...	06018	Custody ...	... ...	06068
Curative ...	... ...	06019	Custom ...	... ...	06069
Curator ...	... ...	06020	Customary	... ...	06070
Curb ...	... ...	06021	Customer	... ...	06071
Curd ...	... ...	06022	Cut	... ...	06072
Curdle ...	... ...	06023	Cutaneous	... ...	06073
Cure ...	... ...	06024	Cute ...	... ...	06074
Cured ...	... ...	06025	Cuticle ...	... ...	06075
Curfew ...	... ...	06026	Cuticular	... ...	06076
Curing ...	... ...	06027	Cutlass ...	... ...	06077
Curiosity...	... ...	06028	Cutler ...	... ...	06078
Curious ...	... ...	06029	Cutlery ...	... ...	06079
Curl... ...	... ...	06030	Cutlet ...	... ...	06080
Curliness...	... ...	06031	Cutter ...	... ...	06081
Curling ...	... ...	06032	Cutting ...	... ...	06082
Curly ...	... ...	06033	Cuttingly	... ...	06083
Curmudgeon ...	...	06034	Cuttle ...	... ...	06084
Currant ...	... ...	06035	Cwt. ...	... ...	06085
Currency...	... ...	06036	Cycle ...	... ...	06086
Current ...	... ..	06037	Cyclopean	... ...	06087
Currently	... ...	06038	Cyclopædia	... ...	06088
Curricle ...	... ...	06039	Cygnet ...	... ...	06089
Curried ...	... ...	06040	Cylinder ...	... ...	06090
Currier ...	... ...	06041	Cylindrical	... ...	06091
Curry ...	... ...	06042	Cymbal ...	... ...	06092
Curse ...	... ...	06043	Cynical ...	... ...	06093
Cursed ..	... ...	06044	Cynic ...	... ...	06094
Cursing ...	... ...	06045	Cynicism...	... ...	06095
Cursitor ...	... ...	06046	Cypress ...	... ...	06096
Cursorily	... ...	06047	Cytherean	... ...	06097
Curt ...	... ...	06048	Czar ...	... ...	06098
Curtail ...	... ...	06049	Czarina ...	... ...	06099
Curtailed	... ...	06050	Czarowitz	... ...	06100

D	(31)	DAR	62

D	06101	Dares 06151
Dab...	06102	Daring 06152
Dabble	06103	Dark 06153
Daffodil	06104	Darken 06154
Daft...	06105	Darkly 06155
Dagger	06106	Darkness 06156
Daguerreotype ...	06107	Darling 06157
Daily	06108	Darn 06158
Daintily	06109	Dart 06159
Daintiness	06110	Darted 06160
Dainty	06111	Darting 06161
Dairy	06112	Dash 06162
Dais...	06113	Dashing 06163
Daisy	06114	Dastard 06164
Dale	06115	Date 06165
Dallied	06116	Dated 06166
Dally	06117	Dating 06167
Dam	06118	Dative 06168
Damage	06119	Daub 06169
Damageable	06120	Daughter 06170
Damaging	06121	Daunt 06171
Damask	06122	Dauntless 06172
Dame	06123	Dauphin 06173
Damn	06124	Dawdle 06174
Damnable	06125	Dawdling 06175
Damnation	06126	Dawn 06176
Damned	06127	Dawning... 06177
Damnify	06128	Day... 06178
Damning...	06129	Daytime 06179
Damp	06130	Dazzle 06180
Dampness	06131	Dazzling 06181
Damsel	06132	Deacon 06182
Damson	06133	Deaconess 06183
Dance	06134	Dead 06184
Dancing	06135	Deaden 06185
Dancer	06136	Deadly 06186
Dandelion	06137	Deadness 06187
Dandify	06138	Deaf 06188
Dandle	06139	Deafen 06189
Dandling	06140	Deafening 06190
Dandy	06141	Deafness... 06191
Danger	06142	Deal 06192
Dangerous	06143	Dealer 06193
Dangle	06144	Dealing 06194
Dangling	06145	Deals 06195
Danish	06146	Dealt 06196
Dank	06147	Dean 06197
Dapper	06148	Deanery 06198
Dapple	06149	Dear 06199
Dare	06150	Dearly 06200

63 DEA	(32)	DEC

Dearness...	06201	Deciding 06251
Dearth	06202	Deciduous 06252
Death	06203	Decimal 06253
Deathless	06204	Decimate 06254
Deathlike	06205	Decipher 06255
Deathly	06206	Deciphered 06256
Debar	06207	Deciphering 06257
Debarring	06208	Decision 06258
Debase	06209	Decisive 06259
Debasing	06210	Deck 06260
Debatable	06211	Decking 06261
Debate	06212	Decked 06262
Debated...	06213	Declaim 06263
Debater	06214	Declaimant 06264
Debating	06215	Declaiming 06265
Debauch...	06216	Declamation 06266
Debauchery	06217	Declaration 06267
Debenture	06218	Declaratory 06268
Debilitate	06219	Declare 06269
Debility	06220	Declared 06270
Debit	06221	Declaring 06271
Debited	06222	Declension 06272
Debiting	06223	Declination 06273
Debouch...	06224	Decline 06274
Debt	06225	Declining 06275
Debtor	06226	Declined 06276
Debutant	06227	Declivity... 06277
Decade	06228	Decoction 06278
Decalogue	06229	Decompose 06279
Decamp	06230	Decomposed 06280
Decant	06231	Decomposing... ... 06281
Decanter	06232	Decorate... 06282
Decapitate	06233	Decorated 06283
Decay	06234	Decorating 06284
Decayed	06235	Decoration 06285
Decaying	06236	Decorator 06286
Decease	06237	Decorous 06287
Deceit	06238	Decorum 06288
Deceitful	06239	Decoy 06289
Deceive	06240	Decoyed... 06290
Deceived	06241	Decoying 06291
Deceiver...	06242	Decrease 06292
Deceiving	06243	Decreased 06293
December	06244	Decreasing 06294
Decency	06245	Decree 06295
Decent	06246	Decreed 06296
Deception	06247	Decrepit 06297
Deceptive	06248	Decrepitude 06298
Decide	06249	Decretal 06299
Decided	06250	Decried 06300

| DEC | (32) | DEG | 64 |

Decry	06301	Deferment	06351
Dedicate...	06302	Deferred...	06352
Dedicated	06303	Deferring	06353
Dedicating	06304	Defiance...	06354
Dedication	06305	Defiatory	06355
Deduce	06306	Deficiency	06356
Deduced...	06307	Deficient	06357
Deducible	06308	Deficit	06358
Deducing	06309	Defied	06359
Deduct	06310	Defile	06360
Deducted	06311	Defilement	06361
Deducting	06312	Defiling	06362
Deduction	06313	Definable	06363
Deductive	06314	Define	06364
Deed	06315	Defined	06365
Deem	06316	Definer	06366
Deemed	06317	Defining...	06367
Deeming...	06318	Definite	06368
Deep	06319	Definition	06369
Deepen	06320	Definitive	06370
Deeply	06321	Definitively	06371
Deer	06322	Deflect	06372
Deface	06323	Deflected	06373
Defaced	06324	Deflecting	06374
Defacing...	06325	Defloration	06375
Defamation	06326	Deflower	06376
Defamatory	06327	Deform	06377
Defame	06328	Deformation	06378
Defamer...	06329	Deformed	06379
Defaming	06330	Deforming	06380
Default	06331	Deformity	06381
Defaulter	06332	Defraud	06382
Defaulting	06333	Defrauded	06383
Defeat	06334	Defrauder	06384
Defeated...	06335	Defrauding	06385
Defeating	06336	Defray	06386
Defect	06337	Defrayed	06387
Defective	06338	Defraying	06388
Defence	06339	Defrayment	06389
Defenceless	06340	Defunct	06390
Defend	06341	Defy	06391
Defendant	06342	Defying	06392
Defended	06343	Degeneracy	06393
Defender	06344	Degenerate	06394
Defending	06345	Degenerated	06395
Defensible	06346	Degenerating... ...	06396
Defensive	06347	Deglutition	06397
Defer	06348	Degradation	06398
Deference	06349	Degrade...	06399
Deferential	06350	Degraded	06400

Degrading	... ...	06401
Degree ...	... ...	06402
Deification	... ...	06403
Deiform ...	... ...	06404
Deify ...	... ...	06405
Deign ...	... ...	06406
Deigning	... ...	06407
Deintegrate	... ...	06408
Deism ...	... ...	06409
Deist ...	... ...	06410
Deity ...	... ...	06411
Deject ...	... ...	06412
Dejected...	... ...	06413
Dejection	... ...	06414
Delay ...	... ...	06415
Delayed ...	... ...	06416
Delaying	... ...	06417
Delayer ...	... ...	06418
Delectable	... ...	06419
Delectation	... ...	06420
Delegate...	... ...	06421
Delegated	... ...	06422
Delegation	... ...	06423
Deleterious	... ...	06424
Delf ...	... ...	06425
Deliberate	... ...	06426
Deliberated	... ...	06427
Deliberately	... ...	06428
Deliberating	... ...	06429
Deliberation	... ...	06430
Delicacy...	... ...	06431
Delicate ...	... ...	06432
Delicately	... ...	06433
Delicious	... ...	06434
Delight ...	... ...	06435
Delightful	... ...	06436
Delineate	... ...	06437
Delineated	... ...	06438
Delineation	... ...	06439
Delineator	... ...	06440
Delinquency	... ...	06441
Delinquent	... ...	06442
Delirious	... ...	06443
Deliriously	... ...	06444
Delirium...	... ...	06445
Deliver ...	... ...	06446
Deliverance	... ...	06447
Delivered	... ...	06448
Delivering	... ...	06449
Delivery	... ...	06450
Dell ...	... ...	06451
Delphine	... ...	06452
Delta ...	... ...	06453
Delude ...	... ...	06454
Deluded ...	... ...	06455
Deludes ...	... ...	06456
Deluding	... ...	06457
Deluge ...	... ...	06458
Delusion...	... ...	06459
Delusively	... ...	06460
Delusory	... ...	06461
Demagogue	... ...	06462
Demand...	... ...	06463
Demanded	... ...	06464
Demanding	... ...	06465
Demarcation ...	...	06466
Demean ...	... ...	06467
Demeaning	... ...	06468
Demeanour	... ...	06469
Demented	... ...	06470
Demerit ...	... ...	06471
Demesne	... ...	06472
Demi ...	... ...	06473
Demisable	... ...	06474
Demise ...	... ...	06475
Demission	... ...	06476
Democracy	... ...	06477
Democrat	... ...	06478
Democratic	... ...	06479
Demolish	... ...	06480
Demolished	... ...	06481
Demolishing ...	...	06482
Demolition	... ...	06483
Demon ...	... ...	06484
Demoniac	... ...	06485
Demonstrable	...	06486
Demonstrate ...	...	06487
Demonstrating	...	06488
Demonstration	...	06489
Demonstrator	...	06490
Demoralization	...	06491
Demoralize	...	06492
Demoralized ...	...	06493
Demulcent	... ...	06494
Demur ...	... ...	06495
Demure ...	... ...	06496
Demurrage	... ...	06497
Demurring	... ...	06498
Den... ...	... ...	06499
Denationalize...	...	06500

DEN	(33)	DEP	66
Denaturalize	06501	Depicted	06551
Deniable...	06502	Depilate	06552
Denial	06503	Depilatory	06553
Denied	06504	Deplete	06554
Denizen	06505	Depletion	06555
Denominate	06506	Deplorable	06556
Denominated... ...	06507	Deplorably	06557
Denomination ...	06508	Deplore	06558
Denominative ...	06509	Deplored	06559
Denominator	06510	Deplorement	06560
Denotable	06511	Deploring	06561
Denote	06512	Deploy	06562
Denoted	06513	Depone	06563
Denoting	06514	Deponent	06564
Denounce	06515	Depopulate	06565
Denounced	06516	Depopulated	06566
Denouncing	06517	Depopulator	06567
Denouncement ...	06518	Deport	06568
Dense	06519	Deported	06569
Density	06520	Deportment	06570
Dent	06521	Depose	06571
Dental	06522	Deposed...	06572
Dentation	06523	Deposing	06573
Dented	06524	Deposit	06574
Dentist	06525	Depositary	06575
Dentition	06526	Deposition	06576
Denude	06527	Depositor	06577
Denuded...	06528	Depository	06578
Denuding	06529	Depot	06579
Denunciate	06530	Depravation	06580
Denunciation... ...	06531	Deprave	06581
Denunciatory	06532	Depraved	06582
Deny	06533	Depravity	06583
Denying	06534	Deprecate	06584
Deodand	06535	Deprecation	06585
Deodorization ...	06536	Deprecatory	06586
Deodorize	06537	Depreciate	06587
Depart	06538	Depreciated	06588
Departed	06539	Depreciation	06589
Departing	06540	Depredate	06590
Department	06541	Depredation	06591
Departmental ...	06542	Depredator	06592
Departure	06543	Depress	06593
Depasture	06544	Depressed	06594
Depend	06545	Depressing	06595
Depended	06546	Depression	06596
Dependence	06547	Deprivable	06597
Dependent	06548	Deprivation	06598
Depending	06549	Deprive	06599
Depict	06550	Depriving	06600

Depth	06601	Designable 06651
Deputation	06602	Designate 06652
Depute	06603	Designated 06653
Deputing	06604	Designation 06654
Deputy	06605	Designed 06655
Derange	06606	Designer... 06656
Deranged	06607	Designing 06657
Derangement... ...	06608	Desirable 06658
Deranging	06609	Desire 06659
Derelict	06610	Desired 06660
Deride	06611	Desiring 06661
Deriding...	06612	Desirous 06662
Derision	06613	Desist 06663
Derivable	06614	Desistance 06664
Derivation	06615	Desk 06665
Derivative	06616	Desolate 06666
Derive	06617	Desolated 06667
Deriving...	06618	Desolating 06668
Derogate	06619	Desolation 06669
Derogation	06620	Despair 06670
Derogatory	06621	Despaired 06671
Descant	06622	Desparing 06672
Descend	06623	Despatch 06673
Descendant	06624	Despatched 06674
Descended	06625	Despatches 06675
Descending	06626	Desperado 06676
Descent	06627	Desperate 06677
Describable	06628	Desperation 06678
Describe	06629	Despicable 06679
Described	06630	Despise 06680
Describing	06631	Despised... 06681
Descried	06632	Despite 06682
Description	06633	Despoil 06683
Descriptive	06634	Despoiler 06684
Descriptively	06635	Despond 06685
Descry	06636	Despondency 06686
Desecrate	06637	Despondent 06687
Desecration	06638	Despondently... ... 06688
Desert	06639	Desponding 06689
Deserted...	06640	Despot 06690
Deserter	06641	Despotic... 06691
Desertion	06642	Despotism 06692
Deserve	06643	Dessert 06693
Deserved...	06644	Destination 06694
Deserving	06645	Destine 06695
Deshabille	06646	Destined... 06696
Desiccate	06647	Destiny 06697
Desiderative	06648	Destitute... 06698
Desideratum	06649	Destitution 06699
Design	06650	Destroy 06700

DES	(34)	DIA	68

Destroyed	... ...	06701	Detonating	... ...	06751
Destroyer	... ...	06702	Detract ...	... ...	06752
Destroying	... ...	06703	Detraction	... ...	06753
Destructible	... ...	06704	Detractor	... ...	06754
Destruction	... ...	06705	Detriment	... ...	06755
Destructive	... ...	06706	Detrimental	... ...	06756
Desuetude	... ...	06707	Deuce	... ...	06757
Desultorily	... ...	06708	Deuteronomy	... ...	06758
Desultory	... ...	06709	Devastate	... ...	06759
Detach ...	... ...	06710	Devastated	... ...	06760
Detached	... ...	06711	Devastating	... ...	06761
Detaching	... ...	06712	Devastation	... ...	06762
Detachment	... ...	06713	Develop ...	... ...	06763
Detail ...	... ...	06714	Developed	... ...	06764
Detain ...	... ...	06715	Developing	... ...	06765
Detained...	... ...	06716	Development	... ...	06766
Detainer...	... ...	06717	Deviate ...	... ...	06767
Detect ...	... ...	06718	Deviated. .	... ...	06768
Detected...	... ...	06719	Deviating	... ...	06769
Detection	... ...	06720	Deviation	... ...	06770
Detecting	... ...	06721	Device ...	... ...	06771
Detective	... ...	06722	Devil ...	... ...	06772
Detention	... ...	06723	Devilish ...	... ...	06773
Deter ...	... ...	06724	Devilishly	... ...	06774
Detergent	... ...	06725	Devious ...	... ...	06775
Deteriorate	... ...	06726	Devisable	... ...	06776
Deteriorated	... ...	06727	Devise ...	... ...	06777
Deteriorates	... ...	06728	Devised ...	... ...	06778
Deteriorating	... ...	06729	Deviser ...	... ...	06779
Deterioration	... ...	06730	Devoid ...	... ...	06780
Determinable	... ...	06731	Devolve ...	... ...	06781
Determinant	... ...	06732	Devote ...	... ...	06782
Determinate	... ...	06733	Devoted ...	... ...	06783
Determination	...	06734	Devotee ...	... ...	06784
Determinative	...	06735	Devotion	... ...	06785
Determine	...	06736	Devour ...	... ...	06786
Determined	... ...	06737	Devourer	... ...	06787
Determining	...	06738	Devouring	... ...	06788
Deterred...	... ...	06739	Devout ...	... ...	06789
Deterrence	... ...	06740	Devoutly	... ...	06790
Deterring	... ...	06741	Dew ...	... ...	06791
Detest ...	... ...	06742	Dewy ...	... ...	06792
Detestable	... ...	06743	Dexter ...	... ...	06793
Detestation	... ...	06744	Dexterity	... ...	06794
Detested ...	... ...	06745	Dexterous	... ...	06795
Detesting	... ...	06746	Diabetes ...	... ...	06796
Dethrone	... ...	06747	Diabolical	... ...	06797
Dethroned	... ...	06748	Diachylum	... ...	06798
Dethronement	...	06849	Diaconal...	... ...	06799
Detonate	... ...	06750	Diaconate	... ...	06800

Diadem	06801	Diffusive... 06851
Diagonal	06802	Diffusiveness 06852
Diagram...	06803	Dig 06853
Dial	06804	Digest 06854
Dialect	06805	Digestible 06855
Dialectics	06806	Digestion 06856
Dialogue	06807	Digit 06857
Diameter	06808	Digital 06858
Diamond ... ...:	06809	Digitalis 06859
Diapason	06810	Dignified 06860
Diaper	06811	Dignify 06861
Diaphanous	06812	Dignitary 06862
Diarrhœa	06813	Dignity 06863
Diary	06814	Digress 06864
Diatribe	06815	Digressing 06865
Dice	06816	Digression 06866
Dickey	06817	Dike 06867
Dictate	06818	Dilapidate 06868
Dictated...	06819	Dilapidated 06869
Dictating	06820	Dilapidation 06870
Dictation	06821	Dilate 06871
Dictator	06822	Dilating 06872
Dictatorial	06823	Dilation 06873
Dictatory	06824	Dilatory 06874
Diction	06825	Dilemma 06875
Dictionary	06826	Dilettantism 06876
Dictum	06827	Diligence 06877
Did	06828	Diligent 06878
Didactic	06829	Diluent 06879
Diddle	06830	Dilute 06880
Die	06831	Diluted 06881
Died	06832	Diluting 06882
Dies	06833	Diluvial 06883
Diet	06834	Dim 06884
Dietary	06835	Dime 06885
Differ	06836	Dimension 06886
Differed	06837	Diminish 06887
Difference	06838	Diminished 06888
Differential	06839	Diminishing 06889
Differently	06840	Diminution 06890
Differing	06841	Diminutive 06891
Difficult	06842	Dimity 06892
Difficulty	06843	Dimly ... ... 06893 .
Diffidence	06844	Dimmed... 06894
Diffident...	06845	Dimness 06895
Diffract	06846	Dimple 06896
Diffuse	06847	Din 06897
Diffused	06848	Dine 06898
Diffusing	06849	Dined 06899
Diffusion	06850	Dinginess 06900

Dingle	06901	Disallowed 06951
Dingy	06902	Disannul... 06952
Dining	06903	Disappear 06953
Dinner	06904	Disappearance ... 06954
Dint	06905	Disappeared 06655
Diocesan...	06906	Disappearing 06956
Diocese	06907	Disappoint 06957
Dip	06908	Disappointed... ... 06958
Diphthong	06909	Disappointing ... 06959
Diploma...	06910	Disappointment ... 06960
Diplomacy	06911	Disappreciate... ... 06961
Diplomatic	06912	Disapprobation ... 06962
Diplomatist	06913	Disappropriate ... 06963
Dipped	06914	Disapproval 06964
Dipping	06915	Disapprove 06965
Dire	06916	Disapproved 06966
Direct	06917	Disapproving... ... 06967
Directed...	06918	Disarm 06968
Directing	06919	Disarming 06969
Direction	06920	Disarrange 06970
Directly	06921	Disarranged 06971
Directness	06922	Disarrangement ... 06972
Director	06923	Disarray 06973
Directorial	06924	Disassociate 06974
Directory	06925	Disaster 06975
Direful	06926	Disastrous 06976
Dirge	06927	Disavow... 06977
Dirk	06928	Disavowal 06978
Dirt...	06929	Disavowed 06979
Dirty	06930	Disband 06980
Disability	06931	Disbarring 06981
Disable	06932	Disbelief... 06982
Disabuse...	06933	Disbelieve 06983
Disaccustom	06934	Disbeliever 06984
Disacknowledge ...	06935	Disburden 06985
Disadvance	06936	Disburse... 06986
Disadvantage... ...	06937	Disbursed 06987
Disadvantageous ...	06938	Disbursing 06988
Disadvantageously	06939	Disc 06989
Disaffect...	06940	Discard 06990
Disaffirm...	06941	Discern 06991
Disafforest	06942	Discerning 06992
Disagree...	06943	Discernment 06993
Disagreeable	06944	Discharge 06994
Disagreeably	06945	Discharged 06995
Disagreed	06946	Discharging 06996
Disagreeing	06947	Disciple 06997
Disagreement... ...	06948	Disciplinarian ... 06998
Disallow...	06949	Disciplinary 06999
Disallowable	06950	Discipline 07000

Disclaim...	07001	Discretionary... ...	07051
Disclaimer	07002	Discriminate	07052
Disclose	07003	Discriminately ...	07053
Disclosure	07004	Discriminating ...	07054
Discolour	07005	Discrimination ...	07055
Discoloration ...	07006	Discursion	07056
Discomfit	07007	Discursive	07057
Discomfiture	07008	Discursory	07058
Discomfort	07009	Discuss	07059
Discompose	07010	Discussed	07060
Discomposed... ...	07011	Discussing	07061
Discomposure ...	07012	Discussion	07062
Disconcert	07013	Disdain	07063
Disconnect	07014	Disdainful	07064
Disconnected... ...	07015	Disdaining	07065
Disconnecting ...	07016	Disease	07066
Disconnection ...	07017	Diseased...	07067
Disconsolate	07018	Disembark	07068
Disconsolation ...	07019	Disembarkation ...	07069
Discontent	07020	Disembarrass... ...	07070
Discontented	07021	Disembellish	07071
Discontinuance ...	07022	Disembody	07072
Discontinue	07023	Disembroil	07073
Discontinued	07024	Disenchant	07074
Discord	07025	Disencumber	07075
Discordance	07026	Disenfranchize ...	07076
Discordant	07027	Disengage	07077
Discount...	07028	Disengaged	07078
Discounted	07029	Disengagement ...	07079
Discountenance ...	07030	Disentangle	07080
Discounter	07031	Disentitle	07081
Discounting	07032	Disentitled	07082
Discourage	07033	Disesteem	07083
Discouragement ...	07034	Disfavour	07084
Discouraging	07035	Disfigure	07085
Discourse	07036	Disfigured	07086
Discoursed	07037	Disfigurement ...	07087
Discoursing	07038	Disforest...	07088
Discourteous	07039	Disfranchise	07089
Discourtesy	07040	Disgorge...	07090
Discover...	07041	Disgrace...	07091
Discoverable	07042	Disgraced	07092
Discovered	07043	Disgraceful	07093
Discovering	07044	Disguise	07094
Discovery	07045	Disguised	07095
Discredit	07046	Disguisedly	07096
Discredited	07047	Disguising	07097
Discreet	07048	Disgust	07098
Discrepancy	07049	Disgusting	07099
Discretion	07050	Dish	07100

| DIS | (36) | DIS | 72 |

Dishearten	07101	Disoblige	07151
Disheartened	07102	Disobliging	07152
Disheartening ...	07103	Disorder...	07153
Dishevel...	07104	Disordered	07154
Dishevelled	07105	Disorderly	07155
Dishonest	07106	Disorganize	07156
Dishonestly	07107	Disown	07157
Dishonesty	07108	Disparage	07158
Dishonour	07109	Disparagement ...	07159
Dishonourable ...	07110	Disparity	07160
Disimprove	07111	Dispassionate... ...	07161
Disinclination ...	07112	Dispel	07162
Disincline	07113	Dispensable	07163
Disinclined	07114	Dispensary	07164
Disinfect...	07115	Dispensation	07165
Disinfectant	07116	Dispense	07166
Disinfecting	07117	Disperse...	07167
Disinherit	07118	Dispersion	07168
Disinheritance ...	07119	Dispirit	07169
Disinherited	07120	Displace...	07170
Disinheriting	07121	Displant...	07171
Disinhume	07122	Display	07172
Disintegrate	07123	Displease	07173
Disinter	07124	Displeased	07174
Disinterested	07125	Displeasing	07175
Disjoin	07126	Displeasure	07176
Disjunction	07127	Disposable	07177
Disjunctive	07128	Disposal...	07178
Dis	07129	Dispose	07179
Dislike	07130	Disposed	07180
Disliked	07131	Disposer...	07181
Disliking	07132	Disposes...	07182
Dislocate	07133	Disposing	07183
Dislocated	07134	Disposition	07184
Dislocation	07135	Dispossess	07185
Dislodge...	07136	Dispossession... ...	07186
Disloyal	07137	Disproof...	07187
Dismal	07138	Disproportion ...	07188
Dismay	07139	Disproportionally ...	07189
Dismember	07140	Disproportionate ...	07190
Dismiss	07141	Disproportioned ...	07191
Dismissal	07142	Disprove...	07192
Dismissed	07143	Disputable	07193
Dismount	07144	Disputant	07194
Dismounted	07145	Disputation	07195
Disobedience... ...	07146	Disputatious	07196
Disobey	07147	Disputative	07197
Disobeyed	07148	Dispute	07198
Disobeying	07149	Disputed	07199
Disobligation... ...	07150	Disputing	07200

Disqualification	...	07201
Disqualified ...	...	07202
Disqualify	...	07203
Disquiet ...	...	07204
Disquisition	...	07205
Disregard	...	07206
Disregarded ...	...	07207
Disregardful ...	...	07208
Disregarding ...	...	07209
Disrepair	...	07210
Disreputable ...	...	07211
Disrepute	...	07212
Disrespect	...	07213
Disrespectful ...	...	07214
Disruption	...	07215
Dissatisfaction	...	07216
Dissatisfactory	...	07217
Dissatisfied	...	07218
Dissatisfy	...	07219
Dissect ...	...	07220
Dissection	...	07221
Dissemble	...	07222
Dissembler	...	07223
Disseminate ...	...	07224
Dissemination	...	07225
Dissension	...	07226
Dissent ...	...	07227
Dissenter	...	07228
Dissentient	...	07229
Dissertate	...	07230
Dissertation ...	...	07231
Dissettlement...	...	07232
Dissever ...	...	07233
Dissevered	...	07234
Dissidence	...	07235
Dissident	...	07236
Dissimilar	...	07237
Dissimilarity ...	...	07238
Dissimulate ...	...	07239
Dissimulation	...	07240
Dissipate	...	07241
Dissipated	...	07242
Dissipating	...	07243
Dissipation	...	07244
Dissociate	...	07245
Dissoluble	...	07246
Dissolute	...	07247
Dissoluteness...	...	07248
Dissolution	...	07249
Dissolve ..	...	07250
Dissolvent	...	07251
Dissonance	...	07252
Dissonant	...	07253
Dissuade...	...	07254
Dissuaded	...	07255
Dissuading	...	07256
Dissuasion	...	07257
Dissuasively ...	...	07258
Dissyllable	...	07259
Distaff ...	...	07260
Distance...	...	07261
Distant ...	...	07262
Distaste ...	...	07263
Distasteful	...	07264
Distemper	...	07265
Distempered ...	...	07266
Distend ...	...	07267
Distention	...	07268
Distich ...	...	07269
Distil	...	07270
Distillation	...	07271
Distiller ...	...	07272
Distillery	...	07273
Distinct ...	...	07274
Distinction	...	07275
Distinctive	...	07276
Distinctly	...	07277
Distinctness ...	...	07278
Distinguish	...	07279
Distinguished...	...	07280
Distinguishing	...	07281
Distinguishingly	...	07282
Distort ...	...	07283
Distortion	...	07284
Distract ...	...	07285
Distracted	...	07286
Distraction	...	07287
Distractive	...	07288
Distrain ...	...	07289
Distrainer	...	07290
Distress ...	...	07291
Distressed	...	07292
Distressing	...	07293
Distribute	...	07294
Distributed	...	07295
Distribution ...	...	07296
Distributive	...	07297
District ...	...	07298
Distrust ...	...	07299
Distrustful	...	07300

| DIS | (37) | DON | 74 |

Distrustingly...	07301	Doctrinal	07351
Disturb	07302	Doctrine	07352
Disturbance	07303	Document	07353
Disturber	07304	Documentary ...	07354
Disunion	07305	Dodge	07355
Disunite...	07306	Doe	07356
Disuse	07307	Doer	07357
Ditch	07308	Does	07358
Ditto	07309	Doff	07359
Ditty	07310	Dog	07360
Diurnal	07311	Doge	07361
Divan	07312	Dogged	07362
Dive	07313	Doggerel	07363
Diver	07314	Dogma	07364
Diverge	07315	Dogmatic	07365
Divergence	07316	Dogmatize	07366
Diverging	07317	Doing	07367
Divers	07318	Doings	07368
Diversely	07319	Dole	07369
Diversified	07320	Doleful	07370
Diversiform	07321	Doll	07371
Diversify	07322	Dollar	07372
Diversion	07323	Dolorous	07373
Diversity	07324	Dolphin	07374
Divert	07325	Dolt	07375
Diverted	07326	Domain	07376
Diverting	07327	Dome	07377
Divest...	07328	Domestic	07378
Divide	07329	Domesticate	07379
Divided	07330	Domicile	07380
Dividend	07331	Domiciliary	07381
Dividing	07332	Dominance	07382
Divination	07333	Dominant	07383
Divine	07334	Dominate	07384
Divinely	07335	Domination	07385
Divinity...	07336	Dominator	07386
Divisible	07337	Domineer	07387
Division...	07338	Domineering... ...	07388
Divisor	07339	Dominical	07389
Divorce	07340	Dominion	07390
Divulge	07341	Domino...	07391
Divulged	07342	Don	07392
Dizziness	07343	Donation	07393
Dizzy	07344	Done	07394
Do	07345	Donjon	07395
Docile	07346	Donkey...	07396
Docility...	07347	Donor	07397
Dock	07348	Doom	07398
Docket	07349	Doomsday	07399
Doctor	07350	Door	07400.

75	DON	(38)	DRI

Doric	... ...	07401	Drake	... ...	07451
Dormant...	... ...	07402	Dram	... ...	07452
Dormitory	... ...	07403	Drama	... ...	07453
Dormouse	... ...	07404	Dramatic	... ...	07454
Dorsal	... ...	07405	Dramatist	... ...	07455
Dose	... ...	07406	Dramatize	... ...	07456
Dot...	... ...	07407	Drank	... ...	07457
Dotage	... ...	07408	Draper	... ...	07458
Dotal	... ...	07409	Drapery...	... ...	07459
Dotard	... ...	07410	Drastic	... ...	07460
Dotation...	... ...	07411	Draught	... ...	07461
Dote	... ...	07412	Draughtsman...	...	07462
Doting	... ...	07413	Draw	... ...	07463
Dotted	... ...	07414	Drawback	... ...	07464
Double	... ...	07415	Drawer	... ...	07465
Doublets...	... ...	07416	Drawing...	... ...	07466
Doubling	... ...	07417	Drawl	... ...	07467
Doubly	... ...	07418	Drawn	... ...	07468
Doubt	... ...	07419	Draws	.. ..	07469
Doubtful...	... ...	07420	Dray	... ...	07470
Doubting	... ...	07421	Dread	... ...	07471
Doubtless	... ...	07422	Dreadful...	... ...	07472
Dough	... ...	07423	Dream	... ...	07473
Doughty...	... ...	07424	Dreaming	... ...	07474
Douse	... ...	07425	Dreamingly	...	07475
Dove	... ...	07426	Dreams ...	... ...	07476
Dowager	... ...	07427	Drearily...	... ...	07477
Dower	... ...	07428	Dreary	... ...	07478
Down	... ...	07429	Dredge	... ...	07479
Downcast	... ...	07430	Dregs	... ...	07480
Downfall	... ...	07431	Drench ...	... ...	07481
Downhill	... ...	07432	Drenching	... ...	07482
Downright	... ...	07433	Dress	... ...	07483
Downwards	... ...	07434	Dresser ...	... ...	07484
Downy	... ...	07435	Dressing...	... ...	07485
Dowry	... ...	07436	Drew	... ...	07486
Doxology	... ...	07437	Dribblet...	... ...	07487
Doze	... ...	07438	Dried	... ...	07488
Dozen	... ...	07439	Drier	... ...	07489
Doziness...	... ...	07440	Drift	... ...	07490
Drab	... ...	07441	Drifting ...	... ...	07491
Drachm ...	... ...	07442	Drill	... ...	07492
Draft	... ...	07443	Drilling ...	... ...	07493
Drafted ...	... ...	07444	Drink	... ...	07494
Drag	... ...	07445	Drinkable	... ...	07495
Draggle ...	... ...	07446	Drinker ...	... ...	07496
Dragon ...	... ...	07447	Drinking	... ...	07497
Dragoon...	... ...	07448	Drinks ...	... ...	07498
Drain	... ...	07449	Drip	... ...	07499
Drainage	... ...	07450	Dripping	... ...	07500

DRI	(38)	DYE	76

Drive	07501	Dudgeon	07551
Driven	07502	Due...	07552
Driver	07503	Duel	07553
Drives	07504	Duelling...	07554
Driving	07505	Duellist	07555
Drizzle	07506	Duenna	07556
Drizzling	07507	Duet	07557
Droll	07508	Dug...	07558
Drollery	07509	Duke	07559
Drone	07510	Dulcet	07560
Dronish	07511	Dull	07561
Droop	07512	Dullness...	07562
Drop	07513	Duly	07563
Dropsical	07514	Dumb	07564
Dropsy	07515	Dummy	07565
Dross	07516	Dump	07566
Drought	07517	Dumpy	07567
Drove	07518	Dun...	07568
Drover	07519	Dunce	07569
Drown	07520	Dune	07570
Drowned	07521	Dung	07571
Drowning	07522	Dungeon...	07572
Drowsiness	07523	Dunnage...	07573
Drowsy	07524	Duodecimal	07574
Drudge	07525	Duodecimo	07575
Drudgery	07526	Dupe	07576
Drug	07527	Duplicate	07577
Drugget	07528	Duplicity	07578
Druggist	07529	Durable	07579
Drum	07530	Duration	07580
Drummer	07531	During	07581
Drunk	07532	Durst	07582
Drunkard	07533	Dusk	07583
Drunken...	07534	Dust	07584
Drunkenness	07535	Duster	07585
Dry...	07536	Dutch	07586
Drying	07537	Dutiful	07587
Dryly	07538	Duty	07588
Dryness	07539	Dwarf	07589
Dub	07540	Dwell	07590
Dubious	07541	Dwelling	07591
Dubiously	07542	Dwells	07592
Ducal	07543	Dwelt	07593
Duchess	07544	Dwindle...	07594
Duchy	07545	Dye...	07595
Duck	07546	Dyer	07596
Ducking	07547	Dying	07597
Duckling	07548	Dynasty	07598
Duct	07549	Dysentery	07599
Ductile	07550	Dyspepsia	07600

E	07601	Ecliptic	07651
Each	07602	Eclogue	07652
Eager	07603	Economical	07653
Eagerly	07604	Economist	07654
Eagerness	07605	Economy	07655
Eagle	07606	Ecstasy	07656
Ear	07607	Ecstatic	07557
Earache	07608	Ecumenical	07658
Earl	07609	Eddy	07659
Earldom	07610	Eden	07660
Early	07611	Edge	07661
Earn	07612	Edged	07662
Earnest	07613	Edgewise	07663
Earnestly	07614	Edible	07664
Earnestness	07615	Edict	07665
Earning	07616	Edification	07666
Earth	07617	Edifice	07667
Earthly	07618	Edified	07668
Earthquake	07619	Edify	07669
Earthy	07620	Edifying	07670
Ease	07621	Edit	07671
Easel	07622	Edition	07672
Easement	07623	Editor	07673
Easily	07624	Editorial	07674
Easiness	07625	Educate	07675
Easing	07626	Education	07676
East	07627	Educe	07677
Easter	07628	Eel	07678
Easterly	07629	Efface	07679
Eastern	07630	Effaced	07680
Eastward	07631	Effect	07681
Easy	07632	Effected	07682
Eat	07633	Effective	07683
Eatable	07634	Effects	07684
Eating	07635	Effectual	07685
Eats	07636	Effeminacy	07686
Eaves	07637	Effeminate	07687
Ebb	07638	Effervesce	07688
Ebbing	07639	Effervescence	07689
Ebony	07640	Effervescing	07690
Ebriety	07641	Effete	07691
Ebullient	07642	Efficacious	07692
Ebullition	07643	Efficacy	07693
Eccentric	07644	Efficient	07694
Eccentricity	07645	Effigy	07695
Ecclesiastic	07646	Effluvium	07696
Ecclesiastical	07647	Efflux	07697
Echo	07648	Effort	07698
Eclectic	07649	Effrontery	07699
Eclipse	07650	Effulgence	07700

EFF	(39)	ELO	78

Effulgent	07701	Electioneerer	07751
Effuse	07702	Electioneering ...	07752
Effusion	07703	Elective	07753
Effusive	07704	Electively	07754
Egg	07705	Elector	07755
Eglantine	07706	Electric	07756
Egotism	07707	Electricity	07757
Egotist	07708	Electrified	07758
Egotistical	07709	Electrify...	07759
Egregious	07710	Electro	07760
Egress	07711	Electrometer	07761
Egyptian	07712	Electrotype	07762
Eh	07713	Eleemosynary ...	07763
Eider	07714	Elegance	07764
Eight	07715	Elegant	07765
Eighteen...	07716	Elegiac	07766
Eighteenth	07717	Elegist	07767
Eighth	07718	Elegy	07768
Eightieth	07719	Element	07769
Eighty	07720	Elemental	07770
Either	07721	Elementary	07771
Ejaculate	07722	Elephant	07772
Ejaculation	07723	Elephantine	07773
Ejaculatory	07724	Elevate	07774
Eject	07725	Elevated...	07775
Ejected	07726	Elevation	07776
Ejecting	07727	Eleven	07777
Ejection	07728	Eleventh...	07778
Ejectment	07729	Elf	07779
Eke...	07730	Elfish	07780
Elaborate	07731	Elicit	07781
Elaboration	07732	Eligible	07782
Elapse	07733	Eligibly	07783
Elastic	07734	Eliminate	07784
Elasticity	07735	Elimination	07785
Elate	07736	Elite	07786
Elated	07737	Elixir	07787
Elatedly	07738	Elk	07788
Elation	07739	Ell	07789
Elator	07740	Elliptic	07790
Elbow	07741	Elm...	07791
Elbowed...	07742	Elocution	07792
Elder	07743	Elocutionary	07793
Elderly	07744	Elocutionist	07794
Eldest	07745	Elogium	07795
Elect	07746	Elongate	07796
Elected	07747	Elongated	07797
Electing	07748	Elongation	07798
Election	07749	Elope	07799
Electioneer	07750	Elopement	07800

Eloquence	07801	Embowel 07851
Eloquent	07802	Embrace... 07852
Eloquently	07803	Embraced 07853
Else...	07804	Embracing 07854
Elsewhere	07805	Embrasure 07855
Elucidate	07806	Embrocate 07856
Elucidation	07807	Embrocation 07857
Elucidative	07808	Embroglio 07858
Elude	07809	Embroider 07859
Elysian	07810	Embroidery 07860
Emaciate	07811	Embroil 07861
Emaciated	07812	Embroilment 07862
Emaciation	07813	Embryo 07863
Emanate...	07814	Emendation 07864
Emanated	07815	Emendator 07865
Emanation	07816	Emerald... 07865
Emanating	07817	Emerge 07867
Emancipate	07818	Emergency 07868
Emancipation ...	07819	Emerging 07869
Emancipationist ...	07820	Emersion 07870
Emasculate	07821	Emetic 07871
Emancipating ...	07822	Emigrant 07872
Embalm...	07823	Emigrate 07873
Embankment... ...	07824	Emigration 07874
Embargo	07825	Eminence 07875
Embark	07826	Eminent 07876
Embarkation	07827	Emissary 07877
Embarked	07828	Emission 07878
Embarrass	07829	Emit 07879
Embarrassed	07830	Emitted 07880
Embarrassing... ...	07831	Emollient 07881
Embarrassment ...	07832	Emolument 07882
Embassy	07833	Emotion... 07883
Embedded	07834	Emotional 07884
Embellish	07835	Empale 07885
Embellishment ...	07836	Empannel 07886
Embers	07837	Emperor... 07887
Embezzle	07838	Emphasis 07888
Embezzlement ...	07839	Emphasize 07889
Embezzling	07840	Emphatic 07890
Emblazon	07841	Empire 07891
Emblazonry	07842	Empiric 07892
Emblem	07843	Empirically 07893
Emblematic	07844	Employ 07894
Emblematize	07845	Employé... 07895
Embodied	07846	Employed 07896
Embody	07847	Employer 07897
Embolden	07848	Employing 07898
Embosom	07849	Employment 07899
Emboss	07850	Emporium 07900

EMP	(40)	ENG	80
Empower	07901	Encumber	07951
Empress...	07902	Encumbrance ...	07952
Emptiness	07903	Encyclical	07953
Empty	07904	Encyclopædia ...	07954
Emptied...	07905	Encyclopedist ...	07955
Empyreal	07906	End...	07956
Emulate...	07907	Endanger	07957
Emulation	07908	Endear	07958
Emulative	07909	Endearment	07959
Emulous...	07910	Endeavour	07960
Emulsive	07911	Endeavoured	07961
Enable	07912	Endeavouring ...	07962
Enabling	07913	Ended	07963
Enact	07914	Endemic...	07964
Enacted	07915	Ending	07965
Enacting...	07916	Endive	07966
Enactment	07917	Endless	07967
Enamel	07918	Endorse	07968
Enameller	07919	Endorsed	07969
Enamour	07920	Endorsement	07970
Enamoured	07921	Endorsing	07971
Encamp	07922	Endow	07972
Encampment... ...	07923	Endowment	07973
Encase	07924	Endue	07974
Encaustic	07925	Endurance	07975
Enceinte...	07926	Endure	07976
Enchant	07927	Enduring	07977
Enchanted	07928	Endways...	07978
Enchanter	07929	Enemy	07979
Enchanting	07930	Energetic	07980
Enchantment	07931	Energy	07981
Enchantress	07932	Enervate...	07982
Enchasing	07933	Enfeeble...	07983
Encircle	07934	Enfilade	07984
Encircling	07935	Enforce	07985
Enclose...	07936	Enforced	07986
Enclosed...	07937	Enforcedly	07987
Enclosing	07938	Enfranchise	07988
Enclosure	07939	Enfranchisement ...	07989
Encomiastic	07940	Engage	07990
Encomium	07941	Engaged...	07991
Encompass	07942	Engagement	07992
Encore	07943	Engaging	07993
Encounter	07944	Engagingly	07994
Encourage	07945	Engender	07995
Encouraged	07946	Engine	07996
Encouragement ...	07947	Engineer	07997
Encouraging	07948	Engineering	07998
Encroach	07949	Enginery...	07999
Encroachment ...	07950	English	08000

F

— 21 —

| 81 | ENG | (41) | ENV |

Englishman	...	08001	Entailing	...	08051
Engrain	...	08002	Entailment	...	08052
Engrave	...	08003	Entangle	...	08053
Engraven	...	08004	Entanglement	...	08054
Engraver	...	08005	Enter	...	08055
Engraving	...	08006	Entered	...	08056
Engross	...	08007	Entering	...	08057
Engrossed	...	08008	Enterprise	...	08058
Engrossing	...	08009	Enterprising	...	08059
Engrossment	...	08010	Enters	...	08060
Engulf	...	08011	Entertain	...	08061
Enhance	...	08012	Entertained	...	08062
Enhancement	...	08013	Entertainer	...	08063
Enigma	...	08014	Entertaining	...	08064
Enigmatic	...	08015	Entertainment	...	08065
Enjoin	...	08016	Enthral	...	08066
Enjoy	...	08017	Enthralment	...	08067
Enjoyable	...	08018	Enthrone	...	08068
Enjoyment	...	08019	Enthusiasm	...	08069
Enlarge	...	08020	Enthusiast	...	08070
Enlarging	...	08021	Enthusiastic	...	08071
Enlargement	...	08022	Entice	...	08072
Enlighten	...	08023	Enticement	...	08073
Enlightenment	...	08024	Enticingly	...	08074
Enlist	...	08025	Entire	...	08075
Enliven	...	08026	Entitle	...	08076
Enlivening	...	08027	Entity	...	08077
Enmity	...	08028	Entomb	...	08078
Ennoble	...	08029	Entomological	...	08079
Ennui	...	08030	Entomologist	...	08080
Enormity	...	08031	Entomology	...	08081
Enormous	...	08032	Entrails	...	08082
Enough	...	08033	Entrance	...	08083
Enquire	...	08034	Entrap	...	08084
Enquiring	...	08035	Entreat	...	08085
Enrage	...	08036	Entreated	...	08086
Enrapt	...	08037	Entreating	...	08087
Enrapture	...	08038	Entreaty	...	08088
Enrich	...	08039	Entry	...	08089
Enrol	...	08040	Entwine	...	08090
Enrolment	...	08041	Enumerate	...	08091
Enshrine	...	08042	Enumerated	...	08092
Ensign	...	08043	Enumerating	...	08093
Ensigncy	...	08044	Enumeration	...	08094
Enslave	...	08045	Enunciate	...	08095
Enslaver	...	08046	Enunciation	...	08096
Ensue	...	08047	Enunciatory	...	08097
Ensuing	...	08048	Envelop	...	08098
Entail	...	08049	Envelope	...	08099
Entailed	...	08050	Envenom	...	08100

ENV	(41)	ERU	82
Enviable...	08101	Equip	08151
Envied	08102	Equipped	08152
Envious	08103	Equipage	08153
Environ	08104	Equipment	08154
Environs...	08105	Equipoise	08155
Envoy	08106	Equiponderance ...	08156
Envy	08107	Equiponderant ...	08157
Envying	08108	Equitable	08158
Epaulet	08109	Equitably	08159
Ephemeral	08110	Equitation	08160
Epic	08111	Equity	08161
Epicure	08112	Equivalent	08162
Epicurean	08113	Equivocal	08163
Epidemic	08114	Equivocate	08164
Epigram...	08115	Equivocation... ...	08165
Epigrammatic ...	08116	Equivocator	08166
Epigraph	08117	Equivoke	08167
Epilepsy...	08118	Era...	08168
Epilogue...	08119	Eradiate	08169
Epiphany	08120	Eradicate	08170
Episcopacy	08121	Eradication	08171
Episcopal	08122	Erase	08172
Episcopalian	08123	Erasement	08173
Episode	08124	Eraser	08174
Epistle	08125	Erasing	08175
Epistolary	08126	Erasure	08176
Epitaph	08127	Erect	08177
Epithet	08128	Erected	08178
Epitome...	08129	Erecting	08179
Epitomize	08130	Erection	08180
Epoch	08131	Erective...	08181
Equability	08132	Erectly	08182
Equable	08133	Erectness	08183
Equal	08134	Ergot	08184
Equality	08135	Ermine	08185
Equalization	08136	Erosion	08186
Equalize	08137	Erotic	08187
Equalizing	08138	Err...	08188
Equally	08139	Erred	08189
Equanimity	08140	Erring	08190
Equation	08141	Errand	08191
Equator	08142	Errata	08192
Equatorial	08143	Erratic	08193
Equerry	08144	Erratum...	08194
Equestrian	08145	Erroneous	08195
Equilateral	08146	Error	08196
Equilibrium	08147	Erudite	08197
Equine	08148	Erudition	08198
Equinoctial	08149	Eruption	08199
Equinox	08150	Eruptive	08200

Erysipelas	...	...	08201	Estuary ...	... ...	08251
Escalade	...	...	08202	Etc	... ...	08252
Escapade	...	...	08203	Etch	... ...	08253
Escape ...	...	...	08204	Etching ...	... ...	08254
Escaped...	...	...	08205	Eternal ...	... ...	08255
Escapement ...	...	08206	Eternity ...	... ...	08256
Escaping	...	...	08207	Eternize ...	... ...	08257
Escarp ...	...	...	08208	Ether	... ...	08258
Escarpment ...	...	08209	Ethereal ...	... ...	08259
Eschalot	...	...	08210	Etherealize	... ...	08260
Escheat ...	...	...	08211	Ethically	... ...	08261
Eschew ...	...	...	08212	Ethics ...	... ...	08262
Escort ...	...	...	08213	Ethnology	... ...	08263
Escritoire	...	...	08214	Etiquette	... ...	08264
Esculapian	...	...	08215	Etymology	... ...	08265
Esculent	...	...	08216	Eucharist	... ...	08266
Escutcheon ...	...	08217	Eulogistic	... ...	08267
Esparto ...	...	...	08218	Eulogium	... ...	08268
Especial	...	...	08219	Eulogize...	... ...	08269
Especially	...	...	08220	Eulogy ...	... ...	08270
Espionage	...	...	08221	Euphemism	... ...	08271
Esplanade	...	...	08222	Euphonism	... ...	08272
Espousal	...	...	08223	Euphony	... ...	08273
Espousals	...	...	08224	European	... ...	08274
Espouse...	...	...	08225	Evacuate	... ...	08275
Espy ...	...	...	08226	Evacuated	... ...	08276
Esquire ...	...	...	08227	Evacuating	... ...	08277
Essay ...	...	...	08228	Evacuation	... ...	08278
Essayed...	...	...	08229	Evacuative	... ...	08279
Essaying	...	...	08230	Evade ...	... ...	08280
Essayist ...	...	...	08231	Evaded ...	... ...	08281
Essence ...	...	...	08232	Evading ...	... ...	08282
Essential	...	...	08233	Evanescence ...	...	08283
Essentially	...	...	08234	Evanescent	... ...	08284
Establish	...	...	08235	Evangelical	... ...	08285
Established ...	...	08236	Evangelicalism	...	08286
Establishing ...	...	08237	Evangelism	... ...	08287
Establishment	...	08238	Evangelist	... ...	08288
Estate ...	...	...	08239	Evangelize	... ...	08289
Esteem ...	...	...	08240	Evaporate	... ...	08290
Esteemed	...	...	08241	Evaporated	... ...	08291
Esteeming	...	...	08242	Evaporating	... ...	08292
Esthetic ...	...	...	08243	Evaporation ...	...	08293
Estimable	...	...	08244	Evasion ...	... ...	08294
Estimate...	...	...	08245	Evasive ...	... ...	08295
Estimated	...	...	08246	Eve ...	... ...	08296
Estimation	...	...	08247	Even ...	... ...	08297
Estrange...	...	...	08248	Evening ...	... ...	08298
Estrangement	...	08249	Evenly ...	... ...	08299
Estreat ...	...	...	08250	Evenness	... ...	08300

EVE	(42)	EXC	84

Event	08301	Examination	08351
Eventful	08302	Examine...	08352
Eventide...	08303	Examined	08353
Eventual...	08304	Examiner	08354
Eventually	08305	Examining	08355
Ever	08306	Example...	08356
Evergreen	08307	Exasperate	08357
Everlasting	08308	Exasperated	08358
Evermore	08309	Exasperating	08359
Every	08310	Exasperation	08360
Everybody	08311	Excavate	08361
Everyday	08312	Excavation	08362
Everywhere	08313	Excavator	08363
Evict	08314	Exceed	08364
Eviction	08315	Exceeded	08365
Evidence	08316	Exceeding	08366
Evident	08317	Exceedingly	08367
Evil...	08318	Excel	08368
Evince	08319	Excellence	08369
Evinced	08320	Excellency	08370
Evincible	08321	Excellent	08371
Evincing...	08322	Excellently	08372
Evitable	08323	Excelling	08373
Evocation	08324	Except	08374
Evoke	08325	Excepted	08375
Evolution	08326	Excepting	08376
Evolve	08327	Exception	08377
Ewe	08328	Exceptionable ...	08378
Ewer	08329	Exceptional	08379
Ex	08330	Exceptive	08380
Exacerbate	08331	Excerpt	08381
Exact	08332	Excess	08382
Exacted	08333	Excessive	08383
Exacter	08334	Excessively	08384
Exacting...	08335	Exchange	08385
Exaction...	08336	Exchequer	08386
Exactitude	08337	Excisable	08387
Exactly	08338	Excise	08388
Exactness	08339	Exciseman	08389
Exactor	08340	Excision	08390
Exaggerate	08341	Excitable	08391
Exaggerated	08342	Excitant	08392
Exaggeration... ...	08343	Excitative	08393
Exaggerative	08344	Excite	08394
Exaggeratory... ...	08345	Excited	08395
Exalt	08346	Exciting...	08396
Exaltation	08347	Excitement	08397
Exalted	08348	Exclaim	08398
Exalting...	08349	Exclamation	08399
Examinant	08350	Exclamatory	08400

Exclude	08401		Exemplar	08451
Excluded	08402		Exemplarily	08452
Excluding	08403		Exemplary	08453
Exclusion	08404		Exemplification ...	08454
Exclusive	08405		Exemplified	08455
Excogitate	08406		Exemplify	08456
Excommunicate ...	08407		Exemplifying ...	08457
Excommunication ...	08408		Exempt	08458
Excommunicator ...	08409		Exempted	08459
Excommunicatory...	08410		Exemption	08460
Excoriate	08411		Exercisable	08461
Excoriation	08412		Exercise...	08462
Excrement	08413		Exercised	08463
Excrescence	08414		Exercising	08464
Excrete	08415		Exert	08465
Excretion	08416		Exerted	08466
Excretory	08417		Exerting	08467
Excruciable	08418		Exertion	08468
Excruciate	08419		Exertive...	08469
Excruciating	08420		Exfoliate	08470
Excruciation	08421		Exhalation	08471
Exculpate	08422		Exhale	08472
Exculpation	08423		Exhaust...	08473
Exculpatory	08424		Exhausted	08474
Excursion	08425		Exhauster	08475
Excursive	08426		Exhaustible	08476
Excursively	08427		Exhaustion	08477
Excusable	08428		Exhaustive	08478
Excusably	08429		Exhibit	08479
Excusatory	08430		Exhibited	08480
Excuse	08431		Exhibiter	08481
Excused	08432		Exhibiting	08482
Excusing	08433		Exhibition	08483
Exeat	08434		Exhibitioner	08484
Execrable	08435		Exhibitory	08485
Execrate...	08436		Exhilarant	08486
Execration	08437		Exhilarate	08487
Execratory	08438		Exhilarating	08488
Executable	08439		Exhilaration	08489
Execute	08440		Exhort	08490
Executed	08441		Exhortation	08491
Execution	08442		Exhorted	08492
Executioner	08443		Exhorter	08493
Executive	08444		Exhorting	08494
Executor	08445		Exhumation	08495
Executory	08446		Exhume...	08496
Executrix	08447		Exigency	08497
Exegesis	08448		Exigent	08498
Exegetical	08449		Exile	08499
Exegetically	08450		Exist	08500

EXI	(43)	EXP	86

Existed	08501	Expense	08551
Existence	08502	Expensive	08552
Existent...	08503	Expensively	08553
Existing...	08504	Experience	08554
Exit	08505	Experienced	08555
Exodus	08506	Experiment	08556
Exonerate	08507	Experimental... ...	08557
Exoneration	08508	Experimentalist ...	08558
Exorbitance	08509	Experimentally ...	08559
Exorbitant	08510	Expert	08560
Exorcise	08511	Expertness	08561
Exorciser	08512	Expiable...	08562
Exorcism	08513	Expiate	08563
Exordial	08514	Expiation	08564
Exordium	08515	Expiator...	08565
Exotic	08516	Expiatory	08566
Expand	08517	Expirable	08567
Expanded	08518	Expiration	08568
Expanding	08519	Expire	08566
Expanse...	08520	Expired	08570
Expansibility ...	08521	Expiring...	08571
Expansion	08522	Explain	08572
Expansive	08523	Explained	08573
Expatiate	08524	Explainer	08574
Expatiatory	08525	Explaining	08575
Expatriate	08526	Explanation	08576
Expatriation	08527	Explanatory	08577
Expect	08528	Expletive	08578
Expectance	08529	Expletory	08579
Expectancy	08530	Explicable	08580
Expectant	08531	Explicit	08581
Expectation	08532	Explicitly	08582
Expected	08533	Explode	08583
Expecting	08534	Exploded	08584
Expectingly	08535	Exploding	08585
Expectorant	08536	Exploit	08586
Expectorate	08537	Exploration	08587
Expediency	08538	Explorator	08588
Expedient	08539	Exploratory	08589
Expedite	08540	Explore	08590
Expeditely	08541	Explorer...	08591
Expedition	08542	Explosion	08592
Expeditious	08543	Explosive	08593
Expeditive	08544	Exponent	08594
Expel	08545	Export	08595
Expelled	08546	Exportation	08596
Expelling	08547	Exported	08597
Expend	08548	Expose	08598
Expended	08549	Exposition	08599
Expenditure	08550	Expositor	08600

Expository	...	...	08601	
Expostulate	...	...	08602	
Expostulation	...	...	08603	
Expostulator	...	...	08604	
Expostulatory	...	...	08605	
Exposure	...	...	08606	
Expound...	...	...	08607	
Express ...	...	...	08608	
Expression	...	...	08609	
Expressive	...	...	08610	
Expressure	...	...	08611	
Expropriate	...	...	08612	
Expropriation	...	...	08613	
Expulsion	...	...	08614	
Expunge...	...	...	08615	
Expunged	...	...	08616	
Expurgate	...	...	08617	
Expurgation	...	...	08618	
Expurgatorial...	...	08619	
Exquisite	...	...	08620	
Exquisitely	...	...	08621	
Exscind ...	...	...	08622	
Exscission	...	...	08623	
Exsudation	...	...	08624	
Exsuscitate	...	...	08625	
Extant ...	...	...	08626	
Extemporaneous	...	08627	
Extemporarily	...	...	08628	
Extemporary ...	...	08629	
Extempore	...	...	08630	
Extemporize ...	...	08631	
Extend ...	...	...	08632	
Extended	...	...	08633	
Extending	...	...	08634	
Extensibility ...	...	08635	
Extension	...	...	08636	
Extensive	...	...	08637	
Extent ...	...	...	08638	
Extenuate	...	...	08639	
Extenuation	...	...	08640	
Extenuatory	...	...	08641	
Exterior ...	...	...	08642	
Exterminate	...	...	08643	
Extermination	...	...	08644	
External...	...	...	08645	
Extinct ...	...	...	08646	
Extinction	...	...	08647	
Extinguish	...	...	08648	
Extinguishable	...	...	08649	
Extinguished ...	...	08650	

Extinguisher ...	...	08651	
Extinguishment	...	08652	
Extirpate	...	...	08653	
Extirpation	...	...	08654	
Extirpator	...	...	08655	
Extol ...	...	...	08656	
Extolled ...	...	...	08657	
Extolling	...	...	08658	
Extorsive	...	...	08659	
Extort ...	...	...	08660	
Extorted ...	...	...	08661	
Extortion	...	...	08662	
Extortionate	...	...	08663	
Extortioner	...	...	08664	
Extra ...	...	...	08665	
Extract ...	...	...	08666	
Extracted	...	...	08667	
Extraction	...	...	08668	
Extradition	...	...	08669	
Extraneous	...	...	08670	
Extraordinarily	...	08671	
Extraordinary	...	08672	
Extravagance...	...	08673	
Extravagant ...	...	08674	
Extravagantly	...	08675	
Extravaganza...	...	08676	
Extreme ...	...	...	08677	
Extremely	...	...	08678	
Extremity	...	...	08679	
Extricate...	...	...	08680	
Extricated	...	...	08681	
Extricating	...	...	08682	
Extrinsic...	...	...	08683	
Extrinsically ...	...	08684	
Extrude ...	...	...	08685	
Extrusion	...	...	08686	
Exuberance	...	...	08687	
Exuberant	...	...	08688	
Exude ...	...	...	08689	
Exult ...	...	...	08690	
Exultant ...	...	...	08691	
Exultation	...	...	08692	
Exulting ...	...	...	08693	
Eye ...	...	...	08694	
Eyed ...	...	...	08695	
Eyeless ...	...	...	08696	
Eyelet ...	...	...	08697	
Eyesight...	...	...	08698	
Eyesore ...	...	...	08699	
Eyry ...	...	...	08700	

F	(44)	FAM	88

F	08701	Fainted	08751
Fabian	08702	Fainting	08752
Fable	08703	Faintly	08753
Fabled	08704	Faintness	08754
Fabric	08705	Fair...	08755
Fabricate	08706	Fairness	08756
Fabricated	08707	Fairway	08757
Fabrication	08708	Fairy	08758
Fabricator	08709	Faith	08759
Fabulist	08710	Faithful	08760
Fabulous	08711	Faithfully	08761
Façade	08712	Faithfulness ...	08762
Face	08713	Faithless... ...	08763
Faced	08714	Faithlessness ...	08764
Facetiæ	08715	Falchion... ...	08765
Facetious	08716	Falcon	08766
Facetiousness... ...	08717	Falconer... ...	08767
Facial	08718	Falconry... ...	08768
Facile	08719	Fall	08769
Facilitate	08720	Fallacious	08770
Facilitated	08721	Fallaciously	08771
Facilitating	08722	Fallacy	08772
Facilities	08723	Fallibility	08773
Facility	08724	Fallible	08774
Facing	08725	Falling	08775
Fac-simile	08726	Fallow	08776
Fact	08727	Fallowness	08777
Faction	08728	Falls	08778
Factious...	08729	False	08779
Factiousness	08730	Falsehood	08780
Factitious	08731	Falsely	08781
Factor	08732	Falseness	08782
Factorage	08733	Falsetto	08783
Factorial	08734	Falsification	08784
Factory	08735	Falsifier	08785
Factotum	08736	Falsify	08786
Faculty	08737	Falsity	08787
Facundity	08738	Falter	08788
Fade	08739	Faltering	08789
Faded	08740	Falteringly	08790
Fading	08741	Fame	08791
Fag...	08742	Famed	08792
Fagot	08743	Familiar	08793
Fahrenheit	08744	Familiarity	08794
Fail...	08745	Familiarize	08795
Failed	08746	Familiarly	08796
Failing	08747	Family	08797
Failure ... ...: ...	08748	Famine	08798
Fain	08749	Famish	08799
Faint	08750	Famished	08800

Famishing	... ...	08801
Famous ...	... ...	08802
Fan...	... ...	08803
Fanatic ...	... ...	08804
Fanaticism	... ...	08805
Fancied ...	... ...	08806
Fanciful ...	... ...	08807
Fancifully	... ...	08808
Fancifulness ...	...	08809
Fancy	... ...	08810
Fanfaronade ...	...	08811
Fang	... ...	08812
Fantasia ...	... ...	08813
Fantastic	... ...	08814
Fantastical	... ...	08815
Far ...	... ...	08816
Farce	... ...	08817
Farcical ...	... ...	08818
Fare	... ...	08819
Fared	... ...	08820
Faring	... ...	08821
Farewell...	... ...	08822
Farina	... ...	08823
Farinaceous	... ...	08824
Farm	... ...	08825
Farmer ...	... ...	08826
Farming...	... ...	08827
Faro	... ...	08828
Farrier ...	... ...	08829
Farrow ...	... ...	08830
Farther ...	... ...	08831
Farthing...	... ...	08832
Fascinate	... ...	08833
Fascinated	... ...	08834
Fascinating	... ...	08835
Fascination	... ...	08836
Fashion ...	... ...	08837
Fashioned	... ...	08838
Fashionable ...	...	08839
Fashionably ...	...	08840
Fast	... ...	08841
Fasten ...	... ...	08842
Fastening	... ...	08843
Fastest ...	... ...	08844
Fastidious	... ...	08845
Fasting ...	... ...	08846
Fat ...	... ...	08847
Fatal	... ...	08848
Fatalism...	... ...	08849
Fatalist ...	... ...	08850
Fatality ...	... ...	08851
Fatally ...	... ...	08852
Fate	... ...	08853
Fated	... ...	08854
Father ...	... ...	08855
Fatherland	... ...	08856
Fatherless	... ...	08857
Fatherly ...	... ...	08858
Fathom ...	... ...	08859
Fathomable	... ...	08860
Fathomless	... ...	08861
Fatigue ...	... ...	08862
Fatigued...	... ...	08863
Fatiguing	... ...	08864
Fatness ...	... ...	08865
Fatten	... ...	08866
Fattiness...	... ...	08867
Fatty	... ...	08868
Fatuitous	... ...	08869
Fatuity ...	... ...	08870
Fault	... ...	08871
Faultily ...	... ...	08872
Faultiness	... ...	08873
Faultless...	... ...	08874
Faulty ...	... ...	08875
Favour ...	... ...	08876
Favourable	... ...	08877
Favourableness	...	08878
Favourably	... ...	08879
Favoured	... ...	08880
Favouring	... ...	08881
Favourite	... ...	08882
Favouritism	... ...	08883
Fawn	... ...	08884
Fawner ...	... ...	08885
Fawningly	... ...	08886
Fealty	... ...	08887
Fear	... ...	08888
Feared ...	... ...	08889
Fearful ...	... ...	08890
Fearfulness	... ...	08891
Fearing ...	... ...	08892
Fearless ...	... ...	08893
Fearlessness	... ...	08894
Feasibility	... ...	08895
Feasible ...	... ...	08896
Feasibly ...	... ...	08897
Feast	... ...	08898
Feasting...	... ...	08899
Feat	... ...	08900

FEA	(45)	FEW	90
Feather 08901	Fen 08951
Feathered 08902	Fence 08952
Feathery 08903	Fenced 08953
Feature 08904	Fencer 08954
Febrifuge 08905	Fencing 08955
Febrile 08906	Fend 08956
February 08907	Fender 08957
Feces 08908	Fenian 08958
Feculence 08909	Fennel 08959
Fecundate 08910	Fenny 08960
Fecundity 08911	Ferment 08961
Fed 08912	Fermentation 08962
Federal 08913	Ferocious 08963
Federalize 08914	Ferocity 08964
Federate 08915	Ferret 08965
Federation 08916	Ferried 08966
Fee 08917	Ferruginous 08967
Feeble 08918	Ferrule 08968
Feebleness 08919	Ferry 08969
Feebly 08920	Fertile 08970
Feed 08921	Fertility 08971
Feeding 08922	Fertilization 08972
Feeds 08923	Fertilize 08973
Feel 08924	Fertilizing 08974
Feeler 08925	Fervency 08975
Feeling 08926	Fervent 08976
Feels 08927	Fervently 08977
Feign 08928	Fervid 08978
Feigned 08929	Fervidly 08979
Feint 08930	Fervidness 08980
Felicitate 08931	Fervour 08981
Felicitation 08932	Festal 08982
Felicitous 08933	Fester 08983
Felicity 08934	Festival 08984
Feline 08935	Festive 08985
Fell 08936	Festivity 08986
Feller 08937	Festoon 08987
Felling 08938	Fetch 08988
Fellness 08939	Fetched 08989
Fellow 08940	Fetching 08990
Fellowship 08941	Fête 08991
Felon 08942	Fetid 08992
Felonious 08943	Fetlock 08993
Feloniously 08944	Fetter 08994
Felony 08945	Fettered 08995
Felt 08946	Feud 08996
Felucca 08947	Feudal 08997
Female 08948	Fever 08998
Feminine 08949	Feverish 08999
Femoral 08950	Few 09000

Fewness	09001	Fill 09051
Fiat...	09002	Filled 09052
Fib	09003	Fillet 09053
Fibre	09004	Filling 09054
Fibrous	09005	Fillip 09055
Fickle	09006	Filly 09056
Fickleness	09007	Film 09057
Fickly	09008	Filter 09058
Fiction	09009	Filtering... 09059
Fictitious	09010	Filth 09060
Fiddle	09011	Filthiness 09061
Fiddler	09012	Filthy 09062
Fiddling...	09013	Filtrate 09063
Fidelity	09014	Filtration 09064
Fidget	09015	Fin 09065
Fidgety	09016	Finable 09066
Fiduciary	09017	Final 09067
Field	09018	Finale 09068
Fiend	09019	Finally 09069
Fiendish...	09020	Finance 09070
Fierce	09021	Financial 09071
Fiercely	09022	Financially 09072
Fierceness	09023	Financier 09073
Fiery	09024	Finch 09074
Fife...	09025	Find 09075
Fifteen	09026	Finder 09076
Fifteenth	09027	Finding 09077
Fifth	09028	Finds 09078
Fiftieth	09029	Fine 09079
Fifty	09030	Fined 09080
Fig	09031	Finely 09081
Fight	09032	Fineness... 09082
Fighter	09033	Finery 09083
Fighting...	09034	Finesse 09084
Fights	09035	Finessing 09085
Figment	09036	Finger 09086
Figurable	09037	Fingering 09087
Figurative	09038	Finical 00088
Figure	09039	Finikin 09089
Figured	09040	Finis 09090
Filament...	09041	Finish 09091
Filbert	09042	Finished... 09092
Filch	09043	Finite 09093
Filchingly	09044	Finny 09094
File...	09045	Fiord 09095
Filial	09046	Fir 09096
Filiation	09047	Fire... 09097
Filibuster	09048	Firing 09098
Filigree	09049	Firkin 09099
Filing	09050	Firm 09100

FIR	(46)	FLI	92

Firmament	...	...	09101	Flank	... ...	09151
Firmly	... ...	...	09102	Flanked	... ...	09152
Firmness	...	...	09103	Flanking	... ...	09153
First	...	... ...	09104	Flannel	... ...	09154
Firstling	...	...	09105	Flap	... ...	09155
Fiscal	...	... ...	09106	Flapping	... ...	09156
Fish	...	... ...	09107	Flare	... ...	09157
Fished	...	... ...	09108	Flaring	... ...	09158
Fisherman	...	...	09109	Flash	... ...	09159
Fishery	...	... ...	09110	Flashed	... ...	09160
Fishing	...	...	09111	Flashing	... ...	09161
Fishy	...	... ...	09112	Flask	... ...	09162
Fissile	...	...	09113	Flat	...	09163
Fissure	...	...	09114	Flatly	... ...	09164
Fist	... ...	...	09115	Flatness	... ...	09165
Fistula	...	...	09116	Flatten	... ...	09166
Fit ...	... ...	...	09117	Flatter	... ...	09167
Fitful	...	...	09118	Flattered	... ...	09168
Fitly	...	...	09119	Flattering	... ...	09169
Fitness	...	...	09120	Flattery	... ...	09170
Fitted	...	...	09121	Flatulency	... ...	09171
Fitting	...	...	09122	Flaunt	... ...	09172
Fittings	...	...	09123	Flavour	... ...	09173
Five	...	...	09124	Flaw	... ...	09174
Fivefold	...	...	09125	Flax	... ...	09175
Fix ...	...	...	09126	Flaxen	... ...	09176
Fixed	...	... ...	09127	Flay	... ...	09177
Fixedness	...	...	09128	Flea	... ...	09178
Fixing	...	...	09129	Fleck	... ...	09179
Fixture	...	...	09130	Fled	... ...	09180
Fizz...	...	...	09131	Fledge	... ...	09181
Flabby	...	...	09132	Fledgeling	... ...	09182
Flaccid	...	...	09133	Flee	... ...	09183
Flag	...	...	09134	Fleece	... ...	09184
Flagellant	...	...	09135	Fleecing	... ...	09185
Flagellate	...	...	09136	Fleecy	... ...	09186
Flagellation	...	...	09137	Fleeing	... ...	09187
Flageolet	...	..	09138	Flees	... ...	09188
Flagged	...	...	09139	Fleet	... ...	09189
Flagging	...	...	09140	Fleeting	... ...	09190
Flagitious	...	...	09141	Fleetly	... ...	09191
Flagon	...	...	09142	Flesh	... ...	09192
Flagrancy	...	...	09143	Fleshly	... ...	09193
Flagrant	...	...	09144	Fleshy	... ...	09194
Flail	...	...	09145	Flew	... ...	09195
Flake	...	...	09146	Flexibility	... ...	09196
Flaky	...	...	09147	Flexible	... ...	09197
Flame	...	...	09148	Flexibly	... ...	09198
Flaming	...	...	09149	Flicker	... ...	09199
Flamingo	...	...	09150	Flickering	... ...	09200

Flight	... ...	09201	
Flighty	... ...	09202	
Flimsy	... ...	09203	
Flinch	... ...	09204	
Flinched	... ...	09205	
Flincher	... ...	09206	
Flinching	... ...	09207	
Fling	... ...	09208	
Flint	... ...	09209	
Flinty	... ...	09210	
Flippancy	... ...	09211	
Flippant	... ...	09212	
Flirt	... ...	09213	
Flirtation	... ...	09214	
Flirting	... ...	09215	
Flit	... ...	09216	
Flitch	... ...	09217	
Float	... ...	09218	
Floated	... ...	09219	
Floating	... ...	09220	
Flock	... ...	09221	
Flocky	... ...	09222	
Flog	... ...	09223	
Flogging	... ...	09224	
Flood	... ...	09225	
Flooded	... ...	09226	
Floor	... ...	09227	
Floored	... ...	09228	
Flop	... ...	09229	
Floral	... ...	09230	
Florescence	... ...	09231	
Floriculture	... ...	09232	
Florid	... ...	09233	
Floridness	... ...	09234	
Florin	... ...	09235	
Florist	... ...	09236	
Floss	... ...	09237	
Flotation	... ...	09238	
Flotilla	... ...	09239	
Flotsam	... ...	09240	
Flounce	... ...	09241	
Flounced	... ...	09242	
Flouncing	... ...	09243	
Flounder	... ...	09244	
Floundering	... ...	09245	
Flour	... ...	09246	
Flourish	... ...	09247	
Flourishing	... ...	09248	
Flout	... ...	09249	
Flouted	... ...	09250	

Flow	... ...	09251	
Flowed	... ...	09252	
Flower	... ...	09253	
Floweriness	... ...	09254	
Flowering	... ...	09255	
Flowery	... ...	09256	
Flowing	... ...	09257	
Flown	... ...	09258	
Fluctuate	... ...	09259	
Fluctuating	... ...	09260	
Fluctuation	... ...	09261	
Flue	... ...	09262	
Fluency	... ...	09263	
Fluent	... ...	09264	
Fluid	... ...	09265	
Fluidity	... ...	09266	
Fluke	... ...	09267	
Flung	... ...	09268	
Flurried	... ...	09269	
Flurry	... ...	09270	
Flush	... ...	09271	
Flushed	... ...	09272	
Flushing	... ...	09273	
Fluster	... ...	09274	
Flute	... ...	09275	
Fluted	... ...	09276	
Flutist	... ...	09277	
Flutter	... ...	09278	
Fluvial	... ...	09279	
Flux	... ...	09280	
Fluxion	... ...	09281	
Fly	... ...	09282	
Flying	... ...	09283	
Foal	... ...	09284	
Foam	... ...	09285	
Foaming	... ...	09286	
Fob	... ...	09287	
Focus	... ...	09288	
Fodder	... ...	09289	
Foe	... ...	09290	
Fœtus	... ...	09291	
Fog	... ...	09292	
Foggy	... ...	09293	
Foible	... ...	09294	
Foil	... ...	09295	
Foiled	... ...	09296	
Foist	... ...	09297	
Fold	... ...	09298	
Folded	... ...	09299	
Folding	... ...	09300	

Foliage	09301	Forearm... 09351
Foliate	09302	Forebode 09352
Foliation...	09303	Foreboding 09353
Folio	09304	Forecast 09354
Folk	09305	Forecastle 09355
Follow	09306	Foreclose 09356
Follower...	09307	Foreclosure 09357
Folly	09308	Forefather 09358
Foment	09309	Forefinger 09359
Fomentation	09310	Forego 09360
Fond	09311	Foregoes... 09361
Fondle	09312	Foregoing 09362
Fondly	09313	Foregone 09363
Fondness	09314	Foreground 09364
Font	09315	Forehead 09365
Food	09316	Foreign 09366
Fool	09317	Foreigner 09367
Foolery	09318	Foreknew 09368
Foolish	09319	Foreknow 09369
Foolscap...	09320	Foreknowledge ... 09370
Foot	09321	Foreland 09371
Footed	09322	Forelock... 09372
Foothold	09323	Foreman... 09373
Footing	09324	Foremost 09374
Footman...	09325	Forenoon 09375
Footstep...	09326	Forensic 09376
Fop...	09327	Forerun 09377
Foppery	09328	Foresail 09378
Foppish	09329	Foresay 09379
For	09330	Foresee 09380
Forage	09331	Foreshadow 09381
Forasmuch	09332	Foreshorten 09382
Foray ... ... ,...	09333	Foreshow 09383
Forbear	09334	Foreshow 09384
Forbearance	09335	Forest 09385
Forbearing	09336	Forestall... 09386
Forbears...	09337	Forester 09387
Forbid	09338	Foretaste 09388
Forbidden	09339	Foretell 09389
Forbidding	09340	Foretelling 09390
Forbids	09341	Forethought 09391
Forbore	09342	Foretold... 09392
Force	09343	Forever 09393
Forced	09344	Forewarn 09394
Forceps	09345	Forewarning 09395
Forcible	09346	Forfeit 09396
Forcibly	09347	Forfeiture 09397
Forcing	09348	Forge 09398
Ford	09349	Forged 09399
Fore	09350	Forger 09400

Forgery	09401	Fortunate 09451
Forget	09402	Fortune 09452
Forgetful	09403	Forty 09453
Forgetfulness	09404	Forward 09454
Forgets	09405	Forwarded 09455
Forgetting	09406	Forwarding 09456
Forging	09407	Fossil 09457
Forgive	09408	Fossilise 09458
Forgiven	09409	Foster 09459
Forgiveness	09410	Fought 09460
Forgiving	09411	Foul 09461
Forgot	09412	Foully 09462
Forgotten	09413	Foulness 09463
Fork	09414	Found 09464
Forked	09415	Foundation 09465
Forlorn	09416	Founded 09466
Form	09417	Founder 09467
Formal	09418	Founding 09468
Formalist	09419	Foundling 09469
Formality	09420	Foundry 09470
Formation	09421	Founds 09471
Formative	09422	Fountain 09472
Formed	09423	Four 09473
Former	09424	Fourfold 09474
Formerly	09425	Fourscore 09475
Formidable	09426	Fourteen 09476
Forming	09427	Fourteenth 09477
Formless	09428	Fourth 00478
Formula	09429	Fourthly 09479
Formulary	09430	Fowl 09480
Fornication	09431	Fowler 09481
Fornicator	09432	Fox 09482
Forsake	09433	Fracas 09483
Forsaken	09434	Fraction 09484
Forswear	09435	Fractious 09485
Forsworn	09436	Fracture 09486
Fort	09437	Fragile 09487
Forth	09438	Fragility 09488
Forthcoming	09439	Fragment 09489
Forthwith	09440	Fragrance 09490
Fortieth	09441	Fragrant 09491
Fortification	09442	Frail 09492
Fortified	09443	Frailty 09493
Fortifier	09444	Frame 09494
Fortify	09445	Framed 09495
Fortitude	09446	Framing 09496
Fortnight	09447	Franchise 09497
Fortnightly	09448	Frank 09498
Fortress	09449	Frankly 09499
Fortuitous	09450	Frankness 09500

FRA	(48)	FRU	96

Frantic ...	...	...	09501	Fried	09551
Fraternal	...	...	09502	Friend	09552
Fraternity	...	...	09503	Friendless	09553
Fraternize	...	...	09504	Friendliness	09554
Fratricidal	...	...	09505	Friendly	09555
Fratricide	...	...	09506	Friendship	09556
Fraud ...	...	...	09507	Frieze	09557
Fraudulence ...	...	...	09508	Frigate	09558
Fraudulent	...	...	09509	Fright	09559
Fraught ...	...	...	09510	Frighten...	09560
Fray ...	...	...	09511	Frightful	09561
Freak ...	...	...	09512	Frigid	09562
Freckle ...	...	...	09513	Frigidity...	09563
Free ...	...	...	09514	Frill	09564
Freebooter	...	...	09515	Fringe	09565
Freeborn	...	...	09516	Frippery...	09566
Freed ...	...	...	09517	Frisk	09567
Freedom...	...	...	09518	Friskiness	09568
Freehold	...	...	09519	Frisky	09569
Freeholder	...	...	09520	Frith	09570
Freely ...	...	...	09521	Fritter	09571
Freeman...	...	...	09522	Frittered...	09572
Freemason	...	...	09523	Frivolity...	09573
Freeze ...	...	...	09524	Frivolous	09574
Freezes ...	...	...	09525	Frivolously	09575
Freezing...	...	...	09526	Frizzle	09576
Freight ...	...	...	09527	Frizzler	09577
Freighted	...	...	09528	Fro	09578
French ...	...	...	09529	Frock	09579
Frenchman	...	...	09530	Frog	09580
Frenzy ...	...	...	09531	Frolic	09581
Frequency	...	...	09532	Frolicsome	09582
Frequent	...	...	09533	From	09583
Frequenter	...	...	09534	Front	09584
Frequently	...	...	09535	Frontage	09585
Fresh ...	...	...	09536	Frontier	09586
Freshen ...	...	...	09537	Fronting...	09587
Freshened	...	...	09538	Frontispiece	09588
Freshly ...	...	...	09539	Frontlet	09589
Freshman	...	...	09540	Frost	09590
Freshness	...	...	09541	Frostily	09591
Fret ...	...	...	09542	Frosty	09592
Fretful ...	...	...	09543	Froth	09593
Fretted ...	...	...	09544	Frothiness	09594
Fretting ...	...	...	09545	Frothy	09595
Fretwork	...	...	09546	Froward...	09596
Friable ...	...	...	09547	Frown	09597
Friar ...	...	...	09548	Froze	09598
Friction ...	...	...	09549	Frozen	09599
Friday ...	...	...	09550	Fructification... ...	09600

Fructify	09601	Fundamental 09651
Frugal	09602	Funded 09652
Frugality	09603	Funeral 09653
Fruit	09604	Funereal 09654
Fruiterer...	09605	Fungus 09655
Fruitful	09606	Funnel 09656
Fruiting	09607	Funny 09657
Fruition	09608	Fur 09658
Fruitless	09609	Furbish 09659
Frump	09610	Furcate 09660
Frustrate	09611	Furcation 09661
Frustrated	09612	Furious 09662
Frustrating	09613	Furiousness 09663
Frustration	09614	Furl... 09664
Frustrative	09615	Furling 09665
Fry	09616	Furled 09666
Frying	09617	Furlong 09667
Fuddle	09618	Furlough 09668
Fudge	09619	Furnace 09669
Fuel	09620	Furnish 09670
Fugacious	09621	Furnished 09671
Fugitive	09622	Furnishing 09672
Fugleman	09623	Furniture 09673
Fugue	09624	Furor 09674
Fulcrum	09625	Furrier 09675
Fulfil	09626	Furrow 09676
Fulfilled	09627	Further 09677
Fulfilling	09628	Furtherance 09678
Fulfilment	09629	Furthered 09679
Fulgency	09630	Furthering 09680
Fulgent	09631	Furthermore 09681
Full...	09632	Furthermost 09682
Fuller	09633	Furthest 09683
Fully	09634	Furtive 09684
Fulminant	09635	Furtively 09685
Fulminate	09636	Fury 09686
Fulmination ...	09637	Furze 09687
Fulminatory ...	09638	Fuse 09688
Fulness	09639	Fusee 09689
Fulsome	09640	Fusible 09690
Fumble	09641	Fusileer 09691
Fume	09642	Fusion 09692
Fumigate	09643	Fuss 09693
Fumigation ...	09644	Fustian 09694
Fuming	09645	Fusty 09695
Fun	09646	Futile 09696
Function... ...	09647	Futility 09697
Functionary ...	09648	Future 09698
Fund	09649	Futurity 09699
Fundament	09650	Fy 09700

G	(49)	GAT	98

G	09701	Gambol	09751
Gab...	09702	Game	09752
Gabardine	09703	Gamester	09753
Gabble	09704	Gaming	09754
Gabion	09705	Gammon	09755
Gable	09706	Gamut	09756
Gad...	09707	Gander	09757
Gaelic	09708	Gang	09758
Gaffer	09709	Ganger	09759
Gag...	09710	Gangrene	09760
Gage	09711	Gangway	09761
Gagged	09712	Gaol	09762
Gaiety	09713	Gaoler	09763
Gain	09714	Gap...	09764
Gained	09715	Gape	09765
Gainings...	09716	Gaper	09766
Gainsay	09717	Gaping	09767
Gainsayer	09718	Garb	09768
Gait	09719	Garbage	09769
Gaiter	09720	Garble	09770
Gala	09721	Garbled	09771
Galaxy	09722	Garden	09772
Gale	09723	Gardener	09773
Galimatia	09724	Gargle	09774
Gall...	09725	Garland	09775
Gallant	09726	Garlic	09776
Gallantly	09727	Garment...	09777
Gallantry	09728	Garner	09778
Galleot	09729	Garnered	09779
Gallery	09730	Garnet	09780
Galley	09731	Garnish	09781
Gallic	09732	Garnished	09782
Gallicism	09733	Garnishee	09783
Galling	09734	Garnishing	09784
Gallipot	09735	Garniture	09785
Gallon	09736	Garret	09786
Galloon	09737	Garrison	09787
Gallop...	09738	Garrote	09788
Galloped	09739	Garroted...	09789
Galloping	09740	Garrulity...	09790
Gallows	09741	Garrulous	09791
Galvanic...	09742	Garter	09792
Galvanism	09743	Gas	09793
Galvanize	09744	Gasconade	09794
Galvanized	09745	Gaseous	09795
Galvanometer ...	09746	Gash	09796
Gamble	09747	Gasket	09797
Gambler	09748	Gasometer	09798
Gambling	09749	Gasp	09799
Gamboge	09750	Gasping	09800

Gastric	09801	Generative	09851
Gastritis	09802	Generator	09852
Gastronomy	09803	Generic	09853
Gate	09804	Generosity	09854
Gateway	09805	Generous	09855
Gather	09806	Generously	09856
Gathered	09807	Genesis	09857
Gatherer	09808	Genet	09858
Gathering	09809	Genetic	09859
Gaudily	09810	Genevese	09860
Gaudy	09811	Genial	09861
Gauge	09812	Genital	09862
Gauger	09813	Genitive	09863
Gaunt	09814	Genius	09864
Gauntlet	09815	Genteel	09865
Gauze	09816	Gentian	09866
Gave	09817	Gentile	09867
Gawky	09818	Gentility	09868
Gay	09819	Gentle	09869
Gaze	09820	Gentleman	09870
Gazed	09821	Gentlemanly	09871
Gazelle	09822	Gentleness	09872
Gazette	09823	Gentlewoman	09873
Gazetteer	09824	Gently	09874
Gazetted	09825	Gentry	09875
Gazing	09826	Genuflection	09876
Gear	09827	Genuine	09877
Gehenna	09828	Genuineness	09878
Gelatine	09829	Genus	09879
Gelatinous	09830	Geocentric	09880
Geld	09831	Geographer	09881
Gelding	09832	Geographical	09882
Gelidity	09833	Geography	09883
Gem	09834	Geological	09884
Genappe	09835	Geologist	09885
Gender	09836	Geologize	09886
Genealogical	09837	Geology	09887
Genealogist	09838	Geometrical	09888
Genealogy	09839	Geometrician	09889
General	09840	Geometry	09890
Generalissimo ...	09841	Georgic	09891
Generality	09842	Geranium	09892
Generalization ...	09843	Germ	09893
Generalize	09844	German	09894
Generally	09845	Germinal	09895
Generalship	09846	Germinant	09896
Generate	09847	Germinate	09897
Generated	09848	Germination	09898
Generating	09849	Gerund	09899
Generation	09850	Gestation	09900

GES	50	GLE	100
Gesticulate	09901	Girdler	09951
Gesticulation	09902	Girdling	09952
Gesticulatory	09903	Girl	09953
Gesture	09904	Girlhood...	09954
Get	09905	Girlish	09955
Getting	09906	Girt...	09956
Gewgaw...	09907	Girth	09957
Ghastliness	09908	Gist...	09958
Ghastly	09909	Give	09959
Gherkin	09910	Given	09960
Ghost	09911	Giver	09961
Ghostliness	09912	Gives	09962
Ghostly	09913	Giving	09963
Ghoul	09914	Gizzard	09964
Giant	09915	Glacial	09965
Giantess...	09916	Glaciation	09966
Giaour	09917	Glacier	09967
Gibberish	09918	Glacis	09968
Gibbet	09919	Glad	09969
Gibe	09920	Gladden	09970
Giblets	09921	Glade	09971
Giddily	09922	Gladiator	09972
Giddiness	09923	Gladiatory	09973
Giddy	09924	Gladly	09974
Gift...	09925	Gladness...	09975
Gifted	09926	Gladsome	09976
Gig	09927	Glamour	09977
Gigantic	09928	Glance	09978
Giggle	09929	Glanced	09979
Gild	09930	Glancing...	09980
Gilded	09931	Gland	09981
Gilder	09932	Glanders	09982
Gilding	09933	Glandular	09983
Gill...	09934	Glare	09984
Gilt...	09935	Glaring	09985
Gimcrack	09936	Glass	09986
Gimlet	09937	Glasses	09987
Gimp	09938	Glassy	09988
Gin	09939	Glaze	09989
Ginger	09940	Glazier	09990
Gingerly...	09941	Glazing	09991
Gingham	09942	Gleam	09992
Gingling	09943	Gleaming	09993
Gipsy	09944	Glean	09994
Giraffe	09945	Gleaner	09995
Girandole	09946	Glebe	09996
Gird	09947	Glee	09997
Girded	09948	Gleeful	09998
Girder	09949	Glen	09999
Girdle	09950	Glenlivet...	10000

Glibly	10001	
Glide	10002	
Glided	10003	
Gliding	10004	
Glimmer...	10005	
Glimmering	10006	
Glimpse	10007	
Glisten	10008	
Glitter	10009	
Glittering	10010	
Gloaming	10011	
Gloat	10012	
Gloated	10013	
Gloating...	10014	
Globe	10015	
Globular...	10016	
Globule	10017	
Gloom	10018	
Gloominess	10019	
Gloomy	10020	
Glorification ...	10021	
Glorified	10022	
Glorify	10023	
Glorious	10024	
Gloriously	10025	
Glory	10026	
Gloss	10027	
Glossarial	10028	
Glossary	10029	
Glossiness	10030	
Glossy	10031	
Glove	10032	
Glover	10033	
Glow	10034	
Glowed	10035	
Glowing	10036	
Gloze	10037	
Glozing	10038	
Glue	10039	
Glum	10040	
Glut	10041	
Gluten	10042	
Glutinate	10043	
Glutinous	10044	
Glutted	10045	
Glutton	10046	
Gluttonous	10047	
Gluttony...	10048	
Glycerine	10049	
Glyphograph... ...	10050	

Glyphography ...	10051	
Gnarled	10052	
Gnash	10055	
Gnashing	10053	
Gnat	10054	
Gnaw	10056	
Gnomon	10057	
Go	10058	
Goad	10059	
Goal	10060	
Goat	10061	
Gobble	10062	
Gobbler	10063	
Gobelin	10064	
Goblet	10065	
Goblin	10066	
God...	10067	
Godchild	10068	
Goddess	10069	
Godfather	10070	
Godhead...	10071	
Godless	10072	
Godlike	10073	
Godliness	10074	
Godly	10075	
Godmother	10076	
Godsend	10077	
Godson	10078	
Goer	10079	
Goes	10080	
Goggle	10081	
Going	10082	
Goitre	10083	
Gold	10084	
Golden	10085	
Goldfinch	10086	
Goldsmith	10087	
Golf	10088	
Goloshes...	10089	
Gondola	10090	
Gondolier	10091	
Gone	10092	
Gonfalon	10093	
Gong	10094	
Gonorrhœa	10095	
Good	10096	
Goodliness	10097	
Goodly	10098	
Goodness	10099	
Goods	10100	

GOO	(51)	GRA	102

Goose	...	10101	Gradually	...	10151
Gooseberry	...	10102	Graduate	...	10152
Gore	...	10103	Graduated	...	10153
Gorge	...	10104	Graduation	...	10154
Gorgeous	...	10105	Graft	...	10155
Gorget	...	10106	Grafting	...	10156
Gorgon	...	10107	Grain	...	10157
Gormandize	...	10108	Graining	...	10158
Gorse	...	10109	Grains	...	10159
Gory	...	10110	Gramineous	...	10160
Gosling	...	10111	Grammar	...	10161
Gospel	...	10112	Grammarian	...	10162
Gospeller	...	10113	Grammatic	...	10163
Gossamer	...	10114	Grammatically	...	10164
Gossip	...	10115	Grammaticize	...	10165
Gossiping	...	10116	Grampus	...	10166
Got	...	10117	Granary	...	10167
Goth	...	10118	Grand	...	10168
Gothic	...	10119	Grandee	...	10169
Gouge	...	10120	Grandeur	...	10170
Gouging	...	10121	Grandiloquence	...	10171
Gourd	...	10122	Grandiloquent	...	10172
Gourmand	...	10123	Grandly	...	10173
Gout	...	10124	Grange	...	10174
Gouty	...	10125	Granger	...	10175
Govern	...	10126	Granite	...	10176
Governable	...	10127	Granitic	...	10177
Governance	...	10128	Granivorous	...	10178
Governed	...	10129	Grant	...	10179
Governess	...	10130	Granted	...	10180
Governing	...	10131	Granting	...	10181
Government	...	10132	Granular	...	10182
Governor	...	10133	Granulate	...	10183
Gown	...	10134	Granulated	...	10184
Grab	...	10135	Granulation	...	10185
Grace	...	10136	Granulous	...	10186
Graced	...	10137	Grape	...	10187
Graceful	...	10138	Grapery	...	10188
Gracefully	...	10139	Graphic	...	10189
Gracefulness	...	10140	Graphically	...	10190
Graceless	...	10141	Grapnel	...	10191
Gracious	...	10142	Grapple	...	10192
Graciously	...	10143	Grappled	...	10193
Graciousness	...	10144	Grappling	...	10194
Gradation	...	10145	Grasp	...	10195
Gradational	...	10146	Grasped	...	10196
Gradatory	...	10147	Grasper	...	10197
Grade	...	10148	Grasping	...	10198
Gradient	...	10149	Grass	...	10199
Gradual	...	10150	Grassy	...	10200

Grate	... ...	10201	Greet	... ...	10251
Grated	... ...	10202	Greeting	... ...	10252
Grateful	... ...	10203	Gregarious	... ...	10253
Gratefully	... ...	10204	Gregorian	... ...	10254
Gratefulness	... ...	10205	Grenade	... ...	10255
Grater	... ...	10206	Grenadier	... ...	10256
Gratification	... ...	10207	Grew	... ...	10257
Gratified	... ...	10208	Grey	... ...	10258
Gratify	... ...	10209	Gridiron	... ...	10259
Gratifying	... ...	10210	Grief	... ...	10260
Grating	... ...	10211	Grievance	... ...	10261
Gratis	... ...	10212	Grieve	... ...	10262
Gratitude	... ...	10213	Grieved	... ...	10263
Gratuitous	... ...	10214	Grieving	... ...	10264
Gratuitously	... ...	10215	Grievous	... ...	10265
Gratuity	... ...	10216	Griffin	... ...	10266
Gravamen	... ...	10217	Grill	... ...	10267
Grave	... ...	10218	Grim	... ...	10268
Gravel	... ...	10219	Grimace	... ...	10269
Gravelly	... ...	10220	Grime	... ...	10270
Gravely	... ...	10221	Grimed	... ...	10271
Graveolent	... ...	10222	Grimly	... ...	10272
Graver	... ...	10223	Grin	... ...	10273
Gravid	... ...	10224	Grind	... ...	10274
Graving	... ...	10225	Grinder	... ...	10275
Gravitate	... ...	10226	Grinding	... ...	10276
Gravitating	... ...	10227	Grinds	... ...	10277
Gravitation	... ...	10228	Grinning	... ...	10278
Gravity	... ...	10229	Grip	... ...	10279
Gravy	... ...	10230	Gripe	... ...	10280
Grayling	... ...	10231	Griping	... ...	10281
Graze	... ...	10232	Grisly	... ...	10282
Grazed	... ...	10233	Grist	... ...	10283
Grazier	... ...	10234	Gristle	... ...	10284
Grazing	... ...	10235	Grit	... ...	10285
Grease	... ...	10236	Groan	... ...	10286
Greasiness	... ...	10237	Groaning	... ...	10287
Greasy	... ...	10238	Groat	... ...	10288
Great	... ...	10239	Grocer	... ...	10289
Greatly	... ...	10240	Grocery	... ...	10290
Greatness	... ...	10241	Grog	... ...	10291
Greaves	... ...	10242	Groin	... ...	10292
Grecian	... ...	10243	Groom	... ...	10293
Greedily	... ...	10244	Groove	... ...	10294
Greediness	... ...	10245	Grope	... ...	10295
Greedy	... ...	10246	Groschen	... ...	10296
Greek	... ...	10247	Gross	... ...	10297
Green	... ...	10248	Grossly	... ...	10298
Greenish	... ...	10249	Grossness	... ...	10299
Greenness	... ...	10250	Grotto	... ...	10300

GRO				(52)	GYR			104
Grotesque	...	...	10301	Guile	...	...	...	10351
Ground ...	...	...	10302	Guileful ...	...	...	10352
Groundless	...	...	10303	Guileless...	...	...	10353
Grounds ...	...	...	10304	Guillotine	...	...	10354
Group	...	...	10305	Guillotined	...	...	10355
Grouped ...	...	...	10306	Guilt	...	...	10356
Grouping	...	...	10307	Guiltiness	...	...	10357
Grouse	...	...	10308	Guiltless...	...	...	10358
Grove	...	...	10309	Guilty	...	...	..	10359
Grovel	...	...	10310	Guinea	...	...	10360
Groveller	...	...	10311	Guise	...	...	10361
Grow	...	...	10312	Guitar	...	...	10362
Grower	...	...	10313	Gulf	...	...	10363
Growing...	...	...	10314	Gull	...	...	10364
Growl	...	...	10315	Gullet	...	...	10365
Grown	...	...	10316	Gully	...	...	10366
Grows	...	...	10317	Gulp	...	...	10367
Growth ...	...	...	10318	Gum	...	...	10368
Grub	...	...	10319	Gummy ...	...	...	10369
Grudge	...	...	10320	Gun...	...	...	10370
Gruel	...	...	10321	Gunner ...	...	...	10371
Gruff	...	...	10322	Gunnery ...	...	...	10372
Gruffness	...	...	10323	Gunpowder	...	...	10373
Grumble...	...	...	10324	Gunshot ...	...	...	10374
Grumbler	...	...	10325	Gunsmith	...	...	10375
Grumbling	...	...	10326	Gunwale...	...	...	10376
Grunt	...	...	10327	Gurgle	...	...	10377
Guano	...	...	10328	Gush	...	...	10378
Guarantee	...	...	10329	Gushed	...	...	10379
Guaranteed	...	...	10330	Gushing ...	...	...	10380
Guard	...	...	10331	Gusset	...	...	10381
Guarded ...	...	...	10332	Gust	...	...	10382
Guardedly	...	...	10333	Gusto	...	...	10383
Guardian	...	...	10334	Gusty	...	...	10384
Guarding	...	...	10335	Gut	...	...	10385
Guava	...	...	10336	Gutter	...	...	10386
Gudgeon...	...	...	10337	Guttering	...	...	10387
Guerdon...	...	...	10338	Guttural ...	...	...	10388
Guerilla ...	...	...	10339	Gutturally	...	...	10389
Guess	...	...	10340	Guzzle	...	...	10390
Guessed ...	...	...	10341	Guzzler ...	...	...	10391
Guessing...	...	...	10342	Gymnasium	...	...	10392
Guesser ...	...	...	10343	Gymnast...	...	...	10393
Guesses ...	...	...	10344	Gymnastic	...	...	10394
Guest	...	...	10345	Gymnastics	...	...	10395
Guidance	...	...	10346	Gypsum ...	...	...	10396
Guide	...	...	10347	Gyral	...	...	10397
Guided	...	...	10348	Gyrate	...	...	10398
Guild	...	...	10349	Gyration...	...	...	10399
Guildhall	...	...	10350	Gyratory...	...	...	10400

H	10401	Halt	10451
Ha	10402	Halted	10452
Habeas	10403	Halter	10453
Haberdasher	10404	Halting	10454
Haberdashery ...	10405	Halve	10455
Habiliment	10406	Halved	10456
Habit , ...	10407	Ham	10457
Habitable	10408	Hamlet	10458
Habitat	10409	Hammer...	10459
Habitation	10410	Hammered	10460
Habited	10411	Hammering	10461
Habitual...	10412	Hammock	10462
Habituate	10413	Hamper	10463
Habituated	10414	Hampered	10464
Habitude	10415	Hand	10465
Hack	10416	Handcuff	10466
Hackneyed	10417	Handed	10467
Had	10418	Handful	10468
Haddock	10419	Handicap	10469
Hæmatoid	10420	Handicraft	10470
Haft	10421	Handicraftsman ...	10471
Hag	10422	Handily	10472
Haggard...	10423	Handiness	10473
Haggis	10424	Handiwork	10474
Haggle	10425	Handkerchief... ...	10475
Haggled	10426	Handle	10476
Haggler	10427	Handled...	10477
Hail	10428	Handling	10478
Hailed	10429	Handmaiden	10479
Hailing	10430	Handsel	10480
Hailstone	10431	Handsome	10481
Hair	10432	Handsomely	10482
Hairless	10433	Handwriting	10483
Hairy	10434	Handy	10484
Halberd	10435	Hang	10485
Halcyon	10436	Hanged	10486
Hale	10437	Hanger	10487
Half	10438	Hanging...	10488
Halibut	10439	Hangman	10489
Hall	10440	Hangs	10490
Hallelujah	10441	Hanker	10491
Halloo	10442	Hankering	10492
Hallooing	10443	Hanseatic	10493
Hallow	10444	Haphazard	10494
Halloween	10445	Hapless	10495
Hallowed	10446	Haply	10496
Hallowmas	10447	Happen	10497
Hallucination... ...	10448	Happened	10498
Hallucinatory... ...	10449	Happening	10499
Halo	10450	Happily	10500

HAP	(53)	HAW	106

Happiness	10501	Harrowing	10551
Happy	10502	Harry	10552
Harangue	10503	Harsh	10553
Harangued	10504	Harshly	10554
Haranguing ...	10505	Hart	10555
Harass	10506	Hartshorn ...	10556
Harassed	10507	Harvest	10557
Harassing	10508	Harvesting	10558
Harbinger	10509	Has...	10559
Harbour	10510	Hash	10560
Harboured	10511	Hashed	10561
Hard	10512	Hasp	10562
Harden	10513	Hassock	10563
Hardihood	10514	Haste	10564
Hardily	10515	Hasten	10565
Hardly	10516	Hastening	10566
Hardness	10517	Hastily	10567
Hardship	10518	Hastiness	10568
Hardware	10519	Hasty	10569
Hardy	10520	Hat...	10570
Hare	10521	Hatch	10571
Harebell...	10522	Hatched... ...	10572
Harem	10523	Hatchet	10573
Haricot	10524	Hatching	10574
Hark	10525	Hatchment	10575
Harlequin	10526	Hatchway	10576
Harlot	10527	Hate	10577
Harm	10528	Hated	10578
Harmless	10529	Hateful	10579
Harmlessly	10530	Hatred	10580
Harmlessness	10531	Hating	10581
Harmonic	10532	Hatter	10582
Harmonica	10533	Haughtily	10583
Harmonics	10534	Haughtiness	10584
Harmonious	10535	Haughty...	10585
Harmonist	10536	Haul	10586
Harmonize	10537	Hauled	10587
Harmonizing	10538	Hauling	10588
Harmony	10539	Haunch	10589
Harness	10540	Haunt	10590
Harnessed	10541	Haunted...	10591
Harp	10542	Hautboy...	10592
Harping	10543	Have	10593
Harpist	10544	Haven	10594
Harpoon...	10545	Haversack	10595
Harpsichord	10546	Having	10596
Harridan	10547	Havoc	10597
Harrier	10548	Haw	10598
Harrow	10549	Hawk	10599
Harrower	10550	Hawker	10600

Hawking	... ...	10601
Hawser ...	... ...	10602
Hawthorn	... ...	10603
Hay	... ...	10604
Hazard ...	... ...	10605
Hazardous	... ...	10606
Haze	... ...	10607
Hazel	... ...	10608
Haziness...	... ...	10609
Hazy	... ...	10610
He ...	... ...	10611
Head	... ...	10612
Headed ...	... ...	10613
Headache	... ...	10614
Headfast	... ...	10615
Heading...	... ...	10616
Headland	... ...	10617
Headless	... ...	10618
Headlong	... ...	10619
Headmost	... ...	10620
Headsman	... ...	10621
Headstrong	... ...	10622
Headway	... ...	10623
Heady ...	... ...	10624
Heal	... ...	10625
Healed ...	... ...	10626
Healing ...	... ...	10627
Health ...	... ...	10628
Healthful	... ...	10629
Healthiness	... ...	10630
Healthy ...	... ...	10631
Heap	... ...	10632
Heaped ...	... ...	10633
Heaping...	... ...	10634
Hear	... ...	10635
Hearer ...	... ...	10636
Heard	... ...	10637
Hearing ...	... ...	10638
Hearken...	... ...	10639
Hears	... ...	10640
Hearsay ...	... ...	10641
Hearse ...	... ...	10642
Heart	... ...	10643
Hearth ...	... ...	10644
Heartily ...	... ...	10645
Heartiness	... ...	10646
Heartless	... ...	10647
Hearty ...	... ...	10648
Heat	... ...	10649
Heated ...	... ...	10650
Heater ...	... ...	10651
Heath	... ...	10652
Heathen...	... ...	10653
Heathendom ...	...	10654
Heathenish	... ...	10655
Heathenism ...	...	10656
Heather ...	... ...	10657
Heating ...	... ...	10658
Heave	... ...	10659
Heaved ...	... ...	10660
Heaven ...	... ...	10661
Heavenly	... ...	10662
Heaves ...	... ...	10663
Heavily ...	... ...	10664
Heaviness	... ...	10665
Heaving...	... ...	10666
Heavy ...	... ...	10667
Hebdomadal ...	...	10668
Hebraist...	... ...	10669
Hebrew ...	... ...	10670
Hectic ...	... ...	10671
Hedge ...	... ...	10672
Hedged ...	... ...	10673
Heed	... ...	10674
Heeded ...	... ...	10675
Heedful ...	... ...	10676
Heeding ...	... ...	10677
Heedless...	... ...	10678
Heel	... ...	10679
Heifer	... ...	10680
Height ...	... ...	10681
Heighten	... ...	10682
Heinous ...	... ...	10683
Heir	... ...	10684
Heirdom ...	...	10685
Heiress ...	... ...	10686
Heirless ...	... ...	10687
Heirloom	... ...	10688
Heirship...	... ...	10689
Held	... ...	10690
Helical ...	... ...	10691
Heliotrope	... ...	10692
Hell	... ...	10693
Hellish ...	... ...	10694
Helm	... ...	10695
Helmet ...	... ...	10696
Helmsman	... ...	10697
Help	... ...	10698
Helped ...	... ...	10699
Helper ...	... ...	10700

HEL	(54)	HIL	108

Helping	10701	Hermit	10751
Helpless	10702	Hermitage	10752
Helpmate	10703	Hero	10753
Helps	10704	Heroic	10754
Helvetic	10705	Heroine	10755
Hem	10706	Heroism	10756
Hemmed	10707	Heron	10757
Hemisphere	10708	Heronry	10758
Hemlock	10709	Herring	10759
Hemming	10710	Hers	10760
Hemorrhage	10711	Herself	10761
Hemp	10712	Hesitancy	10762
Hempen	10713	Hesitate	10763
Hen	10714	Hesitated	10764
Hence	10715	Hesitating	10765
Henceforth ...	10716	Hesitation	10766
Henceforward ...	10717	Heterodox	10767
Henna	10718	Heterodoxy	10768
Heptangular	10719	Heterogeneous ...	10769
Heptarchy	10720	Hew	10770
Her...	10721	Hewed...	10771
Herald	10722	Hewer	10772
Heraldry	10723	Hewing	10773
Herb	10724	Hewn	10774
Herbaceous	10725	Hews	10775
Herbage	10726	Hexagon	10776
Herbal	10727	Hexameter	10777
Herbalist	10728	Hiatus	10778
Herbivora	10729	Hibernate	10779
Herculean	10730	Hiccough	10780
Herd	10731	Hickory	10781
Herded	10732	Hid...	10782
Herdsman	10733	Hidden	10783
Here	10734	Hide	10784
Hereafter	10735	Hideous	10785
Hereditably	10736	Hides	10786
Hereditament ...	10737	Hiding	10787
Hereditary	10738	Hie...	10788
Heresy	10739	Hierarch...	10789
Heretic	10740	Hieroglyphic... ...	10790
Heretical	10741	Higgle	10791
Hereto	10742	Higgling	10792
Heretofore	10743	High	10793
Hereupon	10744	Highest	10794
Herewith	10745	Highland	10795
Heriot	10746	Highlander	10796
Heritage...	10747	Highly	10797
Hermaphrodite ...	10748	Highness	10798
Hermetic	10749	Highway	10799
Hermetically	10750	Hilarious	10800

Hilarity ...	...	...	10801
Hill...	...	...	10802
Hillock ...	...	...	10803
Hilly	...	...	10804
Hilt...	...	...	10805
Him	...	...	10806
Himself ...	...	...	10807
Hind	...	...	10808
Hinder	...	...	10809
Hindoo ...	...	...	10810
Hindrance	...	...	10811
Hindermost	...	...	10812
Hinge	...	...	10813
Hinged ...	...	...	10814
Hint	...	...	10815
Hinted	...	...	10816
Hip...	...	...	10817
Hippodrome ...	...	...	10818
Hippopotamus	...	...	10819
Hire	...	...	10820
Hired	...	...	10821
Hireling...	...	...	10822
Hiring	...	...	10823
Hirsute ...	...	...	10824
His ...	...	...	10825
Hiss	...	...	10826
Hissing ...	...	...	10827
Historian	...	...	10828
Historical	...	...	10829
History ...	...	...	10830
Histrionic	...	...	10831
Hit ...	...	...	10832
Hitch	...	...	10833
Hithe	...	...	10834
Hither	...	...	10835
Hitherto...	...	...	10836
Hits	...	...	10837
Hitting ...	...	...	10838
Hive	...	...	10839
Ho ...	...	...	10840
Hoar	...	...	10841
Hoard	...	...	10842
Hoarded...	...	...	10843
Hoarding	...	...	10844
Hoariness	...	...	10845
Hoarse ...	...	...	10846
Hoarseness	...	...	10847
Hoary	...	...	10848
Hoax	...	...	10849
Hoaxed ...	...	...	10850

Hob	...	...	10851
Hobble ...	...	...	10852
Hobbling	...	...	10853
Hobby ...	...	...	10854
Hobgoblin	...	...	10855
Hobnail ...	...	...	10856
Hobnob ...	...	...	10857
Hock	...	...	10858
Hockey ...	...	...	10859
Hod	...	...	10860
Hoe	...	...	10861
Hoed	...	...	10862
Hog	...	...	10863
Hogged ...	...	...	10864
Hoggish...	...	...	10865
Hogshead	...	...	10866
Hogstye ...	...	...	10867
Hogwash	...	...	10868
Hoiden ...	...	...	10869
Hoist	...	...	10870
Hold	...	...	10871
Holder	...	...	10872
Holdfast...	...	...	10873
Holds	...	...	10874
Holding ...	...	...	10875
Hole	...	...	10876
Holiday ...	...	...	10877
Holiness...	...	...	10878
Holla	...	...	10879
Hollander	...	...	10880
Hollands	...	...	10881
Hollow ...	...	...	10882
Hollowed	...	...	10883
Hollowness	...	...	10884
Holly	...	...	10885
Hollyhock	...	...	10886
Holograph	...	...	10887
Holster ...	...	...	10888
Holy	...	...	10889
Homage...	...	...	10890
Home	...	...	10891
Homeless	...	...	10892
Homeliness	...	...	10893
Homely ...	...	...	10894
Homeopathic...	...	...	10895
Homeopathist	...	...	10896
Homeopathy ...	...	...	10897
Homespun	...	...	10898
Homestead	...	...	10899
Homeward	...	...	10900

HOM	(55)	HOW	110

Homicidal	...	...	10901	Horrific	10951
Homicide	...	...	10902	Horrified	10952
Homilist...	...	...	10903	Horrify	10953
Homily ...	...	...	10904	Horrifying	10954
Homogeneous		...	10905	Horror	10955
Hone	...	...	10906	Horse	10956
Honest ...	...	...	10907	Horseback	10957
Honestly	...	...	10908	Horsemanship ...	10958
Honesty ...	...	...	10909	Horsewhip	10959
Honey ...	...	...	10910	Horsewhipped ...	10960
Honorarium	...	...	10911	Hortation	10961
Honorary	...	...	10912	Hortative	10962
Honour ...	...	...	10913	Horticultural	10963
Honourable	...	...	10914	Horticulture	10964
Honourably	...	...	10915	Horticulturist ...	10965
Honoured	...	...	10916	Hosanna...	10966
Honouring	...	...	10917	Hose	10967
Hood	...	...	10918	Hosier	10968
Hooded ...	...	...	10919	Hosiery	10969
Hoodwink	...	...	10920	Hospitable ... ·	10970
Hool	...	...	10921	Hospital	10971
Hook	...	...	10922	Hospitality	10972
Hooked ...	...	...	10923	Host	10973
Hoop	...	...	10924	Hostage	10974
Hooping...	...	...	10925	Hostess	10975
Hoot	...	...	10926	Hostile	10976
Hop	...	...	10927	Hostility...	10977
Hope	...	...	10928	Hostler	10978
Hoped ...	...	...	10929	Hot	10979
Hopeful ...	...	...	10930	Hotchpot	10980
Hopefulness	...	...	10931	Hotel	10981
Hopeless	...	...	10932	Hotly	10982
Hoping ...	...	...	10933	Hound	10983
Hopingly	...	...	10934	Hour	10984
Hopper ...	...	...	10935	Hourly	10985
Hopping...	...	...	10936	House	10986
Horal	...	...	10937	Housed	10987
Horizon ...	...	...	10938	Household	10988
Horizontal	...	...	10939	Householder	10989
Horn	...	...	10940	Housekeeper	10990
Horned ...	...	...	10941	Housekeeping ...	10991
Hornet ...	...	...	10942	Houseless	10992
Horning ...	...	...	10943	Housewife	10993
Hornpipe	...	...	10944	Housing	10994
Horology	...	...	10945	Hove	10995
Horoscope	...	...	10946	Hovel	10996
Horrible...	·	...	10947	Hover	10997
Horribly...	...	...	10948	How	10998
Horrid ...	...	...	10949	However	10999
Horridly...	...	...	10950	Howitzer	11000

Howl	...	...	11001	Huntsman	 11051
Howsoever	...	...	11002	Hurdle ...	 11052
Hoy	...	...	11003	Hurl	 11053
Hubbub ...	...	...	11004	Hurly	 11054
Huckster	...	...	11005	Hurrah ...	 11055
Huddle ...	...	...	11006	Hurricane	 11056
Hue	...	...	11007	Hurried ...	 11057
Huff	...	...	11008	Hurry	 11058
Huffed ...	...	...	11009	Hurrying	 11059
Huffiness	...	...	11010	Hurt	 11060
Huffish	...	...	11011	Hurtful ...	 11061
Hug	...	...	11012	Hurting ...	 11062
Huge	...	...	11013	Hurts	 11063
Hugeness	...	...	11014	Husband	 11064
Hulk	...	...	11015	Husbanded	 11065
Hum	...	...	11016	Husbanding	 11066
Human ...	...	...	11017	Husbandman...	... 11067
Humane...	...	...	11018	Husbandry	 11068
Humanity	...	...	11019	Hush	 11069
Humanize	...	...	11020	Husk	 11070
Humanly	...	...	11021	Husky	 11071
Humble ...	...	...	11022	Hussar	 11072
Humbling	...	...	11023	Hustings...	 11073
Humbug...	...	...	11024	Hustle	 11074
Humdrum	...	...	11025	Hut...	 11075
Humeral...	...	...	11026	Huzza	 11076
Humid ...	...	...	11027	Hyacinth	 11077
Humiliate	...	...	11028	Hybrid ...	 11078
Humiliated	...	...	11029	Hydraulics	 11079
Humiliating	...	..	11030	Hydrogen	 11080
Humiliation	...	...	11031	Hydrography...	... 11081
Humility	...	...	11032	Hydropathy ...	... 11082
Humming	...	...	11033	Hydrophobia...	... 11083
Humorist	...	...	11034	Hydrostatics ...	... 11084
Humorous	...	...	11035	Hyena	 11085
Humour ...	...	...	11036	Hygieine	 11086
Humoured	...	...	11037	Hymeneal	 11087
Hump	...	...	11038	Hymn	 11088
Hunch	...	...	11039	Hymnal ...	 11089
Hundred...	...	..	11040	Hyperbolical ...	... 11090
Hundredth	...	...	11041	Hypercritical...	... 11091
Hung	...	...	11042	Hypercriticism	... 11092
Hunger ...	...	...	11043	Hyphen ...	 11093
Hungrily	...	...	11044	Hypochondriac	... 11094
Hungry ...	...	...	11045	Hypochondriasis	... 11095
Hunt	...	...	11046	Hypocrisy	 11096
Hunted ...	...	...	11047	Hypocrite	 11097
Hunter	..	...	11048	Hypothesis	 11098
Hunting ...	...	...	11049	Hyssop ...	 11099
Huntress...	...	...	11050	Hysterics	 11100

I	(56)	IMB	112

I	11101	Ignored	11151
Iambic	11102	Ignoring...	11152
Ice	11103	Ilk	11153
Iced	11104	Ill	11154
Iceberg	11105	Illegal	11155
Icelander	11106	Illegality	11156
Ichor	11107	Illegalize	11157
Ichthyology	11108	Illegally	11158
Icicle	11109	Illegibility	11159
Iciness	11110	Illegible	11160
Iconoclast	11111	Illegitimacy	11161
Icy	11112	Illegitimate	11162
Idea...	11113	Illiberal	11163
Ideal	11114	Illiberally	11164
Ideality	11115	Illicit	11165
Idealize	11116	Illimitable	11166
Ideally	11117	Illiterate... · ...	11167
Identical...	11118	Illness	11168
Identification	11119	Illogical	11169
Identify	11120	Illude ... · ...	11170
Identity	11121	Illumine... · ...	11171
Idiom	11122	Illuminate	11172
Idiomatic	11123	Illuminating	11173
Idiosyncrasy	11124	Illumination	11174
Idiot	11125	Illuminative	11175
Idiotcy	11126	Illuminator	11176
Idiotic	11127	Illusion	11177
Idle...	11128	Illusionist	11178
Idleness	11129	Illusive	11179
Idler	11130	Illusory	11180
Idly...	11131	Illustrate	11181
Idol...	11132	Illustrated	11182
Idolater	11133	Illustration	11183
Idolatrous	11134	Illustrative	11184
Idolatry	11135	Illustrator	11185
Idolize	11136	Illustrious	11186
Idyl	11137	Illustriously	11187
If	11138	Image	11188
Igneous	11139	Imagery ... ·	11189
Ignite	11140	Imaginable	11190
Ignited	11141	Imaginary	11191
Ignition	11142	Imagination	11192
Ignoble	11143	Imaginative	11193
Ignominious	11144	Imagine	11194
Ignominy	11145	Imbecile...	11195
Ignoramus	11146	Imbecility	11196
Ignorance	11147	Imbed	11197
Ignorant...	11148	Imbedded	11198
Ignorantly	11149	Imbibe	11199
Ignore	11150	Imbiber	11200

Imbroglio	...	...	11201	Imp	... ...	11251
Imbrue ...	...	...	11202	Impact	... ...	11252
Imbue	... ...	...	11203	Impair	... ...	11253
Imbued ...	...	...	11204	Impaired	... ...	11254
Imitable...	...	...	11205	Impairing	... ...	11255
Imitate ...	...	...	11206	Impale ...	... ...	11256
Imitation	...	...	11207	Impaled ...	... ...	11257
Imitative	...	...	11208	Impalpability...	...	11258
Imitator ...	...	...	11209	Impalpable	... ...	11259
Immaculate	...	...	11210	Impalpably	... ...	11260
Immaculately	...	11211	Impanel ...	... ...	11261
Immanent	...	...	11212	Impanelled	... ...	11262
Immaterial	...	...	11213	Impart ...	... ...	11263
Immaterially ...	...	11214	Imparted	... ...	11264
Immature	...	...	11215	Impartial	... ...	11265
Inimaturely	...	...	11216	Impartiality	... ...	11266
Immaturity	...	...	11217	Impartially	... ...	11267
Immeasurable	...	11218	Imparting	... ...	11268
Immediate	...	...	11219	Impassibility	... ...	11269
Immediately ...	...	11220	Impassionate ...	...	11270
Immemorial ...	...	11221	Impassioned ...	...	11271
Immense	...	...	11222	Impassive	... ...	11272
Immensely	...	...	11223	Impassiveness	...	11273
Immensity	...	...	11224	Impatience	... ...	11274
Immerse...	...	...	11225	Impatient	... ...	11275
Immersion	...	...	11226	Impatiently	... ...	11276
Imminence	...	...	11227	Impeach...	... ...	11277
Imminent	...	...	11228	Impeachable	... ...	11278
Imminently	...	...	11229	Impeached	... ...	11279
Immobility	...	...	11230	Impeacher	... ...	11280
Immoderate	...	...	11231	Impeachment...	...	11281
Immoderately	...	11232	Impede ...	... ...	11282
Immodest	...	...	11233	Impeded...	... ...	11283
Immodesty	...	...	11234	Impediment	... ...	11284
Immolate	...	...	11235	Impedimental	...	11285
Immolated	...	...	11236	Impeding	... ...	11286
Immolation	...	...	11237	Impel	... ...	11287
Immoral...	...	...	11238	Impelled...	... ...	11288
Immorality	...	...	11239	Impelling	... ...	11289
Immortal	...	...	11240	Impend ...	... ...	11290
Immortality	...	...	11241	Impending	... ...	11291
Immortalize	...	...	11242	Impenetrability	...	11292
Immoveability	...	11243	Impenetrable...	...	11293
Immoveable ...	...	11244	Impenitence	... ...	11294
Immoveably ...	...	11245	Impenitent	... ...	11295
Immunity	...	...	11246	Imperative	... ...	11296
Immure ...	...	...	11247	Imperatively ...	...	11297
Immutability...	...	11248	Imperceptible	...	11298
Immutable	...	...	11249	Imperfect	... ...	11299
Inmutably	...	...	11250	Imperfection ...	...	11300

IMP	(57)	IMP	114
Imperfectly	11301	Importunate	11351
Imperial	11302	Importunateness ...	11352
Imperially	11303	Importune	11353
Imperil	11304	Importuned	11354
Imperilled	11305	Importunity	11355
Imperious	11306	Imposable	11356
Imperishable	11307	Impose	11357
Impersonal	11308	Imposed	11358
Impersonation ...	11309	Imposer	11359
Imperspicuity ...	11310	Imposing	11360
Imperspicuous ...	11311	Imposition	11361
Impertinence	11312	Impossibility	11362
Impertinent	11313	Impossible	11363
Impertinently	11314	Impost	11364
Imperturbable ...	11315	Impostor	11365
Impervious	11316	Imposture	11366
Impetuosity	11317	Impotency	11367
Impetuous	11318	Impotent	11368
Impetus	11319	Impound	11369
Impiety	11320	Impoverish	11370
Impinge	11321	Impoverished	11371
Impious	11322	Impoverishment ...	11372
Impish	11323	Impracticable ...	11373
Implacability	11324	Impracticably ...	11374
Implacable	11325	Imprecate	11375
Implant	11326	Imprecated	11376
Implanted	11327	Imprecation	11377
Implead	11328	Impregnable	11378
Impleaded	11329	Impregnably	11379
Implement	11330	Impregnate	11380
Implicate	11331	Impregnated	11381
Implicated	11332	Impregnation	11382
Implication	11333	Impress	11383
Implicit	11334	Impressed	11384
Implicitly	11335	Impressible	11385
Implied	11336	Impressing	11386
Implore	11337	Impression	11387
Implorer	11338	Impressive	11388
Imploringly	11339	Imprimis	11389
Imply	11340	Imprint	11390
Impolicy	11341	Imprinted	11391
Impolite	11342	Imprison	11392
Impolitic	11343	Imprisoned	11393
Import	11344	Imprisoning	11394
Importance	11345	Imprisonment ...	11395
Important	11346	Improbability ...	11396
Importation	11347	Improbable	11397
Imported	11348	Impromptu	11398
Importer	11349	Improper	11399
Importing	11350	Improperly	11400

— 29 —

Impropriety	...	11401	Inarticulate	... ...	11451
Improvable	...	11402	Inasmuch	... ...	11452
Improve...	...	11403	Inattention	... ...	11453
Improved	...	11404	Inattentive	... ...	11454
Improvement...	...	11405	Inaudible	... ...	11455
Improvidence	...	11406	Inaudibly	... ...	11456
Improvident	...	11407	Inaugural	... ...	11457
Improving	...	11408	Inaugurate	... ...	11458
Improvise	...	11409	Inaugurated	... ...	11459
Improvised	...	11410	Inauguration	... ...	11460
Imprudence	...	11411	Inauspicious	... ...	11461
Imprudent	...	11412	Inbred	... ...	11462
Impudence	...	11413	Incalculable	...	11463
Impudent	...	11414	Incandescent	...	11464
Impugn ...	...	11415	Incantation	...	11465
Impugned	...	11416	Incapability	...	11466
Impugning	...	11417	Incapable	...	11467
Impulse ...	...	11418	Incapacious	... ...	11468
Impulsive	...	11419	Incapacitate	... ...	11469
Impunity	...	11420	Incapacitated	...	11470
Impure ...	...	11421	Incapacity	... ...	11471
Imputation	...	11422	Incarcerate	... ...	11472
Impute ...	...	11423	Incarceration	...	11473
Imputed...	...	11424	Incarnate	... ...	11474
Imputing	...	11425	Incarnation	... ...	11475
In	...	11426	Incase ...	... ...	11476
Inability...	...	11427	Incautious	... ...	11477
Inaccessible	...	11428	Incautiously	... ...	11478
Inaccuracy	...	11429	Incendiarism	... ...	11479
Inaccurate	...	11430	Incendiary	... ...	11480
Inaction ...	...	11431	Incense ...	... ...	11481
Inactive ...	...	11432	Incentive	... ...	11482
Inactivity	...	11433	Inception	... ...	11483
Inadequacy	...	11434	Incessant	... ...	11484
Inadequate	...	11435	Incessantly	... ...	11485
Inadequately	...	11436	Incest ...	... ...	11486
Inadmissible	...	11437	Incestuous	... ...	11487
Inadvertence	...	11438	Inch ...	... ...	11488
Inadvertent	...	11439	Incidence	... ...	11489
Inadvertently...	...	11440	Incident ..	.. ...	11490
Inalienable	...	11441	Incidental	.. ...	11491
Inane ...	...	11442	Incidentally	... ...	11492
Inanimate	...	11443	Incipient ..	... ...	11493
Inanity ...	...	11444	Incise ...	... ...	11494
Inapplicable	...	11445	Incised ...	... ...	11495
Inapposite	...	11446	Incision ...	... ...	11496
Inappreciable	...	11447	Incisor ...	... ...	11497
Inappropriate	...	11448	Incite ...	... ...	11498
Inaptitude	...	11449	Incited ...	... ...	11499
Inaptly ...	...	11450	Incitement	... ...	11500

INC	(58)	INC	116

Inciter	11501	Inconsiderable ...	11551
Incivility	11502	Inconsiderably ...	11552
Inclemency	11503	Inconsiderate... ...	11553
Inclement	11504	Inconsideration ...	11554
Inclination	11505	Inconsistency... ...	11555
Incline	11506	Inconsistent	11556
Inclined	11507	Inconsolable	11557
Inclining...	11508	Inconstancy	11558
Inclose	11509	Inconsumable ...	11559
Inclosed	11510	Incontestable... ...	11560
Incloser	11511	Incontestably... ...	11561
Inclosure	11512	Incontinence	11562
Include	11513	Incontrollable ...	11563
Included...	11514	Incontrovertible ...	11564
Including	11515	Inconvenience ...	11565
Inclusive	11516	Inconvenienced ...	11566
Incognito	11517	Inconvenient	11567
Incoherence	11518	Inconvincible... ...	11568
Incoherent	11519	Incorporate	11569
Incombustible ...	11520	Incorporated	11570
Income	11521	Incorporation ...	11571
Incoming	11522	Incorrect	11572
Incommensurable ...	11523	Incorrectly	11573
Incommensurate ...	11524	Incorrectness	11574
Incommodation ...	11525	Incorrigible	11575
Incommode	11526	Incorrigibly	11576
Incommoded	11527	Incorrupt	11577
Incommodious ...	11528	Incorruptible... ...	11578
Incommunicative ...	11529	Incorruptibly... ...	11579
Incommutable ...	11530	Incorruption	11580
Incompact	11531	Increase	11581
Incomparable ...	11532	Increased	11582
Incomparably ...	11533	Increasing	11583
Incompassionate ...	11534	Incredibility	11584
Incompatible... ...	11535	Incredibly	11585
Incompensable ...	11536	Incredible	11586
Incompetence ...	11537	Incredulity	11587
Incompetent	11538	Increment	11588
Incompetently ...	11539	Incrust	11589
Incomplete	11540	Incrustation	11590
Incomprehensible ...	11541	Incrusted	11591
Incomprehensibly...	11542	Incubate...	11592
Incomprehension ...	11543	Incubation	11593
Incompressible ...	11544	Incubus	11594
Incomputable ...	11545	Inculcate	11595
Inconceivable ...	11546	Inculcated	11596
Inconceivably ...	11547	Inculpate	11597
Inconclusive	11548	Incumbency	11598
Incongruity	11549	Incumbent	11599
Incongruous	11550	Incumbrance	11600

117 INC (59) . IND	
Incur 11601	Indication 11651
Incurable 11602	Indicative 11652
Incurably 11603	Indicator 11653
Incurred 11604	Indict 11654
Incurring 11605	Indictable 11655
Incurs 11606	Indicted 11656
Incursion 11607	Indicter 11657
Indebted 11608	Indictment 11658
Indebtedness 11609	Indifference 11659
Indecency 11610	Indifferent 11660
Indecent 11611	Indigence 11661
Indecipherable ... 11612	Indigenous 11662
Indecision 11613	Indigent 11663
Indecisive 11614	Indigestible 11664
Indecorous 11615	Indigestion 11665
Indecorously 11616	Indignant 11666
Indecorum 11617	Indignantly 11667
Indeed 11618	Indignation 11668
Indefatigable ... 11619	Indignity 11669
Indefatigably ... 11620	Indigo 11670
Indefeasible 11621	Indirect 11671
Indefensible 11622	Indirectly 11672
Indefinable 11623	Indiscernible 11673
Indefinite 11624	Indiscreet 11674
Indefinitely 11625	Indiscreetly 11675
Indelible 11626	Indiscretion 11676
Indelibly 11627	Indiscriminate ... 11677
Indelicacy 11628	Indiscriminately ... 11678
Indelicate 11629	Indiscriminative ... 11679
Indemnification ... 11630	Indispensable 11680
Indemnified 11631	Indispensably ... 11681
Indemnify 11632	Indispose 11682
Imdemnity 11633	Indisposed 11683
Indent 11634	Indisposition 11684
Indentation 11635	Indisputable 11685
Indented 11636	Indisputably 11686
Indenture 11637	Indissoluble 11687
Independence ... 11638	Indissolubly 11688
Independent 11639	Indistinct 11689
Independently ... 11640	Indistinctly 11690
Indescribable 11641	Indite 11691
Indestructible ... 11642	Individual 11692
Indeterminable ... 11643	Individuality 11693
Indeterminate ... 11644	Individualize 11694
Indeterminateness ... 11645	Individually 11695
Index 11646	Indivisibility 11696
Indian 11647	Indivisible 11697
Indicate 11648	Indocile 11698
Indicated 11649	Indocility 11699
Indicating 11650	Indoctrinate 11700

IND	(59)	INF	118

Indolence	... ...	11701	Inevitably	11751
Indolent ...	... ...	11702	Inexact	11752
Indolently	... ...	11703	Inexactness	11753
Indomitable	... ...	11704	Inexcusable	11754
Indorse ...	... ...	11705	Inexorable	11755
Indorsed...	... ...	11706	Inexpedience	11756
Indorsement	... ...	11707	Inexpedient	11757
Indubitable	... ...	11708	Inexpensive	11758
Induce ...	... ...	11709	Inexperience	11759
Induced ...	... ...	11710	Inexpert	11760
Inducement	... ...	11711	Inexpiable	11761
Induct ...	... ...	11712	Inexplicable	11762
Inducted...	... ...	11713	Inexplicit	11763
Induction	... ...	11714	Inexpressible	11764
Indue ...	... ...	11715	Inexpressibly	11765
Indued ...	... ...	11716	Inexpressive	11766
Indulge ...	... ...	11717	Inextinguishable ...	11767
Indulged	... ...	11718	Inextricable	11768
Indulgence	... ...	11719	Infallibility	11769
Indulgent	... ...	11720	Infallible	11770
Indulgently	... ...	11721	Infallibly	11771
Indurate...	... ...	11722	Infamous	11772
Indurated	... ...	11723	Infamously	11773
Induration	... ...	11724	Infamy	11774
Industrial	... ...	11725	Infancy	11775
Industrious	... ...	11726	Infant	11776
Industry ...	... ...	11727	Infanticide	11777
Inebriate	... ...	11728	Infantine	11778
Inebriety	... ...	11729	Infantry	11779
Inedited ...	... ...	11730	Infatuate...	11780
Ineffable...	... ...	11731	Infatuated	11781
Ineffably...	... ...	11732	Infatuation	11782
Ineffective	... ...	11733	Infect	11783
Ineffectual	... ...	11734	Infected	11784
Inefficacious ...	...	11735	Infection...	11785
Inefficacy	... ...	11736	Infective	11786
Inefficiency	... ...	11737	Infelicitous	11787
Inefficient	... ...	11738	Infelicity...	11788
Inelegance	... ...	11739	Infer	11789
Inelegant	... ...	11740	Inferable	11790
Ineligibility	... ...	11741	Inference	11791
Ineligible	... ...	11742	Inferentially	11792
Ineptitude	... ...	11743	Inferior	11793
Ineptly ...	... ...	11744	Inferiority	11794
Inequality	... ...	11745	Infernal	11795
Inert ...	... ...	11746	Inferred	11796
Inertia ...	... ...	11747	Inferring...	11797
Inertness	... ...	11748	Infest	11798
Inestimable	... ...	11749	Infested	11799
Inevitable	... ...	11750	Infidel	11800

Infidelity	...	...	11801	Ingenuity 11851
Infinite ...	...,	...	11802	Ingenuous 11852
Infinitely	...	...	11803	Ingenuously 11853
Infinitesimal ...	...	11804	Inglorious 11854
Infinitive	...	...	11805	Ingot 11855
Infinity ...	...	...	11806	Ingraft 11856
Infirm ...	..	...	11807	Ingrain 11857
Infirmary	...	...	11808	Ingrate 11858
Infirmity	...	...	11809	Ingratiate 11859
Inflame ...	..	...	11810	Ingratitude 11860
Inflammability	...	11811	Ingredient 11861
Inflammable ...	...	11812	Ingress 11862
Inflammation...	...	11813	Ingulf 11863
Inflammatory...	...	11814	Inhabit 11864
Inflate ...	...	...	11815	Inhabitable 11865
Inflated ...	...	...	11816	Inhabitant 11866
Inflation...	...	...	11817	Inhabiter 11867
Inflexible	...	...	11818	Inhale 11868
Inflict ...	...	...	11819	Inharmonious ... 11869
Infliction	...	...	11820	Inherent... 11870
Influence	...	...	11821	Inherit 11871
Influenced	...	...	11822	Inheritable 11872
Influential	...	...	11823	Inheritance 11873
Influenza	...	...	11824	Inheritor 11874
Influx ...	...	...	11825	Inhibit 11875
Inform ...	...	...	11826	Inhibition 11876
Informal...	...	...	11827	Inhospitable 11877
Informant	..	...	11828	Inhospitably 11878
Information	...	...	11829	Inhospitality 11879
Informed	...	...	11830	Inhuman 11880
Informer...	...	...	11831	Inhumanity 11881
Informing	...	...	11832	Inhume 11882
Informs ...	...	...	11833	Inhumation 11883
Infract ...	...	...	11834	Inimical 11884
Infraction	...	...	11835	Inimitable 11885
Infractor...	...	...	11836	Inimitably 11886
Infrangible	...	...	11837	Iniquitous 11887
Infrequency	...	...	11838	Iniquity 11888
Infrequent	...	...	11839	Initial 11889
Infringe ...	...	...	11840	Initiate 11890
Infringement ...	...	11841	Initiation 11891
Infuriate...	...	...	11842	Initiative 11892
Infuriated	...	...	11843	Initiatory 11893
Infuse ...	...	...	11844	Inject 11894
Infused ...	...	...	11845	Injected 11895
Infusibility	...	...	11846	Injection... 11896
Infusible...	...	...	11847	Injudicial 11897
Infusion ...	...	...	11848	Injudicious 11898
Ingenious	...	...	11849	Injunction 11899
Ingeniously	...	...	11850	Injure 11900

INJ	(60)	INS	120

Injured	11901	Insatiable 11951
Injurious	11902	Insatiably 11952
Injury	11903	Inscribe 11953
Injustice...	11904	Inscribed 11954
Ink	11905	Inscription 11955
Inkling	11906	Inscrutable 11956
Inky	11907	Insect 11957
Inland	11908	Insecure... 11958
Inlay	11909	Insecurely 11959
Inlaying...	11910	Insecurity 11960
Inlet	11911	Insensate 11961
Inmate	11912	Insensibility 11962
Inmost	11913	Insensible 11963
Inn	11914	Insensibly 11964
Innate	11915	Inseparable 11965
Inner	11916	Inseparably 11966
Innermost	11917	Insert 11967
Innocence	11918	Inserted 11968
Innocent...	11919	Insertion... 11969
Innocently	11920	Inset 11970
Innocuous	11921	Inshore 11971
Innovate...	11922	Inside 11972
Innovation	11923	Insidious... 11973
Innovator	11924	Insight 11974
Innoxious	11925	Insignia 11975
Innuendo	11926	Insignificance ... 11976
Innumerable	11927	Insignificant 11977
Inobservance... ...	11928	Insincere... 11978
Inoculate	11929	Insincerity 11979
Inoculated	11930	Insinuate 11980
Inoculation	11931	Insinuation 11981
Inodorous	11932	Insipid 11982
Inoffensive	11933	Insist 11983
Inoperative	11934	Insolence 11984
Inopportune	11935	Insolent 11985
Inordinate	11936	Insolently 11986
Inquest	11937	Insolidity 11987
Inquietude	11938	Insoluble 11988
Inquire	11939	Insolvency 11989
Inquirer	11940	Insolvent 11990
Inquiring	11941	Insomuch 11991
Inquiry	11942	Inspect 11992
Inquisition	11943	Inspected 11993
Inquisitive	11944	Inspection 11994
Inquisitiveness ...	11945	Inspector 11995
Inquisitorial	11946	Inspirable 11996
Inroad	11947	Inspiration 11997
Insalubrious	11948	Inspire 11998
Insane	11949	Inspired 11999
Insanity	11950	Inspiring 12000

Inspirit	12001	Insuperable 12051
Inspissate	12002	Insupportable ... 12052
Instability	12003	Insuppressible ... 12053
Instal	12004	Insurance 12054
Installation	12005	Insure 12055
Installed...	12006	Insured 12056
Instalment	12007	Insurgent 12057
Instance	12008	Insuring 12058
Instant	12009	Insurmountable ... 12059
Instantaneous ...	12010	Insurrection 12060
Instanter...	12011	Insusceptible 12061
Instantly...	12012	Intact 12062
Instate	12013	Intangible 12063
Instead	12014	Integer 12064
Instep	12015	Integral 12065
Instigate...	12016	Integrity... 12066
Instigated	12017	Integument 12067
Instigation	12018	Intellect 12068
Instigator	12019	Intellectual 12069
Instil	12020	Intellectuality ... 12070
Instillation	12021	Intellectually... ... 12071
Instilled	12022	Intelligence 12072
Instinct	12023	Intelligent 12073
Instinctive	12024	Intelligently 12074
Institute	12025	Intelligible 12075
Institution	12026	Intemperance... ... 12076
Instruct	12027	Intemperate 12077
Instructed	12028	Intemperately ... 12078
Instructing	12029	Intend 12079
Instruction	12030	Intended... 12080
Instructive	12031	Intending 12081
Instructor	12032	Intense 12082
Instructress	12033	Intensify... 12083
Instrument	12034	Intensity... 12084
Instrumental	12035	Intent 12085
Instrumentality ...	12036	Intention 12086
Insubordinate ...	12037	Intentional 12087
Insubordination ...	12038	Intentionally 12088
Insufferable	12039	Intently 12089
Insufferably	12040	Inter 12090
Insufficiency	12041	Intercede 12091
Insufficient	12042	Intercedent 12092
Insular	12043	Interceder 12093
Insulate	12044	Intercept 12094
Insulated	12045	Intercepted 12095
Insulation	12046	Intercepter 12096
Insulator	12047	Interception 12097
Insult	12048	Intercession 12098
Insulted	12049	Intercessor 12099
Insulting...	12050	Intercessory 12100

INT	(61)	INT	122

Interchange	12101	Interpreting	12151
Intercommunicate...	12102	Interregnum	12152
Intercommunion ...	12103	Interrogate	12153
Intercourse	12104	Interrogated	12154
Interdict...	12105	Interrogation... ...	12155
Interdiction	12106	Interrogatively ...	12156
Interest	12107	Interrogatory... ...	12157
Interested	12108	Interrupt	12158
Interesting	12109	Interrupted	12159
Interfere...	12110	Interruptedly... ...	12160
Interfered	12111	Interruption	12161
Interference	12112	Intersect...	12162
Interfering	12113	Intersected	12163
Interim	12114	Intersecting	12164
Interior	12115	Intersection	12165
Interjection	12116	Intersperse	12166
Interlace...	12117	Interspersed	12167
Interleave	12118	Interstice	12168
Interline...	12119	Intertwine	12169
Interlineation... ...	12120	Interval	12170
Interlocutory	12121	Intervene	12171
Interlope	12122	Intervened	12172
Interloper	12123	Intervening	12173
Interlude	12124	Intervention	12174
Intermarry	12125	Interview	12175
Intermeddle	12126	Interweave	12176
Intermediate	12127	Interwoven	12177
Interment	12128	Intestate...	12178
Interminable	12129	Intestinal	12179
Intermingle	12130	Intestine...	12180
Intermission	12131	Intestines	12181
Intermit	12132	Intimacy	12182
Intermittent	12133	Intimate...	12183
Intermix...	12134	Intimated	12184
Intermural	12135	Intimating	12185
Internal	12136	Intimation	12186
International	12137	Intimidate	12187
Internecine	12138	Intimidated	12188
Interpellation ...	12139	Intimidating	12189
Interpolate	12140	Iutimidation	12190
Interpolated	12141	Into...	12191
Interpolation	12142	Intolerable	12192
Interpose	12143	Intolerably	12193
Interposed	12144	Intolerance	12194
Interposing	12145	Intolerant	12195
Interposition	12146	Intonation	12196
Interpret...	12147	Intone	12197
Interpretation ...	12148	Intoned	12198
Interpreted	12149	Intoxicate	12199
Interpreter	12150	Intoxicated	12200

Intoxicating	...	...	12201	Invasion...	12251
Intoxication	...	...	12202	Invective	12252
Intractable	...	...	12203	Inveigh	12253
Intrench ...	...	...	12204	Inveighed	12254
Intrenched	...	...	12205	Inveigle	12255
Intrenchment...	...	12206	Inveigled	12256
Intrepid ...	...	...	12207	Invent	12257
Intrepidity	...	...	12208	Invented...	12258
Intricacy...	...	...	12209	Inventing	12259
Intricate...	...	...	12210	Invention	12260
Intrigue ...	...	...	12211	Inventive	12261
Intriguing	...	...	12212	Inventor...	12262
Intrinsic ...	...	...	12213	Inventory	12263
Introduce	...	...	12214	Inverse	12264
Introduced	...	...	12215	Inversely	12265
Introducing	...	...	12216	Inversion	12266
Introduction ...	...	12217	Invert	12267
Introductory ...	...	12218	Inverted	12268
Intromission ...	...	12219	Invest	12269
Intromit ...	...	...	12220	Invested	12270
Intromitted	...	...	12221	Investing	12271
Intrude ...	...	...	12222	Investigate	12272
Intruded	...	...	12223	Investigated	12273
Intruder ...	...	...	12224	Investigating	12274
Intruding	...	...	12225	Investigation	12275
Intrusion	...	...	12226	Investiture	12276
Intrusive	...	...	12227	Investment	12277
Intrust ...	...	...	12228	Inveterate	12278
Intrusted	...	...	12229	Invidious	12279
Intuition...	...	...	12230	Invidiously	12280
Intuitive...	...	...	12231	Invigorate	12281
Intuitively	...	...	12232	Invigorated	12282
Inundate...	...	...	12233	Invigorating	12283
Inundated	...	...	12234	Invincible	12284
Inundation	...	...	12235	Inviolable	12285
Inure	...	...	12236	Inviolate...	12286
Inured	...	...	12237	Invisible...	12287
Inutility ...	...	...	12238	Invitation	12288
Invade ...	...	...	12239	Invite	12289
Invaded ...	...	...	12240	Invited	12290
Invader ...	...	...	12241	Inviting	12291
Invading...	...	...	12242	Invocation	12292
Invalid ...	...	...	12243	Invoice	12293
Invalided	...	...	12244	Invoiced...	12294
Invalidate	...	...	12245	Invoke	12295
Invalidated	...	...	12246	Invoked	12296
Invaluable	...	...	12247	Invoking	12297
Invariable	...	...	12248	Involuntarily	12298
Invariableness	...	12249	Involuntary	12299
Invariably	...	...	12250	Involuted	12300

INV	(62)	IVY	124
Involution	12301	Irresponsible	12351
Involve	12302	Irretrievable	12352
Involved	12303	Irretrievably	12353
Involving	12304	Irreverence	12354
Invulnerable	12305	Irreverent	12355
Inward	12306	Irreverently	12356
Inwardly	12307	Irrevocable	12357
Inwrought	12308	Irrevocably	12358
Iodine	12309	Irrigate	12359
Ionic	12310	Irrigated	12360
Iota	12311	Irrigating	12361
Ipecacuanha	12312	Irrigation	12362
Irascible	12313	Irritability	12363
Ire	12314	Irritable	12364
Iridescent	12315	Irritant	12365
Iris	12316	Irritate	12366
Irish	12317	Irritated	12367
Irksome	12318	Irritation	12368
Iron	12319	Irruption	12369
Ironed	12320	Is	12370
Ironical	12321	Isinglass	12371
Irons	12322	Island	12372
Irony	12323	Islander	12373
Irradiate	12324	Isle	12374
Irradiated	12325	Islet	12375
Irradiation	12326	Isolate	12376
Irrational	12327	Isolated	12377
Irreclaimable	12328	Isolation	12378
Irreconcilable	12329	Isothermal	12379
Irrecoverable	12330	Israelite	12380
Irrecoverably	12331	Issue	12381
Irredeemable	12332	Issued	12382
Irrefutable	12333	Issuing	12383
Irregular	12334	Isthmus	12384
Irregularity	12335	It	12385
Irregularly	12336	Italian	12386
Irrelevant	12337	Italics	12387
Irreligion	12338	Itch	12388
Irreligious	12339	Itched	12389
Irremediable	12340	Item	12390
Irremovable	12341	Iterate	12391
Irreparable	12342	Iterated	12392
Irreparably	12343	Iteration	12393
Irrepressible	12344	Itinerant	12394
Irreproachable	12345	Itinerary	12395
Irresistible	12346	Itinerate	12396
Irresistibly	12347	Its	12397
Irresolute	12348	Itself	12398
Irresolution	12349	Ivory	12399
Irrespective	12350	Ivy	12400

J	...	...	...	12401	Jeopardy	...	...	12451
Jabber	...	...	...	12402	Jeremiad	...	...	12452
Jack	...	...	...	12403	Jerk	...	...	...	12453
Jackall	...	...	...	12404	Jerking	...	...	...	12454
Jackass	...	...	...	12405	Jerquing	...	...	...	12455
Jackdaw	...	...	...	12406	Jessamine	...	...	12456
Jacket	...	...	...	12407	Jest	...	...	...	12457
Jaconet	...	...	...	12408	Jested	...	...	...	12458
Jade	...	...	...	12409	Jester	...	...	...	12459
Jaded	...	...	...	12410	Jesting	...	...	...	12460
Jagg	...	...	...	12411	Jestingly	...	...	12461
Jagged	...	...	...	12412	Jesuit	...	...	12462
Jail	...	...	...	12413	Jesuitical	...	...	12463
Jailer	...	...	...	12414	Jet	...	...	...	12464
Jam	...	...	...	12415	Jetsam	...	...	...	12465
Jangle	...	...	...	12416	Jettison	...	...	...	12466
Jangler	...	...	...	12417	Jetty	...	...	...	12467
January	...	...	...	12418	Jew	...	...	...	12468
Japanese	...	...	12419	Jewel	...	...	...	12469
Japanned	...	...	12420	Jewelled	...	...	12470
Japanner	...	...	12421	Jeweller	...	...	12471
Japanning	...	...	12422	Jewellery	...	...	12472
Jar	...	...	...	12423	Jewess	...	...	...	12473
Jargon	...	...	...	12424	Jewish	...	...	...	12474
Jargonelle	...	...	12425	Jib	...	...	...	12475
Jarred	...	...	...	12426	Jibe	...	...	...	12476
Jarring	...	...	...	12427	Jibing	...	...	...	12477
Jasmine	...	...	...	12428	Jiffy	...	...	...	12478
Jasper	...	...	...	12429	Jig	...	...	...	12479
Jaundice	...	...	12430	Jilt	...	...	...	12480
Jaunt	...	...	...	12431	Jilted	...	...	...	12481
Jauntily	...	...	12432	Jilting	...	...	...	12482
Jaunty	...	...	...	12433	Jingle	...	...	...	12483
Javanese	...	...	12434	Jingling	...	...	12484
Javelin	...	...	...	12435	Job	...	...	...	12485
Jaw	...	...	...	12436	Jobber	...	...	...	12486
Jay	...	...	...	12437	Jockey	...	...	...	12487
Jealous	...	...	...	12438	Jocose	...	...	...	12488
Jealousy	...	...	12439	Jocosely	...	...	12489
Jean	...	...	...	12440	Jocoseness	...	...	12490
Jeer	...	...	...	12441	Jocular	...	...	12491
Jeered	...	...	...	12442	Jocularly	...	...	12492
Jeering	...	...	...	12443	Jocund	...	...	12493
Jehovah	...	...	12444	Jog	...	...	...	12494
Jelly	...	...	...	12445	Jogged	...	...	...	12495
Jennet	...	...	...	12446	Jogging	...	...	12496
Jenny	...	...	...	12447	Join	...	...	...	12497
Jeopard	...	...	...	12448	Joined	...	...	...	12498
Jeopardize	...	...	12449	Joiner	...	...	...	12499
Jeopardized	...	...	12450	Joinery	...	...	...	12500

JOI	(63)	JUX	126

Joining	12501	Jugular	12551
Joint	12502	Juice	12552
Jointed	12503	Juicy	12553
Jointly	12504	Jujube	12554
Jointure	12505	Julep	12555
Joist	12506	July...	12556
Joke	12507	Jumble	12557
Joking	12508	Jumbled	12558
Jolly	12509	Jumbling	12559
Jolt	12510	Jump	12560
Jolted	12511	Jumped	12561
Jolting	12512	Jumping	12562
Jostle	12513	Jumps	12563
Jostled	12514	Junction	12564
Jostling	12515	Juncture	12565
Jot	12516	June	12566
Jotted	12517	Jungle	12567
Journal	12518	Junior	12568
Journalist	12519	Junk	12569
Journey	12520	Junket	12570
Journeying	12521	Junta	12571
Journeyman	12522	Juridical	12572
Jovial	12523	Jurisconsult	12573
Jovially	12524	Jurisdiction	12574
Joy	12525	Jurisprudence... ...	12575
Joyful	12526	Jurist	12576
Joyfully	12527	Juror	12577
Joyless	12528	Jury...	12578
Joyous	12529	Just	12579
Jubilant	12530	Justice	12580
Jubilation	12531	Justiceship	12581
Jubilee	12532	Justiciary	12582
Judaical	12533	Justifiable	12583
Judaism	12534	Justifiably	12584
Judaize	12535	Justification	12585
Judaizing	12536	Justificatory	12586
Judge	12537	Justified	12587
Judged	12538	Justifier	12588
Judgeship	12539	Justify	12589
Judging	12540	Justifying	12590
Judgment	12541	Justly	12591
Judicature	12542	Justness	12592
Judicial	12543	Jut	12593
Judiciary...	12544	Jute...	12594
Judicious	12545	Jutted	12595
Judiciously	12546	Jutting	12596
Jug	12547	Juvenescence	12597
Juggle	12548	Juvenile	12598
Juggler	12549	Juvenility	12599
Juggling	12550	Juxta	12600

K	12601	
Kaffer	12602	
Kaffrarian	12603	
Kale	12604	
Kaleidoscope... ...	12605	
Kali	12606	
Kalif	12607	
Kalmuck	12608	
Kangaroo	12609	
Kaolin	12610	
Kedge	12611	
Kedger	12612	
Keel	12613	
Keelage	12614	
Keeled	12615	
Keelhaul	12616	
Keeling	12617	
Keen	12618	
Keenly	12619	
Keenness	12620	
Keep	12621	
Keeper	12622	
Keeping	12623	
Keeps	12624	
Keepsake	12625	
Keeve	12626	
Keg...	12627	
Keisar	12628	
Kellow	12629	
Kelp	12630	
Kelpie	12631	
Kelson	12632	
Kemp	12633	
Ken...	12634	
Kennel	12635	
Kentish	12636	
Kentledge	12637	
Kept	12638	
Kerbstone	12639	
Kerchief...	12640	
Kermes	12641	
Kern	12642	
Kernel	12643	
Kerosine...	12644	
Kersey	12645	
Kerseymere	12646	
Kestrel	12647	
Ketch	12648	
Ketchup...	12649	
Kettle	12650	
Key...	12651
Keystone	12652
Khan	12653
Kick	12654
Kicked	12655
Kicking	12656
Kicks	12657
Kickshaw	12658
Kid	12659
Kidderminster ...	12660
Kidnap	12661
Kidnapped	12662
Kidnapper	12663
Kidnapping	12664
Kidneys	12665
Kilderkin	12666
Kill...	12667
Killed	12668
Killer	12669
Killing	12670
Kills	12671
Kiln	12672
Kilogramme	12673
Kilolitre...	12674
Kilometre	12675
Kilt...	12676
Kilted	12677
Kimbo	12678
Kin...	12679
Kind	12680
Kindle	12681
Kindled	12682
Kindler	12683
Kindles	12684
Kindless...	12685
Kindliness	12686
Kindling...	12687
Kindly	12688
Kindness	12689
Kindred	12690
Kine	12691
King	12692
Kingcraft	12693
Kingdom	12694
Kingfisher	12695
Kingless...	12696
Kingly	12697
Kings	12698
Kingship	12699
Kink	12700

Kinked	...	...	...	12701	Kneeling 12751
Kinking	...	...	...	12702	Knell 12752
Kinks	...	...	...	12703	Knelling... 12753
Kino	...	...	...	12704	Knelt 12754
Kinsfolk	...	...	...	12705	Knew 12755
Kinsman	...	...	...	12706	Knicknack 12756
Kinswoman	...	...	12707	Knicknackery ... 12757
Kiosk	...	...	...	12708	Knife 12758
Kip	...	...	...	12709	Knight 12759
Kirb	...	...	...	12710	Knighted 12760
Kirk	...	...	...	12711	Knighthood 12761
Kirschwasser	...	...	12712	Knightly 12762
Kirtle	...	...	...	12713	Knit 12763
Kirtled	...	...	...	12714	Knitted 12764
Kiss	...	...	...	12715	Knitter 12765
Kissed	...	...	...	12716	Knitting... 12766
Kisses	...	...	...	12717	Knob 12767
Kissing	...	...	...	12718	Knobbed 12768
Kit	...	...	...	12719	Knobby 12769
Kitchen	...	...	...	12720	Knock 12770
Kite	...	...	...	12721	Knocked 12771
Kith	...	...	...	12722	Knocker... 12772
Kitten	...	...	...	12723	Knocking 12773
Kittened	...	...	...	12724	Knocks 12774
Kleptomania	...	...	12725	Knoll 12775
Klick	...	...	...	12726	Knot 12776
Klicked	...	...	...	12727	Knotless... 12777
Klicking	...	...	...	12728	Knots 12778
Knab	...	...	...	12729	Knotted 12779
Knabbed	...	...	12730	Knottiness 12780
Knack	...	...	...	12731	Knotting 12781
Knacker	...	...	...	12732	Knotty 12782
Knap	...	...	...	12733	Knout 12783
Knapped	...	...	12734	Knouted... 12784
Knapping	...	...	12735	Know 12785
Knapsack	...	...	12736	Knower 12786
Knarled	...	...	...	12737	Knowing 12787
Knave	...	...	...	12738	Knowingly 12788
Knavery	...	...	...	12739	Knowledge 12789
Knavish	...	...	...	12740	Known 12790
Knavishly	...	...	12741	Knows 12791
Knavishness	...	...	12742	Knuckle... 12792
Knead	...	...	...	12743	Knuckled 12793
Kneaded	...	...	...	12744	Knuckling 12794
Kneading	...	...	12745	Koff 12795
Kneads	...	...	...	12746	Kopeck 12796
Knee	...	...	...	12747	Koran 12797
Kneed	...	...	...	12748	Kremlin 12798
Kneel	...	...	...	12749	Kreutzer... 12799
Kneels	...	...	...	12750	Kyrie 12800

L	12801	Ladder 12851
La	12802	Lade 12852
Labefaction	12803	Laded 12853
Label	12804	Laden 12854
Labelled...	12805	Lades 12855
Labial	12806	Lading 12856
Labiate	12807	Ladle 12857
Laboratory	12808	Lady 12858
Laborious	12809	Ladyship 12859
Laboriously	12810	Lag... 12860
Labour	12811	Laggard... 12861
Laboured	12812	Lagged 12862
Labourer	12813	Lagging 12863
Labouring	12814	Lagoon 12864
Laburnum	12815	Laical 12865
Labyrinth	12816	Laid 12866
Labyrinthian ...	12817	Lain 12867
Lac	12818	Lair... 12868
Lace	12819	Laird 12869
Laced	12820	Laity 12870
Lacerable	12821	Lake 12871
Lacerate...	12822	Lakelet 12872
Lacerated	12823	Lama 12873
Lacerating	12824	Lamb 12874
Laceration	12825	Lambent... 12875
Lacerative	12826	Lambskin 12876
Lachrymal	12827	Lame 12877
Lachrymation ...	12828	Lamed 12878
Lachrymatory ...	12829	Lamely 12879
Lachrymose	12830	Lameness 12880
Lacing	12831	Lament 12881
Lack	12832	Lamented 12882
Lackadaisical... ...	12833	Lamentable 12883
Lacked	12834	Lamentably 12884
Lackey	12835	Lamentation 12885
Lacking	12836	Lamenting 12886
Laconic	12837	Lamentingly 12887
Laconically	12838	Lamina 12888
Laconicism	12839	Laminate 12889
Lacquer	12840	Lammas... 12890
Lacquered	12841	Lamp 12891
Lactation	12842	Lamplight 12892
Lacteal	12843	Lampoon 12893
Lacteous...	12844	Lampooned 12894
Latescent	12845	Lampooner 12895
Lactiferous	12846	Lamprey... 12896
Lactometer	12847	Lance 12897
Lacuna	12848	Lanced 12898
Lacustrine	12849	Lanceolate 12899
Lad...	12850	Lancer 12900

LAN	(65)	LAU	130

Lancet	...	...	12901	Large	...	...	...	12951

Lancet	12901	Large	12951
Lanciform	12902	Largely	12952
Land	12903	Largeness	12953
Landau	12904	Largess	12954
Landed	12905	Lark	12955
Landholder	12906	Larva	12956
Landing	12907	Larynx	12957
Landlady	12908	Lascar	12958
Landlock	12909	Lascivious	12959
Landlocked	12910	Lasciviously	12960
Landlord	12911	Lasciviousness ...	12961
Landmark	12912	Lash	12962
Landscape	12913	Lashed	12963
Landslip	12914	Lashing	12964
Landsman	12915	Lass	12965
Landward	12916	Lassitude	12966
Lane	12917	Lasso	12967
Langrage	12918	Last	12968
Langsyne	12919	Lasted	12969
Language	12920	Lasting	12970
Languid	12921	Lastingly	12971
Languidly	12922	Lastly	12972
Languish	12923	Lasts	12973
Languished	12924	Latch	12974
Languishing	12925	Latchet	12975
Languishingly ...	12926	Late	12976
Languishment ...	12927	Lateen	12977
Languor	12928	Lately	12978
Laniard	12929	Latent	12979
Laniferous	12930	Later	12980
Lank	12931	Lateral	12981
Lankness	12932	Laterally	12982
Lanky	12933	Latere	12983
Lansquenet	12934	Lath	12984
Lantern	12935	Lathe	12985
Lap	12936	Lather	12986
Lapel	12937	Lathered	12987
Lapful	12938	Latin	12988
Lapidary	12939	Latitude	12989
Lappet	12940	Latitudinal	12990
Lapsable	12941	Latitudinarian ...	12991
Lapse	12942	Latter	12992
Lapsed	12943	Latterly	12993
Lapsing	12944	Lattice	12994
Larboard	12945	Latticed	12995
Larceny	12946	Laud	12996
Larch	12947	Lauded	12997
Lard	12948	Laudable	12998
Larded	12949	Laudably	12999
Larder	12950	Laudanum	13000

Laudatory	13001	Laziness 13051
Lauder	13002	Lazulite 13052
Lauding	13003	Lazy 13053
Laugh	13004	Lea 13054
Laughed	13005	Lead 13055
Laughable	13006	Leaden 13056
Laughably	13007	Leader 13057
Laugher	13008	Leadership 13058
Laughing	13009	Leading 13059
Laughingly	13010	Leads 13060
Laughter	13011	Leaf 13061
Launch	13012	Leafiness 13062
Launched	13013	Leafless 13063
Launching	13014	Leafy 13064
Laundress	13015	League 13065
Laundry	13016	Leagued 13066
Laureate	13017	Leaguer 13067
Laurel	13018	Leak 13068
Lava	13019	Leakage 13069
Lavation	13020	Leaked 13070
Lavatory	13021	Leaking 13071
Lave	13022	Leaky 13072
Laved	13023	Lean 13073
Lavement	13024	Leaned 13074
Lavender	13025	Leaning 13075
Laver	13026	Leanly 13076
Lavish	13027	Leanness 13077
Lavished	13028	Leans 13078
Lavishing	13029	Leant 13079
Lavisher	13030	Leap 13080
Lavishly	13031	Leaper 13081
Lavishness	13032	Leaping 13082
Law	13033	Leaps 13083
Lawful	13034	Learn 13084
Lawgiver	13035	Learned 13085
Lawk	13036	Learnedly 13086
Lawless	13037	Learner 13087
Lawn	13038	Learning 13088
Lawsuit	13039	Learns 13089
Lawyer	13040	Leasable 13090
Lax	13041	Lease 13091
Laxative	13042	Leased 13092
Laxity	13043	Leasehold 13093
Laxly	13044	Leash 13094
Lay	13045	Leasing 13095
Layer	13046	Least 13096
Lays	13047	Leather 13097
Layman	13048	Leathern 13098
Lazaroni	13049	Leathery 13099
Lazily	13050	Leave 13100

LEA	(66)	LES	132

Leaven	13101	Legislation	13151
Leavened	13102	Legislative	13152
Leavening	13103	Legislator	13153
Leaves	13104	Legislature	13154
Leaving	13105	Legist	13155
Leavings	13106	Legitimacy	13156
Lecherous	13107	Legitimate	13157
Lecherously	13108	Legitimation	13158
Lechery	13109	Legitimist	13159
Lection	13110	Legitimize	13160
Lecture	13111	Leisure	13161
Lectured	13112	Leisurely	13162
Lecturer	13113	Lemon	13163
Lectureship	13114	Lemonade	13164
Lectum	13115	Lend	13165
Led	13116	Lends	13166
Ledge	13117	Lender	13167
Ledger	13118	Lending	13168
Lee	13119	Length	13169
Leech	13120	Lengthen	13170
Leek	13121	Lengthened	13171
Leer	13122	Lengthening	13172
Leering	13123	Lengthily	13173
Leeringly	13124	Lengthiness	13174
Lees	13125	Lengthwise	13175
Leeward	13126	Lengthy	13176
Leeway	13127	Leniency	13177
Left	13128	Lenient	13178
Leg	13129	Leniently	13179
Legacy	13130	Lenitive	13180
Legal	13131	Lenity	13181
Legality	13132	Lens	13182
Legalize	13133	Lent	13183
Legalized	13134	Lenten	13184
Legally	13135	Lenticular	13185
Legate	13136	Lentil	13186
Legatee	13137	Leonine	13187
Legation	13138	Leopard	13188
Legend	13139	Leper	13189
Legendary	13140	Leprosy	13190
Legerdemain	13141	Leprous	13191
Legged	13142	Lept	13192
Legging	13143	Lesion	13193
Legibility	13144	Less	13194
Legible	13145	Lessee	13195
Legibly	13146	Lessen	13196
Legion	13147	Lesser	13197
Legionary	13148	Lesson	13198
Legislate	13149	Lessor	13199
Legislated	13150	Lest	13200

Let	13201	Liberator 13251
Lethal	13202	Libertine 13252
Lethargic	13203	Libertinism 13253
Lethargically... ...	13204	Liberty 13254
Lethargy	13205	Libidinous 13255
Lethean	13206	Librarian 13256
Lets	13207	Library 13257
Letter	13208	Libration 13258
Lettered...	13209	Libretto 13259
Lettering	13210	License 13260
Letting	13211	Licensed... 13261
Lettuce	13212	Licenser 13262
Levant	13213	Licensing 13263
Levee	13214	Licentiate 13264
Level	13215	Licentious 13265
Levelled...	13216	Licentiously 13266
Leveller	13217	Licentiousness ... 13267
Levelling	13218	Lichen 13268
Lever	13219	Lick 13269
Leverage	13220	Licked 13270
Leveret	13221	Licking 13271
Levied	13222	Lid 13272
Levite	13223	Lie 13273
Levitical...	13224	Lied 13274
Leviticus	13225	Lief... 13275
Levity	13226	Lien 13276
Levy	13227	Lies... 13277
Lewd	13228	Lieu 13278
Lewdly	13229	Lieutenancy 13279
Lexicographer ...	13230	Lieutenant 13280
Lexicography... ...	13231	Life... 13281
Lexicon	13232	Lifeless 13282
Liable	13233	Lifetime 13283
Liability...	13234	Lift 13284
Liaison	13235	Lifted 13285
Liar	13236	Lifter 13286
Lias	13237	Lifting 13287
Libation...	13238	Lifts 13288
Libel	13239	Ligament 13289
Libelled	13240	Ligature 13290
Libeller	13241	Light 13291
Libelling	13242	Lighted 13292
Libellous	13243	Lighten 13293
Liberal	13244	Lighter 13294
Liberality	13245	Lighterman 13295
Liberally	13246	Lighthouse 13296
Liberate	13247	Lighting... 13297
Liberated	13248	Lightly 13298
Liberating	13249	Lightness 13299
Liberation	13250	Lightning 13300

Lights	13301	Lingeringly	13351
Lightsome	13302	Lingual	13352
Ligneous...	13303	Linguiform	13353
Ligniform	13304	Linguist	13354
Lignite	13305	Liniment	13355
Lignitic	13306	Lining	13356
Like	13307	Link	13357
Liked	13308	Linked	13358
Likelihood	13309	Linnet	13359
Likely	13310	Linseed	13360
Liken	13311	Lint...	13361
Likened	13312	Lintel	13362
Likeness...	13313	Lion	13363
Likening	13314	Lioness	13364
Likewise...	13315	Lionize	13365
Liking	13316	Lionized...	13366
Lilac	13317	Lip	13367
Liliputian	13318	Liquefaction	13368
Lily	13319	Liquefied	13369
Limb	13320	Liquefy	13370
Limber	13321	Liquefying	13371
Limbered	13322	Liquescent	13372
Limbo	13323	Liqueur	13373
Lime	13324	Liquid	13374
Limestone	13325	Liquidate	13375
Liming	13326	Liquidated	13376
Limit	13327	Liquidating	13377
Limitable	13328	Liquidation	13378
Limitation	13329	Liquidator	13379
Limited	13330	Liquor	13380
Limiting...	13331	Liquorice	13381
Limner	13332	Lisp...	13382
Limp	13333	Lisped	13383
Limpet	13334	Lisper	13384
Limpid	13335	Lisping	13385
Limping...	13336	Lissom	13386
Linch	13337	List	13387
Linden	13338	Listed	13388
Line	13339	Listen	13389
Lineage	13340	Listened	13390
Lineal	13341	Listener	13391
Lineally	13342	Listening	13392
Lineament	13343	Listless	13393
Linear	13344	Lists	13394
Lined	13345	Lit	13395
Linen	13346	Litany	13396
Linger	13347	Literal	13397
Lingered...	13348	Literally...	13398
Lingerer	13349	Literary	13399
Lingering	13350	Literate	13400

Literati	13401	Loan 13451
Literatim	13402	Loathe 13452
Literature	13403	Loathed 13453
Lithe	13404	Loathing 13454
Litheness	13405	Loathingly 13455
Lithesome	13406	Loathsome 13456
Lithograph	13407	Loathsomeness ... 13457
Lithographed... ...	13408	Loaves 13458
Lithographer ...	13409	Lobbied 13459
Lithography ...	13410	Lobby 13460
Lithotomy	13411	Lobe 13461
Litigant	13412	Lobster 13462
Litigate	13413	Local 13463
Litigated	13414	Locality 13464
Litigation	13415	Localize 13465
Litigious...	13416	Localized 13466
Litmus	13417	Locally 13467
Litre	13418	Locate 13468
Litter	13419	Located 13469
Littered	13420	Location... 13470
Little	13421	Loch 13471
Littleness	13422	Lock 13472
Littoral	13423	Locked 13473
Liturgical	13424	Locker 13474
Liturgy	13425	Locket 13475
Live	13426	Locksmith 13476
Lived	13427	Locomotion 13477
Livelihood	13428	Locomotive 13478
Liveliness	13429	Locust 13479
Lively	13430	Lode 13480
Liver	13431	Lodge 13481
Livery	13432	Lodged 13482
Liveryman	13433	Lodger 13483
Livid	13434	Lodging 13484
Lividness	13435	Lodgment 13485
Living	13436	Loft... 13486
Lizard	13437	Loftily 13487
Llama	13438	Loftiness... 13488
Lloyds	13439	Lofty 13489
Lo	13440	Log... 13490
Load	13441	Logarithm 13491
Loaded	13442	Logged 13492
Loading	13443	Loggerhead 13493
Loads	13444	Logic 13494
Loadstar... ...	13445	Logical 13495
Loadstone	13446	Logically 13496
Loaf	13447	Logician... 13497
Loafing	13448	Logwood 13498
Loam	13449	Loin 13499
Loamy	13450	Loiter 13500

Loitered	13501	Losing 13551
Loiterer	13502	Loss 13552
Loitering	13503	Lost 13553
Loll	13504	Lot 13554
Lolled	13505	Loth 13555
Lolling	13506	Lotion 13556
Lollipop	13507	Lottery 13557
Lone	13508	Lotus 13558
Loneliness	13509	Loud 13559
Lonely	13510	Loudly 13560
Lonesome	13511	Loudness 13561
Lonesomeness	13512	Lough 13562
Long	13513	Lounge 13563
Longed	13514	Lounged 13564
Longer	13515	Lounger 13565
Longest	13516	Lounging 13566
Longevity	13517	Louse 13567
Longing	13518	Lousy 13568
Longish	13519	Lout 13569
Longitude	13520	Loutish 13570
Longitudinal	13521	Lovable 13571
Loo	13522	Love 13572
Look	13523	Loved 13573
Looked	13524	Loveliness 13574
Looking	13525	Lovely 13575
Loom	13526	Lover 13576
Loomed	13527	Loving 13577
Looming	13528	Lovingly 13578
Loon	13529	Low 13579
Loop	13530	Lower 13580
Loose	13531	Lowered 13581
Loosed	13532	Lowering 13582
Loosely	13533	Loweringly 13583
Loosen	13534	Lowest 13584
Looseness	13535	Lowing 13585
Lop	13536	Lowland 13586
Lopped	13537	Lowlily 13587
Lopsided	13538	Lowliness 13588
Loquacious	13539	Lowly 13589
Loquacity	13540	Lowness 13590
Lord	13541	Loyal 13591
Lorded	13542	Loyalist 13592
Lordliness	13543	Loyally 13593
Lordly	13544	Loyalty 13594
Lordship	13545	Lozenge 13595
Lore	13546	Lubber 13596
Lorgnette	13547	Lubberly 13597
Lose	13548	Lubricant 13598
Loser	13549	Lubricate 13599
Loses	13550	Lubricated 13600

Lubricating	13601	Luniform 13651
Lubricator	13602	Lunulate... 13652
Lucid	13603	Lurch 13653
Lucidity	13604	Lurched 13654
Lucidly	13605	Lurcher 13655
Lucifer	13606	Lurching 13656
Luck	13607	Lure 13657
Luckily	13608	Lured 13658
Luckless...	13609	Lurid 13659
Lucky	13610	Luring 13660
Lucrative	13611	Lurk 13661
Lucre	13612	Lurked 13662
Lucubrate	13613	Lurking 13663
Lucubration	13614	Luscious... 13664
Ludicrous	13615	Lust 13665
Ludicrously	13616	Lusted 13666
Lues	13617	Lustful 13667
Luff...	13618	Lustily 13668
Luffed	13619	Lustiness 13669
Lug...	13620	Lusting 13670
Luggage...	13621	Lustre 13671
Lugged	13622	Lustreless 13672
Lugger	13623	Lustrous... 13673
Lugubrious	13624	Lustrously 13674
Lugubriously... ...	13625	Lustrum 13675
Lukewarm	13626	Lusty 13676
Lull...	13627	Lute 13677
Lulled	13628	Lutheran 13678
Lumbago	13629	Luxuriance 13679
Lumbar	13630	Luxuriant 13680
Lumber	13631	Luxuriantly 13681
Lumbered	13632	Luxuriate 13682
Lumbering	13633	Luxuriated 13683
Luminary	13634	Luxuriating 13684
Luminous	13635	Luxurious 13685
Lump	13636	Luxuriousness ... 13686
Lumped	13637	Luxury 13687
Lumping	13638	Lyceum 13688
Lumpish...	13639	Lying 13689
Lumpy	13640	Lyingly 13690
Lunacy	13641	Lymph 13691
Lunar	13642	Lymphate 13692
Lunated	13643	Lymphatic 13693
Lunatic	13644	Lynch 13694
Lunation	13645	Lynched... 13695
Lunch	13646	Lynching 13696
Lunched...	13647	Lynx 13697
Luncheon	13648	Lyre 13698
Lunge	13649	Lyric 13699
Lungs	13650	Lyrical 13700

M	(69)	MAL	138

M	13701	Magnifying	13751
Macadamize	13702	Magniloquence ...	13752
Macadamized... ...	13703	Magniloquent... ...	13753
Macaroni	13704	Magnitude	13754
Mace	13705	Magpie	13755
Macerate	13706	Maharajah	13756
Maceration	13707	Mahogany	13757
Machiavelian... ...	13708	Maid	13758
Machination	13709	Maiden	13759
Machine...	13710	Maidenhood	13760
Machinery	13711	Maidenly	13761
Machinist	13712	Mail	13762
Mackerel	13713	Mailed	13763
Mackintosh	13714	Mails	13764
Mad	13715	Maim	13765
Madam	13716	Maimed	13766
Madden	13717	Maiming...	13767
Maddened	13718	Main	13768
Maddening	13719	Mainly	13769
Madder	13720	Maintain...	13770
Made	13721	Maintainable	13771
Madly	13722	Maintained	13772
Madman...	13723	Maintaining	13773
Madness...	13724	Maintenance	13774
Madrigal	13725	Maize	13775
Magazine	13726	Majestic...	13776
Maggot	13727	Majesty	13777
Magic	13728	Major	13778
Magical	13729	Majority...	13779
Magician	13730	Make	13780
Magisterial	13731	Maker	13781
Magistracy	13732	Makes	13782
Magistrate	13733	Making	13783
Magnanimity	13734	Malady	13784
Magnanimous ...	13735	Malapert	13785
Magnanimously ...	13736	Malaria	13786
Magnate...	13737	Malcontent	13787
Magnesia	13738	Male	13788
Magnet	13739	Malediction	13789
Magnetic	13740	Malefactor	13790
Magnetism	13741	Maleficence	13791
Magnetize	13742	Maleficent	13792
Magnetized	13743	Malevolence	13793
Magnetizer	13744	Malevolent	13794
Magnificence	13745	Malformation... ...	13795
Magnificent	13746	Malice	13796
Magnificently... ...	13747	Malicious	13797
Magnified	13748	Maliciously	13798
Magnifier	13749	Maliciousness... ...	13799
Magnify	13750	Malign	13800

139 MAL	(70)	MAR	
Malignant	13801	Manifesto	13851
Maligned	13802	Manifold	13852
Maligner	13803	Manipulate	13853
Malignity	13804	Manipulated	13854
Mall	13805	Manipulating	13855
Malleability	13806	Manipulation	13856
Malleable	13807	Mankind	13857
Mallet	13808	Manliness	13858
Malpractice	13809	Manly	13859
Malt	13810	Manned	13860
Malting	13811	Manner	13861
Maltreat	13812	Mannerism	13862
Maltreated	13813	Mannerist	13863
Maltreating	13814	Manners	13864
Maltreatment	13815	Manœuvre	13865
Maltster	13816	Manœuvred	13866
Mamma	13817	Manœuvrer	13867
Mammal	13818	Manor	13868
Mammon	13819	Manorial	13869
Mammoth	13820	Manse	13870
Man	13821	Mansion	13871
Manacle	13822	Manslaughter	13872
Manacled	13823	Mantilla	13873
Manage	13824	Mantle	13874
Manageable	13825	Mantled	13875
Manageably	13826	Mantling	13876
Managed	13827	Manual	13877
Management	13828	Manufactory	13878
Manager	13829	Manufacture	13879
Managing	13830	Manufactured	13880
Mandarin	13831	Manufacturer	13881
Mandate	13832	Manufacturing	13882
Mandatory	13833	Manumission	13883
Mane	13834	Manumit	13884
Manfully	13835	Manumitted	13885
Mange	13836	Manure	13886
Manger	13837	Manured	13887
Mangle	13838	Manuring	13888
Mangled	13839	Manuscript	13889
Mangling	13840	Manx	13890
Mangold	13841	Many	13891
Mangy	13842	Map	13892
Manhood	13843	Mapped	13893
Mania	13844	Mar	13894
Maniac	13845	Maranatha	13895
Maniacal	13846	Maraschino	13896
Manifest	13847	Maraud	13897
Manifestation	13848	Marauder	13898
Manifested	13849	Marauding	13899
Manifestly	14850	Marble	13900

MAR	(70)	MAT	140

March	13901	Marvel	13951
Marched...	13902	Marvelled	13952
Marches	13903	Marvellous	13953
Marching	13904	Masculine	13954
Marchioness	13905	Mash	13955
Mare	13906	Mashed	13956
Margin	13907	Mashing...	13957
Marginal	13908	Mask	13958
Marine	13909	Masked	13959
Mariner	13910	Masker	13960
Marital	13911	Masking...	13961
Maritime	13912	Mason	13962
Mark	13913	Masonic	13963
Marked	13914	Masonry...	13964
Marker	13915	Masquerade	13965
Market	13916	Masquerader	13966
Marketable	13917	Mass	13967
Marketing	13918	Massacre	13968
Marking	13919	Massacred	13969
Marksman	13920	Massive	13970
Marlstone	13921	Massiveness	13971
Marmalade	13922	Mast	13972
Maroon	13023	Masted	13973
Marplot	13924	Master	13974
Marque	13925	Mastered	13975
Marquis	13926	Masterly...	13976
Marquetry	13927	Mastery	13977
Marquisate	13928	Masticate	13978
Marred	13929	Masticated	13979
Marriage	13930	Masticating	13980
Marriageable... ...	13931	Mastication	13981
Married	13932	Masticatory	13982
Marrow	13933	Mastiff	13983
Marry	13934	Mat...	13984
Marrying	13935	Match	13985
Marsh	13936	Matched...	13986
Marshal	13937	Matching	13987
Marshalled	13938	Matchless	13988
Marshalling	13939	Mate	13989
Marshy	13940	Mated	13990
Mart	13941	Material	13991
Martello	13942	Materialize	13992
Marten	13943	Materially	13993
Martial	13944	Maternal	13994
Martinet ... ..., ...	13945	Maternally	13995
Martingale	13946	Maternity	13996
Martinmas	13947	Mathematician ...	13997
Martyr	13948	Mathematics	13998
Martyrdom	13949	Matins	13999
Martyrology	13950	Matricidal	14000

Matricide	...	...	14001	Meanly	14051
Matriculate	...	...	14002	Meanness	14052
Matriculated	...	...	14003	Means	14053
Matriculation	...	...	14004	Meant	14054
Matrimonial	...	...	14005	Measles	14055
Matrimonially	...	...	14006	Measly	14056
Matrimony	...	...	14007	Measurable	14057
Matrix	...	...	14008	Measure	14058
Matron ...	...	...	14009	Measured	14059
Matronly	...	...	14010	Measurement	14060
Matted ...	...	...	14011	Measuring	14061
Matter ...	...	...	14012	Meat	14062
Matting ...	...	...	14013	Mechanic	14063
Mattock ...	...	...	14014	Mechanical	14064
Mattress ...	...	...	14015	Mechanically	14065
Mature ...	...	...	14016	Mechanician	14066
Matured ...	...	...	14017	Mechanics	14067
Maturely	...	...	14018	Mechanism	14068
Maturing	...	...	14019	Mechanist	14069
Maturity ...	...	...	14020	Medal	14070
Matutinal	...	...	14021	Medallion	14071
Maudlin ...	...	...	14022	Meddle	14072
Maul ...	...	...	14023	Meddled	14073
Mauled ...	...	...	14024	Meddler	14074
Maunday	...	...	14025	Meddlesome	14075
Mausoleum	...	...	14026	Meddling	14076
Maw ...	...	...	14027	Medial	14077
Mawkish	...	...	14028	Mediate	14078
Mawkishness ...	...	...	14029	Mediated	14079
Maxillary	...	...	14030	Mediating	14080
Maxim ...	...	...	14031	Mediation '	14081
Maximum	...	...	14032	Mediatize	14082
May ...	...	...	14033	Mediator	14083
Maying ...	...	...	14034	Mediatorial	14084
Mayor ...	...	...	14035	Mediatory	14085
Mayoralty	...	...	14036	Medicable	14086
Mayoress	...	...	14037	Medical	14087
Maze ...	...	...	14038	Medically	14088
Mazy ...	...	...	14039	Medicate	14089
Me	...	...	14040	Medicated	14090
Mead ...	...	...	14041	Medicinal	14091
Meadow ...	...	...	14042	Medicinally	14092
Meagre ...	...	...	14043	Medicine	14093
Meagreness	...	...	14044	Medieval	14094
Meal ...	...	...	14045	Mediocre	14095
Mealy ...	...	...	14046	Mediocrity	14096
Mean ...	...	...	14047	Meditate	14097
Meandering ...	...	...	14048	Meditated	14098
Meaning ...	...	...	14049	Meditating	14099
Meaningless ...	...	...	14050	Meditation	14100

Meditative	...	14101	Menacing	... ...	14151
Mediterranean	...	14102	Menagerie	... ...	14152
Medium ...	... ...	14103	Mend ...	... ...	14153
Medlar ...	... ...	14104	Mendacious	... ...	14154
Medley ...	... ...	14105	Mendacity	... ...	14155
Medullary	... ...	14106	Mended ...	... ...	14156
Meek ...	... ...	14107	Mendicancy	... ...	14157
Meekly ...	... ...	14108	Mendicant	... ...	14158
Meekness	... ...	14109	Mendicity	... ...	14159
Meerschaum ...	...	14110	Mending...	... ...	14160
Meet ...	... ...	14111	Menial ...	... ...	14161
Meeting ...	... ...	14112	Menses ...	... ...	14162
Meets ...	... ...	14113	Mensuration ...	...	14163
Melancholic ...	...	14114	Mental ...	... ...	14164
Melancholy	... ...	14115	Mentally...	... ...	14165
Mêlée ...	... ...	14116	Mention ...	... ...	14166
Meliorate	... ...	14117	Mentioned	... ...	14167
Meliorated	... ...	14118	Mentioning	... ...	14168
Melioration	... ...	14119	Mentor ...	... ...	14166
Mellifluous	... ...	14120	Mephitic	... ...	14170
Mellow ...	... ...	14121	Mercantile	... ...	14171
Mellowed	... ...	14122	Mercenary	... ...	14172
Mellowness	... ...	14123	Mercer ...	... ...	14173
Melodious	... ...	14124	Mercery ...	... ...	14174
Melodramatic	...	14125	Merchandise ...	...	14175
Melodrama	... ...	14126	Merchant	... ...	14176
Melody ...	... ...	14127	Merciful ...	... ...	14177
Melon ...	... ...	14128	Mercifully	... ...	14178
Melt ...	... ...	14129	Merciless	... ...	14179
Melted ...	... ...	14130	Mercurial	... ...	14180
Melter ...	... ...	14131	Mercurially ...	...	14181
Melting ...	... ...	14132	Mercury ...	... ...	14182
Melts ...	... ...	14133	Mercy ...	... ...	14183
Member ...	... ...	14134	Mere ...	... ...	14184
Membered	... ...	14135	Merely ...	... ...	14185
Membership ...	...	14136	Meretricious ...	...	14186
Membrane	... ...	14137	Merge ...	... ...	14187
Membraneous	...	14138	Merged ...	... ...	14188
Memento	... ...	14139	Merging ...	... ...	14189
Memoir ...	... ...	14140	Meridian	... ...	14190
Memorable	... ...	14141	Meridional	... ...	14191
Memorably	... ...	14142	Merino ...	... ...	14192
Memorandum	...	14143	Merit ...	... ...	14193
Memorial	... ...	14144	Merited ...	... ...	14194
Memorialist ...	...	14145	Meritorious	... ...	14195
Memorialize ...	...	14146	Merlin ...	... ...	14196
Memorialized...	...	14147	Mermaid	... ...	14197
Memory ...	... ...	14148	Merrily ...	... ...	14198
Menace ...	... ...	14149	Merriment	... ...	14199
Menaced...	... ...	14150	Merry ...	... ...	14200

Mesh	14201	Microscopic 14251
Mesmerism	14202	Mid... 14252
Mesmerist	14203	Middle 14253
Mess	14204	Middling 14254
Message	14205	Midge 14255
Messed	14206	Midland 14256
Messenger	14207	Midnight 14257
Messiah	14208	Midship 14258
Messieurs	14209	Midshipman 14259
Messuage	14210	Midst 14260
Met...	14211	Midsummer 14261
Metal	14212	Midway 14262
Metallic	14213	Midwife 14263
Metallurgic	14214	Midwifery 14264
Metallurgy	14215	Mien 14265
Metamorphose ...	14216	Might 14266
Metamorphosed ...	14217	Mightily 14267
Metamorphosis ...	14218	Mightiness 14268
Metaphor	14219	Mighty 14269
Metaphysical	14220	Migrate 14270
Metaphysician ...	14221	Migrated 14271
Metaphysics	14222	Migration 14272
Mete	14223	Migratory 14273
Meted	14224	Milch 14274
Meteor	14225	Mild 14275
Meteoric...	14226	Mildew 14276
Meteorite	14227	Mildness... 14277
Meteorological ...	14228	Mile 14278
Meteorology	14229	Militant 14279
Meter	14230	Military 14280
Method	14231	Militate 14281
Methodical	14232	Militated 14282
Methodism	14233	Militia 14283
Methodist	14234	Milk 14284
Meting	14235	Milked 14285
Metre	14236	Milking 14286
Metrical	14237	Milky 14287
Metropolis	14238	Mill... 14288
Metropolitan	14239	Millenarian 14289
Mettle	14240	Millenary 14290
Mettlesome	14241	Millennial 14291
Mew	14242	Millennium 14292
Mewing	14243	Miller 14293
Mexican	14244	Milliner 14294
Mezzotint	14245	Millinery 14295
Miasma	14246	Milling 14296
Mica	14247	Million 14297
Micaceous	14248	Millionth 14298
Michaelmas	14249	Millionaire 14299
Microscope	14250	Milt 14300

| MIM | (72) | MIS | 144 |

Mimic	...	...	14301	Miraculous	14351
Mimicry...	...	...	14302	Miraculously	14352
Minaret ...	...	...	14303	Mirage	14353
Minatory	...	...	14304	Mire	14354
Mince	...	...	14305	Mirror	14355
Minced ...	...	...	14306	Mirrored	14356
Mincing ...	...	...	14307	Mirth	14357
Mincingly	...	...	14308	Mirthful	14358
Mind	...	...	14309	Mirthless	14359
Minded ...	...	...	14310	Miry	14360
Mindful ...	...	...	14311	Misadventure... ..	14361
Mindfulness	...	...	14312	Misadvised	14362
Minding ...	...	...	14313	Misaffected	14363
Mindless...	...	...	14314	Misaffirm	14364
Mine	...	...	14315	Misaffirmed	14365
Mined	...	...	14316	Misallege	14366
Miner	...	...	14317	Misalliance	14367
Mineral ...	...	...	14318	Misallied	14368
Mineralogical...	...	14319	Misanthrope	14369
Mineralogist ...	...	14320	Misanthropic	14370
Mineralogy	...	...	14321	Misanthropy	14371
Mingle	...	...	14322	Misapplication ...	14372
Mingled ...	...	...	14323	Misapplied	14373
Mingling	...	...	14324	Misapply	14374
Miniature	...	...	14325	Misapprehend ...	14375
Minimum	...	...	14326	Misapprehended ...	14376
Mining ...	...	...	14327	Misapprehension ...	14377
Minion ...	...	...	14328	Misappropriate ...	14378
Minister ...	...	...	14329	Misappropriated ...	14379
Ministered	...	...	14330	Misappropriation ...	14380
Ministerial	...	..	14331	Misbegotten	14381
Ministering	...	...	14332	Misbehave	14382
Ministrant	...	...	14333	Misbehaved	14383
Ministration ...	...	14334	Misbehaviour... ...	14384
Ministry ...	...	...	14335	Miscalculate	14385
Minnow ...	...	...	14336	Miscalculated... ...	14386
Minor	...	...	14337	Miscalculation ...	14387
Minority...	...	...	14338	Miscall	14388
Minster ...	...	...	14339	Miscalled	14389
Minstrel ...	...	...	14340	Miscarriage	14390
Mint	...	...	14341	Miscarried	14391
Minted ...	...	...	14342	Miscarry... ...	14392
Minter ...	...	...	14343	Miscellaneous ...	14393
Minute ...	...	...	14344	Miscellany	14394
Minuted ...	...	...	14345	Mischance	14395
Minutely	...	...	14346	Mischief	14396
Minuteness	...	...	14347	Mischievous	14397
Minutiæ ...	...	...	14348	Mischievousness ...	14398
Minx	...	...	14349	Miscomputation ...	14399
Miracle ...	...	...	14350	Miscompute	14400

Misconceive	14401
Misconceived	14402
Misconceiving	14403
Misconception	14404
Misconduct	14405
Misconstrue	14406
Misconstrued	14407
Misconstruing	14408
Miscount	14409
Miscounted	14410
Miscreant	14411
Misdate	14412
Misdated	14413
Misdeed	14414
Misdemeanour	14415
Misdescribed	14416
Misdirect	14417
Misdirected	14418
Misdirection	14419
Misdoer	14420
Misemploy	14421
Misemployed	14422
Misentered	14423
Miser	14424
Miserable	14425
Miserably	14426
Miserly	14427
Misery	14428
Misestimate	14429
Misestimated	14430
Misfall	14431
Misformation	14432
Misformed	14433
Misfortune	14434
Misgiving	14435
Misgotten	14436
Misgovern	14437
Misgoverned	14438
Misgovernment	14439
Misguidance	14440
Misguide	14441
Misguided	14442
Misguiding	14443
Mishap	14444
Misinfer	14445
Misinferred	14446
Misinform	14447
Misinformation	14448
Misinformed	14449
Misinstruct	14450
Misinstructed	14451
Misinstruction	14452
Misinterpret	14453
Misinterpretation	14454
Misinterpreted	14455
Misjudged	14456
Misjudgment	14457
Mislaid	14458
Mislay	14459
Mislead	14460
Misleading	14461
Misled	14462
Mismanage	14463
Mismanaged	14464
Mismanagement	14465
Mismanager	14466
Mismanaging	14467
Misname	14468
Misnamed	14469
Misnomer	14470
Misogyny	14471
Misogynist	14472
Mispersuade	14473
Mispersuaded	14474
Mispersuasion	14475
Misplace	14476
Misplaced	14477
Misprint	14478
Misprinted	14479
Misprinting	14480
Misprision	14481
Misproceeding	14482
Mispronounce	14483
Mispronounced	14484
Mispronunciation	14485
Misquotation	14486
Misquote	14487
Misquoted	14488
Misreckon	14489
Misreckoned	14490
Misrelate	14491
Misrelated	14492
Misrelation	14493
Misreport	14494
Misreported	14495
Misrepresent	14496
Misrepresentation	14497
Misrepresented	14498
Misrepresenting	14499
Misrule	14500

| MIS | (73) | MOL | 146 |

Miss	14501	Mizzling...	14551
Missal	14502	Mizzly	14552
Missed	14503	Mnemonics	14553
Misshape	14504	Moan	14554
Misshapen	14505	Moaned	14555
Missile	14506	Moaning...	14556
Missing	14507	Moat	14557
Mission	14508	Moated	14558
Missionary	14509	Mob	14559
Missive	14510	Mobbed	14560
Misspell	14511	Mobility	14561
Misspelling	14512	Mock	14562
Misspelt	14513	Mocked	14563
Misspend	14514	Mocker	14564
Misspent...	14515	Mockery...	14565
Misstatement	14516	Mocking...	14566
Mist	14517	Mode	14567
Mistake	14518	Model	14568
Mistaken	14519	Modelled	14569
Mistaking	14520	Moderate	14570
Mister	14521	Moderated	14571
Mistily	14522	Moderating	14572
Mistimed	14523	Moderation	14573
Mistletoe	14524	Moderator	14574
Mistook	14525	Modern	14575
Mistranslate	14526	Modernize	14576
Mistranslation ...	14527	Modest	14577
Mistress	14528	Modesty...	14578
Mistrust	14529	Modicum	14579
Mistrusting	14530	Modification	14580
Misty	14531	Modified...	14581
Misunderstand ...	14532	Modify	14582
Misunderstanding ...	14533	Modish	14583
Misunderstood ...	14534	Modishness	14584
Misuse	14535	Modulate	14585
Mite	14536	Modulated	14586
Mitigant	14537	Modulation	14587
Mitigate	14538	Mohair	14588
Mitigated	14539	Mohammedan ...	14589
Mitigation	14540	Mohammedanism ...	14590
Mitigative	14541	Moiety	14591
Mitre	14542	Moire	14592
Mitten	14543	Moist	14593
Mix	14544	Moisten	14594
Mixable	14545	Moistened	14595
Mixed	14546	Moistening	14596
Mixing	14547	Moistness	14597
Mixture	14548	Moisture...	14598
Mizen	14549	Molar	14599
Mizzle	14550	Molasses	14600

147	MOL	(74)	MOR	
Mole	14601	Monotonous	14651
Molest	14602	Monotony	14652
Molestation	14603	Monsoon	14653
Molested...	14604	Monster	14654
Molesting	14605	Monstrosity	14655
Mollient	14606	Monstrous	14656
Mollifiable	14607	Month	14657
Mollify	14608	Monthly	14658
Molten	14609	Monument	14659
Moment	14610	Mood	14660
Momentarily	14611	Moodily	14661
Momentary	14612	Moody	14662
Momentous	14613	Moon	14663
Momentum	14614	Moor	14664
Monarch...	14615	Moored	14665
Monarchical	14616	Mooring	14666
Monarchy	14617	Moorish	14667
Monasterial	14618	Moot	14668
Monastery	14619	Mooted	14669
Monastic	14620	Mooting	14670
Monasticism	14621	Mop	14671
Monday	14622	Mope	14672
Monetary	14623	Moped	14673
Money	14624	Moping	14674
Moneyed	14625	Mopish	14675
Mongrel	14626	Mopped	14676
Monition	14627	Moral	14677
Monitive	14628	Moralist	14678
Monitor	14629	Morality	14679
Monitorial	14630	Moralize...	14680
Monitory	14631	Moralized	14681
Monitress	14632	Moralizer	14682
Monk	14633	Moralizing	14683
Monkey	14634	Morally	14684
Monkhood	14635	Morals	14685
Monkish...	14636	Morass	14686
Monogram	14637	Morbid	14687
Monograph	14638	Morbidness	14688
Monolith	14639	Mordant...	14689
Monologue	14640	More	14690
Monomania	14641	Moreover	14691
Monomaniac	14642	Morganatic	14692
Monopolist	14643	Moribund	14693
Monopolize	14644	Morisco	14694
Monopolized	14645	Mormon...	14695
Monopolizing... ...	14646	Mormonism	14696
Monopoly	14647	Morning	14697
Monosyllabic... ...	14648	Morose	14698
Monosyllable... ...	14649	Morosely	14699
Monotone	14650	Moroseness	14700

MOR	(74)	MUL	148

Morphia	... ...	14701	Mounted...	14751
Morris	... ...	14702	Mounting	14752
Morrow	... ...	14703	Mourn	14753
Morsel	... ...	14704	Mourned	14754
Mortal	... ...	14705	Mourner...	14755
Mortality	... ...	14706	Mournful	14756
Mortar	... ...	14707	Mourning	14757
Mortgage	... ...	14708	Mouse	14758
Mortgagee	... ...	14709	Mouth	14759
Mortgager	... ...	14710	Mouthed...	14760
Mortification		14711	Mouthful	14761
Mortified	... ...	14712	Move	14762
Mortify ...	... ...	14713	Moveable	14763
Mortifying	... ...	14714	Moveableness ...	14764
Mortmain	... ...	14715	Moved	14765
Mortuary	... ...	14716	Movement	14766
Mosaic	... ...	14717	Moving	14767
Moslem	... ...	14718	Mow	14768
Mosque	... ...	14719	Mowed	14769
Moss	... ...	14720	Mower	14770
Mossy	... ...	14721	Mowing	14771
Most	... ...	14722	Mown	14772
Mostly	... ...	14723	Much	14773
Moth	... ...	14724	Mucous	14774
Mother	... ...	14725	Mucus	14775
Motherhood		14726	Mud	14776
Motherless	... ...	14727	Muddily	14777
Motherly	... ...	14728	Muddiness	14778
Motion	... ...	14729	Muddle	14779
Motioned	... ...	14730	Muddled...	14780
Motioning	... ...	14731	Muddling	14781
Motionless	... ...	14732	Muddy	14782
Motive	... ...	14733	Muff	14783
Motley	... ...	14734	Muffin	14784
Mottled ...	... ...	14735	Muffle	14785
Motto	... ...	14736	Muffled	14786
Mould	... ...	14737	Muffler	14787
Moulded...	... ...	14738	Mug	14788
Moulder...	... ...	14739	Muggy	14789
Mouldiness	... ...	14740	Mulatto	14790
Moulding	... ...	14741	Mulct	14791
Mouldy ...	... ...	14742	Mule	14792
Moult	... ...	14743	Muleteer...	14793
Moulting	... ...	14744	Mull	14794
Mound	... ...	14745	Mulled	14795
Mount	... ...	14746	Mullett	14796
Mountain	... ...	14747	Mulligatawny ...	14797
Mountaineer		14748	Mullion	14798
Mountainous		14749	Multifarious	14799
Mountebank		14750	Multiform	14800

Multiple...	14801	Musket	14851
Multipliable	14802	Musketeer	14852
Multiplication ...	14803	Musketry	14853
Multiplicity	14804	Musky	14854
Multiplied	14805	Muslin	14855
Multiply...	14806	Musquito	14856
Multiplying	14807	Mussulman	14857
Multitude	14808	Must	14858
Multitudinous ...	14809	Mustaches	14859
Mumble	14810	Mustachioed	14860
Mumbler	14811	Mustard	14861
Mumbling	14812	Muster	14862
Mumm	14813	Mustered	14863
Mummery	14814	Mustering	14864
Mummy	14815	Mustiness	14865
Mumps	14816	Musty	14866
Munch	14817	Mutability	14867
Mundane	14818	Mutation	14868
Municipal	14819	Mute	14869
Municipality	14820	Muteness	14870
Munificence	14821	Mutilate...	14871
Munificent	14822	Mutilated	14872
Muniment	14823	Mutilation	14873
Munition	14824	Mutineer	14874
Mural	14825	Mutinied	14875
Murder	14826	Mutinous	14876
Murdered	14827	Mutiny	14877
Murderer	14828	Mutter	14878
Murdering	14829	Muttered	14879
Murderous	14830	Muttering	14880
Muriatic...	14831	Mutton	14881
Murky	14832	Mutual	14882
Murmur	14833	Mutually	14883
Murmured	14834	Muzzle	14884
Murmurer	14835	Muzzled	14885
Murmuring	14836	My	14886
Murrain	14837	Myriad	14887
Muscatel...	14838	Myrmidon	14888
Muscle	14839	Myrrh	14889
Muscovado	14840	Myrtle	14890
Muscular	14841	Myself	14891
Muse	14842	Mysterious	14892
Mused	14843	Mystery	14893
Museum	14844	Mystic	14894
Mushroom	14845	Mystical...	14895
Music	14846	Mystification	14896
Musical	14847	Myth	14897
Musician	14848	Mythical	14898
Musing	14849	Mythological... ...	14899
Musk	14850	Mythology	14900

N	(75)	NEC	150

N	14901	Naturalist	14951
Nabob	14902	Naturalization ...	14952
Nadir	14903	Naturalize	14953
Nag	14904	Naturalized	14954
Nail	14905	Naturally	14955
Nailed	14906	Nature	14956
Nailing	14907	Naught	14957
Naive	14908	Naughtily	14958
Naivete	14909	Naughtiness	14959
Naked	14910	Naughty...	14960
Nakedness	14911	Nausea	14961
Name	14912	Nauseate	14962
Named	14913	Nauseous	14963
Nameless	14914	Nautical...	14964
Namely	14915	Naval	14965
Namesake	14916	Nave	14966
Naming	14917	Navel	14967
Nap	14918	Navicular	14968
Nape	14919	Navigable	14969
Naphtha...	14920	Navigate	14970
Napkin	14921	Navigated	14971
Napless	14922	Navigating	14972
Napoleon	14923	Navigation	14973
Narcotic...	14924	Navigator	14974
Narrate	14925	Navvy	14975
Narrated	14926	Navy	14976
Narration	14927	Nawab	14977
Narrative	14928	Nay...	14978
Narrator	14929	Naze	14979
Narrow	14930	Neap	14980
Narrowed	14931	Neapolitan	14981
Narrowing	14932	Near	14982
Narrowly	14933	Neared	14983
Narrowness	14934	Nearer	14984
Narwhal...	14935	Nearest	14985
Nasal	14936	Nearly	14986
Nascency	14937	Nearness	14987
Nascent	14938	Neat	14988
Nastiness	14939	Neatly	14989
Nasty	14940	Neatness	14990
Natal	14941	Nebula	14991
Natatory...	14942	Nebulosity	14992
Nation .:.	14943	Nebulous	14993
National...	14944	Necessaries	14994
Nationality	14945	Necessarily	14995
Nationally	14946	Necessary	14996
Native	14947	Necessitate	14997
Nativity	14948	Necessitated	14998
Natty	14949	Necessitous	14999
Natural	14950	Necessity	15000

Neck	15001	Neighbour 15051
Necktie	15002	Neighbourhood ... 15052
Neckerchief	15003	Neighbouring ... 15053
Necklace	15004	Neighbourly 15054
Necrological	15005	Neighed 15055
Necrology	15006	Neither 15056
Necromancer... ...	15007	Neology 15057
Necromancy	15008	Neophyte 15058
Necropolis	15009	Nephew 15059
Nectar	15010	Nepotism 15060
Nectarine	15011	Nerve 15061
Need	15012	Nerved 15062
Needed	15013	Nerveless 15063
Needful	15014	Nervous 15064
Needfully	15015	Nervously 15065
Needily	15016	Nest 15066
Neediness	15017	Nestle 15067
Needing	15018	Nestled 15068
Needle	15019	Nestling 15069
Needless...	15020	Net 15070
Needlessly	15021	Nether 15071
Needy	15022	Netted 15072
Nefarious	15023	Netting 15073
Nefariousness ...	15024	Nettle 15074
Negation	15025	Network... 15075
Negative	15026	Neuralgia 15076
Negatived	15027	Neuter 15077
Negatively	15028	Neutral 15078
Negatory	15029	Neutrality 15079
Neglect	15030	Neutralize 15080
Neglected	15031	Neutralized 15081
Neglectedness ...	15032	Neutrally 15082
Neglectful	15033	Never 15083
Neglecting	15034	Nevertheless 15084
Neglectingly	15035	New 15085
Negligence	15036	Newly 15086
Negligent	15037	Newness... 15087
Negligently	15038	News 15088
Negotiability... ...	15039	Newspaper 15089
Negotiable	15040	Next 15090
Negotiate	15041	Nib 15091
Negotiated	15042	Nibble 15092
Negotiating	15043	Nibbled 15093
Negotiation	15044	Nibbling 15094
Negotiator	15045	Nibblingly 15095
Negotiatory	15046	Nice 15096
Negress	15047	Nicely 15097
Negro	15048	Niceness... 15098
Negus	15049	Nicety 15099
Neigh	15050	Niche 15100

NIC				(76)	NOS			152
Nick	...	...	...	15101	Node	15151
Nickel	...	...	...	15102	Nodded	15152
Nicknacks	...	...	15103	Nodding...	15153
Nickname	...	...	15104	Nodose	15154
Nicknamed	...	...	15105	Noise	15155
Nicotine ...	...	...	15106	Noised	15156
Niece	...	...	...	15107	Noiseless	15157
Niggard ...	...	...	15108	Noiselessly	15158
Niggardly	...	...	15109	Noisily	15159
Nigh	...	...	...	15110	Noisome...	15160
Nighness	...	...	15111	Noisy	15161
Night	...	...	...	15112	Nomadic	15162
Nightingale	...	...	15113	Nomenclature ...	15163
Nightly ...	...	...	15114	Nominal...	15164
Nightmare	...	...	15115	Nominally	15165
Nigrescent	...	...	15116	Nominate	15166
Nil	...	...	15117	Nominated	15167
Nimble ...	...	...	15118	Nomination	15168
Nimbleness	...	...	15119	Nominative	15169
Nimbly ...	...	...	15120	Nominator	15170
Nimbus ...	...	...	15121	Nominee	15171
Nine	...	...	...	15122	Non	15172
Ninefold...	...	...	15123	Nonagenarian ...	15173
Nineteen...	...	...	15124	Nonchalance	15174
Nineteenth	...	...	15125	Nonchalant	15175
Ninetieth	...	...	15126	Nonconformist ...	15176
Ninety	...	...	...	15127	Nonconformity ...	15177
Ninny	...	...	...	15128	Nondescript	15178
Ninth	...	...	...	15129	None	15179
Ninthly ...	...	...	15130	Nonentity	15180
Nip... ...	...	...	15131	Nonesuch	15181
Nipped ...	...	...	15132	Nonpayment	15182
Nippers ...	...	...	15133	Nonplus	15183
Nipping ...	...	...	15134	Nonplussed	15184
Nipple ...	...	...	15135	Nonsense	15185
Nitre	...	...	...	15136	Nonsensical	15186
Nitric	...	...	...	15137	Nonsuit	15187
Nitrogen...	...	...	15138	Nonsuited	15188
Nitrous ...	...	...	15139	Nook	15189
No	...	...	15140	Noon	15190
Nobility ...	...	...	15141	Noose	15191
Noble	...	...	...	15142	Nor...	15192
Nobleman	...	...	15143	Normal	15193
Nobleness	...	...	15144	North	15194
Noblesse...	...	...	15145	Northerly	15195
Nobly	...	...	...	15146	Northern	15196
Nobody ...	...	...	15147	Northward	15197
Nocturnal	...	...	15148	Norwegian	15198
Nocuously	...	...	15149	Nose	15199
Nod	...	...	...	15150	Nosegay...	15200

Nosologist	15201	Nudged	15251
Nostril	15202	Nudity	15252
Nostrum...	15203	Nugatory	15253
Not	15204	Nugget	15254
Notable	15205	Nuisance	15255
Notably	15206	Null	15256
Notarial...	15207	Nullification	15257
Notary	15208	Nullified...	15258
Notation	15209	Nullify	15259
Notch	15210	Nullity	15260
Notched...	15211	Numb	15261
Notching	15212	Numbed...	15262
Note	15213	Number	15263
Noted	15214	Numbered	15264
Nothing	15215	Numbering	15265
Notice	15216	Numberless	15266
Noticeable	15217	Numbers	15267
Noticed	15218	Numbness	15268
Noticing...	15219	Numerable	15269
Notification	15220	Numeral...	15270
Notified	15221	Numerally	15271
Notify	15222	Numerate	15272
Noting	15223	Numerated	15273
Notion	15224	Numeration	15274
Notoriety	15225	Numerator	15275
Notorious	15226	Numerical	15276
Notoriously	15227	Numerically	15277
Notwithstanding ...	15228	Numerous	15278
Noun	15229	Numismatics	15279
Nourish	15230	Numismatist	15280
Nourished	15231	Numskull	15281
Nourishing	15232	Nun	15282
Nourishment	15233	Nuncio	15283
Novel	15234	Nuncupatory	15284
Novelist	15235	Nunnery...	15285
Novelty	15236	Nuptial	15286
November	15237	Nuptials...	15287
Novice	15238	Nurse	15288
Novitiate	15239	Nursed	15289
Now	15240	Nursery	15290
Nowadays	15241	Nursing	15291
Nowhere	15242	Nurture	15292
Nowise	15243	Nurtured	15293
Noxious	15244	Nut...	15294
Noxiousness	15245	Nutmeg	15295
Noyeau	15246	Nutriment	15296
Nozzle	15247	Nutrition	15297
Nucleus	15248	Nutritious	15298
Nude	15249	Nutting	15299
Nudge	15250	Nymph	15300

O	(77)	OCC	154

O	15301	Obloquy	15351
Oak	15302	Obnoxious	15352
Oaken	15303	Obscene	15353
Oakum	15304	Obscenely	15354
Oar	15305	Obscenity	15355
Oarsman...	15306	Obscuration	15356
Oasis	15307	Obscure	15357
Oat	15308	Obscured	15358
Oaten	15309	Obscurely	15359
Oath	15310	Obscuring	15360
Obbligato	15311	Obscurity	15361
Obduracy	15312	Obsequies	15362
Obdurate	15313	Obsequious	15363
Obedience	15314	Observance	15364
Obedient	15315	Observant	15365
Obediently	15316	Observation	15366
Obeisance	15317	Observatory	15367
Obelisk	15318	Observe	15368
Obese	15319	Observed	15369
Obesity	15320	Observer...	15370
Obey	15321	Observing	15371
Obeyed	15322	Obsolete...	15372
Obeying	15323	Obstacle...	15373
Obfuscate	15324	Obstinacy	15374
Obfuscation	15325	Obstinate	15375
Obit	15326	Obstreperous	15376
Obituary...	15327	Obstruct	15377
Object	15328	Obstructed	15378
Objection	15329	Obstructing	15379
Objectionable ...	15330	Obstruction	15380
Objective	15331	Obstructive	15381
Objectless	15332	Obtain	15382
Objector...	15333	Obtained	15383
Objurgation	15334	Obtaining	15384
Oblation...	15335	Obtains	15385
Obligation	15336	Obtrude	15386
Obligatory	15337	Obtruded	15387
Oblige	15338	Obtrusion	15388
Obliged	15339	Obtrusive	15389
Obliging...	15340	Obtuse	15390
Oblique	15341	Obtuseness	15391
Obliquely	15342	Obverse	15392
Obliquity	15343	Obviate	15393
Obliterate	15344	Obviated	15394
Obliterated	15345	Obvious	15395
Obliterating	15346	Obviously	15396
Obliteration	15347	Occasion...	15397
Oblivion	15348	Occasional	15398
Oblivious	15349	Occasioned	15399
Oblong	15350	Occident...	15400

Occidental	15401	Office 15451
Occipital	15402	Officer 15452
Occult	15403	Official 15453
Occultation	15404	Officially 15454
Occupancy	15405	Officiate 15455
Occupant	15406	Officiated 15456
Occupation	15407	Officiating 15457
Occupied	15408	Officious 15458
Occupier	15409	Officiousness 15459
Occupy	15410	Offing 15460
Occupying	15411	Offset 15461
Occur	15412	Offspring 15462
Occurred	15413	Often 15463
Occurrence	15414	Ogle 15464
Occurring	15415	Ogled 15465
Ocean	15416	Ogling 15466
Oceanic	15417	Ogre 15467
Ochre	15418	Ogress 15468
Octagon	15419	Oh 15469
Octave	15420	Oil 15470
Octavo	15421	Oiliness 15471
October	15422	Oily 15472
Octodecimo	15423	Ointment 15473
Octogenarian	15424	Old 15474
Ocular	15425	Olden 15475
Oculist	15426	Older 15476
Odd	15427	Oldness 15477
Oddity	15428	Olfactory 15478
Oddly	15429	Oligarchy 15479
Oddness	15430	Olio 15480
Odds	15431	Olive 15481
Ode	15432	Omega 15482
Odious	15433	Omelet 15483
Odium	15434	Omen 15484
Odoriferous	15435	Ominous 15485
Odorous	15436	Omission 15486
Odour	15437	Omit 15487
Odyssey	15438	Omitted 15488
Of	15439	Omitting 15489
Off	15440	Omnibus 15490
Offal	15441	Omnipotence 15491
Offence	15442	Omnipotent 15492
Offend	15443	Omnipresent 15493
Offended	15444	Omniscience 15494
Offending ...	15445	Omniscient 15495
Offensive	15446	Omnivorous 15496
Offer	15447	On 15497
Offered	15448	Once 15498
Offering	15449	One 15499
Offertory	15450	Oneness 15500

ONE.	(78)	ORD	156

Onerous	15501	Oppressing	15551
Onion	15502	Oppression	15552
Only	15503	Oppressive	15553
Onset	15504	Oppressiveness ...	15554
Onslaught	15505	Oppressor	15555
Onward	15506	Opprobrious	15556
Onyx	15507	Opprobriously ...	15557
Ooze	15508	Opprobrium	15558
Oozing	15509	Optative...	15559
Opacity	15510	Optical	15560
Opal	15511	Optic	15561
Opaque	15512	Optician	15562
Open	15513	Optics	15563
Opened	15514	Optimism	15564
Opening	15515	Optimist...	15565
Openly	15516	Option	15566
Openness	15517	Optional...	15567
Opera	15518	Opulence	15568
Operate	15519	Opulent	15569
Operated	15520	Or	15570
Operatic...	15521	Oracle	15571
Operating	15522	Oracular...	15572
Operation	15523	Oral	15573
Operative	15524	Orange	15574
Operator...	15525	Oration	15575
Ophicleide	15526	Orator	15576
Ophthalmia	15527	Oratorical	15577
Opiate	15528	Oratorio...	15578
Opiated	15529	Oratory	15579
Opine	15530	Orb...	15580
Opined	15531	Orbed	15581
Opinion...	15532	Orbicular	15582
Opinionated	15533	Orbit	15583
Opinionative	15534	Orbital	15584
Opinionist	15535	Orchard	15585
Opium	15536	Orchestra	15586
Opossum	15537	Orchestral	15587
Oppidan...	15538	Orchid	15588
Opponent	15539	Orchilla	15589
Opportune	15540	Ordain	15590
Opportunely	15541	Ordained	15591
Opportunity	15542	Ordaining	15592
Oppose	15543	Ordeal	15593
Opposed...	15544	Order	15594
Opposer	15545	Ordered	15595
Opposing	15546	Ordering...	15596
Opposite...	15547	Orderless	15597
Opposition	15548	Orderly	15598
Oppress	15549	Ordinal	15599
Oppressed	15550	Ordinance	15600

Ordinarily	... ...	15601
Ordinary	... ...	15602
Ordination	... ...	15603
Ordnance	... ...	15604
Ordure ...	... ...	15605
Ore	... ...	15606
Organ ...	... ...	15607
Organic ...	... ...	15608
Organist...	... ...	15609
Organization ...	...	15610
Organize...	... ...	15611
Organized	... ...	15612
Organizing	... ...	15613
Orgies ...	... ...	15614
Oriel ...	... ...	15615
Orient ...	... ...	15616
Oriental ...	... ...	15617
Orientalist	... ...	15618
Orifice ...	... ...	15619
Origin ...	... ...	15620
Original ...	... ...	15621
Originality	... ...	15622
Originally	... ...	15623
Originate	... ...	15624
Originated	... ...	15625
Originating	... ...	15626
Originator	... ...	15627
Orison ...	... ...	15628
Orlop ...	... ...	15629
Ormolu ...	... ...	15630
Ornament	... ...	15631
Ornamented ...	...	15632
Ornamental ...	...	15633
Ornate ...	... ...	15634
Ornateness	... ...	15635
Ornithological	...	15636
Ornithologist...	...	15637
Ornithology ...	...	15638
Orphan ...	... ...	15639
Orphanage	... ...	15640
Orphaned	... ...	15641
Orrery ...	... ...	15642
Orthodox ...	...	15643
Orthographical	...	15644
Orthography ...	...	15645
Ortive ...	... ...	15646
Oscillate...	... ...	15647
Oscillated	... ...	15648
Oscillating	... ...	15649
Oscillation	... ...	15650
Oscillatory	... ...	15651
Osier ...	... ...	15652
Osprey ...	... ...	15653
Osseous ...	... ...	15654
Ossiferous	... ...	15655
Ossification	... ...	15656
Ossified ...	... ...	15657
Ossify ...	... ...	15658
Ostensible	... ...	15659
Ostensibly	... ...	15660
Ostensive	... ...	15661
Ostentation	... ...	15662
Ostentatious ...	...	15663
Ostentatiously	...	15664
Osteology	... ...	15665
Ostrich ...	... ...	15666
Other ..	... ...	15667
Otherwise	... ...	15668
Ottar ...	... ...	15669
Otter ...	... ...	15670
Ottoman...	... ...	15671
Ought ...	... ...	15672
Ounce ...	... ...	15673
Our... ...	... ...	15674
Ourselves	... ...	15675
Oust ...	... ...	15676
Ousted ...	... ...	15677
Out... ...	... ...	15678
Outbreak	... ...	15679
Outburst...	... ...	15680
Outcast ...	... ...	15681
Outcry ...	... ...	15682
Outdo ...	... ...	15683
Outdone...	... ...	15684
Outer ...	... ...	15685
Outermost	... ...	15686
Outfit ...	... ...	15687
Outgo ...	... ...	15688
Outgoing	... ...	15689
Outlandish	... ...	15690
Outlaw ...	... ...	15691
Outlawed	... ...	15692
Outlawry	... ...	15693
Outlay ...	... ...	15694
Outlet ...	... ...	15695
Outline ...	... ...	15696
Outlive ...	... ...	15697
Outlook ...	... ...	15698
Outlying...	... ...	15699
Outpost ...	... ...	15700

Outrage	15701		Overpaid	15751
Outraged	15702		Overpay	15752
Outrageous	15703		Overplus...	15753
Outraging	15704		Overpower	15754
Outré	15705		Overpowered	15755
Outright	15706		Overrate...	15756
Outset	15707		Overrated	15757
Outside	15708		Overreach	15758
Outskirt	15709		Overreached	15759
Outvote	15710		Overrule...	15760
Outvoted	15711		Overruled	15761
Outward...	15712		Oversee	15762
Outwardly	15713		Overseer...	15763
Outwit	15714		Overset	15764
Outwork...	15715		Overshade	15765
Oval	15716		Overshoot	15766
Ovary	15717		Oversight	15767
Ovation	15718		Overt	15768
Oven	15719		Overtake	15769
Over	15720		Overthrew	15770
Overalls	15721		Overthrow	15771
Overbear	15722		Overtook	15772
Overbearing	15723		Overture...	15773
Overbearingly ...	15724		Overturn	15774
Overboard	15725		Overturned	15775
Overcame	15726		Overturning	15776
Overcast	15727		Overwhelm	15777
Overcharge	15728		Overwhelmed ...	15778
Overcharged	15729		Overwhelming ...	15779
Overcharging... ...	15730		Oviform	15780
Overcome	15731		Oviparous	15781
Overdo	15732		Ovum	15782
Overdone	15733		Owe	15783
Overdraw	15734		Owed	15784
Overdrawn	15735		Owing	15785
Overdue	15736		Owl...	15786
Overflow	15737		Own	15787
Overflowed	15738		Owned	15788
Overflowing	15739		Owner	15789
Overhaul	15740		Ownership	15790
Overhauled	15741		Owning	15791
Overhead	15742		Ox	15792
Overhear	15743		Oxide	15793
Overheard	15744		Oxidize	15794
Overlaid	15745		Oxidized...	15795
Overlay	15746		Oxygen	15796
Overlaying	15747		Oxygenated	15797
Overlook	15748		Oyez	15798
Overlooked	15749		Oyster	15799
Overlooking	15750		Ozone	15800

P	15801	Paired	15851
Pabulum...	15802	Pairing	15852
Pace	15803	Palace	15853
Paced	15804	Palanquin	15854
Pacer	15805	Palatable	15855
Pacific	15806	Palate	15856
Pacification	15807	Palatial	15857
Pacificatory	15808	Palatinate	15858
Pacified	15809	Palatine	15859
Pacifier	15810	Palaver	15860
Pacify	15811	Pale	15861
Pacifying	15812	Paled	15862
Pacing	15813	Paleness...	15863
Pack	15814	Palfrey	15864
Package	15815	Paling	15865
Packed	15816	Palisade	15866
Packet	15817	Palisaded	15867
Packing	15818	Pall...	15868
Pact	15819	Palladium	15869
Pad	15820	Palled	15870
Padded	15821	Pallet	15871
Padding	15822	Palliate	15872
Paddle	15823	Palliated...	15873
Paddled	15824	Palliation	15874
Paddler	15825	Palliative	15875
Paddling	15826	Pallid	15876
Paddock...	15827	Palling	15877
Paddy	15828	Palm	15878
Padlock	15829	Palmed	15879
Pæan	15830	Palmer	15880
Pagan	15831	Palmy	15881
Paganism	15832	Palpable...	15882
Page	15833	Palpably...	15883
Pageant	15834	Palpitate	15884
Pageantry	15835	Palpitated	15885
Pagoda	15836	Palpitating	15886
Paid	15837	Palpitation	15887
Pail...	15838	Palsied	15888
Paillasse	15839	Palsy	15889
Pain	15840	Paltry	15890
Pained	15841	Pamper	15891
Painful	15842	Pampered	15892
Painfully...	15843	Pampering	15893
Painless	15844	Pamphlet	15894
Painstaking	15845	Pamphleteer	15895
Paint	15846	Pan...	15896
Painted	15847	Panacea	15897
Painter	15848	Pandemonium ...	15898
Painting	15849	Pane	15899
Pair...	15850	Panegyric	15900

Panegyrical	...	...	15901	Parasite ...	... ...	15951
Panegyrize	...	...	15902	Parasitic...	... ...	15952
Panegyrized	...	...	15903	Parasol ...	... ...	15953
Panel	... ...	...	15904	Parboil ...	... ...	15954
Pang	...	...	15905	Parboiled	... ...	15955
Panic	... ...	...	15906	Parcel ...	... ...	15956
Panoply ...	...	...	15907	Parch ...	... ...	15957
Panopticon	...	...	15908	Parched ...	... ...	15958
Panorama	...	...	15909	Parching	... ...	15959
Pant	... ...	...	15910	Parchment	... ...	15960
Panted ...	...	...	15911	Pardon ...	... ...	15961
Pantaloon	...	...	15912	Pardonable	... ...	15962
Pantechnicon...	...	...	15913	Pardoned	... ...	15963
Panting ...	...	...	15914	Pardoning	... ...	15964
Pantomime	...	...	15915	Pare ...	... ...	15965
Pantomimic	...	...	15916	Pared ...	... ...	15966
Pantry ...	...	...	15917	Paregoric	... ...	15967
Papa	... ...	...	15918	Parent ...	... ...	15968
Papacy ...	...	...	15919	Parentage	... ...	15969
Papal	... ...	...	15920	Parental ...	... ...	15970
Paper	... ...	...	15921	Parenthesis	... ...	15971
Papered ...	...	...	15922	Parenthetical...	...	15972
Papist	... ...	...	15923	Pariah ...	... ...	15973
Papistical	...	...	15924	Parian ...	... ...	15974
Pappy ...	...	...	15925	Paring ...	... ...	15975
Par ...	...	...	15926	Parish ...	... ...	15976
Parable ...	...	...	15927	Parishioner	... ...	15977
Parabolic	...	...	15928	Parisian ...	... ...	15978
Parachute	...	...	15929	Parity ...	... ...	15979
Parade ...	...	...	15930	Park ..	... ...	15980
Paraded ...	...	...	15931	Parlance...	... ...	15981
Parading	...	...	15932	Parley ...	... ...	15982
Paradise...	...	...	15933	Parleying	... ...	15983
Paradox ...	...	...	15934	Parliament	... ...	15984
Paradoxical	...	...	15935	Parliamentary	...	15985
Paraffine...	...	...	15936	Parlied ...	... ...	15986
Paragon ...	...	...	15937	Parlour ...	... ...	15987
Paragraph	...	...	15938	Parochial	... ...	15988
Parallel ...	...	...	15939	Parodied...	... ...	15989
Parallelogram	...	15940	Parody ...	... ...	15990
Paralysis...	...	...	15941	Parole ...	... ...	15991
Paralytic...	...	...	15942	Paroquet	... ...	15992
Paralyze...	...	...	15943	Parotid ...	... ...	15993
Paralyzed	...	...	15944	Paroxysm	... ...	15994
Paramount	...	...	15945	Parquetry	... ...	15995
Paramour	...	...	15946	Parricide	... ...	15996
Parapet ...	...	...	15947	Parried ...	... ...	15997
Paraphernalia	...	15948	Parrot ...	... ...	15998
Paraphrase	...	...	15949	Parry ...	... ...	15999
Paraphrased	...	...	15950	Parrying...	... ...	16000

L

Parse	...	16001	Passing ...	...	16051
Parsee	...	16002	Passion ...	...	16052
Parsimonious...	...	16003	Passionate	...	16053
Parsimony	...	16004	Passionately ...	...	16054
Parsing ...	...	16005	Passionless	...	16055
Parsley ...	...	16006	Passive ...	...	16056
Parsnip ..	...	16007	Passively	...	16057
Parson ...	...	16008	Passiveness	...	16058
Parsonage	...	16009	Passover...	...	16059
Part	...	16010	Passport...	...	16060
Partake ...	...	16011	Past...	...	16061
Partaker...	...	16012	Paste	...	16062
Partaking	...	16013	Pasted	...	16063
Parted	...	16014	Pastern	...	16064
Partial ...	...	16015	Pastime ...	...	16065
Partiality	...	16016	Pastor	...	16066
Partially...	...	16017	Pastoral ...	...	16067
Participant	...	16018	Pastorate	...	16068
Participate	...	16019	Pastry ...	...	16069
Participated ...	...	16020	Pasturage	...	16070
Participation ...	...	16021	Pasture ...	...	16071
Participator	...	16022	Pastured...	...	16072
Participle	...	16023	Pat ...	...	16073
Particle ...	...	16024	Patch	...	16074
Particular	...	16025	Patched ...	...	16075
Particularity ...	...	16026	Patching	...	16076
Particularize ...	...	16027	Pate	...	16077
Particularized	...	16028	Paten	...	16078
Particularly	...	16029	Patent	...	16079
Parting ...	...	16030	Patented...	...	16080
Partisan ...	...	16031	Patentee...	...	16081
Partisanship ...	...	16032	Paternal...	...	16082
Partition	...	16033	Paternity	...	16083
Partitioned	...	16034	Path	...	16084
Partly ...	...	16035	Pathetic ...	...	16085
Partner ...	...	16036	Pathless ...	...	16086
Partnership ...	...	16037	Pathology	...	16087
Partook ...	...	16038	Pathos	...	16088
Partridge	...	16039	Patience...	...	16089
Parts	...	16040	Patient ...	...	16090
Parturition	...	16041	Patiently	...	16091
Party	...	16042	Patriarch	...	16092
Parvenu ...	...	16043	Patriarchal	...	16093
Paschal ...	...	16044	Patrician	...	16094
Pass	...	16045	Patrimonial	...	16095
Passable...	...	16046	Patrimony	...	16096
Passage ...	...	16047	Patriot ...	...	16097
Passed	...	16048	Patriotic...	...	16098
Passenger	...	16049	Patriotism	...	16099
Passim ...	...	16050	Patrol ...	..	16100

Patrolled	16101	Pearl 16151
Patrolling	16102	Peasant 16152
Patron	16103	Peasantry 16153
Patronage	16104	Pease 16154
Patroness	16105	Peat 16155
Patronize	16106	Pebble 16156
Patronized	16107	Pebbly 16157
Patronizing	16108	Peccability 16158
Patronymic	16109	Peccable... 16159
Patted	16110	Peccadillo 16160
Patter	16111	Peck 16161
Pattering	16112	Pecked 16162
Pattern	16113	Pectoral 16163
Patting	16:14	Peculate... 16164
Paucity	16115	Peculated 16165
Paunch	16116	Peculation 16166
Pauper	16117	Peculator 16167
Pauperism	16118	Peculiar 16168
Pauperize	16119	Peculiarity 16169
Pauperized	16120	Peculiarly 16170
Pauperizing	16121	Pecuniary 16171
Pause	16122	Pedagogue 16172
Paused	16123	Pedal 16173
Pausing	16124	Pedant 16174
Pave	16125	Pedantic... 16175
Paved	16126	Pedantry 16176
Pavement	16127	Pedestal 16177
Pavilion	16128	Pedestrian 16178
Paving	16129	Pedestrianism ... 16179
Pavior	16130	Pedigree... 16180
Paw	16131	Pedler 16181
Pawed	16132	Pedobaptist 16182
Pawing	16133	Pedometer 16183
Pawn	16134	Peel 16184
Pawned	16135	Peeled 16185
Pawning...	16136	Peeler 16186
Pay...	16137	Peeling 16187
Payed	16138	Peep 16188
Paying	16139	Peeped 16189
Payment...	16140	Peeping 16190
Pays	16141	Peer 16191
Pea...	16142	Peerage 16192
Peace	16143	Peered 16193
Peaceful...	16144	Peeress 16194
Peacefully	16145	Peerless 16195
Peach	16146	Peevish 16196
Peak	16147	Peg... 16197
Peal	16148	Pegged 16198
Pealing	16149	Pekoe 16199
Pear	16150	Pelf... 16200

Pelican	16201	Penury 16251
Pelisse	16202	People 16252
Pellet	16203	Peopled 16253
Pellicle	16204	Pepper 16254
Pellmell	16205	Peppered 16255
Pellucid	16206	Peppering 16256
Pelt	16207	Peppermint 16257
Pelted	16208	Peppery 16258
Pelting	16209	Per 16259
Pen	16210	Perambulate 16260
Penal	16211	Perambulated ... 16261
Penalty	16212	Perambulation ... 16262
Penance	16213	Perambulator ... 16263
Pence	16214	Perceive 16264
Pencil	16215	Perceived 16265
Pencilled	16216	Perceiving 16266
Pendant	16217	Percentage 16267
Pendent	16218	Perceptible 16268
Pending	16219	Perception 16269
Pendulous	16220	Perceptive 16270
Pendulum	16221	Perch 16271
Penetrability	16222	Perched 16272
Penetrant	16223	Perchance 16273
Penetrate	16224	Percipient 16274
Penetrated	16225	Percolate 16275
Penetrating	16226	Percolated 16276
Penetration	16227	Percolator 16277
Peninsula	16228	Percussion 16278
Peninsular	16229	Perdition 16279
Penitence	16230	Peregrination... ... 16280
Penitent	16231	Peremptorily 16281
Penitential	16232	Peremptoriness ... 16282
Penitentiary	16233	Peremptory 16283
Pennant	16234	Perennial 16284
Penniless	16235	Perfect 16285
Penny	16236	Perfected 16286
Pension	16237	Perfection 16287
Pensionary	16238	Perfectly... 16288
Pensioned	16239	Perfectness 16289
Pensioner	16240	Perfidious 16290
Pensive	16241	Perfidiously 16291
Pensiveness	16242	Perfidy 16292
Pent	16243	Perforate · 16293
Pentagon	16244	Perforated 16294
Pentateuch	16245	Perforating 16295
Pentecost	16246	Perforation 16296
Penultimate	16247	Perforator 16297
Penurious	16248	Perforce 16298
Penuriously	16249	Perform 16299
Penuriousness ...	16250	Performance 16300

PER	(82)	PER	164
Performed	16301	Perpendicularity ...	16351
Performer	16302	Perpendicularly ...	16352
Performing	16303	Perpetrate	16353
Perfume	16304	Perpetrated	16354
Perfumed	16305	Perpetrating	16355
Perfumer	16306	Perpetration	16356
Perfumery	16307	Perpetrator	16357
Perfunctorily	16308	Perpetual	16358
Perhaps	16309	Perpetually	16359
Pericardium	16310	Perpetuate	16360
Peril	16311	Perpetuated	16361
Perilled	16312	Perpetuating	16362
Perilous	16313	Perpetuity	16363
Period	16314	Perplex	16364
Periodical	16315	Perplexed	16365
Periodically	16316	Perplexing	16366
Peripatetic	16317	Perplexity	16367
Perish	16318	Perquisite	16368
Perishable	16319	Perry	16369
Perished	16320	Persecute	16370
Perishing	16321	Persecuted	16371
Periwig	16322	Persecuting	16372
Periwinkle	16323	Persecution	16373
Perjure	16324	Persecutor	16374
Perjured	16325	Perseverance	16375
Perjurer	16326	Persevere	16376
Perjuring	16327	Persevered	16377
Perjury	16328	Persevering	16378
Perk	16329	Persian	16379
Permanence	16330	Persist	16380
Permanent	16331	Persisted	16381
Permanently	16332	Persistence	16382
Permeable	16333	Persistently	16383
Permeate	16334	Persisting	16384
Permeated	16335	Person	16385
Permeating	16336	Personage	16386
Permeation	16337	Personal	16387
Permissible	16338	Personality	16388
Permission	16339	Personally	16389
Permissive	16340	Personalty	16390
Permissively	16341	Personate	16391
Permit	16342	Personated	16392
Permitted	16343	Personating	16393
Permitting	16344	Personation	16394
Permutation	16345	Personification ...	16395
Pernicious	16346	Personified	16396
Perniciously	16347	Personify	16397
Peroration	16348	Perspective	16398
Peroxide	16349	Perspicacious	16399
Perpendicular ...	16350	Perspicacity	16400

Perspicuity	16401	Pessimist 16451
Perspicuous	16402	Pest... 16452
Perspicuously ...	16403	Pester 16453
Perspicuousness ...	16404	Pestering 16454
Perspiration	16405	Pestiferous 16455
Perspire	16406	Pestilence 16456
Perspired	16407	Pestilent... 16457
Perspiring	16408	Pestle 16458
Persuade...	16409	Pet 16459
Persuaded	16410	Petal 16460
Persuading	16411	Petition 16461
Persuasibility... ...	16412	Petitioned 16462
Persuasible	16413	Petitioner 16463
Persuasion	16414	Petrel 16464
Persuasive	16415	Petrifaction 16465
Pert...	16416	Petrified 16466
Pertain	16417	Petrify 16467
Pertained	16418	Petroleum 16468
Pertaining	16419	Petroline... 16469
Pertinacious	16420	Petted 16470
Pertinaciously ...	16421	Petticoat... 16471
Pertinacity	16422	Pettifogger 16472
Pertinency	16423	Pettifogging 16473
Pertinent	16424	Pettiness... 16474
Pertinently	16425	Petting 16475
Pertly	16426	Pettish 16476
Pertness	16427	Petty 16477
Perturb	16428	Petulance 16478
Perturbation	16429	Petulant 16479
Perturbator	16430	Pew... 16480
Perturbed	16431	Pewter 16481
Perusal	16432	Pewterer... 16482
Peruse	16433	Phalanx 16483
Perused	16434	Phantasmagoria ... 16484
Perusing...	16435	Phantom 16485
Peruvian...	16436	Pharisaical 16486
Pervade	16437	Pharisaism 16487
Pervaded	16438	Pharisee 16488
Pervading	16439	Pharmaceutical ... 16489
Perverse	16440	Pharmaceutics ... 16490
Perversely	16441	Pharmacy 16491
Perverseness	16442•	Pharos 16492
Perversion	16443	Phase 16493
Perversity	16444	Pheasant 16494
Perversive	16445	Phenomenon 16495
Pervert	16446	Phial 16496
Perverted	16447	Philanthropic... ... 16497
Perverter	16448	Philanthropist ... 16498
Perverting	16449	Philanthropy 16499
Pervious	16450	Philharmonic... ... 16500

Philippic	...	...	16501	Pickling...	... ...	16551
Philologist	...	...	16502	Picnic	... ...	16552
Philological	...	...	16503	Pictorial...	... ...	16553
Philology	...	...	16504	Picture	... ...	16554
Philoprogenitiveness			16505	Pictured...	... ...	16555
Philosopher	...	...	16506	Picturesque	... ...	16556
Philosophical...	...		16507	Pie	... ...	16557
Philosophize	...	...	16508	Piebald	... ...	16558
Philosophized		...	16509	Piece	... ...	16559
Philosophizer...		...	16510	Pieced	... ...	16560
Philosophizing		...	16511	Pier...	... ...	16561
Philosophy	...	...	16512	Pierce	... ...	16562
Phlebotomy	...	...	16513	Pierced	... ...	16563
Phlegm	...	...	16514	Piercer	... ...	16564
Phlegmatic	...	...	16515	Piercing...	... ...	16565
Phonetic...	...	...	16516	Pierian	... ...	16566
Phosphate	...	...	16517	Piety	... ...	16567
Phosphorescence	...		16518	Pig...	... ...	16568
Phosphorescent	...		16519	Pigeon	... ...	16569
Phosphoric	...	...	16520	Pigment...	... ...	16570
Phosphorus	...	...	16521	Pigmy	... ...	16571
Photogenic	...	...	16522	Pike	... ...	16572
Photograph	...	...	16523	Pilaster	... ...	16573
Photographed		...	16524	Pilchard...	... ...	16574
Photography	...	...	16525	Pile...	... ...	16575
Phrase	...	...	16526	Piled	... ...	16576
Phraseology	...	...	16527	Pilfer	... ...	16577
Phrenological		...	16528	Pilfered	... ...	16578
Phrenology	...	...	16529	Pilferer	... ...	16579
Phthsis	...	...	16530	Pilfering...	... ...	16580
Phylactery	...	...	16531	Pilgrim	... ...	16581
Physic	...	...	16532	Pilgrimage	... ...	16582
Physical...	...	...	16533	Pill...	... ...	16583
Physician	...	...	16534	Pillage	... ...	16584
Physics	...	...	16535	Pillaged	... ...	16585
Physiognomist		...	16536	Pillager	... ...	16586
Physiognomy...		...	16537	Pillaging	... ...	16587
Physiologist	...	...	16538	Pillar	... ...	16588
Physiology	...	...	16539	Pillory	... ...	16589
Pianist	...	...	16540	Pillow	... ...	16590
Piano	...	...	16541	Pillowed...	... ...	16591
Piazza	...	...	16542	Pilot	... ...	16592
Pibroch	...	...	16543	Pilotage	... ...	16593
Pica	...	...	16544	Piloted	... ...	16594
Pick	...	...	16545	Piloting	... ...	16595
Picked	...	...	16546	Pilular	... ...	16596
Picket	...	...	16547	Pimple	... ...	16597
Picking	...	...	16548	Pin...	... ...	16598
Pickle	...	...	16549	Pinafore...	... ...	16599
Pickled	...	...	16550	Pincers	... ...	16600

Pinch	16601	Pitiableness 16651
Pinched	16602	Pitied 16652
Pinchbeck	16603	Pitiful 16653
Pinching	16604	Pitifully 16654
Pine ... -	16605	Pitifulness 16655
Pined	16606	Pitiless 16656
Pining	16607	Pittance 16657
Pinion	16608	Pitted 16658
Pink	16609	Pity... 16659
Pinked	16610	Pitying 16660
Pinking	16611	Pivot 16661
Pinnace	16612	Pix 16662
Pinnacle...	16613	Placable... 16663
Pinned	16614	Placard 16664
Pint	16615	Placarded 16665
Pioneer	16616	Place 16666
Pious	16617	Placed 16667
Piously	16618	Placer 16668
Pip	16619	Placid 16669
Pipe	16620	Placidity... 16670
Piped	16621	Placidly 16671
Piper	16622	Placing 16672
Piping	16623	Plagiarism 16673
Pipkin	16624	Plagiarist 16674
Pippin	16625	Plagiarize 16675
Piquancy	16626	Plagiarized 16676
Piquant	16627	Plague 16677
Pique	16628	Plagued 16678
Piquet	16629	Plaguing... 16679
Piracy	16630	Plaice 16680
Pirate	16631	Plaid 16681
Piratical...	16632	Plain 16682
Pirating	16633	Plainly 16683
Pirouette	16634	Plainness 16684
Piscatory	16635	Plaint 16685
Pistol	16636	Plaintiff 16686
Piston	16637	Plaintive... 16687
Pit	16638	Plaintively 16688
Pitch	16639	Plaintiveness 16689
Pitched	16640	Plait 16690
Pitcher	16641	Plaited 16691
Pitching	16642	Plan 16692
Pitchy	16643	Plane 16693
Piteous	16644	Planet 16694
Piteously	16645	Plank 16695
Pith...	16646	Planked 16696
Pithily	16647	Planned 16697
Pithiness...	16648	Planning... 16698
Pithy	16649	Plant 16699
Pitiable	16650	Plantain 16700

PLA	(84)	PLU	168

Plantation	...	...	16701	Plenarily...	16751
Planted ...	...	...	16702	Plenary	16752
Planter ...	...	...	16703	Plenipotentiary ...	16753
Planting ...	...	...	16704	Plenitude	16754
Plaster ...	...	...	16705	Plenteous	16755
Plastered	...	...	16706	Plentiful	16756
Plasterer...	...	...	16707	Plentifully	16757
Plastering	...	...	16708	Plenty	16758
Plastic ...	...	...	16709	Plethora	16759
Plate ...	...	...	16710	Plethoric	16760
Plated ...	...	...	16711	Pleurisy	16761
Plateau ...	...	...	16712	Pliability	16762
Platform...	...	...	16713	Pliable	16763
Plating ...	...	...	16714	Pliancy	16764
Platinum	...	...	16715	Pliant	16765
Platitude	...	...	16716	Plied	16766
Platonic ...	...	...	16717	Pliers	16767
Platoon ...	...	...	16718	Plight	16768
Plaudit ...	...	...	16719	Plighted...	16769
Plauditory	...	...	16720	Plod	16770
Plausibility	...	...	16721	Plodder	16771
Plausible	...	...	16722	Plodding	16772
Plausibly	...	...	16723	Plot	16773
Play ...	...	...	16724	Plotted	16774
Played ...	...	...	16725	Plotter	16775
Player ...	...	...	16726	Plotting	16776
Playful ...	...	...	16727	Plough	16777
Playfully...	...	...	16728	Ploughed	16778
Playfulness	...	...	15729	Ploughing	16779
Playing ...	...	...	16730	Plover	16780
Plea ...	...	...	16731	Pluck	16781
Plead ...	...	...	16732	Plucked	16782
Pleaded ...	...	...	16733	Plucking	16783
Pleader ...	...	...	16734	Plucky	16784
Pleading...	...	...	16735	Plug	16785
Pleasant ...	...	...	16736	Plugged	16786
Pleasantly	...	...	16737	Plum	16787
Pleasantness ...	...	16738	Plumage	16788
Pleasantry	...	..	16739	Plumb	16789
Please ...	...	...	16740	Plumbago	16790
Pleased ...	...	...	16741	Plumber	16791
Pleasing ...	...	...	16742	Plumbing	16792
Pleasurable	...	...	16743	Plume	16793
Pleasurably	...	...	16744	Plumed	16794
Pleasure ...	...	...	16745	Plummet	16795
Plebeian...	...	...	16746	Plump	16796
Pledge ...	...	...	16747	Plumper	16797
Pledged ...	...	...	16748	Plumply	16798
Pledger ...	...	...	16749	Plumpness	16799
Pledging...	...	...	16750	Plumy	16800

Plunder ...	...	...	16801
Plundered	...	...	16802
Plunderer	...	...	16803
Plundering	...	...	16804
Plunge ...	...	...	16805
Plunged ...	...	...	16806
Plunging...	...	...	16807
Pluperfect	...	...	16808
Plural ...	...	...	16809
Pluralist ...	...	...	16810
Plurality ...	...	...	16811
Plus ...	...	...	16812
Plush ...	...	...	16813
Plutonic ...	...	...	16814
Ply	...	...	16815
Plying ...	...	...	16816
Pneumatic	...	...	16817
Pneumatics	...	...	16818
Pneumonia	...	...	16819
Poach ...	...	...	16820
Poached ...	...	...	16821
Poacher ...	...	..	16822
Poaching	...	...	16823
Pock ...	...	...	16824
Pocket ...	...	...	16825
Pocketed	...	...	16826
Pod... ...	...	...	16827
Poem ...	...	...	16828
Poet ...	...	...	16829
Poetess ...	...	...	16830
Poetic ...	...	...	16831
Poetry ...	...	...	16832
Poignancy	...	...	16833
Poignant	...	...	16834
Point ...	...	...	16835
Pointed ...	...	...	16836
Pointer ...	...	...	16837
Pointing...	...	...	16838
Pointless	...	...	16839
Poise ...	...	...	16840
Poised ...	...	...	16841
Poising ...	...	...	16842
Poison ...	...	...	16843
Poisoned	...	...	16844
Poisoner...	...	...	16845
Poisoning	...	...	16846
Poisonous	...	...	16847
Poke ...	...	...	16848
Poked ...	...	...	16849
Poker ...	...	...	16850

Poking ...	...	...	16851
Polar ...	...	...	16852
Polarity ...	...	...	16853
Polarization	...	...	16854
Polarize ...	...	...	16855
Polarized	...	...	16856
Polarizing	...	...	16857
Pole ...	...	...	16858
Polemical	...	...	16859
Polemics	...	...	16860
Police ...	...	...	16861
Policy ...	...	...	16862
Polish ...	...	...	16863
Polished ...	...	...	16864
Polishing	...	...	16865
Polite ...	..	...	16866
Politely ...	...	...	16867
Politeness	...	...	16868
Politic ...	...	...	16869
Political ...	...	...	16870
Politically	...	...	16871
Politician	...	...	16872
Politics ...	...	...	16873
Polity ...	...	...	16874
Polka ...	...	...	16875
Poll... ...	...	...	16876
Pollard ...	...	...	16877
Pollen ...	...	...	16878
Pollute ...	...	...	16879
Polluted ...	...	...	16880
Pollutor ...	...	...	16881
Polluting	...	...	16882
Pollution	...	...	16883
Poltroon...	...	...	16884
Poltroonery	...	...	16885
Polygamy	...	...	16886
Polyglot...	...	...	16887
Polygon ...	...	...	16888
Polysyllable	...	...	16889
Polytechnic	...	...	16890
Pomade ...	...	...	16891
Pomegranate ...		...	16892
Pommel ...	...	...	16893
Pommelled	...	...	16894
Pommelling	...	...	16895
Pomp ...	...	...	16896
Pomposity	...	...	16897
Pompous	...	...	16898
Pond ...	...	...	16899
Ponder ...	...	...	16900

PON	(85)	POS	170

Ponderable	16901	Porridge...	16951
Pondered	16902	Porringer	16952
Pondering	16903	Port	16953
Ponderosity	16904	Portability	16954
Ponderous	16905	Portable...	16955
Poniard	16906	Portal	16956
Poniarded	16907	Portcullis	16957
Pontiff	16908	Porte	16958
Pontifical	16909	Ported	16959
Pontificate	16910	Portend	16960
Pontoon...	16911	Portended	16961
Pony	16912	Portent	16962
Poodle	16913	Portentous	16963
Pool	16914	Porter	16964
Poop	16915	Porteress	16965
Pooped	16916	Portfolio...	16966
Poor	16917	Portico	16967
Poorly	16918	Porting	16968
Poorness	16919	Portion	16969
Pop...	16920	Portioned	16970
Pope	16921	Portioning	16971
Popedom	16922	Portionless	16972
Popery	16923	Portliness	16973
Popinjay...	16924	Portly	16974
Popish	16925	Portmanteau	16975
Poplar	16926	Portrait	16976
Poplin	16927	Portraiture	16977
Poppy	16928	Portray	16978
Populace	16929	Portuguese	16979
Popular	16930	Pose	16980
Popularity	16931	Posed	16981
Popularize	16932	Poser	16982
Popularized	16933	Posing	16983
Popularly	16934	Position	16984
Populate...	16935	Positive	16985
Populated	16936	Positively	16986
Population	16937	Positiveness	16987
Populous	16938	Possess	16988
Porcelain	16939	Possessed	16989
Porch	16940	Possessing	16990
Porcupine	16941	Possession	16991
Pore	16942	Possessive	16992
Pored	16943	Possessor	16993
Poring	16944	Posset	16994
Pork	16945	Possibility	16995
Porker	16946	Possible	16996
Porosity	16947	Possibly	16997
Porous	16948	Post	16998
Porphyry	16949	Postage	16999
Porpoise...	16950	Posted	17000

Poster	17001	
Posterior	17002	
Posterity	17003	
Postern	17004	
Posthumous	17005	
Postilion	17006	
Posting	17007	
Postpone	17008	
Postponed	17009	
Postponing	17010	
Postponement	17011	
Postscenium	17012	
Postscript	17013	
Postulant	17014	
Postulate	17015	
Posture	17016	
Posy	17017	
Pot	17018	
Potassium	17019	
Potation	17020	
Potato	17021	
Potatory	17022	
Poteen	17023	
Potency	17024	
Potent	17025	
Potentate	17026	
Potential	17027	
Potently	17028	
Pother	17029	
Potion	17030	
Pottage	17031	
Potted	17032	
Potter	17033	
Pottery	17034	
Pottle	17035	
Pouch	17036	
Poulterer	17037	
Poultice	17038	
Poultry	17039	
Pounce	17040	
Pounced	17041	
Pouncing	17042	
Pound	17043	
Poundage	17044	
Pounded	17045	
Pounder	17046	
Pour	17047	
Poured	17048	
Pouring	17049	
Pout	17050	
Pouted	17051	
Pouting	17052	
Poverty	17053	
Powder	17054	
Powdered	17055	
Power	17056	
Powerful	17057	
Powerfully	17058	
Powerless	17059	
Pox	17060	
Practicability	17061	
Practicable	17062	
Practical	17063	
Practically	17064	
Practice	17065	
Practise	17066	
Practised	17067	
Practising	17068	
Practitioner	17069	
Pragmatic	17070	
Prairie	17071	
Praise	17072	
Praised	17073	
Praising	17074	
Prance	17075	
Prancing	17076	
Prank	17077	
Prate	17078	
Prating	17079	
Prattle	17080	
Prattled	17081	
Prattler	17082	
Prattling	17083	
Prawn	17084	
Pray	17085	
Prayer	17086	
Prayed	17087	
Praying	17088	
Preach	17089	
Preacher	17090	
Preaching	17091	
Preadamite	17092	
Preadmonish	17093	
Preadmonished	17094	
Preadmonition	17095	
Preamble	17096	
Prebend	17097	
Prebendal	17098	
Prebendary	17099	
Precarious	17100	

PRE	(86)	PRE	172
Precariously	17101	Predestine	17151
Precatory	17102	Predestined	17152
Precaution	17103	Predeterminate ...	17153
Precautionary ...	17104	Predetermination ...	17154
Precede	17105	Predetermine... ...	17155
Preceded	17106	Predetermined ...	17156
Precedence	17107	Predicable	17157
Precedent	17108	Predicament	17158
Preceding	17109	Predicate	17159
Precentor	17110	Predicated	17160
Precept	17111	Predication	17161
Preceptive	17112	Predict	17162
Preceptor	17113	Predicted	17163
Preceptorial	17114	Predicting	17164
Preceptress	17115	Prediction	17165
Precinct	17116	Predictive	17166
Precious	17117	Predictor	17167
Precipice	17118	Predilection	17168
Precipitancy	17119	Predispose	17169
Precipitant	17120	Predisposed	17170
Precipitate	17121	Predisposition ...	17171
Precipitated	17122	Predominance ...	17172
Precipitating	17123	Predominant	17173
Precipitation	17124	Predominate	17174
Precipitous	17125	Predominated ...	17175
Precise	17126	Pre-eminence... ...	17176
Precisely...	17127	Pre-eminent	17177
Precision	17128	Pre-engage	17178
Preclude...	17129	Pre-engaged	17179
Precluded	17130	Pre-exist...	17180
Precluding	17131	Pre-existing	17181
Preclusion	17132	Preface	17182
Precocious	17133	Prefaced	17183
Precocity	17134	Prefatory	17184
Precognition	17135	Prefect	17185
Precompose	17136	Prefecture	17186
Preconceive	17137	Prefer	17187
Preconceived... ...	17138	Preferable	17188
Preconception ...	17139	Preference	17189
Preconcert	17140	Preferential	17190
Preconcerted	17141	Preferment	17191
Precursor	17142	Preferred	17192
Predatory	17143	Preferring	17193
Predecessor	17144	Prefigure	17194
Predesign	17145	Prefigured	17195
Predesigned	17146	Prefix	17196
Predestinate	17147	Prefixed	17197
Predestinated... ...	17148	Pregnancy	17198
Predestination ...	17149	Pregnant...	17199
Predestinator... ...	17150	Prejudge...	17200

Prejudged	...	...	17201	Preposition	...	...	17251
Prejudication	...	...	17202	Prepossess	...	...	17252
Prejudice	...	...	17203	Prepossessed	...	...	17253
Prejudiced	...	...	17204	Prepossessing	...	17254
Prejudicial	...	...	17205	Preposterous	...	17255
Prelacy	...	...	17206	Preresolve	...	...	17256
Prelate	...	...	17207	Preresolved	...	...	17257
Preliminary	...	...	17208	Prerogative	...	...	17258
Prelude	...	...	17209	Presage	...	...	17259
Preluded	...	...	17210	Presaged	...	...	17260
Prelusive	...	...	17211	Presagement	...	17261
Premature	...	...	17212	Presbyter	...	...	17262
Prematurely	...	...	17213	Presbyterian	...	17263
Prematurity	...	...	17214	Presbyterianism	...	17264
Premeditate	...	...	17215	Presbytery	...	...	17265
Premeditated	...	17216	Prescience	...	...	17266
Premeditation	...	17217	Prescient	...	...	17267
Premier	...	...	17218	Prescribe	...	...	17268
Premiership	...	...	17219	Prescribed	..	...	17269
Premise	...	...	17220	Prescribing	...	...	17270
Premised	...	...	17221	Prescription	...	...	17271
Premises	...	...	17222	Prescriptive	...	...	17272
Premium	...	...	17223	Presence	...	...	17273
Premonish	...	...	17224	Present	...	...	17274
Premonished	...	...	17225	Presented	...	...	17275
Premonitory	...	...	17226	Presentable	...	...	17276
Prenomen	...	...	17227	Presentation	...	...	17277
Preoccupation	...	17228	Presentiment	...	...	17278
Preoccupied	...	...	17229	Presently	...	...	17279
Preoccupy	...	...	17230	Preservable	...	...	17280
Preordain	...	...	17231	Preservation	...	...	17281
Preordained	...	...	17232	Preservative	...	...	17282
Prepaid	...	...	17233	Preserve	...	...	17283
Preparation	...	...	17234	Preserved	...	...	17284
Preparative	...	...	17235	Preserving	...	...	17285
Preparatory	...	...	17236	Preside	...	...	17286
Prepare	...	...	17237	Presided	...	...	17287
Prepared	...	...	17238	Presidency	...	...	17288
Preparedness	...	...	17239	President	...	...	17289
Preparing	...	...	17240	Presidential	...	...	17290
Prepay	...	...	17241	Presiding	...	...	17291
Prepaying	...	...	17242	Press	...	...	17292
Prepayment	...	...	17243	Pressed	...	...	17293
Prepense	...	...	17244	Presser	...	...	17294
Preponderance	...	17245	Pressing	...	...	17295
Preponderant	...	...	17246	Pressure	...	...	17296
Preponderate	...	17247	Prestige	...	...	17297
Preponderated	...	17248	Presto	...	...	17298
Preponderating	...	17249	Presumable	...	...	17299
Preponderation	...	17250	Presume	...	...	17300

Presumed	... ...	17301
Presuming	... ...	17302
Presumption ...	...	17303
Presumptive ...	...	17304
Presumptuous	...	17305
Presuppose	...	17306
Presupposed	... ...	17307
Presupposing...	...	17308
Presupposition	...	17309
Pretence	...	17310
Pretend ...	... ...	17311
Pretended	... ...	17312
Pretender	... ...	17313
Pretending	... ...	17314
Pretension	...	17315
Preterimperfect		17316
Preterit ...	... ...	17317
Pretermission	...	17318
Pretermit	...	17319
Pretermitted	...	17320
Preternatural ...		17321
Preterperfect ...		17322
Preterpluperfect	...	17323
Pretext ...	... ...	17324
Prettily ...	... ...	17325
Prettiness	... ...	17326
Pretty ...	... ...	17327
Prevail ...	... ...	17328
Prevailed	... ...	17329
Prevailing	... ...	17330
Prevalence	...	17331
Prevalent	... ...	17332
Prevaricate	... ...	17333
Prevaricated ...		17334
Prevaricating...		17335
Prevarication...	...	17336
Prevaricator ...	...	17337
Prevent ...	... ...	17338
Prevented	... ...	17339
Preventing	... ...	17340
Prevention	... ...	17341
Preventive	... ...	17342
Previous...	... ...	17343
Previously	... ...	17344
Prevision	... ...	17345
Prey ...	... ...	17346
Preyed ...	... ...	17347
Price ...	... ...	17348
Priced ...	... ...	17349
Priceless	... ...	17350
Prick ...	... ...	17351
Pricked ...	... ...	17352
Pricker ...	... ...	17353
Pricking ...	... ...	17354
Prickle ...	... ...	17355
Prickliness	... ...	17356
Prickly ...	... ...	17357
Pride ...	... ...	17358
Priest ...	...	17359
Priestcraft	... ...	17360
Priestess	... ...	17361
Priesthood	... ...	17362
Priestly ...	... ...	17363
Priestridden	...	17364
Prig... ...	... ...	17365
Priggish ...	... ...	17366
Prim ...	... ...	17367
Primacy ...	... ...	17368
Primage...	... ...	17369
Primary ...	... ...	17370
Primate ...	... ...	17371
Prime ...	... ...	17372
Primed ...	... ...	17373
Primer ...	... ...	17374
Primeval	... ...	17375
Priming ...	... ...	17376
Primitive	... ...	17377
Primitively	... ...	17378
Primly ...	... ...	17379
Primness	... ...	17380
Primo ...	... ...	17381
Primogenitor...	...	17382
Primogeniture	...	17383
Primordial	... ...	17384
Primrose	... ...	17385
Prince ...	... ...	17386
Princelike	... ...	17387
Princedom	... ...	17388
Princely ...	... ...	17389
Princess ...	... ...	17390
Principal	... ...	17391
Principality	... ...	17392
Principally	... ...	17393
Principia	... ...	17394
Principle	... ...	17395
Print ...	... ...	17396
Printed ...	... ...	17397
Printer ...	... ...	17398
Printing ...	... ...	17399
Prior ...	... ...	17400

Prioress	17401	Procrastination ... 17451
Priority	17402	Procrastinator ... 17452
Priory	17403	Procreant 17453
Prism	17404	Procreate 17454
Prismatic	17405	Procreated 17455
Prison	17406	Procreation 17456
Prisoner	17407	Procreative 17457
Pristine	17408	Proctor 17458
Privacy	17409	Procumbent 17459
Private	17410	Procurable 17460
Privateer	17411	Procuration 17461
Privateering	17412	Procurator 17462
Privately	17413	Procure 17463
Privation	17414	Procured 17464
Privilege	17415	Procuring 17465
Privileged	17416	Prod 17466
Privily	17417	Prodigal 17467
Privity	17418	Prodigality 17468
Privy	17419	Prodigious 17469
Prize	17420	Prodigy 17470
Prized	17421	Produce 17471
Probability	17422	Produced 17472
Probable	17423	Producer 17473
Probably	17424	Producible 17474
Probate	17425	Producing 17475
Probation	17426	Product 17476
Probationary	17427	Production 17477
Probe	17428	Productive 17478
Probed	17429	Productiveness ... 17479
Probing	17430	Profanation 17480
Probity	17431	Profane 17481
Problem	17432	Profaned 17482
Problematical ...	17433	Profanely 17483
Proboscis	17434	Profaneness 17484
Procedure	17435	Profaner 17485
Proceed	17436	Profaning 17486
Proceeded	17437	Profanity 17487
Proceeding	17438	Profess 17488
Proceeds	17439	Professed 17489
Process	17440	Professedly 17490
Procession	17441	Professing 17491
Processional	17442	Profession 17492
Proclaim	17443	Professional 17493
Proclamation	17444	Professor 17494
Proclaimed	17445	Professorial 17495
Proclaiming	17446	Proffer 17496
Proclivity	17447	Proffered 17497
Procrastinate	17448	Proffering 17498
Procrastinated ...	17449	Proficiency 17499
Procrastinating ...	17450	Proficient 17500

PRO	88	PRO	176
Profile	17501	Prolonging	17551
Profit	17502	Promenade	17552
Profitable	17503	Promenaded	17553
Profitably	17504	Prominence	17554
Profited	17505	Prominent	17555
Profiting...	17506	Prominently	17556
Profligacy	17507	Promiscous	17557
Profligate	17508	Promiscuously ...	17558
Profligately	17509	Promise	17559
Profound	17510	Promised	17560
Profoundly	17511	Promiser	17561
Profundity	17512	Promises	17562
Profuse	17513	Promising	17563
Profusely	17514	Promissory	17564
Profusion	17515	Promontory	17565
Progenitor	17516	Promote...	17566
Progeny	17517	Promoted	17567
Prognostic	17518	Promoter	17568
Prognosticate ...	17519	Promotes	17569
Prognosticated ...	17520	Promoting	17570
Prognostication ...	17521	Promotion	17571
Prognosticator ...	17522	Promotive	17572
Programme	17523	Prompt	17573
Progress...	17524	Prompted	17574
Progressed	17525	Prompter	17575
Progressing	17526	Promptitude	17576
Progression	17527	Promptly	17577
Progressional	17528	Promptness	17578
Progressive	17529	Promulgate	17579
Prohibit	17530	Promulgated	17580
Prohibited	17531	Promulgating... ...	17581
Prohibiting	17532	Promulgation ...	17582
Prohibition	17533	Promulgator	17583
Prohibitive	17534	Prone	17584
Project	17535	Proneness	17585
Projected	17536	Prong	17586
Projectile	17537	Pronoun...	17587
Projecting	17538	Pronounce	17588
Projection	17539	Pronounceable ...	17589
Projector	17540	Pronounced	17590
Prolapsed	17541	Pronouncing	17591
Proletarian	17542	Pronunciation ...	17592
Prolific	17543	Proof	17593
Prolix	17544	Prop	17594
Prolixity...	17545	Propagandism ...	17595
Prolocutor	17546	Propagandist	17596
Prologue	17547	Propagate	17597
Prolong	17548	Propagated	17598
Prolongation	17549	Propagating	17599
Prolonged	17550	Propagation	17600

Propagator	...	...	17601	Prosaic	17651
Propel ...	...	...	17602	Proscenium	17652
Propelled	...	...	17603	Proscribe	17653
Propelling	...	...	17604	Proscribed	17654
Propensity	...	...	17605	Proscripiton	17655
Proper ...	...	...	17606	Proscriptive	17656
Properly...	...	...	17607	Prose	17657
Property...	...	...	17608	Prosecute	17658
Prophecy	...	...	17609	Prosecuted	17659
Prophesied	...	...	17610	Prosecution	17660
Prophesier	...	...	17611	Prosecuting	17661
Prophesy	...	...	17612	Prosecutor	17662
Prophesying	...	...	17613	Proselyte	17663
Prophet ...	...	...	17614	Proselytism	17664
Prophetess	...	...	17615	Proselytized	17665
Prophetic	...	...	17616	Prosing	17666
Propinquate	...	...	17617	Prosody	17667
Propinquity	...	...	17618	Prospect...	17668
Propitiated	..	...	17619	Prospected	17669
Propitiating	...	...	17620	Prospective	17670
Propitiation	...	...	17621	Prospectively... ...	17671
Propitiator	..	...	17622	Prospectus	17672
Propitiatory	...	...	17623	Prosper	17673
Propitious	...	...	17624	Prospered	17674
Propitiously	...	...	17625	Prospering	17675
Proportion	...	...	17626	Prosperity	17676
Proportionable	...		17627	Prosperous	17677
Proportional	...	...	17628	Prosperously	17678
Proportionally	...		17629	Prostitute	17679
Proportionate	...		17630	Prostituted	17680
Proportionately	...		17631	Prostitution	17681
Proportioned...	...		17632	Prostrate	17682
Proposal...	...	...	17633	Prostrated	17683
Propose ...	...	...	17634	Prostrating	17684
Proposed	...	...	17635	Prostration	17685
Proposing	...	...	17636	Prosy	17686
Proposition	...	...	17637	Protean	17687
Propound	...	...	17638	Protect	17688
Propounded	...	...	17639	Protected	17689
Propounder	...	...	17640	Protecting	17690
Propounding	...	...	17641	Protectingly	17691
Proprietor	...	...	17642	Protection	17692
Propriety	...	...	17643	Protectionist	17693
Propulsion	...	...	17644	Protective	17694
Propulsive	...	...	17645	Protector	17695
Propped...	...	...	17646	Protégé	17696
Propping	...	...	17647	Protest	17697
Prorogation	...	...	17648	Protested	17698
Prorogue	...	...	17649	Protesting	17699
Prorogued	...	...	17650	Protestant	17700

PRO		(89)	PUB	178
Protestantism	...	17701	Provisory	...	...	17751
Protestation ...	...	17702	Provocation	...	...	17752
Protester...	...	17703	Provocative	...	...	17753
Protestingly ...	...	17704	Provokable	...	...	17754
Prothonotary...	...	17705	Provoke ...	...	...	17755
Protocol ...	...	17706	Provoked	...	...	17756
Prototype	...	17707	Provoker	...	...	17757
Protract ...	...	17708	Provoking	...	...	17758
Protracted	...	17709	Provokingly	...	...	17759
Protracting	...	17710	Provost ...	...	...	17760
Protraction	...	17711	Prow ...	...	...	17761
Protractive	...	17712	Prowess ...	...	...	17762
Protrude...	...	17713	Prowl ...	...	...	17763
Protruded	...	17714	Prowled ...	...	...	17764
Protruding	...	17715	Prowler ...	...	...	17765
Protrusion	...	17716	Prowling	...	...	17766
Protrusive	...	17717	Proximate	...	...	17767
Protuberance...	...	17718	Proximately ...	...	17768
Protuberant ...	...	17719	Proximity	...	...	17769
Protuberate ...	...	17720	Proxy ...	...	...	17770
Protuberation	...	17721	Prude ...	...	...	17771
Proud ...	...	17722	Prudence	...	...	17772
Proudly ...	...	17723	Prudent ...	...	...	17773
Provable	...	17724	Prudential	...	...	17774
Prove ...	...	17725	Prudently	...	...	17775
Proved ...	...	17726	Prudery ...	...	...	17776
Provender	...	17727	Prudish ...	...	...	17777
Proverb ...	...	17728	Prune ...	...	...	17778
Proverbial	...	17729	Pruned ...	...	...	17779
Proverbially ...	...	17730	Pruner ...	...	...	17780
Provide ...	...	17731	Pruning ...	...	...	17781
Provided	...	17732	Prurience	...	...	17782
Providence	...	17733	Prurient ...	...	...	17783
Provident	...	17734	Prussian ...	...	...	17784
Providential ...	...	17735	Prussic ...	...	...	17785
Providently	...	17736	Pry ...	...	...	17786
Provider...	...	17737	Pryingly...	...	...	17787
Providing	...	17738	Psalm ...	...	...	17788
Province...	...	17739	Psalmist...	...	...	17789
Provincial	...	17740	Psalmody	...	...	17790
Provincialism	...	17741	Psalter ...	...	...	17791
Provincialist ...	...	17742	Pseudo ...	...	...	17792
Proving ...	...	17743	Psychical	...	17793
Provision	...	17744	Psychological	...	17794
Provisional	...	17745	Psychology	...	17795
Provisionally ...	...	17746	Ptarmigan	...	17796
Provisioned	...	17747	Puberal ...	...	...	17797
Provisioning ...	...	17748	Puberty ...	...	...	17798
Proviso ...	...	17749	Public ...	...	...	17799
Provisor ...	...	17750	Publican	...	...	17800

Publication	... ...	17801
Publicist...	... ...	17802
Publicity	... ...	17803
Publicly ...	... ...	17804
Publish ...	... ...	17805
Published	... ...	17806
Publisher	... ...	17807
Publishing	... ...	17808
Puce	... ...	17809
Pucker ...	... ...	17810
Puckered	... ...	17811
Pudding...	... ...	17812
Puddle ...	... ...	17813
Puddler ...	... ...	17814
Puerile ...	... ...	17815
Puerility...	... ...	17816
Puerperal	... ...	17817
Puff	... ...	17818
Puffed	... ...	17819
Puffiness	... ...	17820
Puffing ...	... ...	17821
Puffy	... ...	17822
Pug	... ...	17823
Pugilism	... ...	17824
Pugilist ...	... ...	17825
Pugilistic	... ...	17826
Pugnacious	... ...	17827
Pugnacity	... ...	17828
Puisne ...	... ...	17829
Puissance	... ...	17830
Puissant	... ...	17831
Puke	... ...	17832
Puking ...	... ...	17833
Pull	... ...	17834
Pulled	... ...	17835
Pullet	... ...	17836
Pulley	... ...	17837
Pulling ...	... ...	17838
Pulmonary	... ...	17839
Pulp	... ...	17840
Pulpiness	... ...	17841
Pulpit ...	... ...	17842
Pulpy ...	... ...	17843
Pulsate ...	... ...	17844
Pulsated	... ...	17845
Pulsating	... ...	17846
Pulsation	... ...	17847
Pulsatory	... ...	17848
Pulse	... ...	17849
Pulseless	... ...	17850

Pulverable	... ...	17851
Pulverization ...	...	17852
Pulverize	... ...	17853
Pulverized	... ...	17854
Pulverous	... ...	17855
Pumice ...	... ...	17856
Pump ...	... ...	17857
Pumped ...	... ...	17858
Pumping	... ...	17859
Pumpkin	... ...	17860
Pun... ...	... ...	17861
Punch ...	... ...	17862
Punched...	... ...	17863
Puncheon	... ...	17864
Puncher ...	... ...	17865
Punchinello ...	...	17866
Punching	... ...	17867
Punchy ...	... ...	17868
Punctilio	... ...	17869
Punctilious	... ...	17870
Punctiliously ...	...	17871
Punctual...	... ...	17872
Punctuality	... ...	17873
Punctually	... ...	17874
Punctuate	... ...	17875
Punctuated	... ...	17876
Punctuation ...	...	17877
Puncture	... ...	17878
Punctured	... ...	17879
Pundit ...	... ...	17880
Pungency	... ...	17881
Pungent ...	... ...	17882
Pungently	... ...	17883
Puniness...	... ...	17884
Punish ...	... ...	17885
Punishable	... ...	17886
Punished	... ...	17887
Punisher...	... ...	17888
Punishing	... ...	17889
Punishment	... ...	17890
Punitive ...	... ...	17891
Punning ...	... ...	17892
Punster ...	... ...	17893
Punt	... ...	17894
Punted ..	... ...	17895
Punter ...	... ...	17896
Puny ...	... ...	17897
Pup... ...	... ...	17898
Pupil ...	... ...	17899
Pupilage...	... ...	17900

Puppet	17901	Pursuant 17951
Puppy	17902	Pursue 17952
Pur	17903	Pursued 17953
Purblind...	17904	Pursuer 17954
Purchasable	17905	Pursuing... 17955
Purchase	17906	Pursuit 17956
Purchased	17907	Pursuivant ... 17957
Purchaser	17908	Pursy 17958
Purchasing	17909	Purulence 17959
Pure	17910	Purulent... 17960
Purely	17911	Purvey 17961
Pureness...	17912	Purveyance 17962
Purgation	17913	Purveyed 17963
Purgative	17914	Purveying 17964
Purgatorial	17915	Purveyor 17965
Purgatory	17916	Pus... 17966
Purge	17917	Puseyism 17967
Purged	17918	Push 17968
Purging	17919	Pushed 17969
Purification	17920	Pushing 17970
Purificative	17921	Pusillanimity... ... 17971
Purified	17922	Pusillanimous ... 17972
Purifier	17923	Pustule 17973
Purify	17924	Pustulous 17974
Purifying	17925	Put 17975
Purist	17926	Putative... 17976
Puritanical	17927	Putrefaction 17977
Purity	17928	Putrefactive 17978
Purl	17929	Putrefied 17979
Purlieu	17930	Putrefy 17980
Purling	17931	Putrefying 17981
Purloin	17932	Putrescence 17982
Purloined	17933	Putrescent 17983
Purloining	17934	Putrid 17984
Purple	17935	Putridity 17985
Purplish	17936	Putty 17986
Purport	17937	Puzzle 17987
Purported	17938	Puzzled 17988
Purporting	17939	Puzzling 17989
Purpose	17940	Pye... 17990
Purposed	17941	Pygmean 17991
Purposeless	17942	Pygmy 17992
Purposely	17943	Pyramid... 17993
Purposing	17944	Pyramidal 17994
Purring	17945	Pyramidally 17995
Purse	17946	Pyre 17996
Purser	17947	Pyrotechnic 17997
Pursiness	17948	Pyrotechny 17998
Pursuable	17949	Python 17999
Pursuance	17950	Pythonic... 18000

Q.	18001	Qualifying 18051
Quack	18002	Quality 18052
Quackery	18003	Qualm 18053
Quackish	18004	Qualmish 18054
Quadragesima ...	18005	Quandary 18055
Quadrangle	18006	Quantitive 18056
Quadrangular ...	18007	Quantity... 18057
Quadrant	18008	Quantum 18058
Quadrate	18009	Quarantine 18059
Quadratic	18010	Quarrel 18060
Quadrature	18011	Quarrelled 18061
Quadrennial	18012	Quarreller 18062
Quadrilateral... ...	18013	Quarrelling 18063
Quadrille	18014	Quarrelsome 18064
Quadrillion	18015	Quarrelsomeness ... 18065
Quadrinomial... ...	18016	Quarry 18066
Quadripartite... ...	18017	Quarrying 18067
Quadrireme	18018	Quart 18068
Quadrisyllable ...	18019	Quartian... 18069
Quadroon	18020	Quarter 18070
Quadrumana	18021	Quartered 18071
Quadruped	18022	Quartering 18072
Quadruple	18023	Quarterly 18073
Quadrupled	18024	Quartern... 18074
Quadruplicate ...	18025	Quarters... 18075
Quadruplication ...	18026	Quartette 18076
Quæstor	18027	Quarto 18077
Quaff	18028	Quartz 18078
Quaffed	18029	Quartzose 18079
Quaffing	18030	Quash 18080
Quagga	18031	Quashed... 18081
Quaggy	18032	Quashing 18082
Quagmire	18033	Quasi 18083
Quail	18034	Quassation 18084
Quailed	18035	Quassia 18085
Quailing...	18036	Quatern 18086
Quaint	18037	Quaternary 18087
Quaintly	18038	Quaternion 18088
Quaintness	18039	Quatrain... 18089
Quake	18040	Quaver 18090
Quaked	18041	Quavered 18091
Quaker	18042	Quavering 18092
Quakerish	18043	Quay 18093
Quakerism	18044	Quean 18094
Quaking...	18045	Queen 18095
Qualifiable	18046	Queenly 18096
Qualification	18047	Queer 18097
Qualified	18048	Queerly 18098
Qualifier...	18049	Queerness 18099
Qualify	18050	Quell 18100

QUE	(91)	QUO	182
Quelled 18101	Quinary 18151
Quelling... 18102	Quince 18152
Quench 18103	Quindecagon 18153
Quenchable 18104	Quinine 18154
Quenched 18105	Quinquagesima ... 18155
Quenching 18106	Quinquangular ... 18156
Quenchless 18107	Quinquennial... ... 18157
Quercitron 18108	Quinquepartite ... 18158
Querist 18109	Quinquina 18159
Quernal 18110	Quinsy 18160
Querulous 18111	Quint 18161
Query 18112	Quintal 18162
Quest 18113	Quintessence 18163
Question... 18114	Quintet 18164
Questionable 18115	Quintillion 18165
Questioned 18116	Quintuple 18166
Questioner 18117	Quintupled 18167
Questioning 18118	Quip 18168
Questionless 18119	Quipping 18169
Quibble 18120	Quire 18170
Quibbled 18121	Quirkish... 18171
Quibbler... 18122	Quit 18172
Quibbling 18123	Quite 18173
Quibblingly 18124	Quits 18174
Quick 18125	Quittance 18175
Quicken 18126	Quitted 18176
Quickened 18127	Quitter 18177
Quickener 18128	Quitting 18178
Quickening 18129	Quiver 18179
Quickly 18130	Quivered 18180
Quickness 18131	Quivering 18181
Quicksand 18132	Quixotic... 18182
Quickset... 18133	Quixotism 18183
Quicksilver 18134	Quiz 18184
Quicksilvered ... 18135	Quizzed 18185
Quid 18136	Quizzing... 18186
Quidnunc 18137	Quodlibet 18187
Quiescence 18138	Quoin 18188
Quiescent 18139	Quoit 18189
Quiet 18140	Quorum 18190
Quieted 18141	Quota 18191
Quieter 18142	Quotable 18192
Quietly 18143	Quotation 18193
Quietness 18144	Quote 18194
Quietude 18145	Quoted 18195
Quietus 18146	Quoter 18196
Quill 18147	Quoting 18197
Quilt 18148	Quoth 18198
Quilted 18149	Quotidian 18199
Quilting 18150	Quotient... 18200

R	...	...	...	18201	Raining ...	...	18251
Rabbi	...	...	...	18202	Rainy ...	...	18252
Rabbinical	...	...	18203	Raise ...	...	18253
Rabbit	...	...	...	18204	Raised ...	...	18254
Rabble	...	...	...	18205	Raisin ...	...	18255
Rabid	...	...	...	18206	Raising ...	...	18256
Rabies	...	...	...	18207	Rajah ...	...	18257
Race	...	...	...	18208	Rajpoot ...	...	18258
Raced	...	...	...	18209	Rake ...	...	18259
Racer	...	...	...	18210	Raked ...	...	18260
Raciness	...	...	...	18211	Raking ...	...	18261
Rack	...	...	...	18212	Rakish ...	...	18262
Racked	...	...	...	18213	Rallied ...	...	18263
Racket	...	...	...	18214	Rally ...	...	18264
Racketing	...	...	18215	Rallying ...	...	18265
Rackety	...	...	...	18216	Ram ...	...	18266
Racking	...	...	...	18217	Ramadan ...	...	18267
Racoon	...	...	...	18218	Ramble ...	...	18268
Racy	...	...	...	18219	Rambled ...	...	18269
Radiance	...	...	18220	Rambler ...	...	18270
Radiant	...	...	...	18221	Rambling ...	...	18271
Radiate	...	...	...	18222	Ramification ...	...	18272
Radiated	...	...	18223	Ramified ...	...	18273
Radiating	...	...	18224	Ramify ...	...	18274
Radiation	...	...	18225	Rammed ...	...	18275
Radiator	...	...	18226	Rampancy ...	...	18276
Radical	...	...	...	18227	Rampant ...	...	18277
Radicalism	...	...	18228	Rampart ...	...	18278
Radically	...	...	18229	Ramrod ...	...	18279
Radius	...	...	...	18230	Ran ...	...	18280
Raffle	...	...	...	18231	Rancid ...	...	18281
Raffled	...	...	...	18232	Rancidity ...	...	18282
Raffling	...	...	...	18233	Rancour ...	...	18283
Raft	...	...	...	18234	Rancorous ...	...	18284
Rafter	...	...	...	18235	Random ...	...	18285
Rag	...	...	...	18236	Rang ...	...	18286
Rage	...	...	...	18237	Range ...	...	18287
Ragged	...	...	...	18238	Ranged ...	...	18288
Raggedness	...	...	18239	Ranger ...	...	18289
Raging	...	...	...	18240	Ranging ...	...	18290
Raid	...	...	...	18241	Rank ...	...	18291
Rail	...	...	...	18242	Ranked ...	...	18292
Railer	...	...	...	18243	Ranking ...	...	18293
Railing	...	...	...	18244	Rankle ...	...	18294
Raillery	...	...	...	18245	Rankled ...	...	18295
Railway	...	...	...	18246	Rankling ...	...	18296
Raiment	...	...	...	18247	Rankly ...	...	18297
Rain	...	...	...	18248	Rankness ...	...	18298
Rainbow	...	...	18249	Ransack ...	...	18299
Rained	...	...	...	18250	Ransacked ...	...	18300

Ransacking	18301	Ratification 18351
Ransom	18302	Ratified 18352
Ramsomed	18303	Ratifier 18353
Ransoming	18304	Ratify 18354
Rant	18305	Ratifying 18355
Ranted	18306	Rating 18356
Ranter	18307	Ratio 18357
Ranting	18308	Ratiocination... ... 18358
Rap...	18309	Ratiocinative... ... 18359
Rapacious	18310	Ration 18360
Rapacity	18311	Rational... 18361
Rape	18312	Rationalism 18362
Rapid	18313	Rationalist 18363
Rapidity...	18314	Rationalistic 18364
Rapidly	18315	Rationally 18365
Rapier	18316	Ratlin 18366
Rapine	18317	Rattle 18367
Rapped	18318	Rattled 18368
Rapper	18319	Rattling 18369
Rapping...	18320	Ravage 18370
Rapt	18321	Ravaged... 18371
Rapture	18322	Ravager 18372
Raptured	18323	Ravaging 18373
Rapturous	18324	Rave 18374
Rare	18325	Raved 18375
Rarefaction	18326	Raven 18376
Rarefied	18327	Ravening 18377
Rarefy	18328	Ravenously 18378
Rarefying	18329	Ravine 18379
Rarely	18330	Raving 18380
Rareness	18331	Ravish 18381
Rarity	18332	Ravished 18382
Rascal	18333	Ravisher... 18383
Rascality	18334	Ravishing 18384
Rascally...	18335	Ravishment 18385
Rash	18336	Raw 18386
Rasher	18337	Rawness... 18387
Rashly	18338	Ray... 18388
Rashness	18339	Rayless 18389
Rasp	18340	Raze 18390
Raspberry	18341	Razed 18391
Rasper	18342	Razing 18392
Rat	18343	Razor 18393
Ratable	18344	Reach 18394
Ratably	18345	Reached... 18395
Ratan	18346	Reaching 18396
Rate	18347	Reaction... 18397
Rated	18348	Reactive... 18398
Rater	18349	Read 18399
Rather	18350	Readable 18400

185	REA	(93)	REC	
Reader		18401	Rebellion	18451
Readily		18402	Rebellious	18452
Readiness		18403	Rebound	18453
Reading		18404	Rebounded	18454
Readjust		18405	Rebounding	18455
Readjusted		18406	Rebuff	18456
Readmission		18407	Rebuffed	18457
Readmitted		18408	Rebuild	18458
Reads		18409	Rebuilt	18459
Ready		18410	Rebuke	18460
Reagent		18411	Rebuked	18461
Real		18412	Rebuking	18462
Reality		18413	Rebukingly	18463
Realization		18414	Rebut	18464
Realize		18415	Rebutted	18465
Realized		18416	Rebutting	18466
Realizing		18417	Recalcitrant	18467
Really		18418	Recall	18468
Realm		18419	Recalled	18469
Ream		18420	Recalling	1847c
Reanimate		18421	Recant	18471
Reanimated		18422	Recantation	18472
Reanimation		18423	Recanted	18473
Reap		18424	Recapacitate	18474
Reaped		18425	Recapacitated	18475
Reaper		18426	Recapitulate	18476
Reaping		18427	Recapitulated	18477
Reappoint		18428	Recapitulating	18478
Reappointed		18429	Recapitulation	18479
Reappointment		18430	Recapitulatory	18480
Rear		18431	Recapture	18481
Reared		18432	Recede	18482
Rearing		18433	Receded	18483
Rearrange		18434	Receding	18484
Rearranged		18435	Receipt	18485
Rearward		18436	Receipted	18486
Reason		18437	Receivable	18487
Reasonable		18438	Receive	18488
Reasonably		18439	Received	18489
Reasoned		18440	Receiver	18490
Reasoner		18441	Receiving	18491
Reasoning		18442	Recent	18492
Reassurance		18443	Recently	18493
Reassure		18444	Receptacle	18494
Reassured		18445	Reception	18495
Reassuring		18446	Recess	18496
Rebate		18447	Recession	18497
Rebel		18448	Recipe	18498
Rebelled		18449	Recipient	18499
Rebelling		18450	Reciprocal	18500

REC	(94)	REC	186

Reciprocally	18501	Recommending ...	18551
Reciprocate	18502	Recommission ...	18552
Reciprocated	18503	Recommissioned ...	18553
Reciprocating ...	18504	Recommit	18554
Reciprocation ...	18505	Recommital ...	18555
Reciprocity	18506	Recommitted	18556
Recital	18507	Recommitting ...	18557
Recitation	18508	Recompense	18558
Recitative	18509	Recompensed... ...	18559
Recite	18510	Recompensing ...	18560
Recited	18511	Recompose	18561
Reciter	18512	Recomposed	18562
Reciting	18513	Recomposing	18563
Reckless...	18514	Reconcilable	18564
Recklessly	18515	Reconcile	18565
Recklessness	18516	Reconciled	18566
Reckon	18517	Reconciling	18567
Reckoned	18518	Reconcilement ...	18568
Reckoner	18519	Reconciler	18569
Reckoning	18520	Reconciliation ...	18570
Reclaim	18521	Reconciliatory ...	18571
Reclaimable	18522	Recondensation ...	18572
Reclaimant	18523	Recondense	18573
Reclaimed	18524	Recondensed	18574
Reclaiming	18525	Recondensing ...	18575
Reclamation	18526	Recondite	18576
Reclination	18527	Reconnoitre	18577
Recline	18528	Reconnoitred	18578
Reclined...	18529	Reconnoitring ...	18579
Reclining	18530	Reconsider	18580
Recluse	18531	Reconsideration ...	18581
Recognisable	18532	Reconsidered... ...	18582
Recognisance... ...	18533	Reconsidering ...	18583
Recognise	18534	Reconstruct	18584
Recognised	18535	Reconstructed ...	18585
Recognising	18536	Reconstructing ...	18586
Recognition	18537	Reconstruction ...	18587
Recoil	18538	Reconvey	18588
Recoiled	18539	Reconveyed	18589
Recoiling	18540	Reconveying	18590
Recoinage	18541	Record	18591
Recollect	18542	Recorded	18592
Recollected	18543	Recorder	18593
Recollecting	18544	Recording	18594
Recollection	18545	Recount	18595
Recommend	18546	Recounted	18596
Recommendable ...	18547	Recounting	18597
Recommendation ...	18548	Recourse...	18598
Recommendatory ...	18549	Recover	18599
Recommended ...	18550	Recoverable	18600

Recovered	...	...	18601	Redemption ...	...	18651
Recovering	...	...	18602	Redemptive ...	...	18652
Recovery	...	...	18603	Redness ...	...	18653
Recreancy	...	...	18604	Redolence	...	18654
Recreant...	...	...	18605	Redolent	...	18655
Recreate...	...	...	18606	Redouble	...	18656
Recreated	...	...	18607	Redoubled	...	18657
Recreating	...	...	18608	Redoubling	...	18658
Recreation	...	...	18609	Redoubt...	...	18659
Recreative	...	...	18610	Redoubtable ...	...	18660
Recriminate	...	...	18611	Redound...	...	18661
Recriminating	...	18612	Redounded	...	18662
Recrimination	...	18613	Redounding	...	18663
Recriminatory	...	18614	Redress ...	...	18664
Recruit ...	...	...	18615	Redressed	...	18665
Recruited	...	...	18616	Redressing	...	18666
Recruiter	...	...	18617	Reduce ...	...	18667
Recruiting	...	...	18618	Reduced...	...	18668
Rectangle	...	...	18619	Reducing	...	18669
Rectangular	...	...	18620	Reducible	...	18670
Rectifiable	...	...	18621	Reduction	...	18671
Rectification	...	...	18622	Redundancy ...	...	18672
Rectified...	...	...	18623	Redundant ...	...	18673
Rectify ...	...	...	18624	Redundantly ...	...	18674
Rectifying	...	...	18625	Reed	...	...	18675
Rectilinear	...	...	18626	Reedy ...	...	..	18676
Rectitude	...	...	18627	Reef ...	...	...	18677
Rector ...	...	...	18628	Reek ...	...	...	18678
Rectorial	...	...	18629	Reeked ...	...	18679
Rectorship	...	...	18630	Reeking ...	...	18680
Rectory ...	...	...	18631	Reel ...	...	...	18681
Recumbence ...	...	18632	Reeled ...	...	...	18682
Recumbent	...	...	18633	Reeling ...	...	...	18683
Recuperative ...	...	18634	Reeve ...	...	...	18684
Recur ...	...	...	18635	Refection	...	...	18685
Recurred	...	...	18636	Refectory	...	...	18686
Recurrence	...	...	18637	Refer ...	...	...	18687
Recurrent	...	...	18638	Referable	...	...	18688
Recurring	...	...	18639	Referee ...	...	18689
Recusant	...	...	18640	Reference	...	...	18690
Red... ...	...	...	18641	Reterred...	...	18691
Redaction	...	...	18642	Referring	...	...	18692
Redan ...	...	...	18643	Refine ...	...	18693
Redden ...	...	...	18644	Refined ...	...	18694
Reddish ...	...	...	18645	Refinement	...	18695
Redeem ...	...	...	18646	Refiner ...	...	18696
Redeemable	...	...	18647	Refinery ...	...	18697
Redeemed	...	...	18648	Refining ...	...	18698
Redeemer	...	...	18649	Refit ...	...	...	18699
Redeeming	...	...	18650	Refitted ...	...	...	18700

REF	(95)	REG	188

Reflect	18701	Refutable 18751
Reflected	18702	Refutation 18752
Reflecting	18703	Refute 18753
Reflection	18704	Refuted 18754
Reflective	18705	Refuting 18755
Reflector	18706	Regain 18756
Reflex	18707	Regained 18757
Reflexible	18708	Regaining 18758
Reflux	18709	Regal 18759
Reform	18710	Regale 18760
Reformation	18711	Regaled 18761
Reformatory	18712	Regaling 18762
Reformed	18713	Regalement 18763
Reformer	18714	Regalia 18764
Reforming	18715	Regality 18765
Refract	18716	Regard 18766
Refracted	18717	Regarded 18767
Refracting	18718	Regardful 18768
Refractive	18719	Regarding 18769
Refractorily	18720	Regardless 18770
Refractoriness ...	18721	Regatta 18771
Refractory	18722	Regency 18772
Refrain	18723	Regeneracy 18773
Refrained	18724	Regenerate 18774
Refraining	18725	Regenerated 18775
Refrangibility ...	18726	Regenerating 18776
Refrangible	18727	Regeneration 18777
Refresh	18728	Regent 18778
Refreshed	18729	Regicide 18779
Refresher	18730	Régime 18780
Refreshing	18731	Regimen 18781
Refreshment	18732	Regiment 18782
Refrigerant	18733	Regimental 18783
Refrigerate	18734	Region 18784
Refrigerated	18735	Register 18785
Refrigerating ...	18736	Registered 18786
Refrigeration ...	18737	Registering 18787
Refrigerative ...	18738	Registrar 18788
Refrigerator ...	18739	Registration 18789
Refuge	18740	Registry 18790
Refugee	18741	Regnant 18791
Refulgence	18742	Regret 18792
Refulgent	18743	Regretful 18793
Refund	18744	Regretted 18794
Refunded	18745	Regretting 18795
Refunding	18746	Regular 18796
Refusal	18747	Regularity 18797
Refuse	18748	Regularly 18798
Refused	18749	Regulate 18799
Refusing	18750	Regulated 18800

Regulating	...	...	18801	Rejoiced... 18851
Regulation	...	...	18802	Rejoicing 18852
Regulator	...	...	18803	Rejoin 18853
Rehabilitate	...	...	18804	Rejoinder 18854
Rehabilitated...	...	18805	Rejoined... 18855
Rehear	...	...	18806	Rejoining 18856
Reheard	...	...	18807	Rejuvenescence ... 18857
Rehearing	...	...	18808	Relapse 18858
Rehearsal	...	...	18809	Relapsed 18859
Rehearse...	...	...	18810	Relate 18860
Rehearsed	...	...	18811	Related 18861
Reign	...	...	18812	Relating 18862
Reigned	...	...	18813	Relation 18863
Reigning...	...	...	18814	Relationship 18864
Reimbody	...	...	18815	Relative 18865
Reimbodied	...	...	18816	Relatively 18866
Reimburse	...	...	18817	Relax 18867
Reimbursed	...	...	18818	Relaxation 18868
Reimbursement	...	18819	Relaxative 18869
Reimburser	...	...	18820	Relaxed 18870
Reimbursing	...	...	18821	Relaxing... 18871
Rein	...	...	18822	Relay 18872
Reined	...	...	18823	Release 18873
Reinforce	...	...	18824	Released... 18874
Reinforced	...	...	18825	Releasing 18875
Reinforcing	...	...	18826	Relent 18876
Reins	...	...	18827	Relented... 18877
Reinstate	...	...	18828	Relenting 18878
Reinstated	...	...	18829	Relentless 18879
Reinstatement	...	18830	Relet 18880
Reinsurance	...	...	18831	Relevant... 18881
Reinsure...	...	...	18832	Reliable 18882
Reinsured	...	...	18833	Reliance... 18883
Reinsuring	...	...	18834	Reliant 18884
Reinvestment...	...	18835	Relic 18885
Reinvigorate	...	...	18836	Relict 18886
Reinvigorated	...	18837	Relied 18887
Reinvigorating	...	18838	Relief 18888
Reissue	...	...	18839	Relieve 18889
Reissued...	...	...	18840	Relieved... 18890
Reiterate	...	...	18841	Relieving 18891
Reiterated	...	...	18842	Relievo 18892
Reiterating	...	...	18843	Religion 18893
Reiteration	...	...	18844	Religionist 18894
Reject	...	...	18845	Religious 18895
Rejectable	...	...	18846	Religiously 18896
Rejected...	...	...	18847	Relinquish 18897
Rejecting	...	...	18848	Relinquished 18898
Rejection	...	...	18849	Relinquishing ... 18899
Rejoice ...	...	...	18850	Relinquishment ... 18900

Reliquary	18901	Remonstrating ... 18951
Relish	18902	Remorse 18952
Relished	18903	Remorseful 18953
Reluctance	18904	Remorseless 18954
Reluctant	18905	Remote 18955
Reluctantly	18906	Remotely 18956
Rely	18907	Removability 18957
Relying	18908	Removable 18958
Remain	18909	Removal 18959
Remainder	18910	Remove 18960
Remained	18911	Removed 18961
Remaining	18912	Removing 18962
Remains	18913	Remunerate 18963
Remand	18914	Remunerated 18964
Remanded	18915	Remunerating ... 18965
Remark	18916	Remuneration ... 18966
Remarkable	18917	Remunerative ... 18967
Remarkably	18918	Remuneratory ... 18968
Remarked	18919	Renal 18969
Remarking	18920	Renascent 18970
Remediable	18921	Rencounter 18971
Remedial	18922	Rend 18972
Remedy	18923	Render 18973
Remember	18924	Rendered 18974
Remembered	18925	Rendering 18975
Rememberer	18926	Rendezvous 18976
Remembering ...	18927	Rending 18977
Remembrance ...	18928	Renegade 18978
Remembrancer ...	18929	Renew 18979
Remind	18930	Renewable 18980
Reminded	18931	Renewal 18981
Reminder	18932	Renewed 18982
Reminding	18933	Renewing 18983
Reminiscence	18934	Renitence 18984
Remise	18935	Rennet 18985
Remiss	18936	Renounce 18986
Remission	18937	Renounced 18987
Remissness	18938	Renouncement ... 18988
Remit	18939	Renouncing 18989
Remittance	18940	Renovate 18990
Remitted	18941	Renovated 18991
Remittent	18942	Renovating 18992
Remitting	18943	Renovation 18993
Remnant	18944	Renovator 18994
Remodel	18945	Renown 18995
Remodelled	18946	Renowned 18996
Remonstrance ...	18947	Rent 18997
Remonstrant	18948	Rentable 18998
Remonstrate	18949	Rental 18999
Remonstrated ...	18950	Rented 19000

Renunciation...	...	19001	Repletion 19051
Reorganization	...	19002	Repleviable 19052
Reorganize ...	...	19003	Replevied 19053
Reorganized ...	...	19004	Replevin... 19054
Repaid	...	19005	Replevy 19055
Repair	...	19006	Replication 19056
Repairable ...	...	19007	Replied 19057
Repaired... ...	...	19008	Reply 19058
Repairer	...	19009	Replying... 19059
Repairing ...	...	19010	Report 19060
Reparable ...	...	19011	Reported 19061
Reparation ...	...	19012	Reporter... 19062
Repartee... ...	...	19013	Reporting 19063
Repast	...	19014	Repose 19064
Repay	...	19015	Reposed 19065
Repaying ...	...	19016	Reposing 19066
Repayment ...	...	19017	Repository 19067
Repeal	...	19018	Reprehend 19068
Repealed ...	...	19019	Reprehended... ... 19069
Repealer... ...	...	19020	Reprehensible ... 19070
Repealing .. '...		19021	Reprehensibly ... 19071
Repeat	...	19022	Reprehension... ... 19072
Repeated ...	...	19023	Reprehensive... ... 19073
Repeatedly ...	...	19024	Represent 19074
Repeater... ...	...	19025	Representation ... 19075
Repeating ...	...	19026	Representative ... 19076
Repel	...	19027	Represented 19077
Repelled... ...	...	19028	Representing 19078
Repellent ...	...	19029	Repress 19079
Repeller... ...	...	19030	Repressed 19080
Repelling ...	...	19031	Represser 19081
Repent	...	19032	Repressing 19082
Repentance ...	...	19033	Repression 19083
Repentant ...	...	19034	Repressive 19084
Repented ...	...	19035	Reprieval 19085
Repenting ...	...	19036	Reprieve... 19086
Repertory ...	...	19037	Reprieved 19087
Repetition ...	...	19038	Reprimand 19088
Repetitional ...		19039	Reprimanded... ... 19089
Repine	...	19040	Reprimanding ... 19090
Repined	...	19041	Reprint 19091
Repining... ...	...	19042	Reprinted 19092
Replace	...	19043	Reprisal 19093
Replaced ...	...	19044	Reproach 19094
Replacing ...	...	19045	Reproachable... ... 19095
Replacement ...	...	19046	Reproached 19096
Replenish ...	...	19047	Reproachful 19097
Replenished ...	...	19048	Reproachfully ... 19098
Replenishing ...	...	19049	Reproaching 19099
Replete	...	19050	Reprobate 19100

Reprobation	19101	Requited	19151
Reproduce	19102	Requiting	19152
Reproducing	19103	Rereward	19153
Reproduction	19104	Rescind	19154
Reproductive	19105	Rescinded	19155
Reproof	19106	Rescission	19156
Reprovable	19107	Rescue	19157
Reprove	19108	Rescued	19158
Reproved	19109	Rescuing	19159
Reprover	19110	Research	19160
Reproving	19111	Reseat	19161
Reptile	19112	Reseated	19162
Republic	19113	Resemblance	19163
Republican	19114	Resemble	19164
Republicanism ...	19115	Resembled	19165
Republication ...	19116	Resembling	19166
Republish	19117	Resent	19167
Republished	19118	Resented	19168
Repudiate	19119	Resentful	19169
Repudiated	19120	Resenting	19170
Repudiating	19121	Resentment	19171
Repudiation	19122	Reservation	19172
Repudiator	19123	Reserve	19173
Repugnance	19124	Reserved	19174
Repugnant	19125	Reserving	19175
Repulse	19126	Reservoir	19176
Repulsed	19127	Reside	19177
Repulsing	19128	Resided	19178
Repulsion	19129	Residing	19179
Repulsive	19130	Residence	19180
Repurchase	19131	Resident	19181
Repurchased	19132	Residential	19182
Reputable	19133	Residual	19183
Reputably	19134	Residuary	19184
Reputation	19135	Residue	19185
Repute	19136	Resign	19186
Reputed	19137	Resignation	19187
Request	19138	Resigned	19188
Requested	19139	Resignedly	19189
Requesting	19140	Resigning	19190
Requiem	19141	Resin	19191
Requirable	19142	Resinous	19192
Require	19143	Resist	19193
Required	19144	Resistance	19194
Requiring	19145	Resistant	19195
Requirement	19146	Resisted	19196
Requisite	19147	Resister	19197
Requisition	19148	Resistibility	19198
Requital	19149	Resistible	19199
Requite	19150	Resisting	19200

Resistive	... ...	19201
Resistless	... ...	19202
Resolute...	... ...	19203
Resolutely	... ...	19204
Resolution	... ...	19205
Resolvable	... ...	19206
Resolve ...	... ...	19207
Resolved	... ...	19208
Resolvent	... ...	19209
Resolving	... ...	19210
Resonance	... ...	19211
Resonant	... ...	19212
Resort ...	... ...	19213
Resorted	... ...	19214
Resorter...	... ...	19215
Resorting	... ...	19216
Resound...	... ...	19217
Resounded	... ...	19218
Resounding	... ...	19219
Resource	... ...	19220
Respect ...	... ...	19221
Respectability	...	19222
Respectable	... ...	19223
Respectably	... ...	19224
Respected	... ...	19225
Respectful	... ...	19226
Respectfully	... ...	19227
Respecting	... ...	19228
Respective	... ...	10229
Respectively	... ...	19230
Respirable	... ...	19231
Respiration	... ...	19232
Respirator	... ...	19233
Respiratory	... ...	19234
Respite ...	... ...	19235
Resplendence	...	19236
Resplendent	... ...	19237
Respond...	... ...	19238
Responded	... ...	19239
Respondent	... ...	19240
Respondentia	...	19241
Responding	... ...	19242
Response	... ...	19243
Responsibility	...	19244
Responsible	... ...	19245
Responsive	... ...	19246
Rest ...	... ...	19247
Rested ...	... ...	19248
Resting ...	... ...	19249
Restitution	... ...	19250
Restive ...	... ...	19251
Restless ...	... ...	19252
Restlessly	... ...	19253
Restoration	... ...	19254
Restorative	... ...	19255
Restore ...	... ...	19256
Restored	... ...	19257
Restorer...	... ...	19258
Restoring	... ...	19259
Restrain...	... ...	19260
Restrained	... ...	19261
Restrainedly ...	...	19262
Restrainer	... ...	19263
Restraining	... ...	19264
Restraint	... ...	19265
Restrict ...	... ...	19266
Restricted	... ...	19267
Restriction	... ...	19268
Restrictive	... ...	19269
Result ...	... ...	19270
Resulted...	... ...	19271
Resulting	... ...	19272
Resume ...	... ...	19273
Resumed	... ...	19274
Resuming	... ...	19275
Resumption	... ...	19276
Resurrection ...	...	19277
Resuscitate	... ...	19278
Resuscitated	... ...	19279
Resuscitating...	...	19280
Resuscitation...	...	19281
Retail ...	... ...	19282
Retailed...	... ...	19283
Retailer ...	... ...	19284
Retailing	... ...	19285
Retain ...	... ...	19286
Retained	... ...	19287
Retainer...	... ...	19288
Retaining	... ...	19289
Retake ...	... ...	19290
Retaken...	... ...	19291
Retaking	... ...	19292
Retaliate	... ...	19293
Retaliated	... ...	19294
Retaliating	... ...	19295
Retaliation	... ...	19296
Retaliatory	... ...	19297
Retard ...	... ...	19298
Retardation	... ...	19299
Retarded	... ...	19300

RET	(97)	REV	194

Retarder...	...	...	19301	Return 19351
Retarding	...	...	19302	Returned 91352
Retch	...	...	19303	Returning 19353
Retched...	...	...	19304	Reunion... 19354
Retching	...	...	19305	Reunite 19355
Retention	...	...	19306	Reunited 19356
Retentive	...	...	19307	Reuniting 19357
Retentiveness		...	19308	Reveal 19358
Reticence	...	...	19309	Revealed 19359
Reticent...	...	...	19310	Revealer... 19360
Reticular	...	...	19311	Revealing 19361
Reticule...	...	...	19312	Reveille 19362
Retina ...	...	...	19313	Revel 19363
Retinue ...	...	...	19314	Revelation 19364
Retire	...	...	19315	Revelled... 19365
Retired ...	...	...	19316	Reveller 19366
Retirement	...	...	19317	Revelling 19367
Retiring ...	...	...	19318	Revelry 19368
Retook ...	...	...	19319	Revenge... 19369
Retort ...	...	...	19320	Revenged 19370
Retorted...	...	...	19321	Revengeful 19371
Retorting	...	...	19322	Revengefully 19372
Retrace ...	...	...	19323	Revenging 19373
Retraced	...	...	19324	Revenue... 19374
Retracing	...	...	19325	Reverberant 19375
Retract ...	...	...	19326	Reverberate 19376
Retractation	...	...	19327	Reverberated... ... 19377
Retracted	...	...	19328	Reverberating ... 19378
Retracting	...	...	19329	Revere 19379
Retractible	...	...	19330	Revered 19380
Retractive	...	...	19331	Reverence 19381
Retreat ...	...	...	19332	Reverend 19382
Retreated	...	...	19333	Reverent 19383
Retreating	...	...	19334	Reverential 19384
Retrench	...	...	19335	Reverie 19385
Retrenchment		...	19336	Revering 19386
Retribution	...	...	19337	Reversal... 19387
Retributive	...	...	19338	Reverse 19388
Retrievable	...	...	19339	Reversed 19389
Retrieve...	...	...	19340	Reversible 19390
Retrieved	...	...	19341	Reversing 19391
Retrieving	...	...	19342	Reversion 19392
Retroactive	...	...	19343	Reversionary... ... 19393
Retrograde	...	...	19344	Revert 19394
Retrogression		...	19345	Reverted 19395
Retrogressive...		...	19346	Revertible 19396
Retrospect	...	...	19347	Reverting 19397
Retrospection		...	19348	Revertive 19398
Retrospective		...	19349	Review 19399
Retrospectively		...	19350	Reviewed 19400

Reviewer	19401	Rib 19451
Reviewing	19402	Ribald 19452
Revile	19403	Ribaldry... 19453
Reviled	19404	Ribbed 19454
Reviler	19405	Ribbon 19455
Reviling...	19406	Rice 19456
Revisal	19407	Rich 19457
Revise	19408	Riches 19458
Revised	19409	Richly 19459
Revising...	19410	Richness 19460
Revision... ...	19411	Rick 19461
Revival	19412	Rickets 19462
Revive	19413	Rickety 19463
Revived	19414	Rid 19464
Revivified	19415	Riddance 19465
Revivify	19416	Ridden 19466
Reviving	19417	Riddle 19467
Revocable	19418	Riddled 19468
Revocation	19419	Riddling... 19469
Revocatory	19420	Ride 19470
Revoke	19421	Rider 19471
Revoked...	19422	Rides 19472
Revoking	19423	Ridge 19473
Revolt	19424	Ridicule 19474
Revolted	19425	Ridiculed 19475
Revolting	19426	Ridiculous 19476
Revolution	19427	Riding 19477
Revolutionary ...	19428	Rife 19478
Revolutionize... ...	19429	Riffraff 19479
Revolutionized ...	19430	Rifle 19480
Revolve	19431	Rifled 19481
Revolved	19432	Rift... 19482
Revolving	19433	Rig 19483
Reward	19434	Rigged 19484
Rewarded	19435	Rigger 19485
Rewarding	19436	Rigging 19486
Rhapsodical	19437	Right 19487
Rhapsodist	19438	Righted 19488
Rhapsody	19439	Righteous 19489
Rhetoric...	19440	Righteously 19490
Rhetorical	19441	Righteousness ... 19491
Rhetorician	19442	Rightful 19492
Rheumatic	19443	Rightfully 19493
Rheumatism	19444	Righting... 19494
Rhinoceros	19445	Rightly 19495
Rhodomontade ...	19446	Rightness 19496
Rhubard...	19447	Rigid 19497
Rhyme	19448	Rigidity 19498
Rhymer	19449	Rigidly 19499
Rhyming	19450	Rigmarole 19500

RIG	(98)	ROG	196

Rigorous	... ...	19501	Rivalled...	... ...	19551
Rigorously	... ...	19502	Rivalling	... ...	19552
Rigour ...	... ...	19503	Rivalry ...	... ...	19553
Rill... ...	... ...	19504	Rive ...	... ...	19554
Rim ...	... ...	19505	Riven ...	... ...	19555
Rime ...	... ...	19506	River ...	... ...	19556
Rimy ...	... ...	19507	Rivet ...	... ...	19557
Rind ...	... ...	19508	Rivetted...	... ...	19558
Ring ...	... ...	19509	Rivetting	... ...	19559
Rings ...	... ...	19510	Rivulet ...	... ...	19560
Ringer ...	... ...	19511	Roach ...	... ...	19561
Ringing ...	... ...	19512	Road ...	... ...	19562
Ringleader	... ...	19513	Roadstead	... ...	19563
Ringlet ...	... ...	19514	Roadster...	... ...	19564
Rinse ...	... ...	19515	Roadway	... ...	19565
Rinsed ...	... ...	19516	Roam ...	... ...	19566
Rinsing ...	... ...	19517	Roamed ...	... ...	19567
Riot ...	... ...	19518	Roamer ...	... ...	19568
Rioted ...	... ...	19519	Roaming	... ...	19569
Rioter ...	... ...	19520	Roan ...	... ...	19570
Rioting ...	... ...	19521	Roar ...	... ...	19571
Riotous ...	... ...	19522	Roared ...	... ...	19572
Riotously	... ...	19523	Roarer ...	... ...	19573
Rip... ...	... ...	19524	Roaring ...	... ...	19574
Ripe ...	... ...	19525	Roast ...	... ...	19575
Ripely ...	... ...	19526	Roasted ...	... ...	19576
Ripen ...	... ...	19527	Roaster ...	... ...	19577
Ripened...	... ...	19528	Roasting...	... ...	19578
Ripening	... ...	19529	Rob... ...	... ...	19579
Ripeness...	... ...	19530	Robbed ...	... ...	19580
Ripped ...	... ...	19531	Robber ...	... ...	19581
Ripping ...	... ...	19532	Robbery ...	... ...	19582
Ripple ...	... ...	19533	Robbing...	... ...	19583
Rippled ...	... ...	19534	Robe ...	... ...	19584
Rippling...	... ...	19535	Robin ...	... ...	19585
Rise ...	... ...	19536	Robust ...	... ...	19586
Risen ...	... ...	19537	Rochet ...	... ...	19587
Rises ...	... ...	19538	Rock ...	... ...	19588
Risibility	... ...	19539	Rocked ...	... ...	19589
Risible ...	... ...	19540	Rocker ...	... ...	19590
Rising ...	... ...	19541	Rocket ...	... ...	19591
Risk ...	... ...	19542	Rockiness	... ...	19592
Risked ...	... ...	19543	Rocking ..	... ...	19593
Risking ...	... ...	19544	Rocky ...	... ...	19594
Rite ...	... ...	19545	Rod... ...	... ...	19595
Ritual ...	... ...	19546	Rode ...	... ...	19596
Ritualism	... ...	19547	Rodent ...	... ...	19597
Ritualist...	... ...	19548	Roebuck...	... ...	19598
Ritualistic	... ...	19549	Rogue ...	... ...	19599
Rival ...	.. ...	19550	Roguery...	... ...	19600

Roguish ...	...	...	19601	Rote	...	...	...	19651
Roguishly	...	...	19602	Rots	...	...	...	19652
Roisterer	...	...	19603	Rotted	...	...	19653
Roll	...	...	...	19604	Rotten	...	...	19654
Rolled	...	...	19605	Rottenness	...	...	19655
Roller	...	...	19606	Rotting ...	...	...	19656
Rolling ...	...	...	19607	Rotund	...	...	19657
Roman ...	...	...	19608	Rotunda...	...	...	19658
Romance	...	...	19609	Rotundity	...	...	19659
Romancer	...	...	19610	Roué	...	...	...	19660
Romancing	...	...	19611	Rouge	...	...	19661
Romanesque ...	...	19612	Rouged	...	...	19662
Romanism	...	...	19613	Rough	...	...	19663
Romanize	...	...	19614	Roughen...	...	...	19664
Romanized	...	...	19615	Roughened	...	...	19665
Romanizing ...	...	19616	Roughish	...	...	19666
Romantic	...	...	19617	Roughly ...	...	...	19667
Romantically...	...	19618	Roughness	...	...	19668
Romp ...	...	...	19619	Rouleau ...	...	...	19669
Romping	...	...	19620	Roulette ...	...	...	19670
Rompish...	...	...	19621	Round ...	...	...	19671
Rood	...	...	...	19622	Rounded...	...	...	19672
Roof	...	...	...	19623	Roundelay	...	...	19673
Roofing ...	...	...	19624	Rounding	...	...	19674
Rook	...	...	...	19625	Roundish	...	...	19675
Rookery...	...	...	19626	Roundly...	...	...	19676
Room	...	...	...	19627	Roundness	...	...	19677
Roominess	...	...	19628	Rounds ...	...	...	19678
Roomy ...	...	...	19629	Roup	...	...	...	19679
Roost	...	...	...	19630	Rouse	...	...	19680
Root	...	...	...	19631	Roused ...	...	...	19681
Rooted	...	...	19632	Rousing ...	...	...	19682
Rope	...	...	...	19633	Rout	...	...	...	19683
Ropy	...	...	...	19634	Route	...	...	19684
Rosary	...	...	19635	Routed	...	...	19685
Rose	...	...	...	19636	Routine ...	...	...	19686
Roseate ...	...	...	19637	Routing ...	...	...	19687
Rosette ...	...	...	19638	Rove	...	...	19688
Rosin	...	...	...	19639	Roved	...	...	19689
Roster	...	...	19640	Rover	...	...	19690
Rostral ...	...	...	19641	Roving ...	...	...	19691
Rostrum...	...	...	19642	Row	...	...	...	19692
Rosy	...	...	...	19643	Rowdy ...	...	...	19693
Rot ...	...	...	...	19644	Rowed ...	...	...	19694
Rotate	...	...	19645	Rowel ...	...	...	19695
Rotated ...	...	...	19646	Rower ...	...	...	19696
Rotating...	...	...	19647	Rowing ...	...	...	19697
Rotation...	...	...	19648	Royal ...	...	...	19698
Rotator ...	...	...	19649	Royally ...	...	...	19699
Rotatory...	...	...	19650	Royalty ...	...	...	19700

Rub...	19701	Rummaged 19751
Rubbed	19702	Rummaging 19752
Rubber	19703	Rumour 19753
Rubbing...	19704	Rumoured 19754
Rubbish	19705	Rump 19755
Rubescent	19706	Rumple 19756
Rubicund	19707	Rumpled 19757
Rubric	19708	Rumpling 19758
Rubrical...	19709	Run... 19759
Ruby	19710	Runagate 19760
Rudder	19711	Runaway 19761
Ruddiness	19712	Rundle 19762
Ruddy	19713	Rung 19763
Rude	19714	Runic 19764
Rudely	19715	Runlet 19765
Rudeness	19716	Runner 19766
Rudiment	19717	Runnet 19767
Rudimentary	19718	Running... 19768
Rue...	19719	Runs 19769
Rued	19720	Rupee 19770
Rueful	19721	Rupture 19771
Ruefully...	19722	Rural 19772
Ruff...	19723	Ruralist 19773
Ruffian	19724	Ruse 19774
Ruffle	19725	Rush 19775
Ruffled	19726	Rushed 19776
Ruffling	19727	Rushing 19777
Rug...	19728	Rushy 19778
Rugged	19729	Rusk 19779
Rugose	19730	Russet 19780
Ruin	19731	Russian 19781
Ruination	19732	Rust 19782
Ruined	19733	Rusted 19783
Ruining	19734	Rustic 19784
Ruinous	19735	Rusticate 19785
Ruinously	19736	Rusticated 19786
Rule	19737	Rustication 19787
Ruled	19738	Rusticity... 19788
Ruler	19739	Rustily 19789
Ruling	19740	Rustiness 19790
Rum	19741	Rusting 19791
Rumble	19742	Rustle 19792
Rumbled	19743	Rustled 19793
Rumbling	19744	Rustling 19794
Ruminant	19745	Rusty 19795
Ruminate	19746	Rut 19796
Ruminated	19747	Ruthless 19797
Ruminating	19748	Rye... 19798
Rumination	19749	Rythm 19799
Rummage	19750	Rythmical 19800

S	19801	Sailor 19851
Sabaoth	19802	Saint 19852
Sabbatarian	19803	Sainted 19853
Sabbath	19804	Saintly 19854
Sabbatical	19805	Sake 19855
Sable	19806	Salaam 19856
Sabre	19807	Salad 19857
Sabred	19808	Salamander ... 19858
Saccharify	19809	Salary 19859
Saccharine	19810	Sale... 19860
Sacerdotal	19811	Saleable 19861
Sachel	19812	Salesman 19862
Sack	19813	Salient 19863
Sacked	19814	Saliferous 19864
Sacking	19815	Salification 19865
Sacrament	19816	Salified 19866
Sacramental	19817	Salify 19867
Sacred	19818	Saline 19868
Sacredly...	19819	Saliva 19869
Sacrificatory	19820	Salivant 19870
Sacrifice	19821	Salivate 19871
Sacrificed	19822	Salivated 19872
Sacrificial	19823	Salivation 19873
Sacrificing	19824	Sallied 19874
Sacrilege	19825	Sallow 19875
Sacrilegious	19826	Sallowness 19876
Sacristan	19827	Sally 19877
Sacristy	19828	Sallying 19878
Sad	19829	Salmon 19879
Sadden	19830	Saloon 19880
Saddle	19831	Salt... 19881
Saddled	19832	Saltation... 19882
Saddler	19833	Salted 19883
Saddlery...	19834	Salter 19884
Sadly	19835	Salting 19885
Sadness	19836	Saltness 19886
Safe	19837	Saltpetre... 19887
Safely	19838	Salts 19888
Safety	19839	Salubrious 19889
Saffron	19840	Salubrity 19890
Sagacious	19841	Salutary 19891
Sagacity	19842	Salutation 19892
Sage	19843	Salute 19893
Sagittate...	19844	Saluted 19894
Sago	19845	Saluting 19895
Said	19846	Salvage 19896
Sail...	19847	Salvation 19897
Sailed	19848	Salve 19898
Sailer	19849	Salved 19899
Sailing	19850	Salver 19900

SAL	(100)	SAV	200

Salvo	19901	Sarcenet...	19951
Salvor	19902	Sarcophagus	19952
Same	19903	Sardine	19953
Samphire	19904	Sardonic...	19954
Sample	19905	Sarsaparilla	19955
Sampler	19906	Sash	19956
Sanatory...	19907	Satan	19957
Sanctification... ...	19908	Satanic	19958
Sanctified	19909	Satchel	19959
Sanctifier	19910	Sate	19960
Sanctify	19911	Satellite	19961
Sanctifying	19912	Satiate	19962
Sanctimonious ...	19913	Satiated	19963
Sanction...	19914	Satiating...	19964
Sanctioned	19915	Satiety	19965
Sanctioning	19916	Satin	19966
Sanctity	19917	Satinet	19967
Sanctuary	19918	Satire	19968
Sand	19919	Satirical	19969
Sandal	19920	Satirist	19970
Sandstone	19921	Satirize	19971
Sandwich	19922	Satirized...	19972
Sandy	19923	Satisfaction	19973
Sane	19924	Satisfactorily	19974
Sang	19925	Satisfactory	19975
Sanguinary	19926	Satisfied	19976
Sanguine	19927	Satisfy	19977
Sanguinely	19928	Satisfying	19978
Sanitary	19929	Satrap	19979
Sanity	19930	Saturate	19980
Sank	19931	Saturday...	19981
Sans	19932	Sauce	19982
Sanscrit	19933	Saucer	19983
Sap	19934	Saucily	19984
Sapience...	19935	Sauciness	19985
Sapient	19936	Saucy	19986
Sapless	19937	Saunter	19987
Sapling	19938	Sauntered	19988
Saponaceous	19939	Saunterer	19989
Saponify...	19940	Sauntering	19990
Sapped	19941	Saurians...	19991
Sapper	19942	Sausage	19992
Sapphire...	19943	Savage	19993
Sappiness	19944	Savagely...	19994
Sapping	19945	Savageness	19995
Sappy	19946	Savant	19996
Saraband	19947	Save	19997
Sarcasm	19948	Saved	19998
Sarcastic...	19949	Saving	19999
Sarcastically	19950	Saviour	20000

201	SAV	(101)	SCI	
Savour	20001	Scare	20051
Savouring	20002	Scared	20052
Savoury	20003	Scarf	20053
Saw...	20004	Scarify	20054
Sawed	20005	Scarified...	20055
Sawn	20006	Scarlatina	20056
Saws	20007	Scarlet	20057
Sawyer	20008	Scath	20058
Saxon	20009	Scathed	20059
Say	20010	Scathing...	20060
Says	20011	Scathless	20061
Saying	20012	Scatter	20062
Scab	20013	Scattered	20063
Scabbard	20014	Scattering	20064
Scaffold	20015	Scavenger	20065
Scaffolding	20016	Scene	20066
Scagliola...	20017	Scenery	20067
Scald	20018	Scenic	20068
Scalded	20019	Scent	20069
Scalding...	20020	Scented	20070
Scale	20021	Scentless...	20071
Scaled	20022	Sceptic	20072
Scaling	20023	Sceptical	20073
Scaliness...	20024	Scepticism	20074
Scallop	20025	Sceptre	20075
Scalp	20026	Schedule...	20076
Scalped	20027	Scheduled	20077
Scalping...	20028	Scheme	20078
Scaly	20029	Schemed...	20079
Scamp	20030	Schemer...	20080
Scamper...	20031	Scheming	20081
Scampered	20032	Schism	20082
Scampering	20033	Schismatic	20083
Scan	20034	Scholar	20084
Scandal	20035	Scholarly	20085
Scandalize	20036	Scholarship	20086
Scandalized	20037	Scholastic	20087
Scandalous	20038	School	20088
Scandalously ...	20039	Schooled	20089
Scant	20040	Schooling	20090
Scantily	20041	Schooner	20091
Scantiness	20042	Sciatica	20092
Scanty	20043	Science	20093
Scape	20044	Scientific	20094
Scapement	20045	Scientifically	20095
Scapular...	20046	Scimitar	20096
Scar	20047	Scintillate	20097
Scarce	20048	Scintillated	20098
Scarcely	20049	Scintillating	20099
Scarcity	20050	Scintillation	20100

SCI	(101)	SCU	202

Scion	20101	Scrap	20151
Scirocco	20102	Scrape	20152
Scissors	20103	Scraped	20153
Scoff	20104	Scraper	20154
Scoffed	20105	Scraping	20155
Scoffer	20106	Scratch	20156
Scoffing	20107	Scratched	20157
Scold	20108	Scratching	20158
Scolded	20109	Scrawl	20159
Scolding	20110	Scrawled	20160
Sconce	20111	Scrawling	20161
Scoop	20112	Scream	20162
Scooped	20113	Screamed	20163
Scooping	20114	Screaming	20164
Scope	20115	Screech	20165
Scorbutic	20116	Screen	20166
Scorch	20117	Screened...	20167
Scorched	20118	Screening	20168
Scorching	20119	Screw	20169
Score	20120	Screwed	20170
Scored	20121	Scribble	20171
Scoria	20122	Scribbled	20172
Scoring	20123	Scribbling	20173
Scorify	20124	Scribe	20174
Scorn	20125	Scrip	20175
Scorned	20126	Script	20176
Scornful	20127	Scriptural	20177
Scornfully	20128	Scripture	20178
Scorning	20129	Scrivener	20179
Scorpion...	20130	Scrofula	20180
Scot...	20131	Scrofulous	20181
Scotch	20132	Scroll	20182
Scotched...	20133	Scrub	20183
Scotticism	20134	Scrubbed	20184
Scoundrel	20135	Scrubbing	20185
Scour	20136	Scruple	20186
Scoured	20137	Scrupled...	20187
Scourer	20138	Scrupling	20188
Scourge	20139	Scrupulous	20189
Scourged	20140	Scrupulously	20190
Scourging	20141	Scrutator	20191
Scouring...	20142	Scrutinize	20192
Scout	20143	Scrutinized	20193
Scowl	20144	Scrutinizing	20194
Scowled	20145	Scrutinous	20195
Scowling	20146	Scrutiny	20196
Scraggy	20147	Scud	20197
Scramble	20148	Scudded	20198
Scrambled	20149	Scudding	20199
Scrambling	20150	Scuffle	20200

| 203 | SCU | (102) | SED |

Scuffling...	20201	Seclude	20251
Sculk	20202	Secluded...	20252
Sculking...	20203	Seclusion	20253
Sculker	20204	Seclusive	20254
Scull	20205	Second	20255
Scullery	20206	Secondary	20256
Scullion	20207	Seconded	20257
Sculptor	20208	Seconder	20258
Sculpture	20209	Seconding	20259
Sculptured	20210	Secrecy	20260
Scum	20211	Secret	20261
Scupper	20212	Secretary	20262
Scurf	20213	Secrete	20263
Scurrile	20214	Secreted...	20264
Scurrilous	20215	Secreting	20265
Scurvy	20216	Secretion	20266
Scutcheon	20217	Secretiveness ...	20267
Scuttle	20218	Secretly	20268
Scuttled	20219	Secretness	20269
Scuttling...	20220	Sect...	20270
Scythe	20221	Sectarian	20271
Sea	20222	Sectary	20272
Seal...	20223	Section	20273
Sealed	20224	Sectional	20274
Sealer	20225	Secular	20275
Sealing	20226	Secularity	20276
Seam	20227	Secularize	20277
Seaman	20228	Secularized	20278
Seamed	20229	Secure	20279
Seaming...	20230	Secured	20280
Seamstress	20231	Securely	20281
Seamy	20232	Securing...	20282
Sear	20233	Security	20283
Search	20234	Sedan	20284
Searched	20235	Sedate	20285
Searcher...	20236	Sedately...	20286
Searching	20237	Sedateness	20287
Seared	20238	Sedative...	20288
Season	20239	Sedentary	20289
Seasonable	20240	Sedge	20290
Seasoned	20241	Sediment	20291
Seasoning	20242	Sedimentary	20292
Seat	20243	Sedition	20293
Seated	20244	Seditious	20294
Seaward...	20245	Seditiously	20295
Secant	20246	Seduce	20296
Secede	20247	Seduced	20297
Seceded	20248	Seducement	20298
Seceding...	20249	Seducer	20299
Secession	20250	Seducing	20300

SED	(102)	SEP	204

Seduction	20301	Selves	20351
Seductive	20302	Semblance	20352
Sedulity	20303	Semi	20353
Sedulous...	20304	Semibreve	20354
See	20305	Semicolon	20355
Seed	20306	Seminal	20356
Seedling	20307	Seminary	20357
Seedsman	20308	Seminate	20358
Seedy	20309	Semination	20359
Seeing	20310	Sempiternal	20360
Seek	20311	Senate	20361
Seeker	20312	Senator	20362
Seeking	20313	Senatorial	20363
Seeks	20314	Send	20364
Seem	20315	Sender	20365
Seemed	20316	Sending	20366
Seeming...	20317	Sends	20367
Seemliness	20318	Seneschal	20368
Seemly	20319	Senile	20369
Seen	20320	Senior	20370
Seer	20321	Seniority	20371
Sees...	20322	Senna	20372
Seethe	20323	Sennight...	20373
Segment	20324	Sensate	20374
Segregation	20325	Sensation	20375
Seigniory	20326	Sense	20376
Seignorage	20327	Senseless	20377
Seisin	20328	Sensibility	20378
Seizable	20329	Sensible	20379
Seize	20330	Sensibly	20380
Seized	20331	Sensitive	20381
Seizing	20332	Sensual	20382
Seizor	20333	Sensualist	20383
Seizure	20334	Sensuality	20384
Selah	20335	Sensualize	20385
Seldom	20336	Sensualizing	20386
Select	20337	Sensuous	20387
Selected	20338	Sent	20388
Selecting	20339	Sentence...	20389
Selection	20340	Sentenced	20390
Selector	20341	Sententious	20391
Self...	20342	Sentient	20392
Selfish	20343	Sentiment	20393
Selfishly	20344	Sentimental	20394
Selfishness	20345	Sentimentality	20395
Sell...	20346	Sentry	20396
Seller	20347	Separable	20397
Selling	20348	Separate...	20398
Sells	20349	Separated	20399
Selvage	20350	Separately	20400

Separating	...	...	20401	Servitor ...	...	...	20451
Separation	...	...	20402	Servitude	...	...	20452
Separatist	...	...	20403	Session ...	...	...	20453
Sepoy ...	...	...	20404	Sessional	...	...	20454
September	...	...	20405	Set	...	...	20455
Septennial	...	...	20406	Setaceous	...	...	20456
Septuagenarian	...	20407	Sets...	...	...	20457
Septuagesima...	...	20408	Settee	...	...	20458
Septuagint	...	...	20409	Setter	...	...	20459
Sepulchral	...	...	20410	Setting ...	...	...	20460
Sepulchre	...	...	20411	Settle	...	...	20461
Sepulture	...	...	20412	Settled ...	...	...	20462
Sequel ...	...	...	20413	Settlement	...	...	20463
Sequence	...	...	20414	Settler ...	...	...	20464
Sequestrate	...	...	20415	Settling ...	...	...	20465
Sequestrated ...	...	20416	Seven	...	...	20466
Sequestration...	...	20417	Seventeen	...	...	20467
Sequin ...	...	...	20418	Seventeenth	...	20468
Seraglio ...	...	...	20419	Seventh ...	:..	...	20469
Seraph ...	...	...	20420	Seventieth	...	...	20470
Seraphic...	...	...	20421	Seventy ...	...	...	20471
Sere	...	...	20422	Sever	...	...	20472
Serenade...	...	...	20423	Several ...	...	...	20473
Serene ...	...	...	20424	Severally	...	...	20474
Serenely ...	...	...	20425	Severance	...	...	20475
Serenity ...	...	...	20426	Severe ...	...	...	20476
Serf... ...	...	...	20427	Severed ...	...	...	20477
Serge	...	...	20428	Severely ...	...	...	20478
Sergeant...	...	...	20429	Severing...	...	...	20479
Serial	...	...	20430	Severity ...	...	...	20480
Seriatim...	...	...	20431	Sew... ...	...	...	20481
Series	...	...	20432	Sewed ...	...	...	20482
Serious ...	...	...	20433	Sewer	...	...	20483
Seriously	...	...	20434	Sewerage	...	...	20484
Seriousness	...	...	20435	Sewing ...	...	...	20485
Sermon ...	...	...	20436	Sews	...	...	20486
Sermonize	...	...	20437	Sex	...	...	20487
Serous ...	...	...	20438	Sexagenarian ...	...	20488
Serpent ...	...	...	20439	Sexagesima	...	...	20489
Serpentine	...	...	20440	Sexangular	...	...	20490
Serrate ...	...	...	20441	Sexennial	...	...	20491
Serried ...	...	...	20442	Sextant ...	...	...	20492
Serum ...	...	...	20443	Sexton ...	...	...	20493
Servant ...	...	...	20444	Sexual ...	...	...	20494
Serve	...	...	20445	Sforzato ...	...	...	20495
Served ...	...	...	20446	Shabbiness	...	...	20496
Service ...	...	...	20447	Shabby ...	...	...	20497
Serviceable	...	...	20448	Shackle ...	...	...	20498
Servile ...	...	...	20449	Shackled	...	...	20499
Serving ...	...	...	20450	Shackles...	...	...	20500

SHA	(103)	SHI	206

Shad	20501	Sharpening	20551
Shaddock	20502	Sharper	20552
Shade	20503	Sharply	20553
Shaded	20504	Sharpness	20554
Shadiness	20505	Shatter	20555
Shading	20506	Shattered	20556
Shadow	20507	Shattering	20557
Shady	20508	Shave	20558
Shaft	20509	Shaved	20559
Shafted	20510	Shaver	20560
Shag	20511	Shaving	20561
Shaggy	20512	Shawl	20562
Shagreen	20513	She	20563
Shah	20514	Sheaf	20564
Shake	20515	Shear	20565
Shaken	20516	Sheared	20566
Shaking	20517	Shearer	20567
Shako	20518	Shearing...	20568
Shaky	20519	Shears	20569
Shall	20520	Sheath	20570
Shallop	20521	Sheathe	20571
Shallow	20522	Sheathed	20572
Shalot	20523	Sheathing	20573
Sham	20524	Shed	20574
Shambles	20525	Shedder	20575
Shambling	20526	Shedding	20576
Shame	20527	Sheen	20577
Shamed	20528	Sheep	20578
Shameful	20529	Sheepish...	20579
Shamefully	20530	Sheer	20580
Shameless	20531	Sheet	20581
Shammed	20532	Sheeting...	20582
Shamming	20533	Shelf	20583
Shampoo	20534	Shell	20584
Shampooed	20535	Shellac	20585
Shampooing	20536	Shelly	20586
Shamrock	20537	Shelter	20587
Shank	20538	Sheltered	20588
Shape	20539	Sheltering	20589
Shaped	20540	Shelve	20590
Shapeless	20541	Shelved	20591
Shapely	20542	Shepherd	20592
Shaping	20543	Shepherdess	20593
Share	20544	Sherbet	20594
Shared	20545	Sheriff	20595
Sharing	20546	Sherry	20596
Shark	20547	Shield	20597
Sharp	20548	Shielded...	20598
Sharpen	20549	Shielding	20599
Sharpened	20550	Shift	20600

Shifted	20601	Shoulder... 20651
Shifting	20602	Shout 20652
Shiftless	20603	Shouted 20653
Shilling	20604	Shouter 20654
Shin	20605	Shouting... 20655
Shine	20606	Shove 20656
Shined	20607	Shoved 20657
Shines	20608	Shovel 20658
Shingle	20609	Shoveller 20659
Shining	20610	Shoving 20660
Shiny	20611	Show 20661
Ship	20612	Showed 20662
Shipmate	20613	Shower 20663
Shipper	20614	Showerless 20664
Shipping	20615	Showery... 20665
Shipwreck	20616	Showily 20666
Shire	20617	Showiness 20667
Shirk	20618	Showing... 20668
Shirked	20619	Shown 20669
Shirking...	20620	Shows 20670
Shirt	20621	Showy 20671
Shirting	20622	Shred 20672
Shiver	20623	Shrew 20673
Shivered...	20624	Shrewd 20674
Shivering	20625	Shrewdly 20675
Shoal	20626	Shriek 20676
Shock	20627	Shrieking 20677
Shocked	20628	Shrievalty 20678
Shocking	20629	Shrill 20679
Shoe	20630	Shrilly 20680
Shone	20631	Shrimp 20681
Shook	20632	Shrine 20682
Shoot	20633	Shrink 20683
Shooter	20634	Shrinking 20684
Shooting...	20635	Shrinks 20685
Shoots	20636	Shrivel 20686
Shop	20637	Shrivelling 20687
Shopping	20638	Shroud 20688
Shore	20639	Shrove 20689
Shored	20640	Shrub 20690
Shorn	20641	Shrubbery 20691
Short	20642	Shrug 20692
Shorten	20643	Shrugged 20693
Shortened	20644	Shrugging 20694
Shortening	20645	Shrunk 20695
Shortly	20646	Shrunken 20696
Shortness	20647	Shudder... 20697
Shot	20648	Shuddered 20698
Shotted	20649	Shuddering 20699
Should	20650	Shuffle 20700

SHU			(104)	SIM			208
Shuffler	...	...	20701	Signally ...	...	...	20751
Shuffling...	...	...	20702	Signatory	...	...	20752
Shun	...	...	20703	Signature	...	...	20753
Shunned ...	...	...	20704	Signed ...	...	...	20754
Shunning	...	...	20705	Signet ...	...	...	20755
Shunt	...	...	20706	Significance	...	...	20756
Shunted ...	...	...	20707	Significant	...	...	20757
Shut	...	...	20708	Signification ...	...	...	20758
Shuts	...	...	20709	Significative ...	...	...	20759
Shutter	...	...	20710	Significatory ...	...	...	20760
Shutting...	...	...	20711	Signified ...	...	...	20761
Shuttle	...	...	20712	Signify ...	...	...	20762
Shy ...	...	...	20713	Signifying	...	...	20763
Shyness ...	...	...	20714	Signing ...	...	...	20764
Sibilant ...	...	...	20715	Signior ...	...	...	20765
Sibilation	...	...	20716	Silence ...	...	...	20766
Sibyl	...	...	20717	Silenced ...	...	...	20767
Sick	...	...	20718	Silencing	...	...	20768
Sicken......	...	...	20719	Silent ...	...	...	20769
Sickish ...	...	...	20720	Silently ...	...	...	20770
Sickle	...	...	20721	Silhouette	...	...	20771
Sickly	...	...	20722	Silica	...	...	20772
Sickness ...	...	...	20723	Silicate ...	...	...	20773
Side	...	...	20724	Silk ...	...	...	20774
Sided	...	...	20725	Silken ...	...	...	20775
Sidereal ...	...	...	20726	Silkiness	...	...	20776
Sideways	...	...	20727	Silky	...	...	20777
Siding	...	...	20728	Sill ...	...	...	20778
Sidle	...	...	20729	Sillabub ...	...	...	20779
Sidling ...	...	...	20730	Sillily	...	...	20780
Siege	...	...	20731	Silliness ...	...	...	20781
Sierra	...	...	20732	Silly	...	...	20782
Siesta	...	...	20733	Silver	...	...	20783
Sieve	...	...	20734	Silvered ...	...	...	20784
Sift ...	...	...	20735	Silvery	...	...	20785
Sifted	...	...	20736	Similar ...	...	...	20786
Sifter	...	...	20737	Similarity	...	...	20787
Sifting	...	...	20738	Similarly	...	...	20788
Sigh	...	...	20739	Simile ...	...	...	20789
Sighed ...	...	...	20740	Similitude	...	...	20790
Sighing ...	...	...	20741	Simmer...	...	...	20791
Sight	...	...	20742	Simmered	...	...	20792
Sighted ...	...	...	20743	Simmering	...	...	20793
Sightless...	...	...	20744	Simony ...	...	...	20794
Sightly ...	...	...	20745	Simoom ...	...	...	20795
Sign	...	...	20746	Simper ...	...	...	20796
Signal	...	...	20747	Simpered	...	...	20797
Signalize...	...	...	20748	Simpering	...	...	20798
Signalized	...	...	20749	Simple ...	...	...	20799
Signalled	...	...	20750	Simpleness	...	...	20800

209	SIM	(105)	SKI	
Simpleton	... ...	20801	Sirocco	20851
Simplicity	... ...	20802	Sirup	20852
Simplification	...	20803	Sister	20853
Simplified	... ...	20804	Sisterly	20854
Simplify	...	20805	Sit	20855
Simplifying	...	20806	Site...	20856
Simply	...	20807	Sits	20857
Simulate	... ...	20808	Sitter	20858
Simulated	... ...	20809	Sitting	20859
Simulating	... ...	20810	Situate	20860
Simulation	... ...	20811	Situated	20861
Simultaneous...	...	20812	Situation...	20862
Simultaneously	...	20813	Six	20863
Sin	...	20814	Sixfold	20864
Since	...	20815	Sixpence...	20865
Sincere	...	20816	Sixteen	20866
Sincerely	... ...	20817	Sixteenth	20867
Sincerity	... ...	20818	Sixth	20868
Sinecure	...	20819	Sixtieth	20869
Sinew	...	20820	Sixty	20870
Sinewy	...	20821	Sizar	20871
Sinful	...	20822	Size...	20872
Sing	...	20823	Skate	20873
Singe	...	20824	Skated	20874
Singed	...	20825	Skating	20875
Singer	...	20826	Skein	20876
Singing	...	20827	Skeleton	20877
Single	...	20828	Sketch	20878
Singleness	... ...	20829	Sketched	20879
Singly	...	20830	Sketching	20880
Sings	...	20831	Sketchy	20881
Singsong... ...	...	20832	Skew	20882
Singular	...	20833	Skewed	20883
Singularity	... ...	20834	Skewer	20884
Singularly	... ...	20835	Skid	20885
Sinister	...	20836	Skiff	20886
Sink	...	20837	Skilful	20887
Sinking	...	20838	Skilfully...	20888
Sinless	...	20839	Skill	20889
Sinner	...	20840	Skim	20890
Sinuosity	... ...	20841	Skimmed	20891
Sinuous	...	20842	Skimmer	20892
Sip	...	20843	Skimming	20893
Siphon	...	20844	Skimmingly	20894
Sipped	...	20845	Skin	20895
Sipping	...	20846	Skinless	20896
Sir	...	20847	Skinner	20897
Sire...	...	20848	Skinny	20898
Siren	...	20849	Skip	20899
Sirloin	...	20850	Skipped	20900

Skipper	20901	Slaughterous ... 20951
Skipping	20902	Slave 20952
Skirmish	20903	Slaver 20953
Skirt	20904	Slavery 20954
Skirted	20905	Slaving 20955
Skirting	20906	Slavish 20956
Skittish	20907	Slay 20957
Skittles	20908	Slayer 20958
Skulk	20909	Slaying 20959
Skulked	20910	Sledge 20960
Skulker	20911	Sleek 20961
Skulking	20912	Sleekly 20962
Skull	20913	Sleep 20963
Skunk	20914	Sleeper 20964
Skurry	20915	Sleeping 20965
Sky	20916	Sleepiness 20966
Slab	20917	Sleepless 20967
Slack	20918	Sleeps 20968
Slacken	20919	Sleepy 20969
Slackened	20920	Sleet 20970
Slackening	20921	Sleeve 20971
Slackly	20922	Sleight 20972
Slackness	20923	Slender 20973
Slain	20924	Slept 20974
Slake	20925	Slice 20975
Slaked	20926	Sliced 20976
Slaking	20927	Slid 20977
Slam	20928	Slide 20978
Slamming	20929	Sliding 20979
Slander	20930	Slight 20980
Slandered	20931	Slightly 20981
Slanderer	20932	Slightingly 20982
Slandering	20933	Slim 20983
Slanderous	20934	Slimness 20984
Slanderously	20935	Slimy 20985
Slang	20936	Sling 20986
Slant	20937	Slink 20987
Slanting	20938	Slinking 20988
Slap	20939	Slip 20989
Slapped	20940	Slipped 20990
Slapping	20941	Slipper 20991
Slash	20942	Slippery 20992
Slate	20943	Slipping 20993
Slater	20944	Slipshod 20994
Slating	20945	Slit 20995
Slattern	20946	Slitting 20996
Slatternly	20947	Sloe 20997
Slaughter	20948	Sloop 20998
Slaughtered	20949	Slop 20999
Slaughtering	20950	Slope 21000

211	SLO	(106)	SNA	
Sloping	21001	Smells	21051
Sloppy	21002	Smelt	21052
Slops	21003	Smelter	21053
Sloth	21004	Smelting...	21054
Slothful	21005	Smile	21055
Slouch	21006	Smiled	21056
Slouched	21007	Smiling	21057
Slouching	21008	Smirk	21058
Slough	21009	Smirking	21059
Sloven	21010	Smite	21060
Slovenliness	21011	Smith	21061
Slovenly...	21012	Smithy	21062
Slow	21013	Smiting	21063
Slowly	21014	Smitten	21064
Slowness	21015	Smock	21065
Slue	21016	Smoke	21066
Slug	21017	Smoked	21067
Sluggard	21018	Smoker	21068
Sluggish...	21019	Smoking...	21069
Sluggishly	21020	Smoky ... .. , ...	21070
Sluice	21021	Smooth	21071
Slumber	21022	Smoothing	21072
Slumbered	21023	Smoothness	21073
Slumbering	21024	Smother	21074
Slunk	21025	Smothered	21075
Slur...	21026	Smothering	21076
Slurred	21027	Smoulder	21077
Slurring	21028	Smouldered	21078
Slush	21029	Smouldering	21079
Slushy	21030	Smuggle...	21080
Sluttish	21031	Smuggled	21081
Sly	21032	Smuggler	21082
Slyly	21033	Smuggling ... ·...	21083
Small	21034	Smut	21084
Smallness	21035	Smutty	21085
Smart	21036	Snaffle	21086
Smarted	21037	Snag	21087
Smarten	21038	Snaggy	21088
Smarting	21039	Snail	21089
Smartly	21040	Snake	21090
Smarts	21041	Snap	21091
Smash	21042	Snapped...	21092
Smashed...	21043	Snapper	21093
Smashing	21044	Snapping	21094
Smattering	21045	Snappish	21095
Smear	21046	Snare	21096
Smeared...	21047	Snared	21097
Smearing	21048	Snaring	21098
Smell	21049	Snarl	21099
Smelling...	21050	Snarled	21100

— **53** —

SNA	(106)	SOL	212
Snarler	21101	Soar	21151
Snarling	21102	Soared	21152
Snatch	21103	Soaring	21153
Snatched	21104	Sob	21154
Snatcher	21105	Sobbed	21155
Snatching	21106	Sobbing	21156
Sneak	21107	Sober	21157
Sneaked	21108	Soberly	21158
Sneaking	21109	Sobriety	21159
Sneer	21110	Sociability	21160
Sneered	21111	Sociable	21161
Sneering	21112	Social	21162
Sneeze	21113	Socialism	21163
Sneezing	21114	Society	21164
Sniff	21115	Socinian	21165
Sniffed	21116	Sock	21166
Sniffing	21117	Socket	21167
Snob	21118	Sod	21168
Snobbish	21119	Soda	21169
Snooze	21120	Sodden	21170
Snore	21121	Sofa	21171
Snored	21122	Soft	21172
Snoring	21123	Soften	21173
Snort	21124	Softened	21174
Snorted	21125	Softening	21175
Snorter	21126	Softly	21176
Snorting	21127	Softness	21177
Snout	21128	Soho	21178
Snow	21129	Soil	21179
Snowed	21130	Soiled	21180
Snowing	21131	Soiling	21181
Snowy	21132	Soirée	21182
Snub	21133	Sojourn	21183
Snubbed	21134	Sojourned	21184
Snuff	21135	Sojourning	21185
Snuffed	21136	Solace	21186
Snuffing	21137	Solaced	21187
Snuffle	21138	Solacing	21188
Snuffled	21139	Solar	21189
Snuffling	21140	Sold	21190
Snuffy	21141	Solder	21191
Snug	21142	Soldier	21192
Snuggery	21143	Soldierly	21193
So	21144	Soldiery	21194
Soak	21145	Sole	21195
Soaked	21146	Solecism	21196
Soaker	21147	Soled	21197
Soaking	21148	Solely	21198
Soap	21149	Solemn	21199
Soapy	21150	Solemnity	21200

— 54 —

213   SOL   (107)   SOU .

Solemnization	...	21201	Soothing	...	...	21251
Solemnize	... ...	21202	Soothsay...	...	...	21252
Solemnized	... ...	21203	Soothsayer	...	...	21253
Solemnizing	...	21204	Soothsaying	...	...	21254
Solemnly	... ...	21205	Sooty	... ...	21255
Solicit	... ...	21206	Sop...	... ...	21256
Solicitation	... ...	21207	Sophism...	... .	21257
Solicited...	... ...	21208	Sophist	... ...	21258
Soliciting	... ...	21209	Sophisticate	... ...	21259
Solicitor...	... ...	21210	Sophisticated...	...	21260
Solicitous	... ...	21211	Sophistry	... ...	21261
Solicitude	... ...	21212	Soporific...	... ...	21262
Solid	... ...	21213	Sopped	... ...	21263
Solidified	... ...	21214	Sopping ...	... ...	21264
Solidify	... ...	21215	Soprano ...	... ...	21265
Solidity	... ...	21216	Sorcery	... ...	21266
Soliloquize	... ...	21217	Sordid	... .	21267
Soliloquized	... ...	21218	Sore	.. ..	21268
Soliloquizing	... ...	21219	Sorely	... ...	21269
Soliloquy	... ...	21220	Soreness...	... ...	21270
Solitary	... ...	21221	Sorrel	... ...	21271
Solitude	... ...	21222	Sorrily	... ...	21272
Solo	... ...	21223	Sorrow	... ...	21273
Solstice	... ...	21224	Sorrowed	... ...	21274
Solubility	... ...	21225	Sorrowful	... ...	21275
Soluble	... ...	21226	Sorrowing	... ...	21276
Solution	... ...	21227	Sorry	... ...	21277
Solvable...	... ...	21228	Sort...	... ...	21278
Solve	... ...	21229	Sorted	... ...	21279
Solved	... ...	21230	Sortie	... ...	21280
Solvency	... ...	21231	Sorting	... ...	21281
Solvent	... ...	21232	Sot ...	... ...	21282
Solver	... ...	21233	Sottish	... ...	21283
Solving	... ...	21234	Souchong	... ...	21284
Sombre	... ...	21235	Sough	... ...	21285
Some	... ...	21236	Sought	... ...	21286
Somersault	... ...	21237	Soul	... ...	21287
Somnambulist	...	21238	Sound	... ...	21288
Somniferous	... ...	21239	Sounded...	... ...	21289
Somnolence	... ...	21240	Sounding	... ...	21290
Son...	... ...	21241	Soundly ...	... ...	21291
Sonata	... ...	21242	Soundness	... ...	21292
Song	... ...	21243	Soup	... ...	21293
Songster...	... ...	21244	Sour	... ...	21294
Sonnet	... ...	21245	Soured	... ...	21295
Sonorous	... ...	21246	Sourly	... ...	21296
Soon	... ...	21247	Source	... ...	21297
Soot	... ...	21248	Sourness...	... ...	21298
Soothe	... ...	21249	Souse	... ...	21299
Soothed	... ...	21250	Soused	... ...	21300

SOU	(107)	SPI	214

Sousing ..	...	...	21301	Spawned...	...	...	21351
South	...	...	21302	Spawning	...	...	21352
Southerly	...	...	21303	Speak	...	...	21353
Southern...	...	...	21304	Speaker ...	...	...	21354
Souvenir	...	...	21305	Speaking	...	...	21355
Sovereign	...	...	21306	Speaks ...	...	...	21356
Sovereignty	...	...	21307	Spear	...	...	21357
Sow...	...	...	21308	Special	...	...	21358
Sowed	...	...	21309	Specially	...	...	21359
Sower	...	...	21310	Specie	...	...	21360
Sowing	...	..	21311	Species ...	...	...	21361
Sown	...	...	21312	Specific ...	...	...	21362
Sows	...	...	21313	Specifically	...	...	21363
Soy ...	...	...	21314	Specify ...	...	...	21364
Spa ...	...	...	21315	Specimen	...	...	21365
Space	...	...	21316	Specious...	...	...	21366
Spacious...	...	...	21317	Speck	...	...	21367
Spade	...	...	21318	Speckled	...	...	21368
Spahi	...	...	21319	Spectacle	...	...	21369
Span	...	...	21320	Spectacles	...	...	21370
Spangle ...	...	...	21321	Spectator	...	...	21371
Spaniel	...	...	21322	Spectre ...	...	...	21372
Spanish ...	...	...	21323	Speculate	...	...	21373
Spank	...	...	21324	Speculated	...	...	21374
Spanker ...	...	...	21325	Speculating	...	...	21375
Spanking	...	...	21326	Speculation	...	...	21376
Spanned...	...	...	21327	Speculative	...	...	21377
Spanning	...	...	21328	Speculator	...	...	21378
Spar	...	...	21329	Speech ...	...	...	21379
Spare	...	...	21330	Speed ...	...	...	21380
Spared	...	...	21331	Speedily ...	...	...	21381
Sparely ...	...	...	21332	Speedy ...	...	...	21382
Spareness	...	...	21333	Spell	...	...	21383
Sparing ...	...	...	21334	Spelling ...	...	...	21384
Spark	...	...	21335	Spells ...	...	...	21385
Sparkle ...	...	...	21336	Spelt	...	...	21386
Sparkled...	...	...	21337	Spend ...	...	...	21387
Sparkling	...	...	21338	Spending	...	...	21388
Sparred ...	...	...	21339	Spends ...	...	...	21389
Sparring ...	...	...	21340	Spendthrift	...	...	21390
Sparrow ...	...	...	21341	Spent ...	...	...	21391
Sparry ...	...	...	21342	Spermaceti	...	...	21392
Sparse ...	...	...	21343	Sphere ...	...	...	21393
Sparsely ...	...	...	21344	Spherical	...	...	21394
Spasm	...	...	21345	Spice ...	...	...	21395
Spasmodic	...	...	21346	Spicy ...	...	...	21396
Spatter ...	...	...	21347	Spider ...	...	...	21397
Spattered	...	...	21348	Spied ...	...	...	21398
Spattering	...	...	21349	Spike ...	...	...	21399
Spawn ...	...	...	21350	Spill ...	...	...	21400

Spilling 21401	Sprayed 21451
Spills 21402	Spread 21452
Spilt 21403	Spreading 21453
Spin 21404	Spreads 21454
Spinach 21405	Sprig 21455
Spine 21406	Sprightliness 21456
Spinning... 21407	Sprightly 21457
Spinster 21408	Spring 21458
Spiral 21409	Springing 21459
Spire 21410	Springs 21460
Spirit 21411	Sprinkle 21461
Spirited 21412	Sprinkling 21462
Spiritual... 21413	Sprout 21463
Spit 21414	Sprouting 21464
Spite 21415	Spruce 21465
Spittle 21416	Sprung 21466
Splash 21417	Spun 21467
Splashing 21418	Spunge 21468
Spleen 21419	Spur 21469
Splendid 21420	Spurious... 21470
Splendidly 21421	Spurn 21471
Splendour 21422	Spurned 21472
Splice 21423	Spurning 21473
Spliced 21424	Spy... 21474
Splicing 21425	Spying 21475
Splinter 21426	Sqnabble 21476
Split 21427	Squadron 21477
Splits 21428	Squalid 21478
Splitting... 21429	Squall 21479
Spoil 21430	Squalled... 21480
Spoiled 21431	Squalling 21481
Spoiling 21432	Squally 21482
Spoilt 21433	Squalor 21483
Spoke 21434	Squander 21484
Spoken 21435	Square 21485
Sponge 21436	Squared 21486
Sponsor 21437	Squaring... 21487
Spontaneous 21438	Squatter 21488
Spontaneously ... 21439	Squeak 21489
Spoon 21440	Squeaking 21490
Sport 21441	Squeamish 21491
Sportfully 21442	Squeeze 21492
Sporting 21443	Squeezed 21493
Spot 21444	Squeezing 21494
Spotted 21445	Squint 21495
Spouse 21446	Squirrel 21496
Sprain 21447	Stab 21497
Sprang 21448	Stabbing... 21498
Sprat 21449	Stability 21499
Spray 21450	Stable 21500

STA	(108)	STE	216

Stack	21501	Startling...	21551
Stacked	21502	Starvation	21552
Staff	21503	Starve	21553
Stag	21504	Starved	21554
Stage	21505	Starving	21555
Stagger	21506	State	21556
Staggered	21507	Stated	21557
Staggering	21508	Stately	21558
Stagnant...	21509	Statement	21559
Stagnate...	21510	States	21560
Staid	21511	Statesman	21561
Stain	21512	Stating	21562
Stained	21513	Station	21563
Staining	21514	Stationary	21564
Stair	21515	Stationed	21565
Stake	21516	Stationer	21566
Stale	21517	Stationery	21567
Stalk	21518	Statistics...	21568
Stall	21519	Statuary	21569
Stallion	21520	Statue	21570
Stalwart...	21521	Stature	21571
Stamina	21522	Statute	21572
Stammer	21523	Staunch	21573
Stammered	21524	Staunched	21574
Stammering	21525	Staunching	21575
Stamp	21526	Stay	21576
Stamped...	21527	Stayed	21577
Stamping	21528	Staying	21578
Stand	21529	Stays	21579
Standard	21530	Stave	21580
Standing	21531	Stead	21581
Stands	21532	Steadily	21582
Stank	21533	Steady	21583
Stanza	21534	Steak	21584
Staple	21535	Steal	21585
Stapler	21536	Stealing	21586
Star...	21537	Steals	21587
Starboard	21538	Stealth	21588
Starch	21539	Stealthily	21589
Starched	21540	Steam	21590
Stare	21541	Steamer	21591
Stared	21542	Steaming	21592
Staring	21543	Steed	21593
Starling	21544	Steel	21594
Starred	21545	Steep	21595
Start	21546	Steeped	21596
Started	21547	Steeping...	21597
Starting	21548	Steeple	21598
Startle	21549	Steer	21599
Startled	21550	Steerage	21600

217	STE	(109)	STR	
Steered ...	... ...	21601	Stipulation	21651
Steering ...	... ...	21602	Stir	21652
Stem ...	... ...	21603	Stirred	21653
Stemming	... ...	21604	Stirring	21654
Stench ...	... ...	21605	Stirrup	21655
Stenography ...	...	21606	Stitch	21656
Step ...	... ...	21607	Stitched	21657
Steppe ...	... ...	21608	Stitching...	21658
Stepped ...	... ...	21609	Stock	21659
Stepping...	... ...	21610	Stocked	21660
Stereotype	... ...	21611	Stocking...	21661
Sterile ...	... ...	21612	Stoical	21662
Sterling ...	... ...	21613	Stoicism...	21663
Stern ...	... ...	21614	Stole	21664
Sternly ...	... ...	21615	Stolen	21665
Stethoscope	... ...	21616	Stolid	21666
Stew ...	... ...	21617	Stomach...	21667
Steward ...	... ...	21618	Stone	21668
Stewing ...	... ...	21619	Stoned	21669
Stick ...	... ...	21620	Stoning	21670
Sticking ...	... ...	21621	Stony	21671
Sticks ...	... ...	21622	Stood	21672
Stiff... ...	... ...	21623	Stool	21673
Stiffly ...	... ...	21624	Stoop	21674
Stiffness ...	... ...	21625	Stooped	21675
Stifle ...	... ...	21626	Stooping...	21676
Stifled ...	... ...	21627	Stop	21677
Stifling ...	... ...	21628	Store	21678
Stigma ...	... ...	21629	Stored	21679
Stile ...	... ...	21630	Storing	21680
Still... ...	... ...	21631	Storm	21681
Stilled ...	... ...	21632	Stormy	21682
Stilling ...	... ...	21633	Story	21683
Stilts ...	... ...	21634	Stout	21684
Stimulant	... ...	21635	Stoutly	21685
Stimulate	... ...	21636	Stove	21686
Stimulated	... ...	21637	Stow	21687
Sting ...	... ...	21638	Stowage	21688
Stinginess	... ...	21639	Straight	21689
Stingy ...	... ...	21640	Strain	21690
Stink ...	... ...	21641	Strained	21691
Stinking...	... ...	21642	Straining	21692
Stinks ...	... ...	21643	Strait	21693
Stint ...	... ...	21644	Straiten	21694
Stinted ...	... ...	21645	Straitened	21695
Stipend ...	... ...	21646	Strand	21696
Stipendiary	... ...	21647	Stranded...	21697
Stipulate...	... ...	21648	Stranding	21698
Stipulated	... ...	21649	Strange	21699
Stipulating	... ...	21650	Strangle	21700

STR			(109)	SUB			218
Strangled	...	...	21701	Strolling...	...	...	21751
Strangling	...	...	21702	Strong	...	...	21752
Strap	...	...	21703	Strongly...	...	...	21753
Strapped...	...	...	21704	Strove	...	...	21754
Strapping	...	...	21705	Struck	...	...	21755
Strata	...	...	21706	Structure	...	...	21756
Stratagem	...	...	21707	Struggle...	...	...	21757
Stratum	..	...	21708	Struggling	...	...	21758
Straw	...	...	21709	Strut	...	...	21759
Strawberry	...	...	21710	Strutting...	...	...	21760
Strawed	..	...	21711	Stubborn	...	...	21761
Stray	...	...	21712	Stuck	...	...	21762
Strayed	...	...	21713	Stucco	...	...	21763
Straying...	...	...	21714	Stud	...	...	21764
Streak	...	...	21715	Student	...	... · ...	21765
Streaked...	...	...	21716	Studied	...	...	21766
Streaky	...	...	21717	Study	...	...	21767
Stream	...	...	21718	Stuff	...	...	21768
Street	...	...	21719	Stuffed	...	...	21769
Strength...	...	...	21720	Stuffing	..	...	21770
Strenuous	...	...	21721	Stultify	...	...	21771
Stress	...	...	21722	Stumble...	...	...	21772
Stretch	...	...	21723	Stumbling	...	...	21773
Stretched	...	...	21724	Stump	...	...	21774
Stretching	...	...	21725	Stun	...	...	21775
Strew	...	...	21726	Stunk	...	...	21776
Strewing...	...	...	21727	Stunning	...	...	21777
Stricken ...	...	...	21728	Stupefied	...	..	21778
Strict	...	...	21729	Stupefy	...	...	21779
Strictly	...	...	21730	Stupendous	...	...	21780
Stride	...	...	21731	Stupid	...	...	21781
Striding ...	...	...	21732	Stupidity	...	...	21782
Strife	...	...	21733	Stupidly ...	...	...	21783
Strike	...	...	21734	Stupor	..	...	21784
Strikes	...	...	21735	Sturdy	...	...	21785
Striking ...	...	...	21736	Sturgeon	...	...	21786
String	...	...	21737	Stutter	...	...	21787
Stringent	...	...	21738	Stuttered	...	...	21788
Strip	...	...	21739	Stuttering	...	...	21789
Stripe	...	...	21740	Sty ...	..	...	21790
Striped	...	...	21741	Style	...	...	21791
Stripped...	...	...	21742	Styled	...	...	21792
Stripping	...	...	21743	Suavity	...	...	21793
Strive	...	...	21744	Subaltern	...	...	21794
Striven	...	...	21745	Subdue	...	...	21795
Strives	...	...	21746	Subdued...	...	...	21796
Striving ...	...	...	21747	Subduing	...	...	21797
Stroke	...	...	21748	Subject ...	..	...	21798
Stroll	...	...	21749	Subjected	..	...	21799
Strolled	...	...	21750	Subjoin	..	...	21800

Subjoined 21801	Succumbed 21851
Subjoining 21802	Such 21852
Subjugate 21803	Suckle 21853
Sublet 21804	Suckled 21854
Sublime 21805	Suckling 21855
Sublunar... 21806	Sudden 21856
Submarine 21807	Suddenly 21857
Submerge 21808	Sue 21858
Submersion 21809	Sued 21859
Submission 21810	Suet 21860
Submit 21811	Suing 21861
Subordinate 21812	Suffer 21862
Suborn 21813	Sufferance 21863
Suborned 21814	Suffered 21864
Subpœna 21815	Sufferer 21865
Subscribe 21816	Suffering 21866
Subscribed 21817	Suffice 21867
Subscriber 21818	Sufficed 21868
Subscribing 21819	Sufficient 21869
Subscription 21820	Sufficiently 21870
Subsequent 21821	Suffocate 21871
Subsequently... ... 21822	Suffocated 21872
Subside 21823	Suffocating 21873
Subsidy 21824	Suffrage 21874
Subsist 21825	Suffuse 21875
Subsisted 21826	Suffused 21876
Subisting 21827	Sugar 21877
Substance 21828	Suggest 21878
Substantial 21829	Suggested 21879
Substantially 21830	Suggesting 21880
Substratum 21831	Suicidal 21881
Subterfuge 21832	Suicide 21882
Subterranean... ... 21833	Suit... 21883
Subtle 21834	Suitable 21884
Subtract 21835	Suitably 21885
Subtracted 21836	Suitor 21886
Subtracting 21837	Sullen 21887
Suburb 21838	Sullenly 21888
Subvert 21839	Sullied 21889
Subverted 21840	Sully 21890
Subverting 21841	Sulphur 21891
Succeed 21842	Sulphurous 21892
Succeeding 21843	Sultan 21893
Success 21844	Sultry 21894
Succinct 21845	Sum 21895
Succour 21846	Summary 21896
Succoured 21847	Summed 21897
Succouring 21848	Summer 21898
Succulent 21849	Summit 21899
Succumb 21850	Summon... 21900

SUM	(110)	SUS	220

Summoned	21901	Suppressed	21951
Summoning	21902	Suppressing	21952
Sumptuous	21903	Supreme	21953
Sun	21904	Supremely	21954
Sunday	21905	Sure	21955
Sung	21906	Surely	21956
Sunk	21907	Surety	21957
Superannuate	21908	Surf	21958
Superannuated	21909	Surface	21959
Superb	21910	Surfeit	21960
Supercilious	21911	Surge	21961
Supererogation	21912	Surgeon	21962
Superficial	21913	Surgery	21963
Superficies	21914	Surgical	21964
Superfine	21915	Surging	21965
Superfluity	21916	Surly	21966
Superfluous	21917	Surmise	21967
Superintend	21918	Surmised	21968
Superintended	21919	Surmising	21969
Superintendent	21920	Surmount	21970
Superintending	21921	Surmounted	21971
Superior	21922	Surmounting	21972
Superiority	21923	Surname	21973
Superlative	21924	Surnamed	21974
Supernatural	21925	Surplice	21975
Supersede	21926	Surplus	21976
Superseded	21927	Surprise	21977
Superseding	21928	Surprised	21978
Superstition	21929	Surprising	21979
Superstructure	21930	Surrender	21980
Supine	21931	Surrendered	21981
Supper	21932	Surrendering	21982
Supplant	21933	Surreptitious	21983
Supple	21934	Surround	21984
Supplement	21935	Surrounded	21985
Suppliant	21936	Surrounding	21986
Supplicate	21937	Survey	21987
Supplicated	21938	Surveyed	21988
Supplicating	21939	Surveying	21989
Supplied	21940	Surveyor	21990
Supply	21941	Survive	21991
Supplying	21942	Survived	21992
Support	21943	Surviving	21993
Supported	21944	Survivor	21994
Supporting	21945	Susceptible	21995
Suppose	21946	Suspect	21996
Supposed	21947	Suspected	21997
Supposing	21948	Suspecting	21998
Supposititious	21949	Suspend	21999
Suppress	21950	Suspended	22000

Suspending	22001	Swim	22051
Suspense...	22002	Swims	22052
Suspension	22003	Swimming	22053
Suspicion	22004	Swimmingly	22054
Suspicious	22005	Swindle	22055
Sustain	22006	Swindled	22056
Sustained	22007	Swindler	22057
Sustaining	22008	Swindling	22058
Sustenance	22009	Swine	22059
Swagger...	22010	Swing	22060
Swaggering	22011	Swinging	22061
Swain	22012	Swings	22062
Swallow...	22013	Swiss	22063
Swallowed	22014	Switch	22064
Swallowing	22015	Swivel	22065
Swam	22016	Swollen	22066
Swamp	22017	Swoon	22067
Swamped	22018	Swooning	22068
Swamping	22019	Swoop	22069
Swan	22020	Swooping	22070
Sward	22021	Sword	22071
Swarm	22022	Swore	22072
Swarmed	22023	Sworn	22073
Swarming	22024	Swum	22074
Swarthy	22025	Swung	22075
Sway	22026	Sybarite	22076
Swaying	22027	Sycamore	22077
Swear	22028	Sycophant	22078
Swearing	22029	Syllable	22079
Swears...	22030	Syllabus	22080
Sweat	22031	Sylph	22081
Sweating	22032	Sylvan	22082
Swedish	22033	Symbol	22083
Sweep	22034	Symbolical	22084
Sweeping	22035	Symbolized	22085
Sweeps	22036	Symmetrical	22086
Sweepstakes	22037	Symmetry	22087
Sweet	22038	Sympathetic	22088
Sweetly	22039	Sympathize	22089
Sweetness	22040	Sympathy	22090
Swell	22041	Symptom	22091
Swelled	22042	Synagogue	22092
Swelling...	22043	Syncope	22093
Swells	22044	Syndic	22094
Swelter	22045	Synod	22095
Sweltering	22046	Synonymous	22096
Swept	22047	Synopsis...	22097
Swerve	22048	Syntax	22098
Swift	22049	System	22099
Swiftly	22050	Systematic	22100

T	(III)	TAX	222

T	...	...	22101	Tangled ...	...	...	22151
Tabernacle	...	...	22102	Tangling...	...	...	22152
Table ...	...	...	22103	Tank ...	...	...	22153
Taboo ...	...	...	22104	Tankard ...	..	...	22154
Tabular ...	...	...	22105	Tanned ...	...	...	22155
Tacit ...	...	...	22106	Tanner ...	...	...	22156
Taciturn ...	...	...	22107	Tannery ...	...	...	22157
Tack ...	...	...	22108	Tanning ...	...	...	22158
Tacked ...	...	...	22109	Tantalize	...	...	22159
Tacking ...	...	...	22110	Tantalized	...	...	22160
Tackle ...	...	...	22111	Tantalizing	...	...	22161
Tackled ...	...	..	22112	Tantamount ...	...	22162
Tackling...	...	...	22113	Tap... ...	...	...	22163
Tact ...	...	...	22114	Tape ...	...	...	22164
Tactics ...	...	...	22115	Taper ...	...	...	22165
Tadpole ...	...	...	22116	Tapering...	...	...	22166
Taffrail ...	...	...	22117	Tapestry...	...	...	22167
Tail ...	...	...	22118	Tapioca ...	...	...	22168
Tailor ...	...	...	22119	Tapped ...	...	...	22169
Taint ...	...	...	22120	Tapping ...	...	...	22170
Tainted ...	...	...	22121	Tar	...	...	22171
Take ...	...	...	22122	Tardy ...	...	...	22172
Taken ...	...	..	22123	Tare ...	...	...	22173
Takes ...	...	...	22124	Target ...	...	...	22174
Taking ...	...	...	22125	Tariff ...	...	...	22175
Talbot ...	...	...	22126	Tarn ...	...	...	22176
Tale ...	...	...	22127	Tarnish ...	...	...	22177
Talent ..	...	...	22128	Tarnished	...	...	22178
Talented...	...	...	22129	Tarred ...	...	...	22179
Talk ...	...	...	22130	Tarried ...	...	...	22180
Talkative	...	...	22131	Tarry ...	...	...	22181
Talked ...	...	...	22132	Tarrying...	...	...	22182
Talking ...	...	...	22133	Tart ...	...	...	22183
Tall...	...	...	22134	Tartan ...	...	...	22184
Tallied ...	...	...	22135	Tartar ...	...	...	22185
Tallow ...	...	...	22136	Tartly ...	...	...	22186
Tally ...	...	...	22137	Task ...	...	...	22187
Talon ...	...	...	22138	Taste ...	...	...	22188
Tambourine	...	...	22139	Tasted ...	...	...	22189
Tame ...	...	...	22140	Tasteful ...	...	...	22190
Tamed ...	...	...	22141	Tasting ...	...	...	22191
Tamely ...	...	...	22142	Tattoo ...	...	...	22192
Taming ...	...	...	22143	Taught ...	...	...	22193
Tamper ...	...	...	22144	Taunt ...	...	...	22194
Tampered	...	...	22145	Tautology	...	...	22195
Tampering	...	...	22146	Tavern ...	...	...	22196
Tan...	...	...	22147	Tawdry ...	...	...	22197
Tangible	...	...	22148	Tawny ...	...	...	22198
Tangibly...	...	...	22149	Tax... ...	...	...	22199
Tangle ...	...	...	22150	Taxation...	...	...	22200

223	TAX	(112)	TEX

Taxed	22201	Tenable	22251
Taxes	22202	Tenacious	22252
Taxing	22203	Tenant	22253
Tea	22204	Tendency	22254
Teach	22205	Tender	22255
Teachable	22206	Tendered	22256
Teacher	22207	Tendering	22257
Teaching	22208	Tenderly...	22258
Team	22209	Tenderness	22259
Tear	22210	Tenement	22260
Tearing	22211	Tenet	22261
Tears	22212	Tenor	22262
Tease	22213	Tense	22263
Teased	22214	Tension	22264
Teasing	22215	Tent	22265
Technical	22216	Tentative	22266
Tedious	22217	Tenth	22267
Tedium	22218	Tenure	22268
Teem	22219	Tepid	22269
Teemed	22220	Term	22270
Teeming...	22221	Termagant	22271
Teetotaler	22222	Termed	22272
Telegram	22223	Terminal	22273
Telegraph	22224	Terminate	22274
Telegraphed ...	22225	Termination	22275
Telegraphic ...	22226	Terminus	22276
Telegraphy	22227	Terrace	22277
Telescope	22228	Terrestrial	22278
Tell...	22229	Terrible	22279
Telling	22230	Terribly	22280
Tells	22231	Terrier	22281
Temerity	22232	Terrified...	22282
Temper	22233	Terrify	22283
Temperament ...	22234	Terrifying	22284
Temperance	22235	Territory	22285
Temperate	22236	Terror	22286
Tempered	22237	Terse	22287
Tempest	22238	Tertian	22288
Tempestuous ...	22239	Test...	22289
Temple	22240	Testament	22290
Temporal	22241	Testator	22291
Temporarily ...	22242	Tested	22292
Temporary	22243	Testify	22293
Temporize	22244	Testimonial	22294
Temporizing ...	22245	Testimony	22295
Tempt	22246	Testing	22296
Temptation	22247	Testy	22297
Tempted...	22248	Tether	22298
Tempting	22249	Tethered...	22299
Ten...	22250	Text	22300

TEX	(112)	THR	224

Textual ...	...	...	22301	Thing	22351
Texture ...	...	...	22302	Think	22352
Than	...	...	22303	Thinking	22353
Thank	...	...	22304	Thinks	22354
Thanked	...	...	22305	Thinly	22355
Thanking	...	...	22306	Third	22356
Thanks ...	...	...	22307	Thirst	22357
That	...	...	22308	Thirsting	22358
Thatch	...	...	22309	Thirsty	22359
Thaw	...	...	22310	Thirteen	22360
Thawed ...	...	...	22311	Thirteenth ...	22361
Thawing...	...	...	22312	Thirtieth ...	22362
The ...	...	...	22313	Thirty	22363
Theatre ...	...	...	22314	This	22364
Thee	...	...	22315	Thither	22365
Theft	...	...	22316	Thorn	22366
Their	...	...	22317	Thorny	22367
Theirs	...	...	22318	Thorough ...	22368
Theist	...	...	22319	Thoroughfare...	22369
Them	...	...	22320	Thoroughly ...	22370
Theme	...	...	22321	Those	22371
Themselves	...	...	22322	Thou	22372
Then	...	...	22323	Though ...	22373
Thence ...	...	...	22324	Thought ...	22374
Theodolite	...	...	22325	Thoughtful ...	22375
Theology	...	...	22326	Thoughtless ...	22376
Theory ...	...	...	22327	Thoughtlessly ...	22377
There	...	...	22328	Thousand ...	22378
Thereby ...	...	...	22329	Thousandth ...	22379
Therefore	...	...	22330	Thraldom ...	22380
Therefrom	...	...	22331	Thrash ...	22381
Therein ...	...	...	22332	Thrashed ...	22382
Thereof ...	...	...	22333	Thrashing ...	22383
Thereon ...	...	...	22334	Thread ...	22384
Thereunto	...	...	22335	Threat ...	22385
Thereupon	...	...	22336	Threaten ...	22386
Therewith	...	...	22337	Threatened ...	22387
Thermal ...	...	...	22338	Threatening ...	22388
Thermometer...	...	...	22339	Three ...	22389
These	..	...	22340	Threshold ...	22390
Thesis	...	...	22341	Threw ...	22391
Thew	...	...	22342	Thrice ...	22392
They	...	...	22343	Thrift ...	22393
Thick	...	...	22344	Thrifty ...	22394
Thicket ...	...	...	22345	Thrill ...	22395
Thickly ...	...	...	22346	Thrilling...	22396
Thief	...	...	22347	Thrive ...	22397
Thigh	...	...	22348	Thriving...	22398
Thin	...	...	22349	Thriven ...	22399
Thine	...	...	22350	Thrives ...	22400

Throat 22401	Tilled 22451
Throb 22402	Tilling 22452
Throbbing 22403	Timber 22453
Throe 22404	Time 22454
Throne 22405	Timed 22455
Throng 22406	Timid 22456
Thronged 22407	Timing 22457
Thronging 22408	Tin 22458
Throttle 22409	Tincture 22459
Throttled 22410	Tinder 22460
Throttling 22411	Tinge 22461
Through 22412	Tinged 22462
Throughout 22413	Tingle 22463
Throve 22414	Tingled 22464
Throw 22415	Tingling 22465
Throwing 22416	Tinsel 22466
Thrown 22417	Tint 22467
Throws 22418	Tinted 22468
Thrust 22419	Tiny 22469
Thumb 22420	Tipple 22470
Thump 22421	Tippled 22471
Thumped 22422	Tippling 22472
Thumping 22423	Tipsy 22473
Thunder 22424	Tire 22474
Thursday 22425	Tired 22475
Thus 22426	Tiresome 22476
Thwart 22427	Tiring 22477
Thwarted 22428	Tissue 22478
Thwarting 22429	Tithe 22479
Thy 22430	Title 22480
Thyme 22431	Titled 22481
Thyself 22432	Tittle 22482
Tick 22433	Titular 22483
Ticket 22434	To 22484
Ticking 22435	Tobacco 22485
Tickle 22436	Toddle 22486
Ticklish 22437	Toe 22487
Tickly 22438	Together 22488
Tide 22439	Toil 22489
Tided 22440	Toiled 22490
Tidy 22441	Toilet 22491
Tie 22442	Toiling 22492
Tied 22443	Token 22493
Tier 22444	Told 22494
Tight 22445	Tolerable 22495
Tighten 22446	Toll 22496
Tightly 22447	Tolled 22497
Tile 22448	Tolling 22498
Tiled 22449	Tomb 22499
Till 22450	Ton 22500

TON	(113)	TRA	226

Tongue	...	...	... 22501	Track	... ...	22551
Tonic	...	...	... 22502	Tracked	... ...	22552
Tonnage	...	...	... 22503	Tract	... ...	22553
Too	...	...	... 22504	Tractable	... ...	22554
Touk	..	...	... 22505	Trade	... ...	22555
Tool	...	...	... 22506	Traded	... ...	22556
Tooth	...	...	... 22507	Trader	... ...	22557
Toothed	...	...	... 22508	Trading	... ...	22558
Topic	...	...	... 22509	Tradition	... ...	22559
Topographer	...	... 22510	Traduce	... ...	22560
Torch	...	...	... 22511	Traduced	... ...	22561
Tore	...	...	... 22512	Traducing	... ...	22562
Torment	...	...	... 22513	Traffic	... ...	22563
Tormented	...	...	... 22514	Tragedy	... ...	22564
Tormenting	...	... 22515	Tragic	... ...	22565
Torn	...	...	... 22516	Trail	... ...	22566
Tornado	...	...	... 22517	Trailed	... ...	22567
Torpid	...	...	... 22518	Trailing	... ...	22568
Torrent	...	...	... 22519	Train	... ...	22569
Torrid	...	...	... 22520	Training	... ...	22570
Tortuous	...	... 22521	Traitor	... ...	22571
Torture	...	...	... 22522	Traitorous	... ...	22572
Tory	...	...	... 22523	Tram	... ...	22573
Toss	...	...	... 22524	Trammel	... ...	22574
Tossed	...	...	... 22525	Trammelled	... ...	22575
Tossing	...	...	... 22526	Trample	... ...	22576
Total	...	...	... 22527	Trampled	... ...	22577
Totally	...	...	... 22528	Trampling	... ...	22578
Totter	...	...	... 22529	Trance	... ...	22579
Tottered	...	...	... 22530	Tranquil	... ...	22580
Tottering	...	... 22531	Tranquilise	... ...	22581
Touch	...	...	... 22532	Tranquilised	... ...	22582
Touched	...	...	... 22533	Tranquilising	...	22583
Touching	...	... 22534	Transact	... ...	22584
Tough	...	...	... 22535	Transaction	...	22585
Tour	...	...	... 22536	Transcend	... ...	22586
Tout	...	...	... 22537	Transcribe	... ...	22587
Touted	...	...	... 22538	Transcript	... ...	22588
Touting	...	...	... 22539	Transept	... ...	22589
Tow	...	...	... 22540	Transfer	... ...	22590
Towards	...	... 22541	Transferable	... ...	22591
Towed	...	...	... 22542	Transferred	... ...	22592
Tower	...	...	... 22543	Transferring	... ...	22593
Towering	...	... 22544	Transfigure	... ...	22594
Towing	...	...	... 22545	Transfix	... ...	22595
Town	...	...	... 22546	Transformation	...	22596
Toy	...	...	... 22547	Transgression	...	22597
Trace	...	...	... 22548	Transient	... ...	22598
Traced	...	...	... 22549	Transition	... ...	22599
Tracing	...	...	... 22550	Transitory	... ...	22600

Translate	22601	Trencher 22651
Translated	22602	Trepan 22652
Translating	22603	Trepidation 22653
Translation	22604	Trespass... 22654
Transmarine	22605	Trespassing 22655
Transmigration	22606	Tret 22656
Transmission	22607	Triad 22657
Transmit... ...	22608	Trial 22658
Transmutation ...	22609	Triangle 22659
Transmute	22610	Triangular 22660
Transparent	22611	Tribe 22661
Transparently ...	22612	Tribulation 22662
Transpire	22613	Tribunal 22663
Transpired	22614	Tribute 22664
Transpiring	22615	Trick 22665
Transplant	22616	Trickle 22666
Transport	22617	Trickling 22667
Transpose	22618	Tricky 22668
Transubstantiation..	22619	Tricolour ... 22669
Transverse	22620	Trident 22670
Trash	22621	Tried 22671
Travail	22622	Triennial 22672
Travel	22623	Trifle 22673
Travelled	22624	Trifling 22674
Traveller	22625	Trigger 22675
Travelling	22626	Trigonometry ... 22676
Traverse	22627	Trim 22677
Tray	22628	Trimmed 22678
Treachery	22629	Trimming 22679
Treacle	22630	Trinity 22680
Tread	22631	Trinket 22681
Treading	22632	Trip 22682
Treads	22633	Triple 22683
Treason	22634	Tripped 22684
Treasure...	22635	Tripping 22685
Treasurer	22636	Trite 22686
Treat	22637	Triumph... 22687
Treated	22638	Triumphant 22688
Treating	22639	Trivial 22689
Treatise	22640	Trod 22690
Treatment	22641	Trodden 22691
Treaty	22642	Troop 22692
Tree	22643	Trooped 22693
Tremble	22644	Trophy 22694
Trembled	22645	Tropical 22695
Trembling	22646	Tropics 22696
Tremendous	22647	Trot 22697
Tremor	22648	Trotting 22698
Trench	22649	Trouble 22699
Trenchant	22650	Troubled 22700

TRO			(114)	TYR			228
Troublesome ...	...		22701	Turf	...	... ...	22751
Troubling	...	...	22702	Turk	...	... ...	22752
Trough ...	...	...	22703	Turkish ...	...	...	22753
Trowel ...	...	...	22704	Turmoil ...	...	...	22754
Trowsers	...	...	22705	Turn	...	... ...	22755
Troy	...	...	22706	Turned ...	...	...	22756
Truant	...	...	22707	Turner ...	...	...	22757
Truce	...	...	22708	Turning ...	...	...	22758
Truck	...	...	22709	Turnip ...	...	...	22759
Truckle ...	...	...	22710	Turnkey ...	...	...	22760
Truculent	...	...	22711	Turnpike	...	...	22761
True	...	...	22712	Turnstile	...	...	22762
Truly	...	...	22713	Turpentine	...	...	22763
Trumpet ...	...	...	22714	Turpitude	...	...	22764
Trumpeted	...	...	22715	Turret	...	...	22765
Truncheon	...	...	22716	Tusk	...	... ...	22766
Trunk	...	...	22717	Tussle	...	...	22767
Truss	...	...	22718	Tussling ...	...	...	22768
Trussed ...	...	...	22719	Tutor	...	...	22769
Trust	...	...	22720	Tweak	...	...	22770
Trusted ...	...	...	22721	Tweezers	...	...	22771
Trusting ...	...	...	22722	Twelfth ...	...	...	22772
Trustee ...	...	...	22723	Twelve ...	...	...	22773
Trusty	...	...	22724	Twentieth	...	...	22774
Truth	...	...	22725	Twenty ...	...	...	22775
Truthful ...	...	...	22726	Twice	...	...	22776
Try ...	...	...	22727	Twig	...	...	22777
Trying	...	...	22728	Twigged	...	...	22778
Tub	...	...	22729	Twilight ...	...	...	22779
Tube	...	...	22730	Twill	...	...	22780
Tubular ...	...	...	22731	Twin	...	...	22781
Tuesday ...	...	...	22732	Twine	...	...	22782
Tuft	...	...	22733	Twinge ...	...	...	22783
Tug	...	...	22734	Twinkle ...	...	...	22784
Tugged ...	...	...	22735	Twinkling	...	...	22785
Tugging ...	...	...	22736	Twirl	...	...	22786
Tuition ...	...	...	22737	Twirling ...	...	...	22787
Tumble ...	...	...	22738	Twist	...	...	22788
Tumbled	...	...	22739	Twisted ...	...	...	22789
Tumbler ...	...	...	22740	Twisting ...	...	...	22790
Tumbling	...	...	22741	Twitch ...	...	...	22791
Tumour ...	...	...	22742	Twitching	...	...	22792
Tumult ...	...	...	22743	Two	...	...	22793
Tumultuous	...	...	22744	Type	...	...	22794
Tune	...	...	22745	Typhoid ...	...	...	22795
Tunic	...	...	22746	Typhus ...	...	...	22796
Tunnel	...	...	22747	Typical ...	...	...	22797
Turbid	...	...	22748	Tyranny ...	...	...	22798
Turbulent	...	...	22749	Tyrian ...	...	...	22799
Tureen ...	...	...	22750	Tyro	...	...	22800

U	22801	Unbelieving	22851
Ubiquitous	22802	Unbend	22852
Udder	22803	Unbending	22853
Ugly	22804	Unbiassed	22854
Ulcer	22805	Unbidden	22855
Ulterior	22806	Unbind	22856
Ultimate ...	22807	Unblemished... ...	22857
Ultimately	22808	Unblushing	22858
Ultimatum	22809	Unbolt	22859
Ultimo	22810	Unbolted	22860
Ultramarine	22811	Unborn	22861
Ultramontane ...	22812	Unbosom	22862
Umber	22813	Unbound	22863
Umbrage	22814	Unbounded	22864
Umbrageous	22815	Unbrotherly	22865
Umbrella	22816	Unbuilt	22866
Umpire	22817	Uncalculating ...	22867
Unable	22818	Unceasing	22868
Unacceptable... ...	22819	Uncertain	22869
Unaccountable ...	22820	Uncertainly	22870
Unaccustomed ...	22821	Uncertainty	22871
Unacquainted ...	22822	Unchain...	22872
Unadulterated ...	22823	Unchangeable ...	22873
Unadvisable	22824	Unchangeably ...	22874
Unaffected	22825	Uncharitable... ...	22875
Unalleviated	22826	Unchaste	22876
Unalterable	22827	Uncivil	22877
Unambitious	22828	Uncle	22878
Unamiable	22829	Unclean	22879
Unanimity	22830	Uncoil	22880
Unanimous	22831	Uncoiled	22881
Unanimously... ...	22832	Uncoiling	22882
Unannounced ...	22833	Uncomfortable ...	22883
Unanswerable ...	22834	Uncomfortably ...	22884
Unappreciated ...	22835	Uncommon	22885
Unapproachable ...	22836	Uncommonly... ...	22886
Unappropriated ...	22837	Unconcern	22887
Unasked...	22838	Unconcerned	22888
Unaspiring	22839	Unconciliatory ...	22889
Unassuming	22840	Uncondemned ...	22890
Unattached	22841	Unconditional ...	22891
Unattested	22842	Unconfined	22892
Unauthorized... ...	22843	Unconquered... ...	22893
Unavailing	22844	Unconscionable ...	22894
Unavenged	22845	Unconscious	22895
Unavowed	22846	Unconsciously ...	22896
Unaware	22847	Unconsecrated ...	22897
Unbearable	22848	Unconsidered... ...	22898
Unbecoming	22849	Unconstitutional ...	22899
Unbelief...	22850	Uncontrollable ...	22900

UNC	(115)	UNG	230

Uncontrolled	22901	Undoing...	22951
Unconverted	22902	Undone	22952
Uncorrupt	22903	Undoubted	22953
Uncourteous	22904	Undress	22954
Uncouth...	22905	Undue	22955
Uncover	22906	Undulate	22956
Uncovered	22907	Undulatory	22957
Uncovering	22908	Unduly	22958
Unction	22909	Undutiful	22959
Uncultivated	22910	Undying...	22960
Uncut	22911	Unearth	22961
Undaunted	22912	Unearthly	22962
Undeceive	22913	Uneasily...	22963
Undecided	22914	Uneasiness	22964
Undefended	22915	Uneasy	22965
Undefinable	22916	Unembarrassed ...	22966
Under	22917	Unequal	22967
Undergo	22918	Unequally	22968
Undergraduate ...	22919	Unequivocal	22969
Underhand	22920	Unerring	22970
Underlet	22921	Uneven	22971
Undermine	22922	Unexceptionable ...	22972
Underneath	22923	Unexpected	22973
Undersell	22924	Unexpectedly ...	22974
Understand	22925	Unfair	22975
Understanding ...	22926	Unfairly...	22976
Understood	22927	Unfaithful	22977
Undersold	22928	Unfashionable ...	22978
Undertake	22929	Unfeeling	22979
Undertaker	22930	Unfeigned	22980
Undertaking	22931	Unfilial	22981
Undertook	22932	Unfit	22982
Underwent	22933	Unfitted	22983
Underwood	22934	Unflagging	22984
Underwriter	22935	Unflinching	22985
Undeservedly ...	22936	Unforeseen	22986
Undeserving	22937	Unfortified	22987
Undesigned	22938	Unfortunate	22988
Undesirable	22939	Unfortunately ...	22989
Undetermined ...	22940	Unfounded	22990
Undeveloped	22941	Unfriendly	22991
Undignified	22942	Unfruitful	22992
Undiscerning... ...	22943	Unfurl	22993
Undisclosed	22944	Unfurled...	22994
Undisguised	22945	Unfurling	22995
Undismayed	22946	Ungainly	22996
Undisturbed	22947	Ungallant	22997
Undid	22948	Ungenerous	22998
Undivided	22949	Ungodly...	22999
Undo	22950	Ungovernable ...	23000

Ungraceful	...	...	23001	Unmanageable ... 23051
Ungrateful	...	...	23002	Unmask 23052
Ungratefully	...	...	23003	Unmasked 23053
Unguarded	...	...	23004	Unmeaning 23054
Unhandsome	...	...	23005	Unmerciful 23055
Unhandy	...	...	23006	Unmerited 23056
Unhappily	...	...	23007	Unmindful 23057
Unhappy	...	...	23008	Unmistakable ... 23058
Unhealthy	...	...	23009	Unmoor 23059
Unhesitating	...	...	23010	Unmoored 23060
Unholy ...	...	...	23011	Unmooring 23061
Unhurt ...	...	...	23012	Unnatural 23062
Unicorn ...	...	...	23013	Unnecessary 23063
Uniform ...	...	...	23014	Unnecessarily... ... 23064
Uniformity	...	...	23015	Unnerve 23065
Uniformly	...	...	23016	Unnerved 23066
Unimportant ...	...	23017	Unobjectionable ... 23067
Unimposing	...	...	23018	Unostentatious ... 23068
Unimpressive...	...	23019	Unpack 23069
Unimproved ...	...	23020	Unpacked 23070
Unincumbered	...	23021	Unpaid 23071
Uninstructed ...	...	23022	Unpalatable 23072
Unintelligible	...	23023	Unparalleled 23073
Unintentional	...	23024	Unpardonable ... 23074
Uninteresting...	...	23025	Unparliamentary ... 23075
Union ...	...	...	23026	Unpitied 23076
Unique ...	...	...	23027	Unpleasant 23077
Unit ...	...	...	23028	Unpopular 23078
Unitarian	...	...	23029	Unprecedented ... 23079
Unite ...	...	...	23030	Unprejudiced... ... 23080
United ...	...	...	23031	Unpremeditated ... 23081
Uniting ...	...	...	23032	Unprepared 23082
Unity ...	...	...	23033	Unpretending ... 23083
Universal	...	...	23034	Unprincipled 23084
Universally	...	...	23035	Unproductive... ... 23085
Universe...	...	...	23036	Unprofessional ... 23086
University	...	...	23037	Unprofitable 23087
Unjust ...	...	...	23038	Unprofitably 23088
Unjustly ...	...	...	23039	Unpronounceable ... 23089
Unkind ...	...	...	23040	Unpropitious 23090
Unkindly	...	...	23041	Unprotected 23091
Unlawful	...	...	23042	Unpublished 23092
Unlawfully	...	...	23043	Unpunished 23093
Unless ...	...	...	23044	Unqualified 23094
Unlike ...	...	...	23045	Unravel 23095
Unlikely...	...	...	23046	Unravelled 23096
Unload ...	...	...	23047	Unread 23097
Unloaded	...	...	23048	Unreasonable ... 23098
Unloading	...	...	23049	Unregenerate ... 23099
Unlucky...	...	...	23050	Unreserved 23100

UNR	(116)	UXO	232

Unrighteous	23101	Unveil	23151
Unripe	23102	Unveiled	23152
Unrivalled	23103	Unwelcome	23153
Unruly	23104	Unworthy	23154
Unsafe	23105	Unyielding	23155
Unsafely...	23106	Up	23156
Unsaid	23107	Upbraid	23157
Unsaleable	23108	Upbraided	23158
Unsatisfactory ...	23109	Upbraiding	23159
Unsatisfied	23110	Upheld	23160
Unsavoury	23111	Uphold	23161
Unscrew	23112	Upholsterer	23162
Unscrewed	23113	Upon	23163
Unscrupulous... ...	23114	Upright	23164
Unsearchable... ...	23115	Uproar	23165
Unseemly	23116	Uproarious	23166
Unseen	23117	Urbane	23167
Unselfish	23118	Urge	23168
Unserviceable ...	23119	Urged	23169
Unsettle	23120	Urgent	23170
Unsettled	23121	Urging	23171
Unsettling	23122	Urine	23172
Unskilfully	23123	Urinal	23173
Unskilled	23124	Urn...	23174
Unsociable	23125	Us	23175
Unsought	23126	Usage	23176
Unsound...	23127	Usance	23177
Unsparing	23128	Use	23178
Unsparingly	23129	Useful	23179
Unspeakable	23130	Usefully	23180
Unstable...	23131	Useless	23181
Unsteady	23132	Usher	23182
Unstudied	23133	Usual	23183
Unsuccessful	23134	Usually	23184
Unsuitable	23135	Usurer	23185
Unsullied	23136	Usurious... ...	23186
Unsusceptible ...	23137	Usurp	23187
Unsuspected	23138	Usurped	23188
Unsuspicious	23139	Usurper	23189
Untaught	23140	Usurping	23190
Untenable	23141	Utensil	23191
Unthankful	23142	Utility	23192
Until	23143	Utmost	23193
Untimely	23144	Utopia	23194
Unto	23145	Utter	23195
Untrue	23146	Utterance	23196
Untruth	23147	Uttered	23197
Unused	23148	Uttering	23198
Unusually	23149	Utterly	23199
Unvarying	23150	Uxorious	23200

233	V	(117)	VEN

V	23201	Variable	23251
Vacancy	23202	Variably	23252
Vacant	23203	Variance	23253
Vacate	23204	Varicose	23254
Vacated	23205	Varied	23255
Vacating	23206	Variegate	23256
Vacation	23207	Variegated	23257
Vacillating	23208	Variety	23258
Vaccinate	23209	Various	23259
Vaccinated	23210	Variously	23260
Vaccination	23211	Varnish	23261
Vaccine	23212	Varnished	23262
Vacillate	23213	Varnishing	23263
Vacuity	23214	Vary	23264
Vagabond	23215	Vassal	23265
Vagrant	23216	Vast	23266
Vague	23217	Vastly	23267
Vaguely	23218	Vat	23268
Vail	23219	Vault	23269
Vain	23220	Vaulted	23270
Vainly	23221	Vaunt	23271
Vale	23222	Vaunted	23272
Valediction	23223	Vaunting	23273
Valet	23224	Veal	23274
Valiant	23225	Veer	23275
Valid	23226	Veered	23276
Validity	23227	Veering	23277
Valley	23228	Vegetable	23278
Valour	23229	Vegetate	23279
Valourous	23230	Vegetation	23280
Valuable	23231	Vehemence	23281
Valuation	23232	Vehement	23282
Value	23233	Vehicle	23283
Valued	23234	Veil	23284
Valuing	23235	Veiled	23285
Valve	23236	Vein	23286
Van	23237	Veined	23287
Vane	23238	Vellum	23288
Vanish	23239	Velocity	23289
Vanished	23240	Velvet	23290
Vanishing	23241	Venal	23291
Vanity	23242	Vend	23292
Vanquish	23243	Vending	23293
Vanquished	23244	Vendor	23294
Vanquishing	23245	Veneer	23295
Vantage	23246	Veneered	23296
Vapid	23247	Veneering	23297
Vaporize	23248	Venerable	23298
Vaporizer	23249	Venerate	23299
Vapour	23250	Venerated	23300

VEN	(117)	VIL	234

Veneration	...	...	23301	Vested	23351
Venetian...	...	...	23302	Vestige	23352
Vengeance	...	...	23303	Vesting	23353
Venial ...	...	...	23304	Vestry	23354
Venison ...	...	...	23305	Veteran	23355
Venom ...	...	...	23306	Veterinary	23356
Venomous	...	...	23307	Vex...	23357
Vent ...	...	...	23308	Vexation	23358
Vented ...	...	...	23309	Vexatious	23359
Ventilate	...	...	23310	Vexed	23360
Ventilated	...	...	23311	Vexing	23361
Ventilating	...	...	23312	Viaduct	23362
Ventilation	...	...	23313	Vial...	23363
Ventriloquism		...	23314	Viands	23364
Venture ...	...	...	23315	Vibrate	23365
Ventured	...	...	23316	Vibrated...	23366
Venturing	...	...	23317	Vibrating	23367
Veracious	...	...	23318	Vibration	23368
Veracity ...	...	...	23319	Vibratory	23369
Verb ...	...	...	23320	Vicar	23370
Verbal ...	...	...	23321	Vicarage...	23371
Verbally...	...	...	23322	Vicarious	23372
Verbatim	...	...	23323	Vice	23373
Verbiage...	...	...	23324	Vicinity	23374
Verdant ...	...	...	23325	Vicious	23375
Verdict ...	...	...	23326	Vicissitude	23376
Verge ...	...	...	23327	Victim	23377
Verger ...	...	...	23328	Victimize	23378
Verging ...	...	...	23329	Victimized	23379
Verification	...	...	23330	Victimizing	23380
Verified ...	...	...	23331	Victor	23381
Verify ...	...	...	23332	Victorious	23382
Verifying	...	...	23333	Victory	23383
Veritable	...	...	23334	Victual	23384
Veritas ...	...	...	23335	Vie	23385
Verity ...	...	...	23336	Vied	23386
Vermilion	...	...	23337	Vieing	23387
Vermin ...	...	...	23338	View	23388
Vernacular	...	...	23339	Viewed	23389
Vernal ...	...	...	23340	Viewing	23390
Versatile...	...	...	23341	Vigilance	23391
Verse ...	...	...	23342	Vigilant	23392
Versification	...	...	23343	Vigilantly	23393
Version ...	...	...	23344	Vigorous...	23394
Vertebral	...	...	23345	Vile	23395
Vertex ...	...	...	23346	Vilified	23396
Vertical ...	...	...	23347	Vilify	23397
Very ...	...	...	23348	Villa	23398
Vessel ...	...	...	23349	Village	23399
Vest ...	...	...	23350	Villain	23400

Vindicate	... ...	23401	
Vindicated	... ...	23402	
Vindicating	... ...	23403	
Vindication	... ...	23404	
Vindictive	... ...	23405	
Vine	... ...	23406	
Vinegar	... ...	23407	
Vintage	... ...	23408	
Vintner	... ...	23409	
Viol...	... ...	23410	
Violate	... ...	23411	
Violation	... ...	23412	
Violence	... ...	23413	
Violent	... ...	23414	
Violently	... ...	23415	
Violet	... ...	23416	
Violin	... ...	23417	
Viper	... ...	23418	
Virgin	... ...	23419	
Virility	... ...	23420	
Virtual	... ...	23421	
Virtually	... ...	23422	
Virtue	... ...	23423	
Virtuous	... ...	23424	
Virulence	... ...	23425	
Virulently	... ...	23426	
Visage	... ...	23427	
Viscid	... ...	23428	
Viscount	... ...	23429	
Viscous	... ...	23430	
Visible	... ...	23431	
Visibly	... ...	23432	
Vision	... ...	23433	
Visit	... ...	23434	
Visited	... ...	23435	
Visiting	... ...	23436	
Visitor	... ...	23437	
Vital	... ...	23438	
Vitality	... ...	23439	
Vitiate	... ...	23440	
Vitiated	... ...	23441	
Vitiating	... ...	23442	
Vitriol	... ...	23443	
Vituperate	... ...	23444	
Vituperation	... ...	23445	
Vivacious	:... ...	23446	
Vivacity	... ...	23447	
Vivid	... ...	23448	
Vividly	... ...	23449	
Vivified	... ...	23450	

Vivify	... ...	23451	
Vivisection	... ...	23452	
Vixen	... ...	23453	
Vocabulary	... ...	23454	
Vocal	... ...	23455	
Vocalist	... ...	23456	
Vocation	... ...	23457	
Vociferate	... ...	23458	
Vociferating	... ...	23459	
Vociferous	... ...	23460	
Vogue	... ...	23461	
Voice	... ...	23462	
Void	... ...	23463	
Volatile	... ...	23464	
Volcano	... ...	23465	
Volcanic	... ...	23466	
Volition	... ...	23467	
Volley	... ...	23468	
Volubility	... ...	23469	
Volume	... ...	23470	
Voluminous	... ...	23471	
Voluntary	... ...	23472	
Voluntarily	... ...	23473	
Volunteer	... ...	23474	
Volunteering	... ...	23475	
Voluptuary	... ...	23476	
Vomit	... ...	23477	
Vomited	... ...	23478	
Vomiting	... ...	23479	
Voracious	... ...	23480	
Vortex	... ...	23481	
Votary	... ...	23482	
Vote	... ...	23483	
Voted	... ...	23484	
Voting	... ...	23485	
Vouch	... ...	23486	
Vouched	... ...	23487	
Voucher	... ...	23488	
Vouching	... ...	23489	
Vow	... ...	23490	
Vowed	... ...	23491	
Vowel	... ...	23492	
Vowing	... ...	23493	
Voyage	... ...	23494	
Vulgar	... ...	23495	
Vulgarity	... ...	23496	
Vulgarly	... ...	23497	
Vulgate	... ...	23498	
Vulnerable	... ...	23499	
Vulture	... ...	23500	

W			(118)	WAS	230

W ...	...	...	23501	Wander ...	...	...	23551
Wade	...	...	23502	Wandered	...	...	23552
Waded	...	...	23503	Wanderer	...	...	23553
Wading	...	...	23504	Wandering	...	...	23554
Wafer	...	...	23505	Wane	...	...	23555
Waft	...	...	23506	Waning ...	...	...	23556
Wafted	...	...	23507	Want	...	...	23557
Wafting	...	...	23508	Wanted	...	...	23558
Wag	...	...	23509	Wanting...	...	...	23559
Wage	...	...	23510	Wanton ...	...	...	23560
Waged	...	...	23511	Wantonly	...	...	23561
Wager	...	...	23512	Wantonness	...	...	23562
Wages	...	...	23513	War	...	...	23563
Waggish...	...	...	23514	Warble ...	...	...	23564
Waggishly	...	...	23515	Warbled...	...	...	23565
Waggon ...	...	...	23516	Warbling	...	...	23566
Waging ...	...	...	23517	Ward	...	...	23567
Waif	...	...	23518	Warded	...	...	23568
Wail	...	...	23519	Warden ...	...	...	23569
Wailed ...	...	...	23520	Warder ...	...	...	23570
Wailing	...	...	23521	Warding...	...	...	23571
Wain	...	...	23522	Wardrobe	...	...	23572
Waist	...	...	23523	Warehouse	...	...	23573
Waistcoat	...	...	23524	Wares	...	...	23574
Wait	...	...	23525	Warfare ...	...	...	23575
Waited ...	...	...	23526	Wariness	...	...	23576
Waiter ...	...	...	23527	Warm	...	...	23577
Waiting ...	...	...	23528	Warmed...	...	...	23578
Waive	...	...	23529	Warming	...	...	23579
Waived ...	...	...	23530	Warlike ...	...	...	23580
Waiving ...	...	...	23531	Warmly ...	...	...	23581
Wake	...	...	23532	Warn	...	...	23582
Waked	...	...	23533	Warning...	...	..	23583
Wakeful ...	...	...	23534	Warp	...	...	23584
Wakefully	...	...	23535	Warped ...	...	...	23585
Waken ...	...	...	23536	Warrant ...	...	...	23586
Wakened	...	...	23537	Warranted	...	...	23587
Wakening	...	...	23538	Warranty	...	...	23588
Waking ...	...	...	23539	Warred ...	...	...	23589
Walk	...	...	23540	Warren ...	...	...	23590
Walked ...	...	...	23541	Warring ...	...	...	23591
Walker ...	...	...	23542	Warrior ...	...	...	23592
Walking	...	...	23543	Wart	...	...	23593
Wall	...	...	23544	Wary	...	...	23594
Walled ...	...	...	23545	Was	...	...	23595
Walnut	...	...	23546	Wash	..	...	23596
Wallow ...	...	...	23547	Washed ...	...	...	23597
Waltz	...	...	23548	Washes ...	...	...	23598
Wan	...	...	23549	Washing...	...	...	23599
Wand	...	...	23550	Wasp	...	...	23600

Waspish ...	...	...	23601	Wedlock...	...	...	23651
Waste	...	...	23602	Wednesday	...	...	23652
Wasted ...	...	...	23603	Weed ...	...	...	23653
Wasteful...	...	...	23604	Weeded ...	...	...	23654
Wasting ...	...	...	23605	Week ...	...	...	23655
Watch ...	...	...	23606	Weekly ...	...	...	23656
Watched...	...	...	23607	Weep ...	...	...	23657
Watchful	...	...	23608	Weeping...	...	...	23658
Watching	...	...	23609	Weeps ...	...	...	23659
Watchman	...	...	23610	Weigh ...	...	...	23660
Water ...	...	...	23611	Weighed...	...	...	23661
Watered ...	...	...	23612	Weighing	...	...	23662
Watering	...	...	23613	Weight ...	...	...	23663
Watery ...	...	...	23614	Weightily	...	...	23664
Wave ...	...	...	23615	Welch ...	...	...	23665
Waved ...	...	...	23616	Welcome	...	...	23666
Waver ...	...	...	23617	Weld ...	...	...	23667
Wavering	...	...	23618	Welded ...	...	...	23668
Waving ...	...	...	23619	Welfare ...	...	...	23669
Wax ...	...	...	23620	Welkin ...	...	...	23670
Waxen ...	...	...	23621	Well ...	...	...	23671
Way ...	...	...	23622	Welling ...	...	...	23672
Waylaid ...	...	...	23623	Went ...	...	...	23673
Waylay ...	...	...	23624	Wept ...	...	...	23674
Wayward	...	...	23625	Were ...	...	...	23675
We	...	...	23626	West ...	...	...	23676
Weak ...	...	...	23627	Westerly...	...	...	23677
Weaken ...	...	...	23628	Western ...	...	...	23678
Weakly ...	...	...	23629	Wet...	...	...	23679
Wealth ...	...	...	23630	Wether ...	...	...	23680
Wealthily	...	...	23631	Wets ...	...	...	23681
Wealthy ...	...	...	23632	Wetted ...	...	...	23682
Wean ...	...	...	23633	Wetting ...	...	...	23683
Weaned ...	...	...	23634	Whale ...	...	...	23684
Weaning	...	...	23635	Wharf ...	...	...	23685
Weapon ...	...	...	23636	Wharfage	...	...	23686
Wear ...	...	...	23637	What ...	...	...	23687
Wearing...	...	...	23638	Whatever	...	...	23688
Wearisome	...	...	23639	Wheat ...	...	...	23689
Wears ...	...	...	23640	Wheaten...	...	...	23690
Weary ...	...	...	23641	Wheel ...	...	...	23691
Weather ...	...	...	23642	Wheeled...	...	...	23692
Weave ...	...	...	23643	Wheeling	...	...	23693
Weaved ...	...	...	23644	Whelp ...	...	...	23694
Weaving...	...	...	23645	When ...	...	...	23695
Web ...	...	...	23646	Whence ...	...	...	23696
Wed ...	...	...	23647	Whenever	...	...	23697
Wedded ...	...	...	23648	Where ...	...	...	23698
Wedding	...	...	23649	Whereas...	...	...	23699
Wedge ...	...	...	23650	Whereat ...	...	...	23700

WHE	(119)		WIN	230
Whereby	23701	Wickedly	23751	
Wherefor	23702	Wickedness	23752	
Wherein...	23703	Wicket	23753	
Whereto...	23704	Wide	23754	
Whereupon	23705	Widely	23755	
Wherever	23706	Widen	23756	
Whet	23707	Widened...	23757	
Whether	23708	Widening	23758	
Whetted	23709	Wider	23759	
Whetting	23710	Widow	23760	
Whey	23711	Widower	23761	
Which	23712	Width	23762	
Whichever	23713	Wield	23763	
Whiff	23714	Wielded...	23764	
While	23715	Wielding	23765	
Whilst	23716	Wife	23766	
Whim	23717	Wig...	23767	
Whine	23718	Wild	23768	
Whined	23719	Wildly	23769	
Whining...	23720	Wilderness	23770	
Whip	23721	Wile	23771	
Whipped	23722	Wilful	23772	
Whipping	23723	Wilfully	23773	
Whirl	23724	Will	23774	
Whirled	23725	Willed	23775	
Whirling	23726	Willing	23776	
Whirlpool	23727	Willingly	23777	
Whirlwind	23728	Willow	23778	
Whisky	23729	Wily	23779	
Whisper...	23730	Win	23780	
Whispered	23731	Winch	23781	
Whispering	23732	Wind	23782	
Whist	23733	Winding...	23783	
Whistle	23734	Windlass	23784	
Whistling	23735	Window...	23785	
White	23736	Winds	23786	
Whited	23737	Windward	23787	
Whither	23738	Windy	23788	
Whiting	23739	Wine	23789	
Who	23740	Wing	23790	
Whoever...	23741	Winged	23791	
Whole	23742	Wink	23792	
Wholesale	23743	Winner	23793	
Wholesome	23744	Winning...	23794	
Wholly	23745	Winnow...	23795	
Whom	23746	Winnowing	23796	
Whoop	23747	Wins	23797	
Whose	23748	Winter	23798	
Why	23749	Wintering	23799	
Wicked	23750	Wintry	23800	

Wipe	23801	
Wiped	23802	
Wiping	23803	
Wire	23804	
Wiry	23805	
Wisdom	23806	
Wise	23807	
Wisely	23808	
Wish	23809	
Wished	23810	
Wishful	23811	
Wishing	23812	
Wisp	23813	
Wistful	23814	
Wistfully	23815	
Wit	23816	
Witch	23817	
With	23818	
Withdraw	23819	
Withdrawing	23820	
Withdrew	23821	
Wither	23822	
Withered	23823	
Withering	23824	
Withheld	23825	
Withhold	23826	
Withholding	23827	
Within	23828	
Without	23829	
Withstand	23830	
Withstanding	23831	
Withstood	23832	
Witness	23833	
Witnessed	23834	
Witted	23835	
Witticism	23836	
Wittily	23837	
Witty	23838	
Wizard	23839	
Woad	23840	
Woe	23841	
Woke	23842	
Wolf	23843	
Woman	23844	
Womanly	23845	
Womb	23846	
Won	23847	
Wonder	23848	
Wondered	23849	
Wonderfully	23850	

Wondering	23851	
Wondrous	23852	
Woo	23853	
Wood	23854	
Wooden	23855	
Wooed	23856	
Wooing	23857	
Woof	23858	
Wool	23859	
Woollen	23860	
Woolly	23861	
Word	23862	
Worded	23863	
Wordy	23864	
Work	23865	
Worker	23866	
Working	23867	
Workman	23868	
Works	23869	
World	23870	
Worldly	23871	
Worm	23872	
Worming	23873	
Worn	23874	
Worried	23875	
Worry	23876	
Worrying	23877	
Worse	23878	
Worship	23879	
Worshipful	23880	
Worshipped	23881	
Worshipper	23882	
Worshipping	23883	
Worst	23884	
Worsted	23885	
Wort	23886	
Worth	23887	
Worthily	23888	
Worthless	23889	
Worthy	23890	
Would	23891	
Wound	23892	
Wounded	23893	
Wounding	23894	
Wove	23895	
Woven	23896	
Wrangle	23897	
Wrangler	23898	
Wrangling	23899	
Wrap	23900	

WRA	(120)	ZOU	240
Wrapped	23901	X	23951
Wrapper...	23902	Y	23952
Wrapping	23903	Yacht	23953
Wrath	23904	Yankee	23954
Wrathful...	23905	Yard	23955
Wreak	23906	Yarn	23956
Wreaking	23907	Yawl	23957
Wreath	23908	Yawn	23958
Weathe...	23909	Ye	23959
Wreck	23910	Year	23960
Wrecked...	23911	Yearling...	23961
Wrecker	23912	Yearly	23962
Wrecking	23913	Yearn	23963
Wren	23914	Yeast	23964
Wrench	23915	Yell...	23965
Wrenched	23916	Yellow	23966
Wrenching	23917	Yeoman	23967
Wrest	23918	Yeomanry	23968
Wresting	23919	Yes	23969
Wrestle	23920	Yesterday	23970
Wrestled...	23921	Yet	23971
Wrestler...	23922	Yew	23972
Wrestling	23923	Yield	23973
Wretch	23924	Yoke	23974
Wretched	23925	Yolk	23975
Wretchedly	23926	Yonder	23976
Wriggle	23927	Yore	23977
Wriggling	23928	You...	23978
Wright	23929	Young	23979
Wring	23930	Younger...	23980
Wringing	23931	Youngest	23981
Wrinkle	23932	Youngster	23982
Wrist	23933	Your	23983
Writ	23934	Yourself	23984
Write	23935	Yourselves	23985
Writer	23936	Youth	23986
Writes	23937	Youthful...	23987
Writhe	23938	Z	23988
Writhing	23939	Zeal...	23989
Writing	23940	Zealous	23990
Written	23941	Zealously	23991
Wrong	23942	Zenith	23992
Wronged	23943	Zephyr	23993
Wrongfully	23944	Zero	23994
Wronging	23945	Zest...	23995
Wrote	23946	Zinc...	23996
Wroth	23947	Zodiac	23997
Wrought	23948	Zone	23998
Wrung	23949	Zoological	23999
Wry...	23950	Zouave	24000

| 241 | AAR | (121) | MAR |

Aaron	24001	Elias	24051
Abraham	24002	Elijah	24052
Absalom	24003	Emile	24053
Adam	24004	Emmanuel	24054
Adolphus	24005	Enoch	24055
Adrian	24006	Eustace	24056
Albert	24007	Everard	24057
Alexander	24008	Ezekiel	24058
Alfred	24009	Ezra	24059
Alan	24010	Ferdinand	24060
Algernon	24011	Fergus	24061
Ambrose	24012	Francis	24062
Andrew	24013	Frederick	24063
Angus	24014	Gabriel	24064
Anthony	24015	George	24065
Archibald	24016	Gerard	24066
Arthur	24017	Giles	24067
Asa	24018	Godfrey	24068
Augustus	24019	Gustavus	24069
Austin	24020	Guy	24070
Baldwin	24021	Harold	24071
Barnabas	24022	Hector	24072
Bartholomew	24023	Herbert	24073
Basil	24024	Henry	24074
Benedict	24025	Hezekiah	24075
Benjamin	24026	Horatio	24076
Bernard	24027	Hosea	24077
Bertram	24028	Hugh	24078
Caleb	24029	Humphrey	24079
Cecil	24030	Isaac	24080
Charles	24031	Isaiah	24081
Christopher	24032	Israel	24082
Claude	24033	Jacob	24083
Clement	24034	James	24084
Conrad	24035	Jeremiah	24085
Constantine	24036	Jocelyn	24086
Cornelius	24037	John	24087
Cuthbert	24038	Jonas	24088
Daniel	24039	Jonathan	24089
David	24040	Joseph	24090
Denis	24041	Joshua	24091
Dominic	24042	Josiah	24092
Donald	24043	Judah	24093
Duncan	24044	Lawrence	24094
Ebenezer	24045	Leonard	24095
Edgar	24046	Leopold	24096
Edmond	24047	Lewis	24097
Edward	24048	Luke	24098
Edwin	24049	Malcolm	24099
Egbert	24050	Marcus	24100

MAR	(121)	SUS	242

Marmaduke	24101	Abigail	24151
Martin	24102	Adelaide...	24152
Matthew...	24103	Agnes	24153
Maurice	24104	Alice	24154
Michael	24105	Amelia	24155
Moses	24106	Ann	24156
Nathaniel	24107	Barbara	24157
Nicholas...	24108	Beatrice	24158
Octavius	24109	Bertha	24159
Oliver	24110	Caroline	24160
Onesimus	24111	Cecilia	24161
Oscar	24112	Charlotte	24162
Otho	24113	Clara	24163
Patrick	24114	Dorothea	24164
Paul	24115	Edith	24165
Percy	24116	Eliza	24166
Peter	24117	Ellen	24167
Philip	24118	Emily	24168
Poyntz	24119	Emma	24169
Ralph	24120	Esther	24170
Randolph	24121	Evangeline	24171
Raphael	24122	Fanny	24172
Reginald	24123	Gertrude...	24173
Reuben	24124	Hannah	24174
Richard	24125	Harriet	24175
Robert	24126	Helen	24176
Roger	24127	Isabella	24177
Roland	24128	Jane	24178
Rupert	24129	Jessie	24179
Samson	24130	Julia	24180
Samuel	24131	Kate	24181
Seth	24132	Laura	24182
Sidney	24133	Louisa	24183
Sigismund	24134	Lucy	24184
Silas	24135	Lydia	24185
Simon	24136	Margaret	24186
Solomon...	24137	Martha	24187
Stephen	24138	Mary	24188
Theobald	24139	Mathilda	24189
Theodore	24140	Maude	24190
Theophilus	24141	Olga	24191
Thomas	24142	Olivia	24192
Timothy...	24143	Penelope	24193
Titus	24144	Priscilla	24194
Toby	24145	Rachel	24195
Valentine	24146	Rebecca	24196
Walter	24147	Rosa	24197
Wilfred	24148	Sarah	24198
William	24149	Sophia	24199
Zachary	24150	Susan	24200

243	AND	(122)	WIL

Anderson	...	...	24201	Irving	24251
Arbuthnot	...	...	24202	Jackson	24252
Armitage	...	...	24203	Jenkins	24253
Barclay ...	...	...	24204	Jones	24254
Baring	...	...	24205	Joyce	24255
Barlow ...	...	...	24206	Kemp	24256
Barnett ...	...	...	24207	Knowles...	24257
Begbie	...	...	24208	Laing	24258
Bompas ...	...	...	24209	Lampson	24259
Boyd	...	...	24210	Lyall	24260
Bruce	...	...	24211	McCalmont	24261
Chalmers	...	...	24212	McDonald	24262
Cohen	...	...	24213	McFarlane	24263
Coutts	...	...	24214	McKenzie	24264
Cunliffe ...	...	...	24215	Matheson	24265
Cunningham ...	...	...	24216	Meyer	24266
Davies ...	...	...	24217	Morgan	24267
Dennistoun	...	...	24218	Morris	24268
Dimsdale	...	...	24219	Murdoch...	24269
Drummond	...	...	24220	Naylor	24270
Elliot	...	...	24221	Oppenheim	24271
Erlanger...	...	...	24222	Overend	24272
Evans	...	...	24223	Paterson...	24273
Fenwick...	...	...	24224	Pickersgill	24274
Fesser	...	...	24225	Pickford	24275
Findlay ...	...	...	24226	Powell	24276
Fletcher ...	...	...	24227	Prescott	24277
Forbes ...	...	...	24228	Ralli	24278
Franklin...	...	...	24229	Rathbone	24279
Fraser	...	...	24230	Reuter	24280
Fruhling...	...	...	24231	Ritchie	24281
Gaines	...	...	24232	Robinson	24282
Gibb	...	...	24233	Rodocanachi	24283
Gilbert ...	...	...	24234	Rothschild	24284
Gillespie ...	...	...	24235	Russell	24285
Glyn	...	...	24236	Sanders	24286
Gordon ...	...	...	24237	Sassoon	24287
Graham ...	...	...	24238	Schröder...	24288
Griffith ...	...	...	24239	Seymour...	24289
Grindlay...	...	...	24240	Simmonds	24290
Gurney ...	...	...	24241	Spence	24291
Halsey ...	...	...	24242	Stanley	24292
Hanbury...	...	...	24243	Stewart	24293
Hankey ...	...	...	24244	Todd	24294
Harris ...	...	...	24245	Tritton	24295
Harvey ...	...	...	24246	Vernon	24296
Hodgson	...	...	24247	Watkins	24297
Howard ...	...	...	24248	Webster	24298
Hughes ...	...	...	24249	Wilkinson	24299
Huth	...	...	24250	Willis	24300

Achilles 24301	Aglaia 24351
Adonis 24302	Amphitrite 24352
Agamemnon 24303	Andromeda 24353
Ajax 24304	Arethusa 24354
Apollo 24305	Ariadne 24355
Argus 24306	Astrea 24356
Bacchus 24307	Atalanta 24357
Bellerophon 24308	Atropos 24358
Castor 24309	Bellona 24359
Charon 24310	Calliope 24360
Cupid 24311	Ceres 24361
Cyclops 24312	Cassandra 24362
Deucalion 24313	Cassiopea 24363
Endymion 24314	Circe 24364
Ganymede 24315	Clio 24365
Hercules... 24316	Cybele 24366
Hymen 24317	Diana 24367
Ixion 24318	Dido 24368
Janus 24319	Euphrosyne 24369
Jason 24320	Eurydice... 24370
Jupiter 24321	Euterpe 24371
Laocoon... 24322	Galatea 24372
Mars 24323	Gorgon 24373
Mercury 24324	Hebe 24374
Minos 24325	Hecate 24375
Nereus 24326	Hermione 24376
Neptune... 24327	Iphigenia 24377
Nestor 24328	Irene 24378
Orion 24329	Juno 24379
Orpheus 24330	Latona 24380
Perseus 24331	Leda 24381
Phœbus 24332	Megaera... 24382
Pluto 24333	Melpomene 24383
Pollux 24334	Minerva 24384
Polyphemus 24335	Nemesis 24385
Priam 24336	Niobe 24386
Prometheus 24337	Pallas 24387
Proteus 24338	Pandora 24388
Pygmalion 24339	Penelope 24389
Rhadamanthus ... 24340	Polyhymnia 24390
Saturn 24341	Pomona 24391
Silenus 24342	Proserpine 24392
Sisyphus... 24343	Psyche 24393
Telemachus 24344	Rhea 24394
Theseus 24345	Terpsichore 24395
Titan 24346	Thalia 24396
Triton 24347	Tisiphone 24397
Ulysses 24348	Urania 24398
Vulcan 24349	Venus 24399
Zeus 24350	Vesta 24400

| 245 | ABY | (123) | LEB |

Abyssinia	... ...	24401	Coromandel ...	... ...	24451
Africa ...	... ...	24402	Corsica ...	... ...	24452
Algoa ...	... ...	24403	Cuba ...	... ...	24453
Amazon ...	... ...	24404	Cyprus ...	... ...	24454
America ...	... ...	24405	Danube ..	... ...	24455
Andes ...	... ...	24406	Darien ...	... ...	24456
Antigua ...	... ...	24407	Dardanelles ...	... ...	24457
Asia ...	... ...	24408	Denmark ...	... ...	24458
Atlantic ...	... ...	24409	Douro ...	... ...	24459
Arabia ...	... ...	24410	Ebro ...	... ...	24460
Algiers ...	... ...	24411	Egypt ...	... ...	24461
Alleghany	... ...	24412	Elbe ...	... ...	24462
Alps ...	... ...	24413	England ...	... ...	24463
Amoor ...	... ...	24414	Erie...	... ...	24464
Apennines	... ...	24415	Etna ...	... ...	24465
Armenia ...	... ...	24416	Europe ...	... ...	24466
Assam ...	... ...	24417	Feejee ...	... ...	24467
Australia	... ...	24418	Formosa ...	... ...	24468
Austria ...	... ...	24419	France ...	... ...	24469
Azof ...	... ...	24420	Fundy ...	... ...	24470
Azores ...	... ...	24421	Gambia ...	... ...	24471
Baden ...	... ...	24422	Ganges ...	... ...	24472
Bahamas ...	... ...	24423	Germany ...	... ...	24473
Baltic ...	... ...	24424	Gibraltar ...	... ...	24474
Barbadoes	... ...	24425	Grampian	... ...	24475
Barbary ...	... ...	24426	Greece ...	... ...	24476
Bavaria ...	... ...	24427	Guadeloupe ...	... ...	24477
Belgium ...	... ...	24428	Guatemala ...	... ...	24478
Bengal ...	... ...	24429	Guiana ...	... ...	24479
Bermuda ...	... ...	24430	Hainan ...	... ...	24480
Biscay ...	... ...	24431	Hayti ...	... ...	24481
Bohemia ...	... ...	24432	Hecla ...	... ...	24482
Bolivia ...	... ...	24433	Heligoland	... ...	24483
Borneo ...	... ...	24434	Himalaya ...	... ...	24484
Bosphorus	... ...	24435	Hindostan ...	... ...	24485
Brazil ...	... ...	24436	Honduras ...	... ...	24486
Brunswick	... ...	24437	Hungary ...	... ...	24487
Burmah ...	... ...	24438	Huron ...	... ...	24488
Canaan ...	... ...	24439	Iceland ...	... ...	24489
Canada ...	... ...	24440	India ...	... ...	24490
Carnatic ...	... ...	24441	Indus ...	... ...	24491
Carpathian	... ...	24442	Ireland ...	... ...	24492
Caspian ...	... ...	24443	Italy ...	... ...	24493
Cattegat ...	... ...	24444	Jamaica ...	... ...	24494
Ceylon ...	... ...	24445	Japan ...	... ...	24495
Champlain	... ...	24446	Java ...	... ...	24496
Cheviot ...	... ...	24447	Labrador ...	... ...	24497
Chili ...	... ...	24448	Lapland ...	... ...	24498
Clyde ...	... ...	24449	La Plata ...	... ...	24499
Columbia	... ...	24450	Lebanon ...	... ...	24500

LEV	(123)	ZEA	246

Levant	24501	Pyrenees	24551
Liffey	24502	Rhine	24552
Loire	24503	Rhone	24553
Lombardy	24504	Russia	24554
Madagascar	24505	Sahara	24555
Madeira	24506	Saldanha	24556
Magdalena	24507	Sardinia	24557
Malacca	24508	Savoy	24558
Malta	24509	Saxony	24559
Manilla	24510	Scotland	24560
Marmora	24511	Seine	24561
Marquesas	24512	Senegal	24562
Mauritius	24513	Shannon	24563
Mediterranean	24514	Severn	24564
Mersey	24515	Siam	24565
Mexico	24516	Siberia	24566
Michigan	24517	Sicily	24567
Mississippi	24518	Silesia	24568
Missouri	24519	Solway	24569
Moldavia	24520	Spain	24570
Moluccas	24521	Sumatra	24571
Montserrat	24522	Sweden	24572
Morocco	24523	Switzerland	24573
Moselle	24524	Syria	24574
Mozambique	24525	Tagus	24575
Nassau	24526	Tartary	24576
Nevis	24527	Tasmania	24577
Newfoundland	24528	Tay	24578
Nicaragua	24529	Teviot	24579
Niger	24530	Thames	24580
Nile	24531	Tiber	24581
Norway	24532	Tobago	24582
Nova Scotia	24533	Tortola	24583
Nubia	24534	Trinidad	24584
Oder	24535	Tripoli	24585
Ohio	24536	Tunis	24586
Ontario	24537	Turkey	24587
Orinoco	24538	Tuscany	24588
Otaheite	24539	Tweed	24589
Palestine	24540	Ural	24590
Panama	24541	Vancouver	24591
Paraguay	24542	Venezuela	24592
Persia	24543	Vesuvius	24593
Peru	24544	Wales	24594
Philippines	24545	Wallachia	24595
Piedmont	24546	Westphalia	24596
Po	24547	Wolga	24597
Poland	24548	Wurtemberg	24598
Portugal	24549	Zanzibar	24599
Prussia	24550	Zealand	24600

Aberdeen	... ...	24601
Anglesea	... ...	24602
Antrim ...	... ...	24603
Argyle ...	... ...	24604
Arklow ...	... ...	24605
Armagh ...	... ...	24606
Arran ...	... ...	24607
Athlone ...	... ...	24608
Ayr	... ...	24609
Banff	... ...	24610
Bedford ...	... ...	24611
Belfast ...	... ...	24612
Berkshire	... ...	24613
Berwick ...	... ...	24614
Boston ...	... ...	24615
Birmingham	... ...	24616
Brecknock	... ...	24617
Brighton ...	... ...	24618
Bristol ...	... ...	24619
Buckingham ...	... ...	24620
Burton ...	... ...	24621
Bute ...	... ...	24622
Caermarthen ...	... ...	24623
Caernarvon	... ...	24624
Caithness	... ...	24625
Cambridge	... ...	24626
Canterbury	... ...	24627
Cardiff ...	... ...	24628
Cardigan	... ...	24629
Carlow ...	... ...	24630
Carstairs ...	... ...	24631
Cavan ...	... ...	24632
Chatham ...	... ...	24633
Chelmsford	... ...	24634
Cheshire ...	... ...	24635
Chichester	... ...	24636
Clackmannan	...	24637
Clare ...	... ...	24638
Coleraine	... ...	24639
Connaught	... ...	24640
Cornwall	... ...	24641
Cromarty	... ...	24642
Coventry	... ...	24643
Cumberland ...	... ...	24644
Cupar ...	... ...	24645
Denbigh ...	... ...	24646
Derby ...	... ...	24647
Derry ...	... ...	24648
Devon ...	... ...	24649
Donaghadee ...	... ...	24650
Donegal ...	... ...	24651
Dorchester	... ...	24652
Dorset ...	... ...	24653
Dover ...	... ...	24654
Drogheda	... ...	24655
Dublin ...	... ...	24656
Dumbarton	... ...	24657
Dumfries	... ...	24658
Dunbar ...	... ...	24659
Dundalk ...	... ...	24660
Dundee ...	... ...	24661
Dunfermline	... ...	24662
Durham ...	... ...	24663
Edinburgh	... ...	24664
Elgin ...	... ...	24665
Ely	... ...	24666
Enniskillen	... ...	24667
Essex ...	... ...	24668
Eton ...	... ...	24669
Exeter ...	... ...	24670
Falkirk ...	... ...	24671
Falmouth	... ...	24672
Fermanagh	... ...	24673
Forfar ...	... ...	24674
Galashiels	... ...	24675
Galloway	... ...	24676
Galway ...	... ...	24677
Glamorgan	... ...	24678
Glasgow ...	... ...	24679
Gloucester	... ...	24680
Greenock	... ...	24681
Guildford	... ...	24682
Haddington	... ...	24683
Hamilton	... ...	24684
Hampshire	... ...	24685
Harwich ...	... ...	24686
Hastings ...	... ...	24687
Hereford ...	... ...	24688
Hertford ...	... ...	24689
Huntingdon	... ...	24690
Inverness	... ...	24691
Ipswich ...	... ...	24692
Jedburgh	..	24693
Kent ...	... ...	24694
Kerry ...	... ...	24695
Kildare ...	... ...	24696
Kilkenny	... ...	24697
Kincardine	... ...	24698
Kinross ...	... ...	24699
Kirkcudbright	...	24700

Lanark	24701	Richmond	24751
Lancashire	24702	Rochester	24752
Launceston	24703	Roscommon	24753
Leeds	24704	Ross	24754
Leicester...	24705	Rothsay	24755
Leinster	24706	Roxburgh	24756
Leith	24707	Rutland	24757
Leitrim	24708	Salford	24758
Limerick	24709	Salisbury	24759
Lincoln	24710	Scarborough	24760
Linlithgow	24711	Selkirk	24761
Liverpool	24712	Sheffield	24762
London	24713	Shetland...	24763
Longford	24714	Shrewsbury	24764
Lothian	24715	Shropshire	24765
Louth	24716	Sligo	24766
Lutterworth	24717	Somerset	24767
Maidstone	24718	Southampton... ...	24768
Margate	24719	Southwark	24769
Manchester	24720	Stafford	24770
Mayo	24721	Stirling	24771
Meath	24722	Stockport	24772
Merioneth	24723	Suffolk	24773
Middlesex	24724	Sunderland	24774
Monaghan	24725	Surrey	24775
Monmouth	24726	Sussex	24776
Montgomery	24727	Sutherland	24777
Montrose	24728	Tewkesbury	24778
Munster	24729	Tipperary	24779
Nairn	24730	Tralee	24780
Norfolk	24731	Truro	24781
Northampton... ...	24732	Tuam	24782
Northumberland ...	24733	Tyrone	24783
Norwich...	24734	Ulster	24784
Nottingham	24735	Valencia...	24785
Orkney	24736	Warrington	24786
Osborne	24737	Warwick	24787
Oxford	24738	Westminster	24788
Paisley	24739	Westmoreland ...	24789
Peebles	24740	Wexford...	24790
Pembroke	24741	Weymouth	24791
Penzance	24742	Wicklow	24792
Perth	24743	Wigton	24793
Peterborough... ...	24744	Wiltshire	24794
Plymouth	24745	Winchester	24795
Portsmouth	24746	Windsor	24796
Preston	24747	Wolverhampton ...	24797
Radnor	24748	Worcester	24798
Ramsgate	24749	Yarmouth	24799
Renfrew	24750	York	24800

249	ABB	(125)	HAR	
Abbeville	... ...	24801	Cairo	24851
Acapulco	... ...	24802	Calais	24852
Aden ...	... ...	24803	Calcutta	24853
Adrianople	... ...	24804	Callao	24854
Agra ...	... ...	24805	Campeachy	24855
Aix-la-Chapelle	...	24806	Canton	24856
Alabama...	... ...	24807	Capua	24857
Albany ...	... ...	24808	Caracas	24858
Aleppo ...	... ...	24809	Carlsruhe	24859
Alexandria	... ...	24810	Carolina	24860
Algiers ...	... ...	24811	Carthagena	24867
Altona ...	... ...	24812	Ceuta	24861
Amsterdam	... ...	24813	Chalons	24863
Ancona ...	... ...	24814	Chambery	24864
Antwerp...	... ...	24815	Coblentz...	24865
Arequipa	... ...	24816	Cologne	24866
Arkansas	... ...	24817	Colombo	24867
Athens ...	.. ...	24818	Connecticut	24868
Augsburg	... ...	24819	Constantinople ...	24869
Austerlitz	... ...	24820	Copenhagen	24870
Avignon ...	... ...	24821	Corfu	24871
Babylon ...	... ...	24822	Corinth	24872
Bagdad ...	... ...	24823	Corunna	24873
Bahia ...	... ...	24824	Cracow	24874
Baltimore	... ...	24825	Cremona...	24875
Barcelona	... ...	24826	Curaçoa	24876
Basel ...	... ...	24827	Dantzic	24877
Batavia ...	... ...	24828	Delaware	24878
Bayonne...	... ...	24829	Delft	24879
Belgrade...	... ...	24830	Detroit	24880
Benin ...	... ...	24831	Dieppe	24881
Berlin ...	... ...	24832	Douai	24882
Berne ...	... ...	24833	Dresden	24883
Bethlehem	... ...	24834	Dusseldorf	24884
Bokhara ...	... ...	24835	Elsinore	24885
Bombay ...	... ...	24836	Emden	24886
Bordeaux	... ...	24837	Florida	24887
Boulogne	... ...	24838	Flushing...	24888
Bourbon ...	... ...	24839	Frankfort	24889
Braganza	... ...	24840	Geneva	24890
Bremen ...	... ...	24841	Genoa	24891
Breslau ...	... ...	24842	Ghent	24892
Brest ...	... ...	24843	Gotha	24893
Brindisi ...	... ...	24844	Grenoble	24894
Brussels ...	... ...	24845	Haerlem...	24895
Bucharest	... ...	24846	Hague	24896
Buenos Ayres	...	24847	Halifax	24897
Cabul ...	... ...	24848	Hamburg	24898
Cadiz ...	... ...	24849	Hanover...	24899
Cahawba	... ...	24850	Hartford...	24900

HAV			(125)	ZUR			250
Havannah	...	...	24901	Odessa	...	...	24951
Havre	...	...	24902	Oldenburg	...	...	24952
Heidelberg	...	...	24903	Oporto	...	...	24953
Hong Kong	...	...	24904	Orleans	...	...	24954
Hudson	...	...	24905	Ostend	...	...	24955
Insbruck	...	...	24906	Ottawa	...	...	24956
Jaffa	...	...	24907	Paris	...	...	24957
Jericho	...	...	24908	Pekin	...	...	24958
Jerusalem	...	...	24909	Pennsylvania	...	...	24959
Kentucky	...	...	24910	Pensacola	...	...	24960
Kiel	...	...	24911	Pernambuco	...	...	24961
Lagos	...	...	24912	Petersburg	...	...	24962
Leghorn	...	...	24913	Philadelphia	...	...	24963
Leipzig	...	...	24914	Potsdam	...	...	24964
Leyden	...	...	24915	Prague	...	...	24965
Liege	...	...	24916	Quebec	...	...	24966
Lille	...	...	24917	Rangoon	...	...	24967
Lima	...	...	24918	Rio Janeiro	...	...	24968
Limoges	...	...	24919	Rome	...	...	24969
Lisbon	...	...	24920	Rotterdam	...	...	24970
Louisiana	...	...	24921	Rouen	...	...	24971
Lubeck	...	...	24922	Salem	...	...	24972
Lucca	...	...	24923	Schwerin	...	...	24973
Lucerne	...	...	24924	Seville	...	...	24974
Luxemburg	...	...	24925	Singapore	...	...	24975
Lyons	...	...	24926	Stockholm	...	...	24976
Macassar	...	...	24927	Strasburg	...	...	24977
Macon	...	...	24928	Strelitz	...	...	24978
Madras	...	...	24929	Stutgard	...	...	24979
Magdeburg	...	...	24930	Suez	...	...	24980
Maine	...	...	24931	Sydney	...	...	24981
Malaga	...	...	24932	Teneriffe	...	...	24982
Malines	...	...	24933	Tennessee	...	...	24983
Marseilles	...	...	24934	Tokay	...	...	24984
Massachusetts		...	24935	Toronto	...	...	24985
Mecca	...	...	24936	Trafalgar	...	...	24986
Mecklenburg	...	...	24937	Trieste	...	...	24987
Melbourne	...	...	24938	Tripoli	...	...	24988
Memel	...	...	24939	Tyre	...	...	24989
Messina	...	...	24940	Valenciennes	...	...	24990
Milan	...	...	24941	Valparaiso	...	...	24991
Miquelon	...	...	24942	Venice	...	...	24992
Mobile	...	...	24943	Vienna	...	...	24993
Mocha	...	...	24944	Virginia	...	...	24994
Montreal	...	...	24945	Warsaw	...	...	24995
Moscow	...	...	24946	Washington	...	...	24996
Munich	...	...	24947	Waterloo	...	...	24997
Naples	...	...	24948	Zambese	...	...	24998
Nashville	...	...	24949	Zion	...	...	24999
Niagara	...	...	24950	Zurich	...	...	25000

www.ingramcontent.com/pod-product-compliance
Lightning Source LLC
Chambersburg PA
CBHW020352030726
47496CB00007B/2111